Law and the Regulation of Scientific Research

Scientific research is fundamental to addressing issues of great importance to the development of human knowledge. Scientific research fuels advances in medicine, technology and other areas important to society and has to be credible, trustworthy and able to command confidence in the face of inevitable uncertainties. Scientific researchers must be trusted and respected when they engage with knowledge acquisition and dissemination and as ethical guardians in their education and training roles of future generations of researchers. The core values of scientific research transcend disciplinary and national boundaries and approaches to the organisation and oversight of research systems can impact significantly upon the ethics and conduct of researchers.

This book draws upon legal expertise to critically analyse issues of regulation, conduct and ethics at the important interface between scientific research and regulatory and legal environments. In so doing it aims to contribute important additional perspectives to the existing literature. Case studies are engaged with to assist with the critical analysis of the current position and the consideration of future possibilities.

The book will be of interest to academics in the fields of science, law and policy; science and law students; and scientific researchers at more advanced stages of their careers. Research professionals in government and the private sector and legal practitioners with interests in the regulation of research should also find the work of interest.

Mark Davies is a reader in law at the University of Sussex, UK. He has written widely in the fields of professional negligence, regulation and liability.

Law and the Regulation of Scientific Research

Trusting Experts

Mark Davies

Routledge
Taylor & Francis Group
a GlassHouse Book

First published 2023
by Routledge
4 Park Square, Milton Park, Abingdon, Oxon OX14 4RN

and by Routledge
605 Third Avenue, New York, NY 10158

A GlassHouse book

Routledge is an imprint of the Taylor & Francis Group, an informa business

British Library Cataloguing-in-Publication Data
A catalogue record for this book is available from the British Library

Library of Congress Cataloging-in-Publication Data
A catalog record for this book has been requested

ISBN: 978-1-138-54979-1 (hbk)
ISBN: 978-1-032-32070-0 (pbk)
ISBN: 978-0-429-49212-9 (ebk)

DOI: 10.4324/9780429492129

Typeset in Bembo
by Apex CoVantage, LLC

Contents

Chapter 1

Introduction and definitions

Scientific research is fundamental to addressing issues of great importance and to the development of human knowledge. Although commissioned some time before the widespread emergence in late 2019 of severe acute respiratory syndrome coronavirus 2 (SARS-CoV-2) and the associated coronavirus disease (COVID-19), the research and writing for this book was completed at the beginning of 2022, when COVID-19 remained of major concern worldwide and much of the world's population had variously endured restricted freedoms and been asked to place their trust in speedily developed vaccines and COVID-19 treatments. This book ranges far more widely in both historical and specific coverage terms and as such engages with wide-ranging considerations about the nature of scientific research ethics and regulation. However, the COVID-19 pandemic has brought further into sharp relief not only the importance of scientific research but the trust which needs to be placed in scientists if measures emerging as necessary or desirable as a result of scientific research findings are to find sufficiently widespread public acceptance.

The term 'science' is not subject to a single universally agreed definition, with significant debate having emerged from discussion within the philosophy of science and sociology of science. The nature of the current work does not require engagement with these debates, but some definitional observations of the words 'science' and 'research' are appropriate to give a flavour of the understanding of these terms as discussed in this work.

Definitions of 'science' commonly include concepts such as pursuing knowledge and understanding of nature and society, utilising a systematic methodology based on organised, methodical experimentation to produce evidence. Definitions also commonly note that science is a branch of study that deals with demonstrated truths and must incorporate trustworthy methods.[1] However,

1 See, for example, Science Council Our definition of science - The Science Council https://sciencecouncil.org/about-science/our-definition-of-science/ (accessed 8 February 2021); Kass, L. (2009). Forbidding science: Some beginning reflections. *Science and Engineering Ethics*, 15, 271–282, 272. doi: 10.1007/s11948-009-9122-9; *Oxford English Dictionary*, 2021: online

DOI: 10.4324/9780429492129-1

science can only offer provisional answers.[2] 'Research' has been described as the 'practice of working in a scientific manner. Research is what is practised, and the result of this work is science.'[3] As well as discovering and formulating new knowledge, credibility is also a central feature of scientific research.[4] The latter is central to the discussion in this book.

Key roles of scientific researchers, in addition to the generation of scientific knowledge, include communicating this knowledge to specialist scientific audiences and, as appropriate, non-specialist audiences, and educating science students, some of whom will constitute the next generation of researchers.[5]

Scientific research is global in nature. Researchers move between jurisdictions to work, and international collaborations both within and between specialisms are increasingly common. National and supranational organisations collectively constitute the global research system. Such organisations are diverse in nature – including universities and other organisations employing researchers, research funders, publishers, professional bodies and learned societies.

The core values of scientific research necessarily transcend both disciplinary and national boundaries, and the policies and approaches of the organisations which make up the global research system can impact widely on the ethics and conduct of researchers.[6]

To fulfil a key societal role, science has to be both credible and trustworthy.[7] Uncertainty is central to science. Scientific understanding advances by means of the 'best' understanding being modified or replaced by updated 'best' understanding. Best scientific understanding today, therefore, will typically turn out to be incorrect as new information and interpretations emerge.[8]

All elements of the scientific process, from the framing of a research question through to the publication of findings, can be susceptible to misbehaviour.[9]

2 Paterson, J. (2003). Trans-science, trans-law and proceduralization. *Social & Legal Studies,* 12(4), 525–545, 531. doi: 10.1177/0964663903012004005, discussing Popper, Karl (1972). *The Logic of Scientific Discovery*. London: Hutchison.

3 Mårtensson, P., Fors, U., Wallin, S-B., Zander, U., & Nilsson, G. H. (2016). Evaluating research: A multidisciplinary approach to assessing research practice and quality. *Research Policy*, 45(3), 593–603, 594. https://doi.org/10.1016/j.respol.2015.11.009.

4 Grinnell, F. (2000). The practice of science at the edge of knowledge. *Chronicle Review*, March 24. The Practice of Science at the Edge of Knowledge (chronicle.com) (accessed 8 February 2021). For further discussion, see Mårtensson, P., Fors, U., Wallin, S-B., Zander, U., & Nilsson, G. H. (2016). Evaluating research: A multidisciplinary approach to assessing research practice and quality. *Research Policy*, 45(3), 593–603, 593. https://doi.org/10.1016/j.respol.2015.11.009.

5 Kirkland, A. (2012). Credibility battles in the autism litigation. *Social Studies of Science*, 42(2), 237–261, 256. https://doi.org/10.1177/0306312711435832.

6 Partnership, Interacademy. (2016). *Doing Global Science*. Princeton, NJ: Princeton University Press, 3.

7 Scheman, N. (2001). Epistemology resuscitated: Objectivity as trustworthiness. In N. Tuana & S. Morgen (Eds.), *Engendering Rationalities* (pp. 23–52). Albany, NY: SUNY Press.

8 Scheman, N. (2001). Epistemology resuscitated: Objectivity as trustworthiness. In N. Tuana & S. Morgen (Eds.), *Engendering rationalities* (pp. 23–52). Albany, NY: SUNY Press

9 Gunsalus, C. K., & Robinson, Aaron D. (2018). Nine pitfalls of research misconduct. *Nature,* 557, 297–299. doi: 10.1038/d41586-018-05145-6

The pollution of scientific information with fabricated data or other manifestations of research misconduct undermines confidence in scientific understanding being the 'best' available at a particular point in time and wastes the time and resources of reputable scientists misled into pursuing research in an attempt to build upon misdirected paths.[10] Research integrity and research ethics are therefore paramount to avoid undermining trust among scientists and the public and to avoid societal harm if, for example, faked research data lead to practical outcomes such as the approval of unsafe medications.[11]

Research integrity and research ethics are closely interconnected. Research integrity focuses upon research behaviour viewed from the perspective of professional standards, whereas research ethics focuses upon research behaviour considered from the perspective of moral principles.[12] At the positive end of the research integrity spectrum lies appropriate and responsible conduct of research in a manner defined, for example, by the Office of Research Integrity in the United States as 'possessing and steadfastly adhering to professional standards, as outlined by professional organizations, research institutions and, when relevant, the government and public' or by the UK Research and Integrity Office as upholding 'values of honesty, rigour, transparency and open communication, as well as care and respect for those involved in research and accountability for a positive research environment.'[13] Towards the middle of this spectrum are questionable research practices – for example, described by the US Office of Research Integrity as 'actions that violate traditional values of the research enterprise and that may be detrimental to the research process.'[14] At the negative end of the spectrum lies behaviour which constitutes deliberate misconduct, including the commonly cited categories of fabrication, falsification and plagiarism.[15] Fabrication and falsification may both be described as forms of lying – making false statements intended to mislead or misleading by omitting

10 See discussion by Jim Woodgett, director of research and senior investigator at the Lunenfeld-Tanenbaum Research Institute in Toronto, discussed in Williams, J. (2016). Is there a problem with academic integrity? *Times Higher Education*, June 30, 2016, www.timeshighereducation.com/features/is-there-a-problem-with-academic-integrity

11 Resnik, D. B. (2014). Data fabrication and falsification and empiricist philosophy of science. *Sci Eng Ethics*, 20, 423–431. doi: 10.1007/s11948-013-9466-z

12 Steneck, N. H. (2006). Fostering integrity in research: Definitions, current knowledge, and future directions. *Sci Eng Ethics*, 12, 53–74. https://doi.org/10.1007/PL00022268

13 Cited by Shaw, D., & Satalkar, P. (2018). Researchers' interpretations of research integrity: A qualitative study. *Accountability in Research*, 25(2), 79–93, 88. doi: 10.1080/08989621.2017.1413940; UK Research and Innovation www.ukri.org/our-work/supporting-healthy-research-and-innovation-culture/research-integrity/

14 Cited by Shaw, D., & Satalkar, P. (2018). Researchers' interpretations of research integrity: A qualitative study. *Accountability in Research*, 25(2), 79–93, 88. doi: 10.1080/08989621.2017.1413940

15 Komić, D., Marušić, S. L., & Marušić, A. (2015). Research integrity and research ethics in professional codes of ethics: Survey of terminology used by professional organizations across research disciplines. *PLoS ONE*, 10(7), e0133662. doi: 10.1371/journal.pone.0133662; Steneck, N. H. (2006). Fostering integrity in research: Definitions, current knowledge, and future directions. *Science and Engineering Ethics*, 12, 53–74. https://doi.org/10.1007/PL00022268.

something of importance.[16] At the extreme, criminal penalties may result if fabrication and falsification include, for example, fraudulently obtaining research grants.[17] Other definitional approaches use terms such as 'misconduct' to describe any behaviour on the part of researchers resulting in outputs which are unreliable, are not presented honestly and should not form part of the research record.[18] Even more broadly, behaviour, whether intentional or unintentional, falling short of good ethical and scientific standards.[19] How specific or precise definitions should be remains open to debate. For example, some critics within scientific communities argue that overreliance on highly specific legalistic provisions may diminish the ethical awareness of individual researchers.[20]

Even if errors are accidental or unintentional, they can still undermine research integrity.[21] In any human endeavour errors are unavoidable, but a scientific error is likely to be viewed with greater understanding and is less likely to face calls for culpability if the researcher acknowledges the error and corrects the scientific record.[22] If such steps are taken to ensure transparency, it has been argued that 'there can be tremendous value in error (indeed the scientific paradigm hangs upon it)' – facilitating the amendment of scientific ideas.[23] However, in cases where recognition and correction of error are absent, procedures to identify unintended error, as well as intended misconduct, are important.[24]

16 Shamoo, A. S., & Resnik, D. B. (2009). *Responsible Conduct of Research* (2nd ed.). New York: Oxford University Press; Bok, S. (1979). *Lying: Moral Choice in Public and Private Life*. New York: Pantheon Books.

17 See, for example, the discussion by Shamoo and Resnik of Eric Poehlman, a researcher at the University of Vermont. Shamoo, A. S., & Resnik, D. B. (2009). *Responsible Conduct of Research* (2nd ed.). New York: Oxford University Press.

18 Wager, E., Kleinert, S., Garfinkel, M., Volker Bahr, C., et al. (2017). Cooperation & Liaison between Universities & Editors (CLUE): Recommendations on best practice. *bioRxiv*. doi: https://doi.org/10.1101/139170.

19 Kakuk, P. (2009). The legacy of the Hwang case: research misconduct in biosciences. *Resources*, 15, 545–562, 556. Doi: 10.1007/s11948-009-9121-x

20 Shaw, D., & Satalkar, P. (2018). Researchers' interpretations of research integrity: A qualitative study. *Accountability in Research*, 25(2), 79–93, 88. doi: 10.1080/08989621.2017.1413940

21 Shaw, D., & Satalkar, P. (2018). Researchers' interpretations of research integrity: A qualitative study. *Accountability in Research*, 25(2), 79–93, 86–87. doi: 10.1080/08989621.2017.1413940

22 See, for example, the observations of Professor Stephan Lewandowsky and Professor Dorothy Bishop (RIN0046) para 20, House of Commons Science and Technology Committee, Research integrity, Sixth Report of Session 2017–19, 11 July 2018 HC 350. There are counter arguments that all misuses of scientific method are by their very nature intentional as every researcher, from Ph.D. onwards, should know the principles of scientific method and appropriate scientific practice. See discussion in Shaw, D., & Satalkar, P. (2018). Researchers' interpretations of research integrity: A qualitative study. *Accountability in Research*, 25(2), 79–93, 86. doi: 10.1080/08989621.2017.1413940.

23 Priaulx, N. M., & Weinel, M. (2014). Behavior on a beer mat: Law, interdisciplinarity & expertise. *Journal of Law, Technology & Policy*, (2), 361–391, 389.

24 Shaw, D., & Satalkar, P. (2018). Researchers' interpretations of research integrity: A qualitative study. *Accountability in Research*, 25(2), 79–93, 86. doi: 10.1080/08989621.2017.1413940.

Overall, the precise intersection between integrity, error and incompetence remains unclear. Compared with many other areas of professional misbehaviour, comparatively little attention has been paid by experts such as criminologists to scientific misconduct, notwithstanding the significant societal harms which can result.[25] All researchers are likely to occasionally make mistakes during the course of a career, but if this develops into regular errors, the question will arise of whether the researcher is guilty of misconduct, for example, on the basis of continuing to practise knowing that their competence is impaired.[26] Such approaches are established in other areas of professional regulation, for example, that pertaining to the legal and medical professions, where repeated errors which give rise to questions of competence may give rise to regulatory action.[27] The narrow border between innocent error and a breach of integrity is illustrated by the 'great pentaretraction' – the retraction by a research team of several papers due to a software error invalidating their findings.[28] This gave rise to divided opinion within the research community regarding whether this was a forgivable error or an example of irresponsibility of such magnitude that it gave rise to questions of misconduct.[29]

It is essential that the culture underpinning scientific research supports the ethical pursuit of high-quality work.[30] Creating a necessary culture in science that rewards integrity and professional excellence, in an environment which is committed to transparency, honesty and integrity, requires appropriate organisational and psychological developments in both national and global research cultures.[31]

Society frequently benefits from scientific innovation, but the public have little direct input in setting research agendas or contributing to the interpretations of research findings.[32] In such an environment a vast amount of scientific

25 Faria, R. (2014). Science under pressure: Problematic behaviors and social harms. *Crítica penal y poder*, 65(7), 64–84.

26 See, for example, Penders, B., Vos, R., & Horstman, K. (2009). A question of style: Method, integrity and the meaning of proper science. *Endeavour*, 33, 93–98. doi: 10.1016/j.endeavour.2009.07.001.

27 See, for example, Davies, M. (2007). *Medical Self-regulation, Crisis and Change*. London and New York: Routledge; Davies, M. (2010). The demise of professional self-regulation? Evidence from the 'ideal type' professions of medicine and law. *Tottels Journal of Professional Negligence*, 26(1), 3–38.

28 Miller, G. (2006). A scientist's nightmare: Software problem leads to five retractions. *Science*, 314, 1856–1857; Miller, C. (2007). Pretty structures, but what about the data? *Science*, 315(5811) (January 26), 459. doi: 10.1126/science.315.5811.459b. PMID: 17255494; Myers, N. (2015). *Rendering Life Molecular: Models, Modelers, and Excitable Matter*. Durham, NC: Duke University Press.

29 See, for example, Penders, B., Vos, R., & Horstman, K. (2009). A question of style: Method, integrity and the meaning of proper science. *Endeavour*, 33, 93–98. doi: 10.1016/j.endeavour.2009.07.001

30 Nuffield Council on Bioethics (2014). *The Culture of Scientific Research in the UK*, December 2014, Foreword

31 Kretser, A., Murphy, D., Bertuzzi, S., Abraham, T., Allison, D., Boor, K., Dwyer, J., Grantham, A., Harris, L., Hollander, R., Jacobs-Young, C., Rovito, S., Vafiadis, D., Woteki, C., Wyndham, J., & Yada, R. (2019). Scientific integrity principles and best practices: Recommendations from a scientific integrity consortium. *Science and Engineering Ethics*, 25. doi: 10.1007/s11948-019-00094-3.

32 Kitcher, P. (2011). *Science in a Democratic Society*. New York: Prometheus Books

knowledge is taken on trust.[33] Public trust in scientists and the scientific community collectively may be regarded as a form of belief leading to expectations of particular behaviour and ethical outlook.[34] The public rely on very many outputs of scientific research, for example, in the fields of medicine and engineering, given the nature of knowledge inequalities. Reliance is distinct from trust, and the two do not inevitably occur in combination.[35] Trust remains vital if scientific endeavour is to comply fully with wider societal norms.[36] Appropriate ethics and research integrity used to create a responsible culture is therefore central to the highest-quality research and innovation and the maintenance of public trust.[37]

Scientists, in seeking to discover and certify knowledge, face the constant challenge of establishing credibility and authority. Such challenges are exacerbated when, for example, it is suggested that scientists may be hired guns in the legal process or influenced as a result of being in the pay of powerful commercial bodies.[38] More broadly, if scientific assertions and counter-assertions find themselves being fought out in the political, media and legal arenas, this can be at the expense of robust, evidence-driven science, with an associated erosion in the creation and maintenance of public trust.[39]

33 Ranalli, B. (2013). Science communication as communication about persons. In J. Goodwin, M. F. Dahlstrom, & S. Priest (Eds.). *Ethical Issues in Science Communication: A Theory-Based Approach*. https://doi.org/10.31274/sciencecommunication-180809–46

34 See, for example, Gambetta, D. (1988). Can we trust trust? In D. Gambetta (Ed.), *Trust. Making and Breaking Cooperative Relations* (pp. 213–237). Oxford: Basil Blackwell. The term 'public' is not one with a precise or single definition. As well as individuals, it can be used to refer to groups with collective interests or official bodies such as law courts. See further, Irzik, G., & Kurtulmus, F. (2018). Well-ordered science and public trust in science. *Synthese*. https://doi.org/10.1007/s11229-018-02022-7

35 For further discussion of the distinction between trust and reliance see Baier, A. (1986). Trust and antitrust. *Ethics*, 96(2) (January), 231–260. https://doi.org/10.1086/292745

36 Ranalli, B. (2013). Science communication as communication about persons. In J. Goodwin, M. F. Dahlstrom, & S. Priest (Eds.). *Ethical Issues in Science Communication: A Theory-Based Approach*. https://doi.org/10.31274/sciencecommunication-180809–46

37 *UK Research and Innovation Delivery Plan 2019*, www.ukri.org/about-us/delivery-plans/ (accessed 14 June 2019) pp 28–29

38 A cited example is that of the tobacco industry and allegations that scientists were recruited and paid to 'maintain controversy' within the scientific community and beyond about the effects of tobacco smoke, Oreskes, N., & Conway, E. M. (2010). *Merchants of Doubt: How a Handful of Scientists Obscured the Truth on Issues from Tobacco Smoke to Global Warming*. New York: Bloomsbury.

39 See, for example, Oreskes, N., & Conway, E. M. (2010). *Merchants of Doubt: How a Handful of Scientists Obscured the Truth on Issues from Tobacco Smoke to Global Warming*. New York: Bloomsbury. Attempts have been made to address some of these challenges. For example, from 2012 onwards the InterAcademy Council and InterAcademy Partnership (IAP) – The Global Network of Science Academies has published recommendations and guidance to the global research community. This guidance addresses what are suggested to be the fundamental values of research – honesty, fairness, objectivity, reliability, scepticism, accountability, and openness – applicable across national and disciplinary boundaries, *Responsible Conduct in the Global Research Enterprise: A Policy Report*,

Discussion of the term 'trust' draws from debates about the character of trust in different contexts. In particular, the importance of trust in areas where complexity of understanding meets uncertainty about motivations and risk levels if trust proves to be misplaced. In communicating scientific information to the public, scientists possess no inherent special powers to change minds, and so in the context of providing information which may be opaque to members of the public, the symbolic signs of expertise may be vital to facilitate trust.[40] For such symbols to be meaningful, the ethical and regulatory underpinnings of scientific research, and the extent to which a shared ethical and regulatory identity can be found or created within research communities, is of central importance.[41] Therefore, focus on research integrity has in recent years increasingly come to be seen as an important priority underpinning trust in science.[42]

As the public have little direct input in setting research agendas or contributing to the interpretations of research findings, the usual mechanisms adopted to ensure the credibility of scientific information are contained within the internal mechanisms of the scientific community.[43] Conflicting scientific ideas and interpretation are explored in the scientific literature and at scientific conferences. Such exploration is expected to be underpinned by quality control mechanisms such as peer review and the replication of findings. Within the scientific community the assumption tends to be that other scientists can be relied upon to be rigorous and trustworthy, both with their own work and in roles which involve checking the work of others.[44] These activities are largely

October 2012; *Doing Global Science: A Guide to Responsible Conduct in the Global Research Enterprise*, February 2016 accessible from publications | IAP (interacademies.org) (accessed 15 January 2021).

40 Kirkland, A. (2012). Credibility battles in the autism litigation. *Social Studies of Science*, 42(2), 237–261, 256. https://doi.org/10.1177/0306312711435832; Giddens, A. (1991). *Modernity and Self-identity: Self and Society in the Late Modern Age*. Cambridge: Polity Press.

41 For discussion in the context of healthcare, see Gilson, L. (2006). Trust in health care: Theoretical perspectives and research needs. *Journal of Health Organization Management*, 20(5), 359–375. https://doi.org/10.1108/14777260610701768

42 For example, European Commission (2019). Open Science Policy Platform. Research integrity is one of the '8 prioritised Open Science ambitions' https://ec.europa.eu/research/openscience/index.cfm?pg=open-science-policy-platform (accessed 9 February 2020). The extent to which communities may or may not be gripped by a 'crisis of public trust' in, for example, experts or institutions is a subject of considerable debate. O'Neill, for example, has argued that concerns about a crisis in trust are somewhat overstated. Expressed levels of trust or distrust may not manifest in actual behaviour – for example, expressions of distrust in the medical profession may not be borne out in practice when individuals are seeking prompt, sometimes highly invasive, medical treatment, O'Neill, N., Reith Lectures 2002 Radio 4 (www.bbc.co.uk/radio4/reith2002/).

43 Kitcher, P. (2011). *Science in a Democratic Society*. New York: Prometheus Books.

44 Moher, D., Bouter, L., Kleinert, S., Glasziou, P., Sham, M. H., Barbour, V., et al. (2020). The Hong Kong principles for assessing researchers: Fostering research integrity. *PLoS Biol*, 18(7), e3000737. https://doi.org/10.1371/journal.pbio.3000737, citing Funk, C., Hefferon, M., Kennedy, B., & Johnson, C. Pew Research Centre. Trust and Mistrust in Americans' Views of Scientific Experts [Internet]. Available from: www.pewresearch.org/science/2019/08/02/trust-and-mistrust-in-americans-views-of-scientific-experts/

invisible to the general public. The public tend to enter the arena when the scientific consensus view is presented. Acceptance of such a consensus requires trust, a 'leap of faith' even, that the scientific community and the individuals within it have acted diligently and reported responsibly.[45] Public reliance on media reporting of purported scientific findings is also of importance, with the risk that some media reporting may be skewed in the direction of capturing public interest rather than towards the rigour of the research. Effective regulatory mechanisms can offer a source of reassurance in this and other respects.[46]

Trust in scientific research may also be influenced by perceptions of the role of the state and suspicion of the state on the part of some members of the public. For example, a sample of UK consumers were asked to estimate the safety of a genetically modified (GM) food product. When subsequently told that the government had stated that the product was safe, the levels of public confidence in the safety of that product fell significantly, a response the researchers attributed to public suspicion of institutions with a history of misrepresenting scientific risk, rather than a mistrust of science itself.[47] However, the risk remains that interconnectivity of science and state, for example, in the context of research funding or perceptions that universities may be subject to increasing levels of state interference, will result in some sections of the public remaining suspicious that the state and scientific communities are not sufficiently distinct. Similarly, if the state largely controls the dissemination of certain scientific information, public trust in the scientific findings may decrease.[48] Scientists employed directly by the state may also encounter lower levels of public trust.[49] In essence, if members of the public suspect that scientific representations are

45 Goldenberg, Maya J. (2016). Public misunderstanding of science? Reframing the problem of vaccine hesitancy. *Perspectives on Science*, 24(5), 552–581. https://doi.org/10.1162/POSC_a_00223

46 Wang, M. T. M., Bolland, M. J., Gamble, G., & Grey, A. (2015). Media coverage, journal press releases and editorials associated with randomized and observational studies in high-impact medical journals: A cohort study. *PLoS ONE*, 10(12), e0145294. https://doi.org/10.1371/journal.pone.0145294; Selvaraj, S., Borkar, D. S., & Prasad, V. (2014). Media coverage of medical journals: Do the best articles make the news? *PLoS ONE*, 9(1), e85355. https://doi.org/10.1371/journal.pone.0085355

47 Millstone, E., & van Zwanenberg, P. (2000). A crisis of trust: For science, scientists or for institutions? *Nat Med*, 6, 1307–1308. https://doi-org.ezproxy.sussex.ac.uk/10.1038/82102, citing Greenberg, S. *The British Test* (Report to Monsanto, 5 October 1998).

48 Millstone, E., & van Zwanenberg, P. (2000). A crisis of trust: For science, scientists or for institutions? *Nat Med*, 6, 1307–1308. https://doi-org.ezproxy.sussex.ac.uk/10.1038/82102, citing by way of example the suppression by the UK government for political reasons of information about BSE Phillips, Lord of Worth Matravers, Bridgeman, J., Ferguson-Smith, M. *The BSE Inquiry* Vol. 1, Findings and Conclusions, 233 (The Stationary Office, London, 2000); Grove White, R., McNaughton, P., Mayer, S. D., & Wynne, B. (1997). *Uncertain World, Genetically Modified Organisms, Food and Public Attitudes in Britain*. Lancaster, UK: CSEC, Lancaster University.

49 Millstone, E., & van Zwanenberg, P. (2000). A crisis of trust: For science, scientists or for institutions? *Nat Med*, 6, 1307–1308. https://doi-org.ezproxy.sussex.ac.uk/10.1038/82102, citing Grove

being subordinated to political considerations, they are unlikely to trust the scientists associated with those representations.[50]

While replication or reproducibility of results are core tenets of the scientific method and can replace the need to unquestioningly trust,[51] in practical terms scientists often lack the time, resources or motivation to fully engage in such activities, and so trust in their peers remains vital.[52] Trust between scientists is also important in other respects. Research papers with tens or even hundreds of authors drawn from complex research networks are possible only because high levels of trust exist within the scientific community.[53] In team-based projects –especially large teams – no one individual has enough evidence or even knowledge to justify the research conclusions – 'accepting each other's testimony' is necessary to accumulate sufficient research evidence to justify the mutual conclusion arising from the project.[54]

Moral character and epistemic character each have important roles to play. Truthfulness is part of a researcher's moral character, while competence, conscientious work and epistemic self-assessment are aspects of their epistemic character.[55] Often scientists must rely on scientific testifiers who are not

White, R., McNaughton, P., Mayer, S. D., & Wynne, B. (1997). *Uncertain World, Genetically Modified Organisms, Food and Public Attitudes in Britain*. Lancaster, UK: CSEC, Lancaster University.

50 Millstone, E., & van Zwanenberg, P. (2000). A crisis of trust: For science, scientists or for institutions? *Nat Med*, 6, 1307–1308. https://doi-org.ezproxy.sussex.ac.uk/10.1038/82102.

51 Hendriks, F., Kienhues, D., & Bromme, R. (2016). Trust in science and the science of trust. In B. Blöbaum (Ed.), *Trust and Communication in a Digitized World. Progress in IS*. Cham: Springer. https://doi.org/10.1007/978-3-319-28059-2_8

52 The importance of trust is not exclusive to science. As Webb argues, we would know very little in many spheres of life if such knowledge was based upon each individual's direct experience. Webb, M. O. (1993). Why I know about as much as you: A reply to Hardwig. *The Journal of Philosophy*, 90(5), 260–270. Such observation is not disputed, but for the purposes of this work it is argued that scientific knowledge and the impact of scientific research in a very wide range of societal fields place the necessity of trust in science at a particularly high level.

53 See, for example, Hardwig, J. (1991). The role of trust in knowledge. *Journal of Philosophy*, 88(12), 693–708. Extremely large author teams, sometimes running into thousands, have been criticised as rendering the concept of academic authorship on such papers meaningless, Jack Grove. (2015). Is mass authorship destroying the credibility of papers? *Times Higher Education*, August 24, www.timeshighereducation.com/news/mass-authorship-destroying-credibility-papers. For example, in the field of medical research the Vancouver Convention on authorship has sought to manage the proliferation of authorship claims by requiring the contribution of each named author to meet certain identifiable requirements, ICMJE | Recommendations | Defining the Role of Authors and Contributors (accessed 20 November 2020)

54 Hardwig, J. (1991). The role of trust in knowledge. *The Journal of Philosophy*, 88(12), (December), 693–708, 695–697. www.jstor.org/stable/2027007; Enserink, M. (2017). Researcher in Swedish fraud case speaks out: 'I'm very disappointed by my colleague'. *Science*, December 8, 2017, www.sciencemag.org/news/2017/12/researcher-swedish-fraud-case-speaks-out-i-m-very-disappointed-my-colleague.

55 Hardwig, J. (1991). The role of trust in knowledge. *The Journal of Philosophy*, 88(12), (December), 693–708, 700. www.jstor.org/stable/2027007

personally known to them, either at all or well. This is often the case for scientific testimony embodied in the research literature, but can also be true among members of large research teams, divided across institutions, countries, even continents.[56] Among the scientific community each may be categorised as a lay person outside of their own area of expertise, and so placing epistemic trust in a co-researcher to trust them as providers of information is a key element of trust.[57] Appropriate dialogue is critical within research teams in a manner understandable to all in order to facilitate critical judgements to determine levels of trustworthiness.[58] The integrity necessary to maintain such trust requires collective engagement to establish and maintain an appropriate research culture as 'a scaffold which facilitates responsibility.'[59]

With a multi-authored work, if misconduct is suspected it may be difficult in some instances to identify who is directly responsible.[60] While multi-expertise and multi-jurisdictional team-based research projects present enhanced challenges and potential risks in research misconduct terms, there are some counterbalancing observations. For example, a survey of the scientific research community in the United Kingdom gave rise to consistent themes of interdisciplinary, intersectoral and international collaborations as presenting positive incentives for research integrity 'by increasing openness, honesty and rigour' and by reducing the risks to research integrity from 'disciplinary siloes' and 'cliques.'[61] Individual disciplines each foster research cultures which in turn have the potential to influence broader-ranging research integrity – those disciplines which have more developed approaches to fostering good research practices having the opportunity to influence other disciplines when researchers work in interdisciplinary communities.[62]

56 Hardwig, J. (1991). The role of trust in knowledge. *The Journal of Philosophy*, 88(12), (December), 693–708, 701. www.jstor.org/stable/2027007

57 For further discussion, see ALLEA (2018). *Loss of Trust? Loss of Trustworthiness? Truth and Expertise*. ALLEA discussion paper #1, May 2018, https://allea.org/wp-content/uploads/2018/05/ALLEA_Discussion_Paper_1_Truth_and_Expertise_Today-digital.pdf

58 For further discussion, see ALLEA (2018). *Loss of Trust? Loss of Trustworthiness? Truth and Expertise*. ALLEA discussion paper #1, May 2018, https://allea.org/wp-content/uploads/2018/05/ALLEA_Discussion_Paper_1_Truth_and_Expertise_Today-digital.pdf

59 Zwart, H. (2017). *Tales of Research Misconduct. Library of Ethics and Applied Philosophy* (Vol 36, p. 34). Cham: Springer.

60 See, for example, Abbott, A. (2000). German fraud inquiry casts a wider net of suspicion . . .. *Nature*, 405, 871–872. https://doi.org/10.1038/35016207; Schiermeier, Q. (2002). German task force outraged by changes to science fraud report. *Nature*, 415, 3. https://doi.org/10.1038/415003a

61 Metcalfe, J., Wheat, K., Munafò. M., Parry, J. (2020). *Research Integrity: A Landscape Study*. Vitae/UK Research Integrity Office/UK Reproducibility Network, www.ukri.org/files/legacy/documents/research-integrity-main-report/

62 Metcalfe, J., Wheat, K., Munafò. M., Parry, J. (2020). *Research Integrity: A Landscape Study* (p. 25). Vitae/UK Research Integrity Office/UK Reproducibility Network, www.ukri.org/files/legacy/documents/research-integrity-main-report/; Ancker, J., & Flanagin, A. (2007). A comparison of conflict of interest policies at peer-reviewed journals in different scientific disciplines. *Science and Engineering Ethics*, 13, 147–157. doi: 10.1007/s11948-007-9011-z.

Also, from the perspective of fostering greater trust and in recent times communicating scientific ideas and public understanding of science, public participation or public engagement with science has taken a prominent position, for example, with the creation of university chairs in the public understanding of science and state-sponsored committees along similar lines.[63] Some within the scientific community have suggested that there are very significant challenges in this regard. For example, Nobel Laureate for Physics, Michael Kosterlitz, is reported as saying that physicists attempting to explain their work to the general public are faced with an 'almost impossible task' in trying to communicate meaningfully something to an audience which lacks the 'background at all in these logical steps that are natural to, are part of, any scientist's psyche, [but] which are alien to most other people.'[64] However, such sentiments have been questioned. For example, observations to the House of Lords Select Committee on Science and Technology:

> [T]he expression 'public understanding of science' may not be the most appropriate label. Sir Robert May called it a 'rather backward-looking vision'. . . . It is argued that the words imply a condescending assumption that any difficulties in the relationship between science and society are due entirely to ignorance and misunderstanding on the part of the public; and that, with enough public-understanding activity, the public can be brought to greater knowledge, whereupon all will be well.[65]

Scientific communication and associated instilling of trust also faces challenges arising from the predisposition of different audiences and tensions between localised 'anecdotal' knowledge and the search by scientists for universal, generalisable knowledge.[66] If public discourse about controversial matters such as potential risks to health from mobile phone use or the MMR (measles,

63 For example, the chair at the University of Oxford, created in 1995 and, until 2002 in the UK, COPUS, the Committee on the Public Understanding of Science created in 1986 by the Royal Society. See further, The Royal Society (1985). *Public Understanding of Science*, chaired by Sir Walter Bodmer FRS, 1985; The Royal Society, The Public Understanding of Science, https://royalsociety.org/~/media/Royal_Society_Content/policy/publications/1985/10700.pdf (accessed 22 July 2019).

64 Matthews, D. (2019). Nobel winner: Explaining physics to public a 'waste of time'. *Times Higher Education*, July 22, 2019, www.timeshighereducation.com/news/nobel-winner-explaining-physics-public-waste-time

65 House of Lords Select Committee on Science and Technology Third Report, Chapter 3, https://publications.parliament.uk/pa/ld199900/ldselect/ldsctech/38/3801.htm (accessed 22 July 2019)

66 Moore, A., & Stilgoe, J. (2009). Experts and anecdotes: The role of "anecdotal evidence" in public scientific controversies. *Science Technology Human Values*, 34, 654. doi: 10.1177/0162243908329382, citing, inter alia, Irwin, A. (1995). *Citizen Science. A Study of People, Expertise and Sustainable Development*. London and New York: Routledge; Irwin, A., & Michael, M. (2003). *Science, Social Theory and Public Knowledge*. Maidenhead and Philadelphia: Open University Press.

mumps, rubella) vaccine gains sufficient momentum, cumulatively anecdotal accounts may vie with accounts from within the scientific community such that the boundary lines between the two become contested, and anecdotes may be transformed 'as they pass into scientific discourse.'[67] For example, when considering the influence of Andrew Wakefield's views about the MMR vaccine, account has to be taken of the fact that his audiences start with beliefs and values which influence how they assess the information communicated to them. Ongoing trust in Wakefield, and a reluctance to replace this for trust in his critics, arises not simply from the possibility of a confused picture emerging from disagreeing apparent experts but more fundamentally a greater tendency to reject the account which fits least well with prior beliefs.[68] By tapping into a pre-existing narrative and, for example, providing an apparently credible explanation as to why a child is autistic, the challenge Wakefield presents to his critics goes beyond attempts to highlight badly conducted research. His critics will be expected by the audiences who have adopted Wakefield's narrative to provide an alternative and better account of the apparent causal relationship for the life events which the parents are experiencing.[69] In this context, Wakefield's narrative in response to his critics tends towards presenting himself as an advocate for children against a medical establishment and pharmaceutical industry, characterised as seeking to protect their vested interests in the widespread adoption of the MMR vaccine.[70] As reported from a meeting hosted by the Science Media Centre in 2002, a narrative nurtured by Wakefield's research and by the media reporting of it viewed parents of autistic children as experts on the condition, rather than as experts on its symptoms.[71] The activities of parent groups advocating for families whose belief was that their children had suffered

67 Moore, A., & Stilgoe, J. (2009). Experts and anecdotes: The role of "anecdotal evidence" in public scientific controversies. *Science Technology Human Values*, 34, 654. doi: 10.1177/0162243908329382.

68 Sorell, T. (2007). Parental choice and expert knowledge in the debate about MMR and autism. In A. Dawson & M. Verweij (Eds.), *Ethics, Prevention and Public Health* (pp. 95–110). Oxford: Oxford University Press. Cited by Tindale, C. W. (2012). Dismantling expertise: Disproof, retraction, and the persistence of belief. In J. Goodwin (Ed.), *Between Scientists & Citizens*. https://doi.org/10.31274/sciencecommunication-180809-87. Wakefield's retention of a public relations firm may be seen as further complicating the narrative between the opposing scientific positions and public understanding, Speers, T., & Lewis, J. (2004). Journalists and jabs: Media coverage of the MMR vaccine. *Communication & Medicine*, 1, 171–181. doi: 10.1515/come.2004.1.2.171.

69 Tindale, C. W. (2012). Dismantling expertise: Disproof, retraction, and the persistence of belief. In J. Goodwin (Ed.), *Between Scientists & Citizens*. https://doi.org/10.31274/sciencecommunication-180809-87

70 Tindale, C. W. (2012). Dismantling expertise: Disproof, retraction, and the persistence of belief. In J. Goodwin (Ed.), *Between Scientists & Citizens*. https://doi.org/10.31274/sciencecommunication-180809-87

71 MMR Lessons Meeting, www.sciencemediacentre.org/release-of-report-from-mmr-lessons-meeting-2/ (accessed 12 June 2021), discussed in Moore, A., & Stilgoe, J. (2009). Experts and anecdotes: The role of "anecdotal evidence" in public scientific controversies. *Science Technology Human Values*, 34, 654. doi: 10.1177/0162243908329382.

harm resulting from the vaccine have been criticised for adding to public misinformation.[72] Some elements of the media reinforce that side of the argument by giving equal weight or even primacy to 'first person experience' compared with 'objective knowledge' from the scientific community.[73] Sections of the media have been criticised for over-zealous adherence to the convention of seeking balanced reporting by giving equal coverage to each side's account. By not engaging with the science and recognising where consensus opinion lay, the media coverage gave the impression that there was equal support for and against Wakefield's claims.[74] Conflicting 'credibility zones,' spaces where 'knowledge' is produced within a community drawing from its own sources, can undermine the prospect of consensus. The network of parents identifying autism as a result of vaccine harm and scientists rejecting that idea provide an example of opposing 'zones.'[75]

In terms of trust from some sections of the public, Wakefield's credibility appears to have been enhanced by the weight of opinion within the scientific community against him: the image of a 'maverick' taking on the establishment by 'speaking truth to power' and listening to the patient or the patient's parents as the source of 'the answer.'[76]

These observations have a common feature – the need for public trust in the work and findings of scientists, research outputs projecting the author's competence and credibility, irrespective of the extent to which individual members of the public understand the depth and subtleties of the work in question.[77] That the Wakefield case was more about trust than the detail of the science may be illustrated by the observation that those parents who believed Wakefield's account might also have been expected to factor into their decision making that

72 Goldenberg, Maya J. (2016). Public misunderstanding of science? Reframing the problem of vaccine hesitancy. *Perspectives on Science*, 24(5), 552–581 https://doi.org/10.1162/POSC_a_00223, citing, inter alia, Offit, Paul A. 2011. Deadly Choices: How the Anti-Vaccine Movement Threatens Us All. New York: Basic Books.

73 Tallis, R. (2004). *Hippocratic Oaths: Medicine and Its Discontents* (pp. 200–201). London: Atlantic Books, cited by Brazier, M. (2011). How the media presents medicine and science. *Medical Law International*, 11(3), 187–196. https://doi.org/10.1177/096853321101100303

74 Wilholt, T. (2013). Epistemic trust in science. *The British Journal for the Philosophy of Science*, 64(2) (June), 233–253, 17, https://doi.org/10.1093/bjps/axs007, citing Boyce, T. (2007). *Health, Risk and News: The MMR Vaccine and the Media* (pp. 71–94). New York: Peter Lang Publishing.

75 Kirkland, A. (2012). Credibility battles in the autism litigation. *Social Studies of Science*, 42(2), 237–261, 240. https://doi.org/10.1177/0306312711435832, citing Jasanoff, S. (2004). *States of Knowledge: The Co-Production of Science and Social Order*. New York: Routledge.

76 Goldenberg, Maya J. (2016). Public misunderstanding of science? Reframing the problem of vaccine hesitancy. *Perspectives on Science*, 24(5), 552–581. https://doi.org/10.1162/POSC_a_00223; Wakefield, A. J. (1998). Autism, inflammatory bowel disease and MMR vaccine, letter. *Lancet*, 351(9106) (March 21), https://doi.org/10.1016/S0140-6736(05)70322-6

77 Ranalli, B. (2013). Science communication as communication about persons. In J. Goodwin, M. F. Dahlstrom, & S. Priest (Eds.). *Ethical Issues in Science Communication: A Theory-Based Approach*. https://doi.org/10.31274/sciencecommunication-180809–46

Wakefield's claim was that the MMR vaccine causes autism in a tiny proportion of cases, in which case the risks from not vaccinating an individual child might be expected to outweigh the risk of autism.[78] Instead, having believed Wakefield rather than other sections of the scientific community, it appears to have become an all or nothing, 'which side do we trust?' decision. Media representations which emphasised that the scientists opposing Wakefield refused to express a certainty that the vaccine was safe may have played into some public misconceptions about the nature of science and scientific uncertainty.[79]

The work of scientists as experts may be viewed as being akin to that of other professions, with the principle of *credat emptor* applying.[80] Misinformation may be far more difficult to correct with the lay public than within the scientific community. When scientific ideas are revised, the relevant scientific community follows established protocols in order to seek to restore balance. In contrast, public opinion can be far more resistant to revision, especially if some within the scientific community continue to adopt a stance which sits in opposition to the otherwise consensus scientific view.[81]

Levels of trust in science

In the UK university professors and scientists are relatively highly rated by the public in terms of trust. For example, in 2011 professors scored 74 per cent in terms of being trusted to tell the truth.[82] This had risen to 84 per cent by 2017. Scientists were scored at 83 per cent in 2017, a rise of 20 per cent since 1997.[83]

78 John, S. (2011). Expert testimony and epistemological free-riding: The MMR controversy. *The Philosophical Quarterly*, 61, 496–517, 498. doi: 10.1111/j.1467-9213.2010.687.x

79 John, S. (2011). Expert testimony and epistemological free-riding: The MMR controversy. *The Philosophical Quarterly*, 61, 496–517, 501. doi: 10.1111/j.1467-9213.2010.687.x, citing Hargreaves, I. et al. (2003). *Towards a Better Map: Science, the Public and the Media*. Swindon: ESRC; Boyce, T. (2007). *Health, Risk and News: The MMR Vaccine and the Media*. New York: Peter Lang; Sorell, T. (2007). Parental choice and expert knowledge in the debate about MMR and autism. In A. Dawson & M. Verweij (Eds.), *Ethics, Prevention and Public Health* (pp. 95–110). Oxford: Oxford University Press. At least some of those parents who favoured Wakefield's position may have been well aware of the uncertainties of scientific testing, which in turn may have constituted the basis of their choices, John, S. (2011). Expert testimony and epistemological free-riding: The MMR controversy. *The Philosophical Quarterly*, 61, 496–517, 501. doi: 10.1111/j.1467-9213.2010.687.x

80 Let the buyer trust, in contrast to let the buyer beware – *caveat emptor*.

81 Tindale, C. W. (2012). Dismantling expertise: Disproof, retraction, and the persistence of belief. In J. Goodwin (Ed.), *Between Scientists & Citizens*. https://doi.org/10.31274/sciencecommunication-180809-87, citing Harmon, K. (2010, March 4). Impact factor: Can a scientific retraction change public opinion? *Scientific American*, 1–4. www.scientificamerican.com/article.cfm?id=retraction-impact-lancet

82 Castell, S., Charlton, A., Clemence, M., Pettigrew, N., Pope, S., Quigley, A., Navin Shah, J., & Silman, T. (2014). *Public Attitudes to Science 2014*, www.gov.uk/government/publications/public-attitudes-to-science-2014 (accessed 9 May 2019)

83 *The 2017 Ipsos MORI Veracity Index*, https://www.ipsos.com/ipsos-mori/en-uk/politicians-remain-least-trusted-profession-britain

Public trust in science and scientists also remained robust during the COVID-19 pandemic, according to a global survey undertaken by the Wellcome Trust between August 2020 and February 2021.[84] These figures were higher than, for example, judges and clergy/priests and a little below teachers, doctors and nurses.[85] However, a significant minority, 35 per cent of respondents, considered that scientists would adjust their findings to get the results they wanted.[86]

The House of Commons Science and Technology Committee made the following observations about trust in science:

> [I]n the UK research has an enviable record of excellence and public trust, but this should not be taken for granted. There is a risk that public trust in science could be eroded in the future through high-profile examples of research misconduct, and a risk that this could lead to demands for knee-jerk and ill-advised changes to the research system in the UK. There is a need for the research community – including funders, publishers, and employers of researchers – to stay ahead of research integrity issues and how they are dealt with in public policy. The UK's position of international high regard and public trust in researchers is strengthened if the community has the confidence to admit that no area of human endeavour is immune to misconduct and error at some scale.[87]

Ipsos MORI research over three decades demonstrates that trust levels have the potential to shift dramatically in either direction and that maintaining a public reputation for trustworthiness is something which has continually to be worked on. Public trust in science has remained reasonably consistent over time, although figures from 2016 showed only 21 per cent of adults in the United States had 'a great deal of confidence' that scientists would act in the best interests of the public and 40 per cent expressed 'a great deal of confidence in the

84 *Wellcome Global Monitor: How Covid-19 Affected People's Lives and Their Views About Science, 2020*, https://wellcome.org/sites/default/files/2021-11/Wellcome-Global-Monitor-Covid.pdf

85 *The 2017 Ipsos MORI Veracity Index*, www.ipsos.com/ipsos-mori/en-uk/politicians-remain-least-trusted-profession-britain

86 Castell, S., Charlton, A., Clemence, M., Pettigrew, N., Pope, S., Quigley, A., Navin Shah, J., & Silman, T. (2014). *Public Attitudes to Science 2014*, www.gov.uk/government/publications/public-attitudes-to-science-2014 (accessed 9 May 2019)

87 House of Commons Science and Technology Committee, Research integrity, Sixth Report of Session 2017–19, 11 July 2018 HC 350, page 47. The need to maintain public and peer confidence remains especially important for the UK in light of its global positioning. Accounting for 6.3 per cent of journal articles globally, in 2014, the UK represented 0.9 per cent of global population, 2.7 per cent of research and development (R&D) expenditure and 4.1 per cent of researchers, while accounting for 6.3 per cent of journal articles globally, 9.9 per cent of downloads, 10.7 per cent of citations and 15.2 per cent of the most highly cited articles, Department for Business, Energy & Industrial Strategy (BEIS) and Elsevier, *International Comparative Performance of the UK Research Base – 2016*, www.elsevier.com/research-intelligence/research-initiatives/beis2016

scientific community.'[88] Trust has also been found to vary between areas of scientific research, for example, 39 per cent on climate change but 55 per cent on the risks associated with vaccination.[89] Globally, the level of trust in scientists has been placed at 72 per cent overall, 18 per cent at a high level of trust and 54 per cent at a medium level.[90] The figures were higher in Central Asia, Northern and Western Europe and the United States and Canada than the average for the world as a whole, but in all of these areas high levels of trust still remained well below 50 per cent (the highest being Central Asia at 32 per cent).[91]

Scientists themselves quite often have concerns about each other's work. In a survey of over 3,000 academic researchers, 37 per cent of respondents reported that half or more of the research outputs they studied in a representative period were considered to be untrustworthy. Only 14 per cent of respondents trusted all of the work that they had read.[92] Research was considered to be untrustworthy for a number of reasons, key amongst these being exaggerated findings from the data presented; absence of peer review; flawed methodology; bias; absence of supporting data/supplementary material to allow checking of findings; and errors ranging from grammatical errors, errors relating to citations, 'inflated statistical power,' and errors in code to errors in calculations.[93]

Drawing from research which identifies a correlation between personal behaviour and trustworthiness, reports about 'mean and aggressive' research working cultures in some areas of science threatens the public's respect for scientists.[94] A survey of UK scientists found that incidents of bullying and harassment were considered to have the most negative influence on research

88 Iyengar, S., & Massey, D. S. (2018). Scientific communication in a post-truth society. *Proceedings of the National Academy of Sciences*, 201805868. doi: 10.1073/pnas.1805868115, citing Funk, C., & Kennedy, B. (2017). *Public Confidence in Scientists Has Remained Stable for Decades*. Washington, DC: Pew Research Center, www.pewresearch.org/fact-tank/2017/04/06/public-confidence-in-scientists-has-remained-stable-for-decades/. Disaggregated figures showed confidence levels were 28 per cent for those without a high school degree and 61 per cent of those with an advanced degree.

89 National Science Board (2018). *Science and Technology: Public Attitudes and Understanding*. Science and Engineering Indicators 2018. Washington, DC: Natl Sci Found, Chap 7, cited in Iyengar, S., & Massey, D. S. (2018). Scientific communication in a post-truth society. *Proceedings of the National Academy of Sciences*, 201805868. doi: 10.1073/pnas.1805868115

90 Wellcome Global Monitor 2018, https://wellcome.ac.uk/reports/wellcome-global-monitor/2018 (accessed 19 June 2019)

91 Wellcome Global Monitor 2018, https://wellcome.ac.uk/reports/wellcome-global-monitor/2018 (accessed 19 June 2019)

92 Matthews, D. (2019). Do researchers trust each other's work? *Times Higher Education*, August 27, 2019, www.timeshighereducation.com/news/do-researchers-trust-each-others-work.

93 Matthews, D. (2019). Do researchers trust each other's work? *Times Higher Education*, August 27, 2019, www.timeshighereducation.com/news/do-researchers-trust-each-others-work.

94 Cardew, G. (2020). People will not trust unkind science. *Nature*, February 4, 2020, www.nature.com/articles/d41586-020-00269-0; Wellcome (2020). *What Researchers Think about the Culture They Work in*, https://wellcome.ac.uk/sites/default/files/what-researchers-think-about-the-culture-they-work-in.pdf

integrity and that a significant number of researchers identified incidences of bullying to be widespread.[95] A survey report from Wellcome found that 43 per cent of researchers had experienced bullying or harassment, while 61 per cent had witnessed it.[96] Pressure and the stress it can create have been associated with research misconduct. Bullied researchers may feel under pressure to cut corners to be seen to be achieving results.[97] For example, researchers perceive one of the causes for plagiarism is connected to a constant 'pressure to publish.'[98] Large funding bodies have the potential to positively influence institutional and individual behaviour. For example, Wellcome has introduced a policy as part of its grant conditions which requires organisations submitting grant applications to confirm that the lead applicant (and sponsor and supervisor if relevant) has not had an allegation of bullying or harassment upheld against them for which there is a current formal disciplinary warning or an active sanction.[99] In the case of newer appointees, Wellcome expects organisations to check the position with the previous employer. Allegations of bullying and harassment within organisations should be investigated in an impartial, fair and timely manner, with appropriate sanctions if proven.[100] Investigations should be concluded even if the subject of the investigation resigns during the process.[101] Wellcome reserves the right to impose its own sanctions on individuals and on organisations which fail to respond promptly and objectively to a bullying and/ or harassment complaint.[102] If such policies are adopted sufficiently widely by funding bodies, any temptation by institutions to ignore or downplay bullying behaviour presents significant risks to their research funding.

In the United States in 2018 the US National Institutes of Health (NIH) instituted a mechanism which allowed it to cut off the grant funding of researchers and remove researchers from peer review panels if they had committed

95 Metcalfe, J., Wheat, K., Munafò. M., Parry, J. (2020). *Research Integrity: A Landscape Study*. Vitae/ UK Research Integrity Office/UK Reproducibility Network, www.ukri.org/files/legacy/documents/research-integrity-main-report/, 21

96 Wellcome (2020). *What Researchers Think about the Culture They Work in* (p. 27), https://wellcome.ac.uk/sites/default/files/what-researchers-think-about-the-culture-they-work-in.pdf

97 See, for example, Davis, M., Riske-Morris, M., & Diaz, S. (2007). Causal factors implicated in research misconduct: Evidence from ORI case files. *Science and Engineering Ethics*, 13, 395–414. doi: 10.1007/s11948-007-90452.

98 Faria, R. (2014). Science under pressure. Problematic behaviours and social harms. *Revista Crítica Penal y Poder*, nº 7, 64–84. *Revista Crítica Penal y Poder*, 72.

99 Wellcome, *Bullying and Harassment Policy*, https://wellcome.ac.uk/funding/guidance/bullying-and-harassment-policy (accessed 8 March 2020).

100 Wellcome, *Bullying and Harassment Policy*, https://wellcome.ac.uk/funding/guidance/bullying-and-harassment-policy (accessed 8 March 2020).

101 Wellcome, *Bullying and Harassment Policy*, https://wellcome.ac.uk/funding/guidance/bullying-and-harassment-policy (accessed 8 March 2020).

102 Wellcome, *Bullying and Harassment Policy*, https://wellcome.ac.uk/funding/guidance/bullying-and-harassment-policy (accessed 8 March 2020).

sexual harassment or certain other forms of personal misbehaviour.[103] By 2021 action had been taken against over 70 researchers, although criticisms remain that some researchers were able to escape full investigation by resigning from their employment but remained free to seek employment elsewhere.[104] While some commentators have expressed concerns that the NIH initiative is not progressing sufficiently rapidly, some institutions have been identified as pushing back against those advances which have been made in an attempt to preserve grant income.[105]

The nature and scope of this work

A work of this type cannot cover every aspect of scientific misconduct across every jurisdiction. The focus therefore is on key principles and case examples which permit analysis, critique and the drawing together of key themes. Chapter 2 builds upon this introductory chapter by considering the centrality of trust to the process of science and the regulation of research. Chapter 3 considers the categorisation of scientific misconduct, including debates and disagreement about the boundaries of misconduct. Chapter 4 addresses the importance of education as a means of maximising ethical behaviour and addressing misconduct. Chapter 5 considers self-regulation within the scientific community, including the role of scientific method in the process of quality control. Chapter 6 focuses upon institutional regulation, the role of universities and other employers of researchers in regulating science. Chapter 7 builds upon Chapter 6 by considering regulatory sources external to individual employers, with particular focus on the courts and the judicial process. Chapters 8 and 9 bring the work to a close by drawing together concluding observations and considering prospects for the future, including technological developments which may offer prospects for advances in the processes of scientific regulation.

103 See ACD Working Group on Changing the Culture to End Sexual Harassment, https://acd.od.nih.gov/working-groups/sexual-harassment.html;

104 Lauer, M., MD (2021), *Update on the ACD Working Group Recommendations on Changing the Culture to End Sexual Harassment*, Meeting of the Advisory Committee to the Director June 10, 2021 (Virtual), https://acd.od.nih.gov/documents/presentations/06102021_Lauer.pdf; Basken, P. (2021). National Institutes of Health axes 75 grants over harassment. *Times Higher Education*, June 15, 2021, www.timeshighereducation.com/news/national-institutes-health-axes-75-grants-over-harassment; Kaiser, J. (2020). NIH requires disclosure about sexual harassment by grantees. *Science*, 368(6497) (19 June), 1301. doi: 10.1126/science.368.6497.1301

105 See, for example, The Federation of American Societies for Experimental Biology (FASEB) letter dated February 2, 2021, www.faseb.org/uploadimagefolder/CustomerImages/_FOLDER_FASEBArticles/ArticleImages/img_FASEB_TaCO_NIH_ACDLetter_20210202.pdf?cache=637479653589952357; Health Care Compliance Association (2020). *Institutions Pushing Back against Removing PIs from Awards, Despite Harassment Findings*, June 26, 2020, www.jdsupra.com/legalnews/institutions-pushing-back-against-22419/

Chapter 2

The centrality of trust

Trust may be seen as a public good which, inter alia, facilitates the need to cope with uncertainty and vulnerability.[1] As such, trust is a hard-earned but potentially easily lost good which represents valuable social capital.[2] Because recovery of lost trust can be extremely challenging, it has been argued that maintaining trust against loss must be 'ruthless.'[3]

Trust and risk are closely connected – the placing of trust almost inevitably involves an element of risk.[4] In the terminology of professions, in complex scenarios where outcomes cannot be guaranteed, outsiders will have trouble assessing the accuracy of what is presented to them, and trust therefore takes on a vital importance.[5]

In deciding where to place trust, competence, extent of knowledge and integrity play key roles and come together to constitute expertise – also expressed as motivation towards truthfulness and sincerity, described as benevolence or warmth.[6] A perceived lack of benevolence or warmth can be a

1 Hirsch, F. (1978). *Social Limits to Growth* (pp. 78–79). Cambridge, MA: Harvard University Press; Barber, B. (1983). *The Logic and Limits of Trust* (p. 8). New York: Rutgers.

2 O'Neill, O. *Reith Lectures 2002*, radio 4, www.bbc.co.uk/radio4/reith2002/ONora O'Neill

3 See Solomon, R. C., & Fernando, F. (2001). *Building Trust* (p. 5). Oxford: Oxford University Press and Luhmann, N. (1980). *Trust and Power*. New York: Wiley; Handy, C. (1998). *The Hungry Spirit* (pp. 187, 191). London: Arrow.

4 Earle, T. C., & Cvetkovich, G. T. (1995). *Social Trust: Toward a Cosmopolitan Society*. Westport, CT: Praeger. An expression of trust or distrust in 'scientists' may be directed at specific individuals, but more often is directed at a 'social type' – the accredited scientist, John, S. (2018). Epistemic trust and the ethics of science communication: Against transparency, openness, sincerity and honesty. *Social Epistemology*, 32(2), 75–87. doi: 10.1080/02691728.2017.1410864, 78

5 See, for example, Barber, B. (1983). *The Logic and Limits of Trust* (p. 131). New York: Rutgers; Sztompka, P. (1998). Trust, distrust and two paradoxes of democracy. *European Journal of Social Theory*, 1, 19.

6 van der Bles, A. M., van der Linden, S., Freeman, A. L. J., Mitchell, J., Galvao, A. B., Zaval, L., & Spiegelhalter, D. J. (2019). Communicating uncertainty about facts, numbers and science. *R. Soc. Open Sci.*, 6, 181870. http://dx.doi.org/10.1098/rsos.181870, citing, inter alia Fiske, S. T., Cuddy, A. J. C., & Glick, P. (2007). Universal dimensions of social cognition: Warmth and competence. *Trends Cogn. Sci.*, 11, 77–83. doi: 10.1016/j.tics.2006.11.005; Wiener, J. L., & Mowen, J. C. (1986).

DOI: 10.4324/9780429492129-2

factor impacting upon trust placed in science, although it remains an open question whether this may be ameliorated by means of increased transparency and the communication of scientific uncertainty or whether such transparency could risk undermining the perceived competence element of trust.[7] Research findings in that regard have been mixed, with studies finding trends in the direction of perceived honesty and others in the opposite direction.[8] To add to the complexity, uncertainty relayed in the message may not undermine trust in the messenger, but again, this also varies between different research studies.[9]

Long-standing professions such as medicine and law have traditionally relied on 'status trust,' deriving from the trust necessary in the absence of patient or

---

Source credibility: On the independent effects of trust and expertise. *Adv. Consum. Res.*, 13, 306–310; Fiske, S. T., & Dupree, C. (2014). Gaining trust as well as respect in communicating to motivated audiences about science topics. *Proc. Natl Acad. Sci. USA*, 111(13), 593–513, 597. doi: 10.1073/pnas.1317505111; Baier, A. (1986). Trust and antitrust. *Ethics*, 96, 231–260, cited by Ben; Hendriks, F., Kienhues, D., & Bromme, R. (2015). Measuring laypeople's trust in experts in a digital age: The muenster epistemic trustworthiness inventory (METI). *PLoS ONE*, 10(10), e0139309. doi: 10.1371/journal.pone.0139309; Resnik, D. B. (2011). Scientific research and the public trust. *Science and Engineering Ethics*, 17(3) (September), 399–409. doi: 10.1007/s11948-010-9210-x. Epub 2010 Aug 29. PMID: 20803259; PMCID: PMC3151305. Almassi, Public Understanding of Climate Science and the Ethics of Expertise, conference paper January 2012

7 van der Bles, A. M., van der Linden, S., Freeman, A. L. J., Mitchell, J., Galvao, A. B., Zaval, L.,& Spiegelhalter, D. J. (2019). Communicating uncertainty about facts, numbers and science. *R. Soc. Open Sci.*, 6, 181870. http://dx.doi.org/10.1098/rsos.181870

8 van der Bles, A. M., van der Linden, S., Freeman, A. L. J., Mitchell, J., Galvao, A. B., Zaval, L., & Spiegelhalter, D. J. (2019). Communicating uncertainty about facts, numbers and science. *R. Soc. Open Sci.*, 6, 181870. http://dx.doi.org/10.1098/rsos.181870, citing, inter alia, Fiske, S. T., Cuddy, A. J. C., & Glick, P. (2007). Universal dimensions of social cognition: Warmth and competence. *Trends Cogn. Sci.*, 11, 77–83. doi: 10.1016/j.tics.2006.11.005; Fiske, S. T., & Dupree, C. (2014). Gaining trust as well as respect in communicating to motivated audiences about science topics. *Proc. Natl Acad. Sci. USA*, 111(13), 593–513, 597. doi: 10.1073/pnas.1317505111; Johnson BB, Slovic, P. (1995). Presenting uncertainty in health risk assessment: Initial studies of its effects on risk perception and trust. *Risk Analysis*, 15, 485–494. doi: 10.1111/j.1539-6924.1995. tb00341.x. Johnson, B. B., & Slovic P. (1998). Lay views on uncertainty in environmental health risk assessment. *J. Risk Res.*, 1, 261–279. doi: 10.1080/136698798377042; Wiener, J. L., & Mowen, J. C. (1986). Source credibility: On the independent effects of trust and expertise. *Adv. Consum. Res.*, 13, 306–310.

9 van der Bles, A. M., van der Linden, S., Freeman, A. L. J., & Spiegelhalter, D. J. (2018). *The Effects of Uncertainty Communication*. https://ebm.bmj.com/content/23/Suppl_1/A9.2; van der Bles, A. M., van der Linden, S., Freeman, A. L. J., Mitchell, J., Galvao, A. B., Zaval, L., & Spiegelhalter, D. J. (2019). Communicating uncertainty about facts, numbers and science. *R. Soc. Open Sci.*, 6, 181870. http://dx.doi.org/10.1098/rsos.181870, citing, inter alia Jensen, J. D., & Hurley, R. J. (2012). Conflicting stories about public scientific controversies: Effects of news convergence and divergence on scientists' credibility. *Public Underst. Sci.*, 21, 689–704. doi: 10.1177/0963662510387759; Jensen, J. D., Carcioppolo, N., King, A. J., Bernat, J. K., Davis, L., Yale, R., & Smith, J. (2011). Including limitations in news coverage of cancer research: Effects of news hedging on fatalism, medical skepticism, patient trust, and backlash. *J. Health Commun.*, 16, 486–503. doi: 10.1080/10810730.2010.546491; Smithson, M. (1999). Conflict aversion: Preference for ambiguity vs conflict in sources and evidence. *Organ. Behav. Hum. Decis. Process.*, 79, 179–198. doi: 10.1006/obhd.1999.2844

client expertise to assess competence.[10] Scientists similarly occupy positions of complexity, often beyond realistic day-to-day regulatory oversight, and so trust is similarly central. For trust to be effective, transparency with an openness to scrutiny is important.[11] However, transparency can be double edged – information overload risks reducing rather than enhancing understanding by external observers. Explanation and contextualisation of information which is chosen for disclosure may also be important in aiding understanding and therefore to the maintenance of trust, with trust in those making disclosure choices itself being of importance.[12] The balance between formal regulations and the audit of the application of these, on the one hand, and trust, on the other, is also important – if regulations become 'surrogates for trust,' the ethical underpinnings of trust may be reduced.[13]

Trust in science

Trust in science may be compared to a credit economy in the world of finance – activities in which if credibility is subtracted, 'there is just no product left, neither a currency nor a body of scientific knowledge. Skepticism in science is like a run on the currency.'[14]

The scientific community collectively is the source of objectivity in science. Researchers verify and validate each other's work if it is correct, and such self-correction mechanisms are seen as central to the credibility of science.[15] However, peer reviewers and editors have to take a great deal on trust, from author identity to the authenticity of the work submitted, for no journal can easily verify every aspect of each paper.[16]

10 For example, in the context of lawyers, see Webb, J., & Nicolson, D. (1999). Institutionalising trust: Ethics and the responsive regulation of the legal profession. *Legal Ethics*, 2(2) (Winter), 148–168.

11 Sztompka, P. (1998). Trust, distrust and two paradoxes of democracy. *European Journal of Social Theory*, 1, 19, 23.

12 O'Neill, N. Reith lectures 2002. *Radio 4*, www.bbc.co.uk/radio4/reith2002/. See also, Tallis, R. (2004). *Hippocratic Oaths* (p. 103). London: Atlantic.

13 Harre, R. (1999). Trust and its surrogates. In M. Warren (Ed.), *Democracy and Trust* (pp. 249–272). Cambridge: Cambridge University Press. Cited by Groundwater-Smith, S., & Sachs, J. (2002). The activist professional and the reinstatement of trust. *Cambridge Journal of Education*, 32(3), 345.

14 Shapin, Steven (2010). *Never Pure: Historical Studies of Science as if It Was Produced by People with Bodies, Situated in Time, Space, Culture, and Society, and Struggling for Credibility and Authority* (p. 19). Baltimore: Johns Hopkins University Press.

15 Grinnell, F. (2013). Research integrity and everyday practice of science. *Science and Engineering Ethics*, 19, 685–701. doi: 10.1007/s11948-012-9376-5.

16 Edmond, G. (2008). Judging the scientific and medical literature: Some legal implications of changes to biomedical research and publication. *Oxford Journal of Legal Studies*, 28(3), 523, at 529. doi: 10.1093/ojls/gqn021. The average time a reviewer spends on a submission has been found to be two hours – far too little time to enable the numerous tasks and assumptions placed upon peer review to be undertaken thoroughly. Edmond at 531, citing Yankauer, A. (1990). Who are the peer

Society places trust in scientists to engage in the quest for knowledge reliably and transparently, and scientists should be receptive to the necessity of trust by remaining aware that society is counting on them to merit the trust they receive.[17] Mechanisms to detect misbehaviour cannot be perfect, so being able to trust in the moral and epistemic character of their scientists, 'their competence, honesty and adequate epistemic self-assessment,' is vital.[18]

Misplacing trust in those with whom they collaborate may result in significant reputational consequences to scientists. However, some who find themselves in this position also highlight that because of the importance of trust to multi-researcher scientific endeavours, once a cooperative bond has been formed, 'it takes a lot before you really change your opinion. . . . It takes some time to going from trusting . . . to accusing . . .' as condemning evidence mounts.[19]

Psychological literature indicates that people are averse to ambiguous information.[20] There are various taxonomies of uncertainty, for example, uncertainty about scientific model structure, the weighting or values assigned to outcomes or indirect uncertainty about the quality of the underlying knowledge that forms a basis for claims made.[21] These ideas have comparators in the sphere of legal reasoning – direct uncertainty regarding the relative value of evidence to the probability of guilt or liability and indirect uncertainty in terms of the credibility to be given to an individual testimony or piece of evidence.[22] The

reviewers and how much do they review? *JAMA*, 263, 1338–1340; Lock, S., & Smith, J. (1990). What do peer reviewers do? *JAMA*, 263, 1341–1343.

17 Jones, K. (1996). Trust as an affective attitude. *Ethics*, 107(1) (October), 4–25. See also discussion by Ben Almassi, Public Understanding of Climate Science and the Ethics of Expertise, Conference Paper Iowa State University Digital Repository - Iowa State University Summer Symposium on Science Communication: Public Understanding of Climate Science and the Ethics of Expertise (iastate.edu) (accessed 31 January 2021)

18 Simon, J. (2013). Trust. In D. Pritchard (Ed.), *Oxford Bibliographies in Philosophy*. New York: Oxford University Press, www.oxfordbibliographies.com/view/document/obo-9780195396577/obo-9780195396577-0157.xml, engaging with the ideas in Hardwig, J. (1991). The role of trust in knowledge. *The Journal of Philosophy*, 88(12), 693–708; Enserink, M. (2017). Researcher in Swedish fraud case speaks out: 'I'm very disappointed by my colleague'. *Science*, December 8, 2017, www.sciencemag.org/news/2017/12/researcher-swedish-fraud-case-speaks-out-i-m-very-disappointed-my-colleague

19 Enserink, M. (2017). Researcher in Swedish fraud case speaks out: 'I'm very disappointed by my colleague'. *Science*, December 8, 2017, www.sciencemag.org/news/2017/12/researcher-swedish-fraud-case-speaks-out-i-m-very-disappointed-my-colleague

20 Keren, G., & Gerritsen, L. E. M. (1999). On the robustness and possible accounts of ambiguity aversion. *Acta Psychol. (Amst)*, 103, 149–172. doi: 10.1016/S0001-6918(99)00034-7.

21 See, for example, Walker, W. E., Harremoe¨s, P., Rotmans, J., van der Sluijs, J. P., van Asselt, M. B. A., Janssen, P., & Krayer von Krauss, M. P. (2003). Defining uncertainty: a conceptual basis for uncertainty management in model-based decision support. *Integr. Assess.*, 4, 5–17. doi: 10.1076/iaij.4.1.5.16466, cited by van der Bles, A. M., van der Linden, S., Freeman, A. L. J., Mitchell, J., Galvao, A. B., Zaval, L., & Spiegelhalter, D. J. (2019). Communicating uncertainty about facts, numbers and science. *R. Soc. Open Sci.*, 6, 181870. http://dx.doi.org/10.1098/rsos.181870

22 van der Bles, A. M., van der Linden, S., Freeman, A. L. J., Mitchell, J., Galvao, A. B., Zaval, L., & Spiegelhalter, D. J. (2019). Communicating uncertainty about facts, numbers and science. *R. Soc. Open Sci.*, 6, 181870. http://dx.doi.org/10.1098/rsos.181870

terminology of balance of probabilities and beyond reasonable doubt is devised to communicate levels of uncertainty in the legal sphere.[23]

Criticisms that some journals prefer 'a cohesive story' rather than 'a full (and likely messy) account of the research as it was conceptualised and conducted'[24] give rise to important considerations about the communication of scientific uncertainty and its effect on trust, whether divulging uncertainty may signal incompetence and a lowering of trust, or whether such transparency might increase trust.[25]

Generally, the legal arena focuses on words rather than numbers to communicate levels of uncertainty. In the scientific field attempts to increase the accessibility of communication by moving away from numbers can give rise to communication issues and from there trust issues. For example, when the Intergovernmental Panel on Climate Change (IPCC) reports on climate change, lay recipients of this information may misinterpret linguistic terms when assessing probability. For example, the IPCC's use of 'very likely' to indicate probabilities of 90 per cent or more has been shown to have been misinterpreted by many people as presenting much lower risks – in the region of 60 per cent.[26] Use by the International Agency for Research on Cancer (IARC) of linguistic terms such as 'Carcinogenic to humans,' 'Probably carcinogenic to humans,' 'Not classifiable,' and 'Probably not carcinogenic to humans' leaves uncertain the interpretation both of 'probably' and of the size of any carcinogenic effect.[27] Further complications arise from such linguistic uncertainty when variations in understanding resulting, for example, from education levels and pre-existing beliefs, between recipients of communications are factored in, resulting in uncertainty

23 van der Bles, A. M., van der Linden, S., Freeman, A. L. J., Mitchell, J., Galvao, A. B., Zaval, L., & Spiegelhalter, D. J. (2019). Communicating uncertainty about facts, numbers and science. *R. Soc. Open Sci.*, 6, 181870. http://dx.doi.org/10.1098/rsos.181870

24 Fraser, H., Parker, T., Nakagawa, S., Barnett, A., & Fidler, F. (2018). Questionable research practices in ecology and evolution. *PLoS ONE*, 13(7), e0200303. https://doi.org/10.1371/journal.pone.0200303

25 van der Bles, A. M., van der Linden, S., Freeman, A. L. J., Mitchell, J., Galvao, A. B., Zaval, L., & Spiegelhalter, D. J. (2019). Communicating uncertainty about facts, numbers and science. *R. Soc. Open Sci.*, 6, 181870. http://dx.doi.org/10.1098/rsos.181870

26 Budescu, D. V., Por, H-H., & Broomell, S. B. (2012). Effective communication of uncertainty in the IPCC reports. *Clim. Change*, 113, 181–200. doi: 10.1007/s10584-011-0330-3, cited by van der Bles, A. M., van der Linden, S., Freeman, A. L. J., Mitchell, J., Galvao, A. B., Zaval, L., & Spiegelhalter, D. J. (2019). Communicating uncertainty about facts, numbers and science. *R. Soc. Open Sci.*, 6, 181870. http://dx.doi.org/10.1098/rsos.181870. Misinterpretation of verbal quantifiers against IPCC guidelines has been found to cross jurisdictions and languages.

27 van der Bles, A. M., van der Linden, S., Freeman, A. L. J., Mitchell, J., Galvao, A. B., Zaval, L., & Spiegelhalter, D. J. (2019). Communicating uncertainty about facts, numbers and science. *R. Soc. Open Sci.*, 6, 181870. http://dx.doi.org/10.1098/rsos.181870, citing International Agency for Research on Cancer. 2006 IARC monographs on the evaluation of carcinogenic risks to humans: preamble.

in communication not be understood identically by all recipients.[28] The provision of numbers will likely aid understanding and therefore trust by some recipients but be alienating and confusing for others, potentially decreasing trust.[29]

Climate science presents an example of particular challenges, as 'the weather' and climatological phenomena more generally may seem to be understandable to the non-expert observer. For both climate change sceptics and climate change advocates among the general population, personal observation can be a key determinant of their beliefs.[30] In such an environment the overlapping trust relations within the climate researcher community and between researchers and the public are key.[31] Researchers must resist neglecting or even abusing the trust placed in them to avoid the destabilisation and even destruction of the trust relationship.[32] Epistemic trust is morally corrupted when a trusted researcher takes advantage of unfamiliarity by trusting recipients of the range of alternative viewpoints within the research community.[33] Experts must therefore resist

28 See, for example, Han, P. K. J., Klein, W. M. P., Lehman, T. C., Massett, H., Lee, S. C., & Freedman, A. N. (2009). Laypersons' responses to the communication of uncertainty regarding cancer risk estimates. *Med. Decis. Mak.*, 29, 391–403. doi: 10.1177/0272989X08327396; discussed in van der Bles, A. M., van der Linden, S., Freeman, A. L. J., Mitchell, J., Galvao, A. B., Zaval, L., & Spiegelhalter, D. J. (2019). Communicating uncertainty about facts, numbers and science. *R. Soc. Open Sci.*, 6, 181870. http://dx.doi.org/10.1098/rsos.181870. Motivated cognition and confirmation bias may lead to information which underpins prior beliefs being processed more fluently and the opposite with information which challenges prior beliefs.

29 Dieckmann, N. F., Gregory, R., Peters, E., & Hartman, R. (2017) Seeing what you want to see: How imprecise uncertainty ranges enhance motivated reasoning. *Risk Anal.*, 37, 471–486. doi: 10.1111/risa.12639; Myers, T. A., Maibach, E., Peters, E., & Leiserowitz, A. (2015). Simple messages help set the record straight about scientific agreement on humancaused climate change: The results of two experiments. *PLoS ONE*, 10, 1–17. doi: 10.1371/journal.pone.0120985, cited by van der Bles, A. M., van der Linden, S., Freeman, A. L. J., Mitchell, J., Galvao, A. B., Zaval, L., & Spiegelhalter, D. J. (2019). Communicating uncertainty about facts, numbers and science. *R. Soc. Open Sci.*, 6, 181870. http://dx.doi.org/10.1098/rsos.181870. See also Jenkins, S. C., Harris, A. J. L., & Lark, R. M. (2018). Understanding 'unlikely (20% likelihood)' or '20% likelihood (unlikely)' outcomes: The robustness of the extremity effect. *J. Behav. Decis. Mak.*, 31, 572–586. doi: 10.1002/bdm.2072.

30 Borick, C. (2010). American public opinion and climate change. In B. Rabe (Ed.), *Greenhouse Governance: Addressing Climate Change in America* (pp. 24–57). Washington, DC: The Brookings Institution, cited by Almassi, B. (2012). *Public Understanding of Climate Science and the Ethics of Expertise*, conference paper January 2012. doi: 10.31274/sciencecommunication-180809-55 (accessed 5 October 2019)

31 Solomon, R., & Flores, F. (2001). *Building Trust in Business, Politics, Relationships, and Life*. Oxford: Oxford University Press; Baier, A. (1986). Trust and antitrust. *Ethics*, 96, 231–260, cited by Almassi, B. (2012). *Public Understanding of Climate Science and the Ethics of Expertise*, conference paper January 2012. doi: 10.31274/sciencecommunication-180809-55 (accessed 5 October 2019). In contrast, a lack of trust 'erodes the moral health of citizen-scientist epistemic dependency'. Almassi, B. (2012). *Public Understanding of Climate Science and the Ethics of Expertise*, conference paper January 2012. doi: 10.31274/sciencecommunication-180809-55 (accessed 5 October 2019).

32 Baier, A. (1986). Trust and antitrust. *Ethics*, 96, 231–260, 255–256. doi: 10.31274/science communication-180809–55

33 Almassi, B. (2012). *Public Understanding of Climate Science and the Ethics of Expertise*, conference paper January 2012. doi: 10.31274/sciencecommunication-180809-55 (accessed 5 October 2019)

any temptation to use the lack of expertise of those who place trust in them to improperly propagate their favoured scientific interpretation or to express opinions which stray beyond their expertise.[34]

However, disclosing expert disagreement within fields such as climate science may risk increasing perceptions of uncertainty among the public.[35] An example is the hack and email leak in November 2009 from the Climate Research Unit at the University of East Anglia, one of the world's foremost centres of climate science research. The disclosure of information revealed aspects of the inner debates of the climate change community. Internet discussion following the leak alleged improper collusion among climate scientists and deletion or manipulation of data in order to falsely support evidence of global warming.[36] Climate-change sceptics utilised the leaked information to argue that the field of climate science was 'broken' and that 'non-' or 'anti-' scientific practices were prevalent, for example, in the selection of data and in refusing to publish papers by certain authors.[37] Investigations within this scientific community exonerated the scientists of wrongdoing relating to participating in 'directly or indirectly, any actions with an intent to suppress or to falsify data.' However, some public suspicions and concerns remained, with some sections of the public who previously had no strongly held views about climate science potentially having their trust in the climate science community diminished because of the arguments surrounding the leaked information.[38]

34 Baier, A. (1986). Trust and antitrust. *Ethics*, 96, 231–260, 255–256; Almassi, B. (2012). *Public Understanding of Climate Science and the Ethics of Expertise*, conference paper January 2012. doi: 10.31274/sciencecommunication-180809-55 (accessed 5 October 2019)

35 Shrader-Frechette, K. (2011). *What Will Work: Fighting Climate Change with Renewable Energy, Not Nuclear Power*. Oxford: Oxford University Press. van der Bles, A. M., van der Linden, S., Freeman, A. L. J., Mitchell, J., Galvao, A. B., Zaval, L., & Spiegelhalter, D. J. (2019). Communicating uncertainty about facts, numbers and science. *R. Soc. Open Sci.*, 6, 181870. http://dx.doi.org/10.1098/rsos.181870, citing, inter alia, Dixon, G. N., & Clarke, C. E. (2012). Heightening uncertainty around certain science: Media coverage, false balance, and the autism-vaccine controversy. *Sci. Commun.*, 35, 358–382. doi: 10.1177/1075547012458290; van der Linden, S., Leiserowitz, A., Rosenthal, S., & Maibach, E. (2017). Inoculating the public against misinformation about climate change. *Glob. Challenges*, 1, 1600008. doi: 10.1002/gch2.201600008

36 House of Commons Science and Technology Committee. *The Disclosure of Climate Data from the Climatic Research Unit at the University of East Anglia*, Eighth Report of Session 2009–10 HC 387-I, para 1

37 John, S. (2018). Epistemic trust and the ethics of science communication: Against transparency, openness, sincerity and honesty. *Social Epistemology*, 32(2), 75–87, 81. doi: 10.1080/02691728.2017.1410864, citing McAllister, J. W. 2012. Climate science controversies and the demand for access to empirical data. *Philosophy of Science*, 79(5), 871–880.

38 RA-1O Final Investigation Report Involving Dr. Michael E. Mann, The Pennsylvania State University, June 4, 2010, http://news.sciencemag.org/scienceinsider/Final Investigation Report.pdf (accessed 31 January 2021). For further commentary see Brahic, C. (2010). US 'climategate' scientist all but cleared of misconduct. *New Scientist*, February 3, 2010; Oxburgh Report (2010). *Report of the International Panel Set Up by the University of East Anglia to Examine the Research of the Climatic Research Unit*. University of East Anglia; Almassi, B. *Public Understanding of Climate Science and the Ethics of Expertise*, Conference Paper Iowa State University Digital Repository - Iowa State University

The House of Commons Science and Technology Committee, while emphasising that it wasn't its role to adjudicate on the validity of the science relating to the UEA disclosures, noted the importance of transparency and public perception:

> [B]ecause climate science is a matter of global importance and of public interest . . . the quality and transparency of the science should be irreproachable. We therefore consider that climate scientists should take steps to make available all the data used to generate their published work, including raw data; and it should also be made clear and referenced where data has been used but, because of commercial or national security reasons is not available. . .. In addition, scientists should take steps to make available in full their methodological workings, including the computer codes. . . . There should be enough information published to allow verification.[39]

It has been suggested that improved communication between the scientific community and the public remains important but is no longer the central issue of concern.[40] Instead, the ready availability of misleading and biased information has taken centre stage. Primary scientifically factual information is typically published in specialist sources which members of the general public are unlikely to see and written in linguistic and numerical form which even if seen may be difficult for many to understand. In contrast, potentially misleading claims may much more readily find themselves in general media sources, written in a more understandable manner and in terms which may seek to persuade rather than inform.[41] Expansion in media outlets, especially the proliferation of online social media, has resulted in an explosion of sources of information but without the balance, or at least journalistic accuracy, more common historically from traditional media sources.[42] Social media is also accused of risking a collapse of context, meaningful dialogue and debate to facilitate the challenging of

---

Summer Symposium on Science Communication: Public Understanding of Climate Science and the Ethics of Expertise (iastate.edu) (accessed 31 January 2021); Maibach, E., Leiserowitz, A., Cobb, S., Shank, M., Cobb, K. M., & Gulledge, J. (2012). The legacy of Climategate: Undermining or revitalizing climate science and policy? *WIREs Climate Change*, 3, 289–295. Wiley Online Library (accessed 31 January 2021)

39 House of Commons Science and Technology Committee. *The Disclosure of Climate Data from the Climatic Research Unit at the University of East Anglia*. Eighth Report of Session 2009–10 HC 387-I, para 54

40 Iyengar, S., & Massey, D. S. (2018). Scientific communication in a post-truth society. *Proceedings of the National Academy of Sciences*, 201805868; doi: 10.1073/pnas.1805868115

41 For example, in the context of communicating concerns about acid rain see Oreskes, N., & Conway, E. M. (2010). *Merchants of Doubt: How a Handful of Scientists Obscured the Truth on Issues from Tobacco Smoke to Global Warming*. New York: Bloomsbury, 101

42 Iyengar, Shanto, & Massey, D. S. (2018). Scientific communication in a post-truth society. *Proceedings of the National Academy of Sciences*, 201805868; doi: 10.1073/pnas.1805868115

ideas.[43] Some media sources may even be categorised as fostering a 'culture of contempt' – lurid headlines may change emphasis, and 'sensational embellishments' and disregard of factual accuracy may significantly change the account of scientific development.[44]

In the words of another commentator, the development of a polarized, partisan culture segregated within the social sphere has resulted in an environment such that:

> whenever scientific findings clash with a person or group's political agenda ... scientists can expect to encounter a targeted campaign of fake news, misinformation, and disinformation in response, no matter how clearly the information is presented or how carefully and convincingly it is framed. Under these circumstances, the information is unlikely to penetrate the cognitive structures of those it threatens and therefore is likely to be either rejected or ignored by otherwise open-minded people who have absorbed the campaign of false and misleading information.[45]

Even in the absence of 'fake' or intentionally misleading information, proportionately selective reporting is still likely to distort public perception. Oreskes and Conway cite the example of acid rain science and one particular study, which they identify as moving against the overall flow of research in the area, receiving disproportionate coverage from those sections of the media and from commentators on social media who disagree with the majority scientific view.[46]

43 See, for example, For further discussion, see ALLEA., *Loss of Trust? Loss of Trustworthiness? Truth and Expertise*, ALLEA discussion paper #1, May 2018, 5, https://allea.org/wp-content/uploads/2018/05/ALLEA_Discussion_Paper_1_Truth_and_Expertise_Today-digital.pdf; Sunstein, Cass R. (2017). *#republic: Divided Democracy in the Age of Social Media*. Princeton and Oxford: Princeton University Press.

44 Tallis, R. (2004). *Hippocratic Oaths: Medicine and Its Discontents* (pp. 200–201). London: Atlantic Books, cited by Brazier, M. (2011). How the media presents medicine and science. *Medical Law International*, 11(3), 187–196. https://doi.org/10.1177/096853321101100303

45 Iyengar, S., & Massey, D. S. (2018). Scientific communication in a post-truth society. *Proceedings of the National Academy of Sciences*, 201805868; doi: 10.1073/pnas.1805868115

46 Oreskes, N., & Conway, E. M. (2010). *Merchants of Doubt: How a Handful of Scientists Obscured the Truth on Issues from Tobacco Smoke to Global Warming* (p. 101). New York: Bloomsbury. O'Keefe & Kueter, challenge what they perceive to be a consensus model of scientific advancement adopted by Oreskes and Conway when compared with the idea that the idea of even a lone individual can overturn the consensus view of thousands. O'Keefe, W., & Kueter, J. (2010). Clouding the truth: A critique of *Merchants of doubt*. *Marshall Institute Policy Outlook*, 1–8, June. http://scienceandpublicpolicy.org/wp-content/uploads/2010/07/clouding_the_truth.pdf. See also, Nierenberg, N., Tschinkel, W., & Tschinkel, V. (2010). An independent thinker, willing to say what he thought. *Nature*, 466, 435. https://doi.org/10.1038/466435c; Oreskes, N., & Conway, E. (2010). Difference between interim and final acid-rain reports. *Nature*, 466, 815. https://doi.org/10.1038/466815d

The plethora of modern communication routes also requires the process of scientific debate and its propagation to address breakthroughs, perhaps paradigm-shifting ones, which come from outside the majority view. Compared with the historical position, communication opportunities are greater, but so is the prospect of a revolutionary idea becoming lost in the noise of misinformation.[47]

As illustrated by the Andrew Wakefield case, in communicating ideas to the public, the scientific community should take into account the attempts by some sections of the public to formulate their own accounts and explanations of the risks. Rather than simply being ignorant of the dominant scientific view, these sections of the public may incorporate their own personal experience and that of friends and family to attempt to fill a causal knowledge gap – in the case of Wakefield's ideas, parents feeling personal responsibility to undertake their own research on behalf of their children.[48] Rather than being demonstrative of a selfish disregard for public health, such parental approaches could instead be characterised as manifestations of a public health discourse which adopts ideas of choice, empowerment, personal responsibility and participation.[49] Simply presuming public ignorance can therefore undermine appropriate responses by the scientific community to engage with the public and maximise the chances of engendering trust.

In terms of the handling of scientific misconduct, when seeking to counter misleading information and in so doing potentially accusing the purveyors of such information of being unscrupulous, as near to an unblemished record as possible within the scientific community is essential to avoid accusations of hypocrisy. Debates about contentious issues, vaccination or global warming, for example, have proved to be particularly challenging, extending beyond disagreements about the appropriate interpretation of data to more fundamental disagreements about the trustworthiness of the medico-scientific community and its methods.[50] Some objectors may be more inclined to review their position if satisfied that scientific practice and its practitioners are, as far as is

47 O'Keefe, W., & Kueter, J. (2010). Clouding the truth: A critique of *Merchants of doubt*. *Marshall Institute Policy Outlook*, 1–8, June. http://scienceandpublicpolicy.org/wp-content/uploads/2010/07/clouding_the_truth.pdf

48 Goldenberg, M. J. (2016). Public misunderstanding of science? Reframing the problem of vaccine hesitancy. *Perspectives on Science*, 24(5), 552–581. https://doi.org/10.1162/POSC_a_00223, citing, Brown, K. F., Kroll, S., Hudson, M. J. et al. (2010). Factors underlying parental decisions about combination childhood vaccinations including MMR: A systematic review. *Vaccine*, 28, 4235–4248.

49 Goldenberg, M. J. (2016). Public misunderstanding of science? Reframing the problem of vaccine hesitancy. *Perspectives on Science*, 24(5), 552–581. https://doi.org/10.1162/POSC_a_00223, citing, Lupton, D. (1995). *The Imperative of Health: Public Health and the Regulated Body*. London: Sage; Petersen, A., & Lupton, D. (1996). *The New Public Health: Health and Self in the Age of Risk*. London: Sage.

50 Dare, T. (2014). Disagreement over vaccination programmes: Deep or merely complex and why does it matter? *HEC Forum*, 26(1), 43–57, 46.

possible in any human activity, beyond reproach both in terms of the avoidance of questionable practices and embracing aspirational standards of scientific conduct.[51]

Failure on the part of the scientific community to effectively address social media and other sources of problematic communications not only risks undermining trust, but without effective challenge, biased communication may lead to 'witch hunts' and drive accountability underground.[52] Members of the scientific community seeking to anticipate campaigns of misleading information and to develop proactive strategies to counteract them have been suggested as one way forward.[53] In practical terms scientific organisations could collectively fund the creation of an organisation to monitor media and online sources for false and misleading scientific information to facilitate prompt responses and, as necessary, mount a countervailing campaign.[54]

51 See, for example, National Academies – Institute of Medicine. (2002). *Integrity in Scientific Research: Creating an Environment That Promotes Responsible Conduct*. Washington, DC: National Academy Press. Cited by Grinnell, F. (2013). Research integrity and everyday practice of science. *Science and Engineering Ethics*, 19, 685–701. doi: 10.1007/s11948-012-9376-5.

52 Metcalfe, J., Wheat, K., Munafò. M., Parry, J. (2020). *Research Integrity: A Landscape Study* (p. 41). Vitae/UK Research Integrity Office/UK Reproducibility Network, www.ukri.org/files/legacy/documents/research-integrity-main-report/

53 Iyengar, S., & Massey, D. S. (2018). Scientific communication in a post-truth society. *Proceedings of the National Academy of Sciences*, 201805868. doi: 10.1073/pnas.1805868115

54 Iyengar, S., & Massey, D. S. (2018). Scientific communication in a post-truth society. *Proceedings of the National Academy of Sciences*, 201805868. doi: 10.1073/pnas.1805868115. In the context of US society it has been suggested that this could be: 'much easier said than done . . . given what research tells us about how the tribalization of US society has closed American minds . . .'

Chapter 3

Categories of scientific misconduct

The nature of research integrity and research misconduct

The development of what today is recognised as the scientific method created a formal basis for scrutiny of the scientific process and a reliable scientific record – a collective history of discovery which can be subject to critical scrutiny.[1]

The practice of science has continued to provide a focus for philosophers of science, but scientists are both practitioners and authors, with the authorship aspect of the role tending to provide the focus for research misconduct with 'misconduct typically [emerging] in the gap between research as conducted and research as reported.'[2]

A weakness in the objectivity of scientific method is the human element – for example, personal interests and ulterior motives undermine its purity.[3] Certain behaviours undermine the advancing of scientific knowledge, discredit scientific activity in the eyes of the public and waste or misallocate funding.[4] Regulatory challenges therefore include separating innocent and acceptable risks from behaviours and outcomes which may be categorised as misconduct.

1 Ayala, F. (1994). On the scientific method, its practice and pitfalls. *History and Philosophy of the Life Sciences*, 16(2), 205–240. Retrieved October 21, 2020, from www.jstor.org/stable/23331738

2 Zwart, H. (2017). *Tales of Research Misconduct. Library of Ethics and Applied Philosophy* (Vol 36, p. 34). Cham: Springer.

3 Shaw, D., & Satalkar, P. (2018). Researchers' interpretations of research integrity: A qualitative study. *Accountability in Research*, 25(2), 79–93 (R11, Senior researcher (M) in health sciences), 83 doi: 10.1080/08989621.2017.1413940. Shaw and Satalkar also cite the provocatively titled paper 'Is the Scientific Paper a Fraud?' in which Medawar concludes that, in general terms, all published research findings are, by their nature, problematic – human researchers driven by passions, interests and desire that their hypotheses are true may rely upon leaps of intuition rather than entirely stepwise logic. Medawar, P. B. (1963). Is the scientific paper a fraud? *The Listener*, 70(12), 377–378.

4 Chubin, D. E. (1985). Research malpractice. *BioScience*, 35, 80–89; De Vries, R., Anderson, M. S., & Martinson, B. C. (2006). Normal misbehavior: Scientists talk about the ethics of research. *Journal of Empirical Research on Human Research Ethics*, 1(1), 43–50.

DOI: 10.4324/9780429492129-3

There can be a tendency to look backwards, focusing on misconduct after the event, at the expense of facing forwards to what constitutes integrity to maximise desirable behaviour.[5]

Challenges arise in identifying consistent aspects of researcher understanding of integrity and the degree of coherence between an individual researcher's set of values and the coherence between these values and actions.[6] There are common attributes researchers identify with their understanding of integrity, such as honesty and objectivity, but the order of importance and individual researcher understanding of what each attribute means is not consistent.[7] Objective meanings of terms such as 'misconduct' and 'unethical' are not clear cut or culturally heterogeneous in content and function, as within science perceived demarcation lines between appropriate and unethical conduct involve ambiguities.[8]

At its simplest definitional level, research misconduct reflects a spectrum of behaviours ranging from the minor incursions to the extremes of malpractice. However, once attempts at definitions become more sophisticated, they can give rise to a significant degree of disagreement and controversy within research communities.[9] Some definitions have a very long history. For example, in the nineteenth century Babbage identified 'hoaxing,' 'forging, 'trimming,' and 'cooking' as the key types of scientific misconduct.[10] Modern terminology includes fabrication of data, misappropriating the work of others, manipulation of observations and the misleading reporting of findings or outright suppression of data.[11] FFP is a key acronym for fabrication, falsification and plagiarism.[12] Other categories include redundant publication or

5 Shaw, D., & Satalkar, P. (2018). Researchers' interpretations of research integrity: A qualitative study. *Accountability in Research*, 25(2), 79–93. doi: 10.1080/08989621.2017.1413940

6 Meriste, H., Parder, M. L., Lõuk, K., Simm, K., Lilles-Heinsar, L., Veski, L., Soone, M., Juurik, M., & Sutrop, M. (2016). Normative analysis of research integrity and misconduct. *Printeger*. http://printeger.eu/wp-content/uploads/2016/10/D2.3.pdf

7 Shaw, D., & Satalkar, P. (2018). Researchers' interpretations of research integrity: A qualitative study. *Accountability in Research*, 25(2), 79–93, 87. doi: 10.1080/08989621.2017.1413940.

8 Johnson, D. R., & Ecklund, E. H. (2016). Ethical ambiguity in science. *Science and Engineering Ethics*, 22(4), 989–1005, 990. doi: 10.1007/s11948-015-9682-9

9 Kaiser, J. (1999). Policing of science: A misconduct definition that finally sticks? *Science*, 286(5439), 391. doi: 10.1126/science.286.5439.391a.

10 Babbage, C. (1989). The decline of science in England. *Nature*, 340, 499–502. https://doi.org/10.1038/340499a0; Babbage, C. (1969). *Reflections on the Decline of Science in England and on Some of Its Causes* (Facsimile reprint of 1st ed.). Farnborough, London: Fellowes, 1830.

11 Barber, B. (1987). Trust in science. *Minerva*, 25, 123, https://doi.org/10.1007/BF01096860, citing Babbage, C. (1976). *Reflections on the Decline of Science in England and on Some of Its Causes* (pp. 177–182). New York: Scholarly Books. (Published originally in 1830).

12 A common definition of fabrication is the making up of data or results; falsification is the manipulating of research materials or the changing or omitting of data or results; plagiarism is the appropriation of the ideas or words of others without giving appropriate acknowledgment. To constitute

self-plagiarism, invalid authorship, inappropriate approaches to conflict of interest, misrepresentation in funding applications or mismanagement of funding awards and breach of peer review processes.[13] An example of an organisational attempt at defining unacceptable scientific practice is that from the Nuffield Council on Bioethics, which includes design, analytic or reporting practices used to present evidence biased in favour of a particular assertion; poor experimental design; inappropriately slicing up data to create several papers; plagiarism and other issues around authorship; overclaiming the significance of work when seeking grants or to publish findings; from the peer review perspective, inappropriate behaviour such as failing to declare a conflict of interest; cherry-picking data; and the selective reporting hypotheses and rounding down a 'p value' in order to increase the statistical significance of a result.[14]

Such categories remain important descriptors for some commentators and in some jurisdictions but are seen as overly simplistic by others. For example, the borderlines between manipulating data, falsification and fabrication are blurred. The term 'research misconduct' itself can be problematic, with terms such as 'detrimental research practice' being favoured in some quarters as a useful addition to cover situations where researcher behaviour falls short of traditional ideas of misconduct but nevertheless is damaging.[15]

Challenges to achieving agreed definitional approaches to research misconduct also include the variability of common practices between different research

misconduct, typically the behaviour must be committed intentionally, knowingly or without adherence to accepted practices. See, for example The European Code of Conduct for Research Integrity; The US Federal Policy on Research Misconduct; National Science Foundation OIG - Key Regulations | NSF - National Science Foundation; Loikith, L., & Bauchwitz, R. (2016)., The essential need for research misconduct allegation audits. *Science and Engineering Ethics*, 22, 1027–1049. doi: 10.1007/s11948-9798-6; Helgesson, G., & Eriksson, S. (2014). Plagiarism in research. *Medicine, Health Care, and Philosophy*, 18, 91–101, 92. doi: 10.1007/s11019-014-9583-8.

13 See, for example, Canadian Institutes of Health Research, Natural Sciences and Engineering Research Council of Canada, & Social Sciences and Humanities Research Council of Canada. (2016). *Tri-Agency Framework: Responsible Conduct of Research;* Kretser, A., Murphy, D., Bertuzzi, S., Abraham, T., Allison, D., Boor, K., Dwyer, J., Grantham, A., Harris, L., Hollander, R., Jacobs-Young, C., Rovito, S., Vafiadis, D., Woteki, C., Wyndham, J., & Yada, R. (2019). Scientific integrity principles and best practices: Recommendations from a scientific integrity consortium. *Science and Engineering Ethics*, 25. doi: 10.1007/s11948-019-00094-3; National Academies of Sciences, Engineering, and Medicine (US). 2002. Integrity in scientific research. National Academies Press, cited by Shaw, D., & Satalkar, P. (2018). Researchers' interpretations of research integrity: A qualitative study. *Accountability in Research*, 25(2), 79–93, 89. doi: 10.1080/08989621.2017.1413940.

14 Nuffield Council on Bioethics, *The Culture of Scientific Research in the UK*, December 2014.

15 National Academies of Sciences, Engineering, and Medicine. (2017). *Fostering Integrity in Research* (p. 1). Washington, DC: National Academies Press. https://doi.org/10.17226/21896; John, L. K., Loewenstein, G., & Prelec, D. (2012). Measuring the prevalence of questionable research practices with incentives for truth telling. *Psychological Science,* 23(5), 524–532, cited by Kretser, A., Murphy, D., Bertuzzi, S., Abraham, T., Allison, D., Boor, K., Dwyer, J., Grantham, A., Harris, L., Hollander, R., Jacobs-Young, C., Rovito, S., Vafiadis, D., Woteki, C., Wyndham, J., & Yada, R. (2019). Scientific integrity principles and best practices: Recommendations from a scientific integrity consortium. *Science and Engineering Ethics*, 25. doi: 10.1007/s11948-019-00094-3.

fields and socialisation within each field, which can dictate levels of acceptability of different forms of conduct.[16] For example, behaviours which some scientists may identify as normal, routine occurrences include activities such as withholding selected results from publications, overhyping research, exploiting hierarchy relationships in the workplace, cronyism, misusing research funds and inadequate keeping of research records.[17] Ethical boundaries are not universally agreed within scientific communities, resulting in the flexibility and ambiguity of ethical interpretation associated with some behaviours and associated weak social control in terms of determining fault and applying sanctions.[18]

Entrenchment of certain behaviours within a research community may therefore blur boundaries between acceptable behaviour and misconduct. For example, in the fields of psychiatry and psychology Jellison et al found that 56 per cent of papers reporting randomised controlled trials in leading journals contained evidence of attempted 'spin' in reporting their results.[19] If the latter leads to reporting apparently positive results from data which do not support this and downplaying non-supporting data, the scientific record can be harmed. The so-called 'gold standard' of randomized controlled trials, and even patient treatment, can also suffer as a result. For example, spin was found in 49 per cent of abstract conclusion sections in 2 per cent of titles.[20] Figures as high as 84 per cent in abstracts have been found in other studies.[21] While preferences by some

16 Szomszor, M., & Quaderi, N. (2020). *Global Research Report Research Integrity: Understanding Our Shared Responsibility for a Sustainable Scholarly Ecosystem* (p. 5), October 2020. Institute for Scientific Information, https://clarivate.com/webofsciencegroup/wp-content/uploads/sites/2/2020/10/ISI-Research-Integrity-Report.pdf (accessed 21 October 2020)

17 Johnson, D. R., & Ecklund, E. H. (2016). Ethical ambiguity in science. *Science and Engineering Ethics,* 22(4), 989–1005, 990. doi: 10.1007/s11948-015-9682-9, citing De Vries, R., Anderson, M. S., & Martinson, B. C. (2006). Normal misbehavior: Scientists talk about the ethics of research. *Journal of Empirical Research on Human Research Ethics,* 1(1), 43–50

18 See, for example, Hobson-West, P. (2012). Ethical boundary-work in the animal research laboratory. Sociology, 46(4), 649–663; Wainwright, S. P., Williams, C., Michael, M., Farsides, B., & Cribb, A. (2006). Ethical boundary-work in the embryonic stem cell laboratory. *Sociology of Health and Illness,* 28(6), 732–748.

19 Spin is defined as including only those results which the authors wish to highlight or selective conclusions they wish to draw even though these may not accurately summarise the findings of the study. Many practices contribute to spin, including the selective reporting of outcomes, p-hacking, inappropriate application of statistical analysis and manipulation of figures or graphs. Jellison, S., Roberts, W., Bowers, A. et al. (2019). Evaluation of spin in abstracts of papers in psychiatry and psychology journals. *BMJ Evidence-Based Medicine.* Published Online First: 05 August 2019. doi: 10.1136/bmjebm-2019-111176

20 Jellison, S., Roberts, W., Bowers, A. et al. (2019). Evaluation of spin in abstracts of papers in psychiatry and psychology journals. *BMJ Evidence-Based Medicine.* Published Online First: 05 August 2019. doi: 10.1136/bmjebm-2019-111176

21 Lazarus, C., Haneef, R., Ravaud, P. et al. (2015). Classification and prevalence of spin in abstracts of non-randomized studies evaluating an intervention. *BMC Med Res Methodol,* 15, 85. doi: 10.1186/s12874-015-0079-x; Patel, S. V., Van Koughnett, J. A., Howe, B. et al. (2015). Spin is common in studies assessing robotic colorectal surgery: an assessment of reporting and interpretation of study results. *Dis Colon Rectum,* 58, 878–84. doi: 10.1097/DCR.0000000000000425

publications for positive results may encourage spin, it sits uncomfortably with ideas that good research practice requires findings to be reported honestly and accurately, and while some aspects of spin may be evident on reading an article, it nevertheless can mislead or, at best, waste the time of busy readers.[22]

Approaches also differ in definitional terms between countries and between research institutions and professional groupings within countries. In the UK and some other European jurisdictions, approaches to definitions of research misconduct have favoured flexibility, whereas in the United States, calls from within research communities have tended towards greater precision to aid individual researchers to determine what is and is not permitted.[23] The focus in the United States has remained on FFP due, it has been argued, to 'intense lobbying by American scientists' to limit its extension.[24] This has at least two important consequences. One relates to the international influence of the United States and so proliferation of a limited definition to other jurisdictions. The other is more legalistic in nature. While there may be some attempts to act against alleged misconduct beyond the narrowness of the definition, in terms of natural justice, prohibited behaviour should be clearly defined along with the requisite mental state, for example, intention or recklessness.[25] Alternative definitional approaches, for example, risk-based regulation, are intentionally less precise but enable greater breadth of regulatory enforcement.

In terms of common categories of misconduct, studies have found that around 2 per cent of researchers admit to having fabricated or falsified data.[26] Fourteen per cent of researchers in one study reported knowing of a colleague who had behaved in such a way.[27] Another study found that the rate of such

22 Jellison, S., Roberts, W., Bowers, A. et al. (2019). Evaluation of spin in abstracts of papers in psychiatry and psychology journals. *BMJ Evidence-Based Medicine*. Published Online First: 05 August 2019. doi: 10.1136/bmjebm-2019-111176; Boutron, I., & Ravaud, P. (2018). Misrepresentation and distortion of research in biomedical literature. *Proc Natl Acad Sci U S A,* 115, 2613–2619. doi: 10.1073/pnas.1710755115; Shinohara, K., Aoki, T., So, R. et al. (2017). Influence of overstated abstract conclusions on clinicians: A web-based randomised controlled trial. *BMJ Open*, 7, e018355. doi: 10.1136/bmjopen-2017–018355

23 Smith, R. (2006). Research misconduct: The poisoning of the well. *Journal of the Royal Society of Medicine*, 99, 232–237, 233–234.

24 Breen, K. J. (2016). Research misconduct: Time for a re-think? *Internal Medicine Journal,* 46, 728–733. doi: 10.1111/imj.13075, 728, citing Rennie, D., & Gunsalus, C. K. (2008). What is research misconduct? In F. Wells & M. Farthing (Eds.), *Fraud and Misconduct in Biomedical Research* (4th ed., pp. 29–51). London: The Royal Society of Medicine Press.

25 Breen, K. J. (2016). Research misconduct: Time for a re-think? *Internal Medicine Journal,* 46, 728–733. doi: 10.1111/imj.13075, 729.

26 Fanelli, D. (2009). How many scientists fabricate and falsify research? A systematic review and meta-analysis of survey data. *PLoS One,* 4; Fraser, H., Parker, T., Nakagawa, S., Barnett, A., & Fidler, F. (2018). Questionable research practices in ecology and evolution. *PLoS ONE*, 13(7), e0200303. https://doi.org/10.1371/journal. pone.0200303

27 Fanelli, D. (2009). How many scientists fabricate and falsify research? A systematic review and meta-analysis of survey data. *PLoS One,* 4.

awareness is higher for plagiarism than for data fabrication and falsification.[28] Experiences can differ between research areas. For example, in the fields of ecology and evolution, around 50 per cent of those researchers questioned reported that they had encountered questionable research practices or scientific misconduct 'once or twice' or 'often' among researchers in their own and other institutions. Such observations included both junior and senior researchers in roughly equal numbers.[29] In the same field, 64 per cent of respondents reported cherry-picking statistically significant results; 42 per cent reported *p* hacking by means of first checking the statistical significance of results before collecting more data and 51 per cent engaged in 'P-hacking' and 'HARKing.'[30]

28 Pupovac, V., & Fanelli, D. (2015). Scientists admitting to plagiarism: A meta-analysis of surveys. *Science and Engineering Ethics,* 21, 1331–1352. https://doi.org/10.1007/s11948-014-9600-6

29 Fraser, H., Parker, T., Nakagawa, S., Barnett, A., & Fidler, F. (2018). Questionable research practices in ecology and evolution. *PLoS ONE,* 13(7), e0200303. https://doi.org/10.1371/journal.pone.0200303

30 'P-hacking' and 'HARKing' relate to the running of multiple tests in the search for a statistically significant result to report and hypothesising after the results are known. In the latter context researchers create a plausible-sounding explanation for the result that was obtained after the data have been obtained, presenting unexpected findings as if predicted and presenting exploratory work as if confirmatory hypothesis testing. Such approaches can result in statistically significant findings by chance alone. Activities may include checking the statistical significance in advance of deciding whether or not to continue collecting data; stopping data collection at the point results reach statistical significance; choosing to exclude data after checking the statistical effect; and failing to report the data exclusion, Fraser, H., Parker, T., Nakagawa, S., Barnett, A., & Fidler, F. (2018). Questionable research practices in ecology and evolution. *PLoS ONE,* 13(7), e0200303. 2 https://doi.org/10.1371/journal. pone.0200303; Norbert, L. Kerr (1998). HARKing: Hypothesizing after the results are known. *Personality and Social Psychology Review,* 2(3) (February), 196–217. doi: 10.1207/s15327957pspr0203_4. P-hacking can be intentional, for example, the hypothetical example by Simmons et al that appropriately selected data could 'prove' that listening to The Beatles could make undergraduates younger, Simmons, J. P., Nelson, L. D., & Simonsohn, U. (2011). False-positive psychology: Undisclosed flexibility in data collection and analysis allows presenting anything as significant (May 23, 2011). *Psychological Science.* Available at SSRN: https://ssrn.com/abstract=1850704. P-hacking can also be unintentional, for example, Rohrer et al, in their study of self-retraction of questionable research findings, had three respondents who identified their own work where P-hacking was an issue but which had resulted from poor understanding, at the time the research was undertaken, of the relevant statistical considerations. In each case, the researchers had come to realise that their reported findings 'would not have held up had all researcher degrees of freedom been properly accounted for.' Rohrer, J. M., DeBruine, L. M., Heyman, T., Jones, B. C., Schmukle, S. C., Silberzahn, R., . . . Yarkoni, T. (2018). *Putting the Self in Self-Correction.* December 12. osf.io/ps8nt. P-hacking can also be an unintended side effect of the drive by journals to enhance the reproducibility of research by ensuring that original material such as study protocols, datasets and code are available when an article is published. Such open data can, however, be misused by other researchers, House of Commons Science and Technology Committee, Research integrity, Sixth Report of Session 2017–19, 11 July 2018 HC 350, paras 69–70. Ideally, open access to data permits the rigorous retesting of purported findings and in turn allows external validation of claims. In reality, further controls may be needed, such as researchers specifying their research question and intended methodology before being granted access to data. One approach to implementing such safeguards would be to empower a council or centre on data ethics to coordinate such controls.

Concerns connected to individual behaviour include examples of institutional approaches which may deter whistle-blowers and obstruct investigations.[31] Accusations have also arisen of institutional investigatory or adjudicatory processes failing to properly address alleged misconduct in order, for example, to protect a 'star' researcher.[32]

Codes of good practice and education about research ethics and integrity offer alternative or additional approaches to reliance upon definitional lists of bad practices and associated sanctions.[33] Attempts to introduce overarching codes include the Concordat to Support Research Integrity, described as the UK's national policy statement on research integrity, devised by a range of stakeholders and the UK Research Integrity Office (UKRIO). The Concordat seeks to provide a national framework for good research conduct and its governance. Signatories to the concordat commit to:

1 Upholding the highest standards of rigour and integrity in all aspects of research
2 Ensuring that research is conducted according to appropriate ethical, legal and professional frameworks, obligations and standards
3 Supporting a research environment that is underpinned by a culture of integrity and based on good governance, best practice, and support for the development of researchers
4 Using transparent, timely, robust and fair processes to deal with allegations of research misconduct should they arise
5 Working together to strengthen the integrity of research and to review progress regularly and openly[34]

For such a recommendation see Science and Technology Committee, Fourth Report of Session 2015–16, *The big data dilemma*, HC 468, para 102. In regulatory terms p-hacking has tended to be downplayed, but evidence is emerging that attitudes and approaches might be changing, Grove, J. (2020). Reprimand for 'p-hacking' is 'important moment' for science. *Times Higher Education*, October 6, 2020, www.timeshighereducation.com/news/reprimand-p-hacking-important-moment-science. This article reports what was considered to be 'a first for the Netherlands, and possibly for Europe, a researcher at Leiden University was found to have "acted in violation of scientific integrity by incorrectly using statistical methods (*p*-hacking) by continuously conducting statistical tests during the course of an experiment."'

31 Partnership, Interacademy. (2016). *Doing Global Science*, Princeton, NJ: Princeton University Press, 4

32 Cabbolet, M. J. T. F. (2014). Scientific misconduct: Three forms that directly harm others as the modus operandi of Mill's Tyranny of the prevailing opinion. *Science and Engineering Ethics*, 20(1), 41–54. doi: 10.1007/s11948-013-9433, Martin, B. (1998). Advice for the dissident scholar. *Thought & Action*, 14(1), 119–130. A suggested response to this is that such behaviour should itself constitute misconduct.

33 Smith, R. (2006). Research misconduct: The poisoning of the well. *Journal of the Royal Society of Medicine*, 99, 232–237, 233–234.

34 The Concordat to Support Research Integrity, www.universitiesuk.ac.uk/policy-and-analysis/reports/Documents/2019/the-concordat-to-support-research-integrity.pdf (accessed 12 October 2020)

For national policy statements such as the Concordat to be effective, they need to be fully integrated into the day-to-day thinking of individual researchers. A survey of UK-based researchers found that while the provisions of the Concordat were seen as valuable in general terms, only a minority of respondents referred to it specifically, and when questioned directly 42 per cent had no awareness of it.[35] Other attempts at overarching policy approaches have similarly low awareness rates. For example, the San Francisco Declaration of Research Assessment (DORA) had an even lower level of awareness than the UK Concordat, with over 65 per cent of respondents saying they had never heard of it. Awareness of their employer's institutional ethics processes was much higher, but over 10 per cent of respondents had no awareness of their employer's ethics processes and a higher number were unaware of the institutional policy for reporting suspected misconduct.[36]

Undue focus upon traditional definitional approaches such as FFP may detract from newer issues which threaten to harm research integrity. It has been argued that developments such as the measurement of research performance, intense competition for career advancement and research funding have resulted in the emergence of new behaviours 'that are more epiphenomena around research activity and publication than phenomena of the type traditionally monitored, such as FFP.'[37] Traditional ideas of altruism from members of the scientific community, focused primarily on the public good, face challenges presented by the intensely competitive environment to secure and build a research career.[38] Funding and career recognition systems which may inadvertently tend towards favouring poor practices and risky methods can lead to 'the natural selection of bad science.'[39] This is directly harmful to the scientific record but may also inhibit further the creation of good science if scientists with higher levels of integrity are squeezed out in career advancement and funding terms.

35 Metcalfe, J., Wheat, K., Munafò. M., Parry, J. (2020). *Research Integrity: A Landscape Study*. Vitae/UK Research Integrity Office/UK Reproducibility Network, www.ukri.org/files/legacy/documents/research-integrity-main-report/ (accessed 14 October 2020)

36 Metcalfe, J., Wheat, K., Munafò. M., Parry, J. (2020). *Research Integrity: A Landscape Study*. Vitae/UK Research Integrity Office/UK Reproducibility Network, www.ukri.org/files/legacy/documents/research-integrity-main-report/ (accessed 14 October 2020)

37 Edwards, M. A., & Roy, S. (2017). Academic research in the 21st century: Maintaining scientific integrity in a climate of perverse incentives and hypercompetition. *Environmental Engineering Science*, 34(1), 51–61. www.liebertpub.com/doi/10.1089/ees.2016.0223, cited by Szomszor, M., & Quaderi, N. (2020). *Global Research Report Research Integrity: Understanding Our Shared Responsibility for a Sustainable Scholarly Ecosystem* (p. 6). October 2020. Institute for Scientific Information. https://clarivate.com/webofsciencegroup/wp-content/uploads/sites/2/2020/10/ISI-Research-Integrity-Report.pdf (accessed 21 October 2020)

38 See, for example, Jones, N. (2007). A code of ethics for the life sciences. *Science and Engineering Ethics*, 13, 25–43. doi: 10.1007/s11948-006-0007-x.

39 Gunsalus, C. K., & Robinson, Aaron D. (2018). Nine pitfalls of research misconduct. *Nature*, 557, 297–299. doi: 10.1038/d41586-018-05145-6, citing Smaldino, P. E., & McElreath, R. (2016). The natural selection of bad science. *Royal Society Open Science*, 3, 160384.

Deliberate gaming of the system can arise from desires for prestige, status advancement and material gain and is one explanation for some research misconduct.[40] The desire on the part of a researcher to work fast and become famous can undermine integrity.[41] The overall picture of the publication of 'exciting' findings in high-profile journals feeds into a reward system of promotions, speaking invitations and other current esteem markers. A shift from the traditional model of 'discovery' as the main focus of researcher reward to the expectation of an outstanding publication and citation profile can lead to new models of misconduct, such as the manipulation of the publication and citation record.[42] This presents a challenge to instilling a culture of scientific integrity which necessitates different priorities, one in which the system of rewards and normative ideals is in alignment.[43] The tension between the current reward model and the norms of science, it has been argued, is the real threat to ethical research conduct.[44] An alternative model designed to address this would see incentives based on commitment to appropriate research processes and a focus on research integrity.[45]

40 See, for example, Hoover, G. A. (2005). *A Game-theoretic Model of Plagiarism*. Working Paper No. 05–06–01, Economics, Finance and Legal Studies, University of Alabama; Riis, P. (2000). Sociology and psychology within the scope of scientific dishonesty. *Science and Engineering Ethics,* 6, 35–39.

41 Shaw, D., & Satalkar, P. (2018). Researchers' interpretations of research integrity: A qualitative study. *Accountability in Research*, 25(2), 79–93, 88. doi: 10.1080/08989621.2017.1413940.

42 Szomszor, M., & Quaderi, N. (2020). *Global Research Report Research Integrity: Understanding Our Shared Responsibility for a Sustainable Scholarly Ecosystem* (p. 6). October 2020. Institute for Scientific Information. https://clarivate.com/webofsciencegroup/wp-content/uploads/sites/2/2020/10/ISI-Research-Integrity-Report.pdf (accessed 21 October 2020), citing Biagioli, M., Kenney, M., Martin, B., & Walsh, J. (2019). Academic misconduct, misrepresentation, and gaming. *Research Policy*, 48(2), 401–413; Biagioli, M. (2020). Fraud by numbers: Metrics and the new academic misconduct. *Los Angeles Review of Books*, September 7, 2020; Biagioli, M., & Lippman, A. (Eds.) (2020). *Gaming the Metrics: Misconduct and Manipulation in Academic Research*. Cambridge, MA: MIT Press; Chapman, C. A., Bicca-Marques, J. C., CalvignacSpencer, S., Fan, P. F., Fashing, P. J., Gogarten, J., Guo, S. T., Hemingway, C. A., Leendertz, F., Li, B. G., Matsuda, I., Hou, R., Serio-Silva, J. C., & Stenseth, N. C. (2019). Games academics play and their consequences: how authorship, h-index and journal impact factors are shaping the future of academia. *Proceedings of the Royal Society B – Biological Sciences*, 286(1916), article number 20192047.

43 Devereaux, M. L. (2014). Rethinking the meaning of ethics in RCR education. *Journal of Microbiology and Biology Education,* 15(2), 165–168, 168. doi: http://dx.doi.org/10.1128/jmbe.v15i2.857; Kretser, A., Murphy, D., Bertuzzi, S., Abraham, T., Allison, D., Boor, K., Dwyer, J., Grantham, A., Harris, L., Hollander, R., Jacobs-Young, C., Rovito, S., Vafiadis, D., Woteki, C., Wyndham, J., & Yada, R. (2019). Scientific integrity principles and best practices: Recommendations from a scientific integrity consortium. *Science and Engineering Ethics*, 25. doi: 10.1007/s11948-019-00094-3.

44 Devereaux, M. L. (2014). Rethinking the meaning of ethics in RCR education. *Journal of Microbiology and Biology Education,* 15(2), 165–168, 168. doi: http://dx.doi.org/10.1128/jmbe.v15i2.857

45 Metcalfe, J., Wheat, K., Munafò. M., Parry, J. (2020). *Research Integrity: A Landscape Study* (p. 43). Vitae/UK Research Integrity Office/UK Reproducibility Network, www.ukri.org/files/legacy/documents/research-integrity-main-report/

Objectivity in a publish-or-perish climate can pose particular challenges in terms of determining the limits of where results might take a hypothesis, acknowledging limitations rather than trying to manipulate data to fit a hypothesis and being willing to admit that a hypothesis was wrong.[46] This requires resisting 'target science' – seeking to target certain findings which would result in a higher publication rate or publications in higher-impact-factor journals. From this perspective, publishing should be an outcome which arises naturally if research proves to be fruitful, not a target to be achieved at (almost) any cost.[47]

Gunsalus uses the mnemonic TRAGEDIES: Temptation; Rationalization; Ambition; Group and authority pressure; Entitlement; Deception; Incrementalism; Embarrassment and Stupid systems to summarise various interlocking factors that can lead scientists astray.[48] Kornfeld attributes examples of research misconduct to one or more psychological traits or circumstantial factors. The categories identified are:

> The desperate, whose fear of failure overcame a personal code of conduct
> The perfectionist, for whom any failure was a catastrophe
> The ethically challenged, who succumbed to temptation,
> The grandiose, who believed that his or her superior judgment did not require verification,
> The sociopath, who was totally absent a conscience.[49]

However, in the absence of extensive systematic research into the motives of researchers who have committed research misconduct, determining reasons remains at least in part speculative.[50]

46 Shaw, D., & Satalkar, P. (2018). Researchers' interpretations of research integrity: A qualitative study. *Accountability in Research*, 25(2), 79–93, 84. doi: 10.1080/08989621.2017.1413940.

47 Shaw, D., & Satalkar, P. (2018). Researchers' interpretations of research integrity: A qualitative study. *Accountability in Research*, 25(2), 79–93, 84. doi: 10.1080/08989621.2017.1413940.

48 Gunsalus, C. K. (2012). *The Young Professionals' Survival Guide* (pp. 12, 78). Cambridge, MA: Harvard University Press; Gunsalus, C. K., & Robinson, Aaron D. (2018). Nine pitfalls of research misconduct. *Nature,* 557, 297–299. doi: 10.1038/d41586-018-05145-6. Gunsalus defines the component terms as follows: Temptation – "Getting my name on this article would look really good on my CV."; Rationalization -"It's only a few data points, and those runs were flawed anyway."; Ambition – "The better the story we can tell, the better a journal we can go for."; Group and authority pressure – "The PI's instructions don't exactly match the protocol approved by the ethics review board, but she is the senior researcher."; Entitlement – "I've worked so hard on this, and I know this works, and I need to get this publication."; Deception – "I'm sure it would have turned out this way (if I had done it)."; Incrementalism – "It's only a single data point I'm excluding, and just this once."; Embarrassment – "I don't want to look foolish for not knowing how to do this."; Stupid systems – "It counts more if we divide this manuscript into three submissions instead of just one."

49 See, for example, case studies from Kornfeld, D. S. (2012). Perspective: Research misconduct: The search for a remedy. *Acad Med,* 87, 877–882, 879.

50 Breen, K. J. (2016). Research misconduct: Time for a re-think? *Internal Medicine Journal,* 46, 728–733. doi: 10.1111/imj.13075, 728.

It is important to distinguish between the integrity of research and the integrity of the researchers. The integrity of the research record can be undermined accidently without any intentional misconduct and, if recognised by the researchers involved, corrected voluntarily. Transparency in reporting research findings is both an ethical responsibility and a scientific obligation, it being incumbent upon all within the scientific community to maintain an ecosystem directed towards reproducibility through transparency.[51] Research can be untidy and mistakes happen – the transparent remedying of errors is key.[52]

Publication misconduct

Scientific findings can gain no traction unless they are disseminated. In the words of one commentator, 'when discoveries are not made public, it is as if the work was never performed.'[53] The veracity of the publication record is a vital component of the research process and its long-term sustainability.[54] For scientists themselves, career development will stall, or even collapse, without an impressive publication record.[55] The desired aim of original research activity is that it should be rigorously and honestly undertaken, accurate and transparent.[56] Even everyday research practice takes scientists into vulnerable territory – presentation of data may often involve it being 'arranged to tell the best story,' papers tend to be drafted in a manner which presents as logical and internally consistent and failed experiments and discarded hypotheses may be omitted.[57] Such selectivity has the potential to blur the boundary between creative insight and fabrication.[58] In each case, the intellectual honesty of a research

51 Kretser, A., Murphy, D., Bertuzzi, S., Abraham, T., Allison, D., Boor, K., Dwyer, J., Grantham, A., Harris, L., Hollander, R., Jacobs-Young, C., Rovito, S., Vafiadis, D., Woteki, C., Wyndham, J., & Yada, R. (2019). Scientific integrity principles and best practices: Recommendations from a scientific integrity consortium. *Science and Engineering Ethics*, 25. doi: 10.1007/s11948-019-00094-3.

52 Dr Elizabeth Moylan, representing the Committee on Publication Ethics, in evidence to the House of Commons Science and Technology Committee, Research integrity, Sixth Report of Session 2017–19, 11 July 2018 HC 350, page 13

53 Grinnell, F. (2013). Research integrity and everyday practice of science. *Science and Engineering Ethics*, 19, 685–701. doi: 10.1007/s11948-012-9376-5.

54 Szomszor, M., & Quaderi, N. (2020). *Global Research Report Research Integrity: Understanding Our Shared Responsibility for a Sustainable Scholarly Ecosystem* (p. 4). October 2020. Institute for Scientific Information, https://clarivate.com/webofsciencegroup/wp-content/uploads/sites/2/2020/10/ISI-Research-Integrity-Report.pdf (accessed 21 October 2020)

55 Grinnell, F. (2013). Research integrity and everyday practice of science. *Science and Engineering Ethics*, 19, 685–701. doi: 10.1007/s11948-012-9376-5.

56 See, for example, Nuffield Council on Bioethics, The Culture of Scientific Research in the UK; Universities UK, 'The concordat to support integrity in research' (2012)

57 Grinnell, F. (2013). Research integrity and everyday practice of science. *Science and Engineering Ethics*, 19, 685–701. doi: 10.1007/s11948-012-9376-5.

58 See, for example, National Academies – Institute of Medicine. (2002). Integrity in scientific research: Creating an environment that promotes responsible conduct. Washington, DC: National Academy Press.

output will be determined by the approach of the researchers when writing up results and, more broadly, the suitability and rigour or the conventions of everyday practice.[59] As the number of papers making up the scientific record increases, each drawing upon and citing earlier work, pollution of the record risks frustrating the efforts of those who place reliance on it and damaging future research.[60]

Plagiarism gives rise to reputational damage to the research community as a whole and poses some harm to the plagiarised author. In theory, fear of detection and associated punishment are strong deterrents against publication misconduct such as plagiarism. However, the realities can be somewhat different. If plagiarism comes to the attention of the original author, the author is faced with the choice of whether or not to challenge it. Disincentives to challenge include the risk that the allegation will not be substantiated, the original author having devoted time and energy which could have been devoted to other pursuits. Financial costs will also accrue if lawyers are engaged.[61] The disincentive will be greater if the accusation of plagiarism is against a more senior and powerful member of the research community.[62] Cost to the original author of not challenging plagiarism includes citations lost by unfair attribution and the potential mental discomfort of knowing that work has been misappropriated and that the plagiarist has profited.[63] Overall, from a game theory perspective, the risks and uncertainty faced by the original author in challenging plagiarism, compared with, at best, modest gains if successful, point in the direction away from challenge.[64]

The onus of deciding whether or not to pursue plagiarism may rest with the plagiarised author because of the absence of a professional regulatory body and

59 For further discussion, see Grinnell, F. (2013). Research integrity and everyday practice of science. *Science and Engineering Ethics*, 19, 685–701. doi: 10.1007/s11948-012-9376-5. Grinnell argues that selectivity of this type, even if complying with accepted conventions, results 'an absolute sense' in a paper which is 'false.'

60 Szomszor, M., & Quaderi, N. (2020). *Global Research Report Research Integrity: Understanding Our Shared Responsibility for a Sustainable Scholarly Ecosystem* (p. 4). October 2020. Institute for Scientific Information, https://clarivate.com/webofsciencegroup/wp-content/uploads/sites/2/2020/10/ISI-Research-Integrity-Report.pdf (accessed 21 October 2020)

61 Hoover, G. A. (2006). A game-theoretic model of plagiarism. *Atl Econ J*, 34, 449. https://doi.org/10.1007/s11293-006-9029-7

62 Hoover, G. A. (2006). A game-theoretic model of plagiarism. *Atl Econ J*, 34, 449. https://doi.org/10.1007/s11293-006-9029-7, citing Enders, W., & Hoover, G. A. (2004). *Plagiarism in Economics: A Problem Needing Attention!* University of Alabama Working Paper; List, J., Bailey, C. B., Euzent, P., & Martin, T. (2001). Academic economists behaving badly? A survey on three areas of unethical behavior. *Economic Inquiry*, 39(1), 162–170.

63 Hoover, G. A. (2006). A game-theoretic model of plagiarism. *Atl Econ J*, 34, 449. https://doi.org/10.1007/s11293-006-9029-7

64 Hoover, G. A. (2006). A game-theoretic model of plagiarism. *Atl Econ J*, 34, 449. https://doi.org/10.1007/s11293-006-9029-7, citing Arce, D. M. (2005). *The Whistle Blower: Hero or Rat?* Rhodes College Working Paper.

associated code of ethics to provide a reliable alternative mechanism.[65] Certain ad hoc provisions have emerged. For example, the UKRIO emphasises the importance of integrity in the publication process, with journal editors, referees and ultimately readers as part of the research community each playing an important role in detecting and addressing publication misconduct.[66] The Council of Science Editors White Paper on Promoting Integrity in Scientific Journal Publications discusses the responsibility of editors when they encounter suspected misconduct, as well as aiming to open dialogue about ethical publishing practices and foster informed decision making by editors.[67]

Committee on Publication Ethics

In 1997, the Committee on Publication Ethics (COPE) emerged from a relatively informal coming together of a small number of journal editors and developed into an organisation with the purpose to advise editors and publishers and to produce a code of conduct.[68] The COPE code of conduct provides that editors have a duty to act if they suspect misconduct or an allegation of misconduct is reported to them. Papers giving rise to concerns about misconduct should not simply be rejected by editors. Specific editorial obligations include seeking to ensure that journal policies applied to authors and reviewers are such that they encourage responsible behaviour and discourage misconduct; maintenance of the integrity of the academic record; and publishing corrections, clarifications, retractions and apologies when necessary.[69] In terms of best practice, journal editors should provide support for authors who have been victims of plagiarism or whose copyright has been breached.[70]

Editors are ethically obliged to pursue alleged cases, initially with those suspected of misconduct, but if they are not satisfied with the responses, they should contact the employing institution or other appropriate body to facilitate a fuller investigation.[71] Anticipating the absence of satisfactory employer action

65 Hoover, G. A. (2006). A game-theoretic model of plagiarism. *Atl Econ J*, 34, 449. https://doi.org/10.1007/s11293-006-9029-7, citing Enders, W., & Hoover, G. A. (2004). *Plagiarism in Economics: A Problem Needing Attention!* University of Alabama Working Paper.

66 Martin, B. (2007) Keeping plagiarism at bay – A salutary tale. *Research Policy*, 36(7), 905–911, 906, citing Fox, M. F. (1994). Scientific misconduct and editorial and peer review processes. *The Journal of Higher Education*, 65, 298–309.

67 Council of Science Editors. White Paper on Publication Ethics. www.councilscienceeditors.org/resource-library/editorial-policies/white-paper-on-publication-ethics/ (accessed 15 August 2020)

68 History of COPE. https://publicationethics.org/node/2/revisions/13678/view (accessed 1 December 2021)

69 https://publicationethics.org/guidance (accessed 1 December 2001)

70 https://publicationethics.org/guidance (accessed 1 December 2001)

71 Cooperation between research institutions and journals on research integrity cases: guidance from the Committee on Publication Ethics (COPE), https://publicationethics.org/files/Research_institutions_guidelines_final_0_0.pdf (accessed 1 December 2001)

in some situations and the absence of an alternative regulatory body, the COPE guidance also recommends that journal editors consider the appointment of an ombudsperson as ultimate adjudicator of complaints that cannot be resolved by other means.

The guidance recognises the potentially onerous nature of requiring editors to make all reasonable efforts to ensure that a proper investigation is undertaken.[72] It may be unrealistic to place such obligations on individual editors, who will often be full-time academics undertaking their editorial role on a part-time basis. Retractions as a result of misconduct have been increasing in number in recent years, reflecting an increased editorial workload in this regard.[73]

An ombudsperson acting across a number of journals may be more realistic and could even constitute the basis for a wider-ranging adjudicatory process to consider issues of research misconduct. This might resemble the type of autonomous or semi-autonomous regulatory bodies common to professions such as medicine or law, although these usually focus on a single geographical jurisdiction, rather than being international in nature. The latter may be more appropriate for scientific research, but more complex and challenging to organise.[74]

As well as the need to withdraw research findings which are produced as a result of misconduct such as data fabrication or manipulation, other examples cited in combined UKRIO/COPE guidance on behaviour which, if sufficiently serious, might warrant retraction include plagiarism, redundant publication (multiple publishing of the same information without justification or acknowledgment) or the failure to disclose conflicts of interest likely to influence interpretation.[75] Retraction plays an important role in ensuring the integrity of the research record and associated public trust in scientific findings. Even with matters such as redundant publication, retraction can be important to prevent inappropriate multiple counting in meta-analyses.[76] The fact of

72 *Code of Conduct and Best Practice Guidance for Journal Editors,* https://publicationethics.org/files/Code_of_conduct_for_journal_editors_Mar11.pdf (accessed 1st December 2021), paras 7.2, 11.1–11.5

73 Sonfield, M. C. (2014). Academic plagiarism at the faculty level: Legal versus ethical issues and a case study. *J Acad Ethics*, 12, 75–87. Doi: 10.1007/s10805-014-9205-3, citing Ioannides, J. (2005). Why most published research findings are false. *PLoS Medicine*, 2(8), e124. It has been noted that the reason for a retraction cannot always be ascertained with certainty, as publishers rarely explicitly state reasons on retraction notices that a particular study is fraudulent because of the difficulties with proof, Else, H., & Van Noorden, R. (2021). The fight against fake-paper factories that churn out sham science. *Nature,* 591, 516–519, doi: https://doi.org/10.1038/d41586-021-00733-5

74 See, for example, Marks, D. F. (2019). The Hans Eysenck affair: Time to correct the scientific record, Editorial. *Journal of Health Psychology*, 24(4), 409–420. https://doi.org/10.1177/1359105318820931; Marks, D. F., & Buchanan, R. (2020). King's College London's enquiry into Hans J Eysenck's "unsafe" publications must be properly completed. *Journal of Health Psychology,* 25, 3–6 with regard to a suggested independent Ombudsperson responsible for research integrity.

75 *UKRIO Information Note: guidance for researchers on retractions in academic journals*, 2010, para 3.3

76 It is worth noting that the direct harm caused by plagiarism is limited. As Biagioli observes, unlike the passing off of an inferior product under the trademark of a superior one, the content knowledge derived from an accurately plagiarised piece is identical to the knowledge the reader would gain

retraction should be readily available – not, for example, being placed behind a pay wall or available only to subscribers of the journal.[77]

Techniques available to seek to detect publication misconduct include statistical analysis of patterns in datasets, image checking tools, linguistic analysis and post-publication peer review, as well as policies that require full reporting of methods and results and the sharing of data.[78] An example of the latter is the requirement by PLOS journals that authors make all data supporting the findings described their manuscript fully available without restriction at the time of publication. If legal or ethical prohibitions restrict the public sharing of a dataset, indications must be given by authors regarding how researchers may obtain access to the data.[79] Plagiarism detection software can highlight copying, but detecting the appropriation of ideas is more problematic. Detection failures and under-reporting continue to be of concern.[80] Historical estimates of under-reporting suggest a figure as high as 90 per cent.[81] There may be limited incentive for journals to invest appropriately in tools to aid the detection of misconduct – 'a journal may have to retract a paper . . . but that is about as bad as it gets for them.'[82]

The UK House of Commons Science and Technology Committee identified a continuing need for publishers to make the necessary investment to detect problems with research papers. The sector has a responsibility to take 'reasonable steps to ensure that technology to detect problems is developed and

from the original piece. The harm which is or may be caused therefore revolves around public trust and peripheral (but not unimportant) costs such as time wasted in the reviewing and publication process of a plagiarised piece and honest scientists being deprived career advancement in favour of dishonest counterparts. Biagioli, M. (2012). Recycling texts or stealing time? Plagiarism, authorship, and credit in science. *International Journal of Cultural Property*, 19, 453–476, 465–466. Retraction of a multi-authored piece will usually impact upon all authors, however modest their input, *UKRIO Information Note: guidance for researchers on retractions in academic journals*, 2010, para 3.4. A published correction rather than full retraction may mitigate against all authors being affected, but this will depend upon the misconduct being limited in extent to a relatively small part of the piece, para 3.7.

77 *UKRIO Information Note: guidance for researchers on retractions in academic journals*, 2010

78 House of Commons Science and Technology Committee, Research integrity, Sixth Report of Session 2017–19, 11 July 2018 HC 350, para 78 citing evidence from the British Medical Journal. For further discussion of policy and ethical consideration relating to plagiarism see, for example, Parrish, D. (2006). Research misconduct and plagiarism. *Journal of College and University Law*, 33, 1–32; Latourette, A. (2010). Plagiarism: legal and ethical implications for the university. *Journal of College and University Law*, 37, 9–80

79 https://journals.plos.org/plosone/s/data-availability (accessed 24 July 2020)

80 Titus, S. L., Wells, J. A., & Rhoades, L. J. (2008). Repairing research integrity. *Nature*, 453, 980–982.

81 Titus, S. L., Wells, J. A., & Rhoades, L. J. (2008). Repairing research integrity. *Nature*, 453, 980–982.

82 House of Commons Science and Technology Committee, Research integrity, Sixth Report of Session 2017–19, 11 July 2018 HC 350, para 81.

put to good use.'[83] Market forces are unlikely to ensure this, so a Concordat-style set of commitments from academic publishers may be necessary, with an oversight body such as the UKRIO taking a lead in exploring this.[84]

Defective or false knowledge is as significant to the knowledge economy as manufacturing defects are to the industrial economy.[85] Culturally, therefore, retraction is an important element to maintaining the research record, not only as a result of misconduct but also innocent errors. Retractions clearly signal false science and in doing so help to create a norm of regular correction in scientific journals.[86] From this perspective, larger numbers of retractions may be seen as evidence that the self-corrective nature of science is working effectively.[87] However, in terms of the effectiveness of retractions in protecting the accuracy of future research, it has been found that, historically, retraction may not significantly and in a timely manner reduce future citation of the retracted work.[88] For example, it has been observed on behalf of the *British Medical Journal* that 'the original, erroneous versions of papers that have subsequent published corrigenda are cited at roughly the same rate as the corrected versions.'[89] Using one example of scientific misconduct as a case study, that involving Scott S. Reuben, Bornemann-Cimenti et al note that the current approach to retraction as a mechanism for control of the scientific record has limitations.[90] Twenty-one major publications, produced over a period of 15 years, had included fabricated data. These had influenced the scientific record, having been cited almost 1,200 times. Bornemann-Cimenti et al identified significant

83 House of Commons Science and Technology Committee, Research integrity, Sixth Report of Session 2017–19, 11 July 2018 HC 350, para 82. The focus is upon image manipulation software, but the sentiments can be extended more broadly.

84 House of Commons Science and Technology Committee, Research integrity, Sixth Report of Session 2017–19, 11 July 2018 HC 350, para 82.

85 Furman, J., Jensen, K., & Murray, F. (2011). Governing knowledge in the scientific community: Exploring the role of retractions in biomedicine. *Research Policy*, 41, 277. doi: 10.2139/ssrn.2014481.

86 Furman, J., Jensen, K., & Murray, F. (2011). Governing knowledge in the scientific community: Exploring the role of retractions in biomedicine. *Research Policy*, 41, 278. doi: 10.2139/ssrn.2014481.

87 Pulverer, B. (2015). When things go wrong: Correcting the scientific record. *The EMBO Journal*, 34(20), 2483–2485. https://doi.org/10.15252/embj.201570080

88 See, for example, Pfeifer, M. P., & Snodgrass, G. L. (1990). The continued use of retracted, invalid scientific literature. *JAMA*, 263(10), 1420–1423. doi: 10.1001/jama.1990.03440100140020; Thomsen, M., & Resnik, D. (1995). The effectiveness of the erratum in avoiding error propagation in physics. *Sci Eng Ethics*, 1, 231–240. https://doi.org/10.1007/BF02628800; Redman, B. K., Yarandi, H. N., & Merz, J. F. (2008). Empirical developments in retraction. *J Med Ethics.*, 34(11) (November), 807–809. doi: 10.1136/jme.2007.023069. PMID: 18974415.

89 House of Commons Science and Technology Committee, Research integrity, Sixth Report of Session 2017–19, 11 July 2018 HC 350, para 92.

90 Bornemann-Cimenti, H., Szilagyi, I. S., & Sandner-Kiesling, A. (2016). Perpetuation of retracted publications using the example of the Scott S. Reuben case: Incidences, reasons and possible improvements. *Sci Eng Ethics*, 22, 1063. https://doi.org/10.1007/s11948-015-9680-y

continued citation of retracted articles, without showing awareness of the retractions.[91] In the period 2009–2014 Reuben's retracted articles were cited 267 times in 122 different journals, with clear indication of retracted status occurring in only 25.8 per cent of cases.[92] Citations decreased markedly over this period, although to a lesser degree in less specialised journals. The latter suggested that while the fact of Reuben's misconduct may have become better known in his specialist field of anaesthesia and pain management, communication within medicine more broadly was slower.[93]

The estimated proportion of retractions due to misconduct varies depending upon source. A study of 742 English-language research papers retracted from the PubMed database between 2000 and 2010 found that a little over 26 per cent were retracted for fraud, with roughly 53 per cent of fraudulent papers written by a first author who had other papers retracted.[94] Other sources suggest that around half of retractions result from research misconduct and that the rate of retractions globally has been increasing – one estimation suggests 'doubling every few years.'[95] Given the propensity of some observers to equate retraction with misconduct, there is a value in more clearly separating the 'honourable' retraction of innocent errors, a commendable act to clean up the

91 Bornemann-Cimenti, H., Szilagyi, I. S., & Sandner-Kiesling, A. (2016). Perpetuation of retracted publications using the example of the Scott S. Reuben case: Incidences, reasons and possible improvements. *Sci Eng Ethics*, 22, 1063. https://doi.org/10.1007/s11948-015-9680-y

92 Bornemann-Cimenti, H., Szilagyi, I. S., & Sandner-Kiesling, A. (2016). Perpetuation of retracted publications using the example of the Scott S. Reuben case: Incidences, reasons and possible improvements. *Sci Eng Ethics*, 22, 1063. https://doi.org/10.1007/s11948-015-9680-y

93 Bornemann-Cimenti, H., Szilagyi, I. S., & Sandner-Kiesling, A. (2016). Perpetuation of retracted publications using the example of the Scott S. Reuben case: Incidences, reasons and possible improvements. *Sci Eng Ethics*, 22, 1063 at 1066. https://doi.org/10.1007/s11948-015-9680-y. It was also noted that while the number of citations per year decreased significantly, the percentage of these citations which correctly indicated that the cited article had been retracted also decreased. In contrast, Furman et al conclude that when problematic knowledge is identified to a research community by means of retraction, this leads to an 'immediate and long-lived decline in citations.' Further their qualitative evidence indicates that, whilst the decline in citation is not complete, many post-retraction citations do not draw from the false knowledge contained within the retracted work. Furman, J., Jensen, K., & Murray, F. (2011). Governing knowledge in the scientific community: Exploring the role of retractions in biomedicine. *Research Policy*, 41, 278. doi: 10.2139/ssrn.2014481.

94 Steen, R. (2010). Retractions in the scientific literature: Is the incidence of research fraud increasing? *Journal of Medical Ethics*, 37, 249–253, 249. doi: 10.1136/jme.2010.040923; Steen, R. (2010). Retractions in the scientific literature: Do authors deliberately commit research fraud? *Journal of Medical Ethics*, 37, 113–117, 113. doi: 10.1136/jme.2010.038125.

95 Dr Ivan Oransky, co-founder of Retraction Watch, in evidence to the House of Commons Science and Technology Committee, Research integrity, Sixth Report of Session 2017–19, 11 July 2018 HC 350, page 13; Alberts, B., Cicerone, R. J., Fienberg, S. E., Kamb, A., McNutt, M., Nerem, R. M., Schekman, R., Shiffrin, R., Stodden, V., Suresh, S., Zuber, M. T., Pope, B. K., & Jamieson, K. H. (2015). Self-correction in science at work. *Science,* 348(6242) (June 26), 1420–1422.

research literature, and retractions which signal misconduct.[96] Retraction constitutes a blunt instrument applied to cases both extremely serious and relatively trivial.[97] However, in total still only a small fraction of the scientific literature is retracted. Calculations indicate that globally there are 0.44 retractions per billion US dollars spent on research. The figure for the UK is 0.75 retractions per billion US dollars spent.[98] Both numbers are extremely low, but in terms of the higher figure for the UK, it has been suggested that this could reflect lower levels of spending on research, compared with some other jurisdictions, and could therefore be a counterintuitive side effect of lower-cost/more efficient research programmes.[99]

It has been suggested that the increase in retractions worldwide may be attributable to, inter alia, a greater use of detection software, alertness by a wider online readership and an increased willingness by journals to retract articles.[100] However, in the absence of conclusive evidence, an increase in the prevalence of research misconduct as a factor in the observed increase in retractions cannot be ruled out.[101]

Notwithstanding the fact that many retractions occur in order to correct the research record following innocent error, retraction remains associated with suspicion of misbehaviour and as such for some researchers is viewed as 'a considerable sanction in its own right.'[102] Given this potential stigma, a number of honest researchers may be reluctant to see their work retracted,

96 Graham, F. (2020). Daily briefing: How it feels to retract a paper. *Nature* (March 3). doi: 10.1038/d41586-020-00631-2. Epub ahead of print. PMID: 33654253; Van Noorden, R. (2011). Science publishing: The trouble with retractions. *Nature*, 478. 26–28, 28. doi: 10.1038/478026a.

97 Bik, E. M., Casadevall, A., & Fang, F. C., (2016). The prevalence of inappropriate image duplication in biomedical research publications. *mBio*, 7(3) (June), e00809–16. doi: 10.1128/mBio.00809-16; Steen, R. (2010). Retractions in the scientific literature: Do authors deliberately commit research fraud? *Journal of Medical Ethics*, 37, 113–117, 117. doi: 10.1136/jme.2010.038125.

98 Dr Ivan Oransky, co-founder of Retraction Watch, in evidence to the House of Commons Science and Technology Committee, Research integrity, Sixth Report of Session 2017–19, 11 July 2018 HC 350, page 13.

99 Dr Ivan Oransky, co-founder of Retraction Watch, in evidence to the House of Commons Science and Technology Committee, Research integrity, Sixth Report of Session 2017–19, 11 July 2018 HC 350, page 13.

100 Fanelli, D. (2013) Why growing retractions are (mostly) a good sign. *PLoS Med*, 10(12), e1001563. https://doi.org/10.1371/journal.pmed.1001563; Van Noorden, R. (2011). Science publishing: The trouble with retractions. *Nature*, 478, 26–28, 28. doi: 10.1038/478026a. As software develops further, in the medium term retraction numbers could reduce because pre-publication screening will better detect issues at that stage.

101 Dr Ivan Oransky, co-founder of Retraction Watch, in evidence to the House of Commons Science and Technology Committee, Research integrity, Sixth Report of Session 2017–19, 11 July 2018 HC 350, page 13.

102 Jacob, M.-A. (2017). The strikethrough: An approach to regulatory writing and professional discipline. *Legal Studies*, 37(1), 137–161. doi: 10.1111/lest.12142.

even though this is the 'right thing' in terms of protecting the research record and the integrity of science.[103] A significant number of retraction notices also fail to comply with good-practice standards. For example, notices may lack explicit authorship attribution and may fail specifically to identify the content to be retracted, the reasons for the retraction and the division of responsibility between authors.[104]

Suggested ways forward include a change in vocabulary – the creation of a new term – reserving 'retraction' exclusively for misconduct.[105] A number of journals and organizations, for example, the COPE, are considering ways to standardise the language and processes for corrections and retractions.[106] New terminology would clearly identify the reason for the retraction or correction process, for example, 'honest error' or 'proven research misconduct.'[107]

A move towards clearly labelling retraction in all databases is desirable, although technically challenging. The latter is particularly challenging if publications continue to appear on an author's own or other private websites. Citations of the paper prior to retraction will also continue to influence subsequent researchers.[108] With the proliferation of online sources of access to published research, it is likely that the problem will remain until a technical solution can be implemented. In the meantime, authors can minimise the risk that they will unknowingly cite a retracted source by always accessing the (usually free) abstract of the source via the publisher website. Publishers, in turn, must

103 Van Noorden, R. (2011). Science publishing: The trouble with retractions. *Nature*, 478, 26–28, 28. doi: 10.1038/478026a

104 Hu, G. (2017). Authorship of retraction notices: "If names are not rectified, then language will not be in accord with truth". *Publications*, 5, 10. 10.3390/publications5020010.

105 Barbour, V., Bloom, T., Lin, J., & Moylan, E. (2017). Amending published articles: Time to rethink retractions and corrections? [version 1; peer review: 2 approved with reservations]. *F1000Research*, 6, 1960. https://f1000research.com/articles/6-1960/v1; Fanelli, D. (2016). Set up a 'self-retraction' system for honest errors. *Nature*, 531, 415–415. doi: 10.1038/531415a; Van Noorden, R. (2011). Science publishing: The trouble with retractions. *Nature*, 478, 26–28, 28. doi: 10.1038/478026a

106 Kretser, A., Murphy, D., Bertuzzi, S., Abraham, T., Allison, D., Boor, K., Dwyer, J., Grantham, A., Harris, L., Hollander, R., Jacobs-Young, C., Rovito, S., Vafiadis, D., Woteki, C., Wyndham, J., & Yada, R. (2019). Scientific integrity principles and best practices: Recommendations from a scientific integrity consortium. *Science and Engineering Ethics*, 25. doi: 10.1007/s11948-019-00094-3, citing Allison, D. B., Brown, A. W., George, B. J., & Kaiser, K. A. (2016). Reproducibility: A tragedy of errors. *Nature,* 530(7588), 27–29.

107 Kretser, A., Murphy, D., Bertuzzi, S., Abraham, T., Allison, D., Boor, K., Dwyer, J., Grantham, A., Harris, L., Hollander, R., Jacobs-Young, C., Rovito, S., Vafiadis, D., Woteki, C., Wyndham, J., & Yada, R. (2019). Scientific integrity principles and best practices: Recommendations from a scientific integrity consortium. *Science and Engineering Ethics*, 25. doi: 10.1007/s11948-019-00094-3., citing Allison, D. B., Brown, A. W., George, B. J., & Kaiser, K. A. (2016). Reproducibility: A tragedy of errors. *Nature,* 530(7588), 27–29.

108 House of Commons Science and Technology Committee, Research integrity, Sixth Report of Session 2017–19, 11 July 2018 HC 350, para 94, citing evidence from Dr Trish Groves, representing the BMJ.

ensure that concerns about a paper are highlighted as promptly as possible via such free-access sources.[109] Even more proactively, as part of the copy editing process, publishers can check all references in case any retractions or corrections have been missed by the author or the retraction has occurred in the gap between the author submitting a piece for publication and the final stages of the publishing process. Some publishers do this, but not all.[110]

Publishers have a vital role in maintaining the integrity of the research record, whether by retraction, publishing correction notices or publishing notices of concern. They also have the capacity to prohibit an author from future publication and to bring concerns to the attention of other publishers.[111] However, there are hurdles to an effective system for retractions. Even when serious concerns have been raised with a journal, it can take many months before retraction occurs – during which time potentially harmful misinformation continues to be disseminated.[112] Obstacles can also be placed in the way, for example, legal threats by authors fearing career detriment if retraction of their work occurs. Even if such threats have little legal substance, they may act as a deterrent with little by way of counterbalancing incentives for journals to push for retraction.[113] Editors may look to investigations by employing institutions – a formal institutional finding of research misconduct helps to counter fears of, for example, defamation claims arising from retraction notices.[114] Institutions

109 Grey, A., Bolland, M., Gamble, G. et al. (2019). Quality of reports of investigations of research integrity by academic institutions. *Res Integr Peer Rev*, 4, 3 https://doi.org/10.1186/s41073-019-0062-x

110 House of Commons Science and Technology Committee, Research integrity, Sixth Report of Session 2017–19, 11 July 2018 HC 350, para 94, citing evidence from Dr Trish Groves, representing the BMJ.

111 House of Commons Science and Technology Committee, Research integrity, Sixth Report of Session 2017–19, 11 July 2018 HC 350, para 92

112 Grey, A., Avenell, A., Klein, A. A., & Gunsalus, C.K. (2020). Check for publication integrity before misconduct. *Nature*, 577, 167–169 doi: https://doi.org/10.1038/d41586-019-03959-6; Korpela, K.M. (2010). How long does it take for the scientific literature to purge itself of fraudulent material? The Breuning case revisited. *Current Medical Research and Opinion*, 26(4), 843–847. doi: 10.1185/03007991003603804; van der Vet, P. E., & Nijveen, H. (2016). Propagation of errors in citation networks: A study involving the entire citation network of a widely cited paper published in, and later retracted from, the journal Nature. *Res Integr Peer Rev*, 1, 3. https://doi.org/10.1186/s41073-016-0008-5

113 Kretser, A., Murphy, D., Bertuzzi, S., Abraham, T., Allison, D., Boor, K., Dwyer, J., Grantham, A., Harris, L., Hollander, R., Jacobs-Young, C., Rovito, S., Vafiadis, D., Woteki, C., Wyndham, J., & Yada, R. (2019). Scientific integrity principles and best practices: Recommendations from a scientific integrity consortium. *Science and Engineering Ethics*, 25. doi: 10.1007/s11948-019-00094-3, citing Allison, D. B., Brown, A. W., George, B. J., & Kaiser, K. A. (2016). Reproducibility: A tragedy of errors. *Nature*, 530(7588), 27–29.

114 Wager, E., Kleinert, S., Garfinkel, M., Volker Bahr, C., et al. (2017). Cooperation & Liaison between Universities & Editors (CLUE): Recommendations on best practice. *bioRxiv*. doi: https://doi.org/10.1101/139170.

should permit journals to quote from reports of misconduct investigations in retraction statements, editorial commentaries and suchlike.[115]

Institutions also play an important role in ensuring that resources are available to undertake investigations fairly and with due process. However, institutional responses have not always been appropriate, with some examples of a failure to respond at all.[116] For example, one journal editor observed that in relation to the COPE guidance to editors to report concerns to employing institutions:

> Unfortunately, I have rarely received the impression that an institution has responded in an appropriate manner. In one case, an institution [named] . . . did not follow the procedure it had published on its website for the investigation of scientific misconduct. In the majority of cases, the institutional response has been to deny any fault, even in cases of blatant lying by authors, and they recommend no correction, retraction or retraining and no other steps to prevent further misconduct. . . . Academic institutions have a conflict of interest concerning allegations of misconduct.[117]

In an example from Australia, it was observed that some institutional investigations may lack coordination, with different panels more or less simultaneously considering accusations against the same researcher or team without being aware of each other. Each panel may conclude that there had been some misdemeanours, but with extenuating circumstances which mitigated against a finding of research misconduct. The institution in turn may direct critics to each individual finding as evidence of effective internal investigation and all being fine.[118] However, had a single panel considered all allegations and a pattern of behaviour been observed, a different conclusion regarding the overall seriousness of the behaviour may have been reached.[119]

If prompt institutional action is not forthcoming, or if there is uncertainty between different aspects of the investigatory process, one relatively novel way forward has been an editorial response which seeks comment from the authors in response to the allegations from their accusers. No adjudication is undertaken

115 Wager, E., Kleinert, S., Garfinkel, M., Volker Bahr, C., et al. (2017). Cooperation & Liaison between Universities & Editors (CLUE): Recommendations on best practice. *bioRxiv*. doi: https://doi.org/10.1101/139170.

116 House of Commons Science and Technology Committee, Research integrity, Sixth Report of Session 2017–19, 11 July 2018 HC 350, para 92

117 House of Commons Science and Technology Committee, Research integrity, Sixth Report of Session 2017–19, 11 July 2018 HC 350, para 92

118 Worthington, E., & Taylor, K. UNSW skin cancer researcher Levon Khachigian hit with string of retractions. *ABC News*, www.abc.net.au/news/2019-10-17/unsw-skin-cancer-levon-khachigian-allegations-and-retractions/11585768

119 Worthington, E., & Taylor, K. UNSW skin cancer researcher Levon Khachigian hit with string of retractions. *ABC News*, www.abc.net.au/news/2019-10-17/unsw-skin-cancer-levon-khachigian-allegations-and-retractions/11585768

at the editorial level, but the different sides of the argument are presented to the journal readership to decide on an individual basis whether or not they accept the content of the piece as reliable.[120]

Plagiarism

Building upon the discussion earlier in this work, plagiarism is categorised as a form of cheating which goes to the heart of academic integrity. Concerns about plagiarism in science have a long history; for example, questions about Leibniz allegedly plagiarising the work of Newton date back to the eighteenth century. Compared with the significant developments over time in intellectual property law, little progress has been made with a clear and consistent conceptualisation of plagiarism.[121] Plagiarism is not a universal concept, with approaches and definitions varying between jurisdictions. For example, while English law has recognised the idea of an 'originating author' since the early eighteenth century, approaches and timelines in some other jurisdictions differ. For example, the ability to memorise and reproduce without attribution the work of esteemed thinkers and leaders continues to constitute a demonstration of education and intelligence in some cultures.[122] Considerations of cultural differences helps to contextualise variations in approach to matters of ethics and misconduct.

Plagiarism is categorised by some commentators as residing at the most serious end of the research misconduct spectrum because it involves the stealing of words or ideas to be passed off as an original contribution to knowledge.[123] Plagiarism does not distort the scientific record in knowledge terms, only in attribution terms.[124] Denying original authors the full attribution to which

120 Herth, F. (2018). How journals treat scientific misconduct allegations: Should articles be retracted? *Respiration*, 96, 1–13. doi: 10.1159/000489981.

121 Biagioli, M. (2012). Recycling texts or stealing time? Plagiarism, authorship, and credit in science. *International Journal of Cultural Property*, 19, 453–476, 453. Citing Moore Howard, R. (1999). *Standing in the Shadow of Giants: Plagiarists, Authors, Collaborators* (p. 157). Stamford, CT: Ablex, Biagioli notes that 'neat definitions to be cleanly applied to all cases cannot be fulfilled' even within disciplines, let alone between them.

122 Pennycook, A. (1996). Borrowing others' words: Text ownership, memory, and plagiarism. *TESOL Quarterly*, 30(2) (Summer), 205, citing Willinsky, J. (1990). Intellectual property rights and responsibilities: The state of the text. *The Journal of Educational Thought*, 24, 68–82.

123 Martin, B. (2007) Keeping plagiarism at bay – A salutary tale. *Research Policy*, 36(7), 905–911, 905–906, citing Rosamond, B. (2002). Plagiarism, academic norms and the governance of the profession. *Politics*, 22, 167–174.

124 Even if they escape detection, it is argued that plagiarists are treading water in career development terms because scientific rewards are disproportionately made for work that alters the scope of accepted knowledge. Foster, J. G., Rzhetsky, A., & Evans, J. A. (2013). Tradition and innovation in scientists' research strategies. *American Sociological Review*, 80(5) (February). doi: 10.1177/0003122415601618

they are entitled undermines to some extent the importance of recognition and priority in scientific discovery.[125]

Opinions differ with regard to the boundaries of plagiarism – for example, the differentiation between using without attribution phrases which are background in nature only compared to misappropriating substantive ideas, whether using the original author's exact words or paraphrasing.[126] It has also been suggested that the copying of text is not all of equal severity. For example, misuse of original research findings would be placed at the serious end of the scale, whereas copying a literature review section or the limited use of text which describes a commonly used methodology may sit towards the less serious end of a spectrum or, according to some definitions, not constitute plagiarism at all.[127] The US Office of Research Integrity definition of plagiarism, for example, mentions 'substantial unattributed textual copying' which 'materially mislead the ordinary reader.'[128]

Even experienced editors and other senior members of the research community have been found to differ in their understanding of what constitutes plagiarism.[129] Whether or not intention is a necessary factor is also subject to debate.[130] If plagiarism can be committed without intentional wrongdoing, honorary authorship could constitute plagiarism, as this involves claiming or accepting merit for work done by others – even though those undertaking the work approve the act.[131]

125 Biagioli, M. (2012). Recycling texts or stealing time? Plagiarism, authorship, and credit in science. *International Journal of Cultural Property,* 19, 453–476, 458 and 460–461. Misappropriation by those entrusted pre-publication as part of the peer review process takes on greatest significance. In this context, Biagioli notes that in the period 1992–2006 the majority of plagiarism allegations in US biomedicine related to peer review and grant applications (in this latter scenario, facilitating the misappropriation of an earlier stage idea and/or research methodology), not published work – citing, inter alia, Price, A. (2006). Cases of plagiarism handled by the United States office of research integrity 1992–2005. *Plagiary: Cross-Disciplinary Studies in Plagiarism, Fabrication, and Falsification,* 1, 1–11; De Vries, R., Anderson, M. S., & Martinson, B. C.. (2006). Normal misbehavior: Scientists talk about the ethics of research. *Journal of Empirical Research on Human Research Ethics,* 1, 43–50, 47.

126 Bouville, M. (2008). Plagiarism: Words and ideas. *Science and Engineering Ethics,* 14, 311–322, 312. doi: 10.1007/s11948-008-9057-6.

127 Biagioli, M. (2012). Recycling texts or stealing time? Plagiarism, authorship, and credit in science. *International Journal of Cultural Property,* 19, 453–476, 459; ORI Newsletter, Vol 3, No. 1, December 1994, cited at https://ori.hhs.gov/ori-policy-plagiarism

128 ORI Newsletter, Vol 3, No. 1, December 1994, cited at https://ori.hhs.gov/ori-policy-plagiarism

129 See, for example, the case study discussed by Zhang, X-X., Huo, Z-L., & Zhang, Y-H. (2013). Detecting and (not) dealing with plagiarism in an engineering paper: Beyond CrossCheck-A case study. *Science and Engineering Ethics,* 20. doi: 10.1007/s11948-013-9460-5. At page 441

130 Helgesson, G., & Eriksson, S. (2014). Plagiarism in research. *Medicine, Health Care, and Philosophy,* 18, 91–101, 94. doi: 10.1007/s11019-014-9583-8.

131 Helgesson, G., & Eriksson, S. (2014). Plagiarism in research. *Medicine, Health Care, and Philosophy,* 18, 91–101, 94. doi: 10.1007/s11019-014-9583-8, citing Anekwe, T.D. 2010. Profits and plagiarism: The case of medical ghostwriting. *Bioethics* 24(6): 267–272.

Given the definitional disagreements, the blanket term 'plagiarism' has been described as 'useless,' grouping behaviours which are very different in nature and significance under a single heading and then treating them as alike because they share a label rather than because they share sufficiently significant wrongful characteristics.[132]

Possible motivating factors which lead to plagiarism vary, but one contributing factor may be the importance within scientific communities placed upon remaining visibly productive.[133] Plagiarising already published work, if undertaken discreetly, may facilitate the plagiariser with an enhanced curriculum vitae (CV).[134] This is the opposite of wanting one's research findings to be widely read and to make impact – the plagiarist, once the CV enhancement has been achieved, is likely to want the actual publication to be 'as invisible as possible.'[135]

In an academic environment where there is increasing pressure to publish and, more recently, in some jurisdictions, pressure to achieve 'impact,' the dissemination of research findings has extended in a variety of ways beyond traditional refereed articles – for example, blogs, press releases and other forms of dissemination prior to formal refereed publication. However, such multiple publication approaches raise new challenges in terms of defining appropriate conduct. The issue of repeat publication, sometimes – more problematically given typical definitions of plagiarism – described as 'self-plagiarism' can, in relatively modern terms, be traced back to 1969 and the policy adopted by Franz J. Ingelfinger, when editor of *The New England Journal of Medicine*. The policy was to consider only manuscripts the substance of which had not been reported elsewhere. Key purposes behind the policy were to protect the interests of the journal in terms of the originality of its content but also to

132 Bouville, M. (2008). Plagiarism: Words and ideas. *Science and Engineering Ethics*, 14, 311–322, 320. doi: 10.1007/s11948-008-9057-6.

133 The idea of productive tradition derives from ideas developed by Kuhn, Kuhn, T. S. ([1959] 1977). The essential tension: Tradition and innovation in scientific research. In C. W. Taylor (Ed.), *The third (1959) University of Utah Research Conference on the Identification of Scientific Talent* (pp. 162–174). Salt Lake City: University of Utah Press. Reprint in *The Essential Tension: Selected Studies in Scientific Tradition and Change* (pp. 225–239). Chicago: University of Chicago Press ([1959] 1977), cited by Foster, J. G., Rzhetsky, A., & Evans, J. A. (2013). Tradition and innovation in scientists' research strategies. *American Sociological Review*, 80(5) (February). doi: 10.1177/0003122415601618

134 Biagioli, M. (2012). Recycling texts or stealing time? Plagiarism, authorship, and credit in science. *International Journal of Cultural Property*, 19, 453–476, 462–464. Biagioli identifies subtlety as including publishing translated plagiarised work in sources produced in another language or publication in sources which are lesser ranking and therefore less likely to be read by the same audience as the original version.

135 Biagioli, M. (2012). Recycling texts or stealing time? Plagiarism, authorship, and credit in science. *International Journal of Cultural Property*, 19, 453–476, 464. It is also suggested that such deceitful approaches can be inadvertently facilitated by career advancement processes in many institutions focusing upon the publication list itself, rather a close and critical reading of the publications themselves.

discourage dissemination of research findings before they have undergone the rigours of the peer review process.[136]

Self-citation also raises challenges because of the impact it can have on artificially inflating citation rates.[137] Self-citation can also distort the measurement of scientific impact, given that such citations reveal nothing about the impact of a work beyond its relevance to those who produced it.[138] However, appropriate self-citation is a regular part of scientific communication, reflecting the developmental nature of the research process. A key distinction between self-citation and self-plagiarism is that the latter constitutes reuse by authors of their own previously published ideas, text or datasets in different publishing venues without any or sufficient acknowledgement.[139]

Self-citation has increased in recent decades. For example, fewer than 4 per cent of all papers in 1950 contained one or more self-citations. By 2014 this had more than doubled to over 8 per cent. The average number of self-citations per paper had also increased more than seven-fold, and the maximum number of self-citations discovered in a single paper also rose, from 10 in a 1950 paper to over 250 in a 2013 paper.[140] In these circumstances it has been argued that the relationship of authors to their own text has changed, with a move from direct quotation to more subtle incorporation – the 'reference may still be there, but there is a slipperiness over the reusability of one's own words.'[141]

136 See, for example, Marcia Angell, M. D., & Kassirer, J. P. MD (1991). The Ingelfinger rule revisited. *N Engl J Med*, 325, 1371–1373. doi: 10.1056/NEJM199111073251910. Arnold, S., & Relman, M. D. (1981). The Ingelfinger rule. *N Engl J Med,* 305, 824–826. doi: 10.1056/NEJM198110013051408. During the COVID-19 pandemic from 2020 onwards, it was common for the results of scientific research relevant to COVID to be released to news sources and then be published in summary form in that way, typically with the caveat that the finding remain subject to peer review and more formal publication.

137 Costas, R., van Leeuwen, T. N., & Bordons, M. (2010). Self-citations at the meso and individual levels: effects of different calculation methods. *Scientometrics* (82), 517–537. doi: 10.1007/s11192-010-0187-7. Citing, inter alia Pichappan, P., & Sarasvady, S. (2002). The other side of the coin: The intricacies of author self-citations. *Scientometrics,* 54(2), 285–290; Schubert, A., Glänzel, W., & Thijs, B. (2006). The weight of author self-citations. A fractional approach to self-citation counting. *Scientometrics,* 67(3), 503–514.

138 Costas, R., van Leeuwen, T. N., & Bordons, M. (2010). Self-citations at the meso and individual levels: effects of different calculation methods *Scientometrics* (82), 517–537 doi: 10.1007/s11192-010-0187-7. Citing, inter alia Pichappan, P., & Sarasvady, S. (2002). The other side of the coin: The intricacies of author self-citations. *Scientometrics,* 54(2), 285–290; Schubert, A., Glänzel, W., & Thijs, B. (2006). The weight of author self-citations. A fractional approach to self-citation counting. *Scientometrics,* 67(3), 503–514.

139 Andreescu, L. (2012). Self-plagiarism in academic publishing: The anatomy of a misnomer. *Science and Engineering Ethics,* 19. doi: 10.1007/s11948-012-9416-1.

140 Fire, M., & Guestrin, C. (2019). Over-optimization of academic publishing metrics: Observing Goodhart's law in action. *GigaScience*, 8(6) (June), giz053. https://doi.org/10.1093/gigascience/giz053

141 Pennycook, A. (1996). Borrowing others' words: Text ownership, memory, and plagiarism. *TESOL Quarterly*, 30(2) (Summer), 217.

There are differing views from within the scientific community about the wrongs, or otherwise, of duplicate publication by researchers who may feel themselves to be under intense pressure to maximise published outputs and to disseminate their findings. At one end of the scale duplicate publication – the repetition of key findings, often with an attempt to conceal the fact by the use of differently written and structured text – has been described as both infringement of copyright and a scientific deception.[142] From this perspective, it is the misrepresentation and deceit which make plagiarism and self-plagiarism close bedfellows.[143] Harm which can arise from this includes a distortion of meta-analyses if undetected duplicated ideas and findings lead to magnification of perceived importance.[144]

For those who view self-plagiarism as a serious issue, there are limited coordinated response mechanisms. Individual editors may take steps in terms of, for example, restricting future submissions from the author. However, there is no centralised mechanism to adjudicate in a just and balanced way an allegation and to impose an appropriate sanction if proven,[145] although there are some emerging national initiatives, such as the Swiss Academy of Arts and Sciences updated *Code of Conduct for Scientific Integrity* which prohibits unjustified self-citation.[146]

There is a subtle balance to be drawn. Too readily making accusations of self-plagiarism could stifle academic creativity and the development of ideas over a lengthy period and numerous publications.[147] Some arguments focus upon those plagiarism definitions which necessitate the appropriation of the work of others, definitions which cannot include a researcher reproducing their own

142 Roig, M. (2005). Re-using text from one's own previously published papers: An exploratory study of potential self-plagiarism. *Psychol. Rep.*, 97, 43.

143 Andreescu, L. (2012). Self-plagiarism in academic publishing: The anatomy of a misnomer. *Science and Engineering Ethics*, 19, 781. doi: 10.1007/s11948-012-9416-1. citing Hexham, I. (1999). *The Plague of Plagiarism*, http://c.web.umkc.edu/cowande/plague.htm; Scanlon, P. M. (2007). Song from myself: An anatomy of self-plagiarism. *Plagiary: Cross-Disciplinary Studies in Plagiarism, Fabrication, and Falsification*, 2, 57–66.

144 Andreescu, L. (2012). Self-plagiarism in academic publishing: The anatomy of a misnomer. *Science and Engineering Ethics*, 19, 781. doi: 10.1007/s11948-012-9416-1, citing Habibzadeh, F., & Winker, M. A. (2009). Duplicate publication and plagiarism: Causes and cures. *Notfall und Rettungsmedizin*, 12, 415–418.

145 Berlin, L. (2009). Plagiarism, salami slicing, and Lobachevsky. *Skeletal Radiology*, 38, 1–4. https://doi.org/10.1007/s00256-008-0599-0 citing Farthing, M. J. (1997). Research misconduct. *Gut* 41, 1–2; Rogers, L. F. (2000). Duplicate publication or not? Case 1. Letter. *AJR*, 174, 1789–1790; Rogers, L. A. (1999). Protocol for investigating alleged duplicate publications. *AJR*, 172, 2.

146 Swiss Academy of Arts and Sciences (2021). *Code of Conduct for Scientific Integrity*, https://api.swiss-academies.ch/site/assets/files/25709/kodex_layout_en_web.pdf

147 Prof. Z. W. Dr hab J. Sieńczyło-Chlabicz Dr Joanna Banasiuk (2014). The issue and nature of self-plagiarism in academic work. *Intellectual Property Quarterly*, 2, 113–124, 120.

work.[148] There is also a focus on the risks of suppressing the dissemination of scientific knowledge. For example, one editor observes:

> Ethical writing in relation to self-plagiarism should be defined by full disclosure and ensuring that there is no violation of copyright law. If duplication of content helps the author to reach a new or larger readership, or if a text recycling helps to present the same idea more accurately across several publications, they become legitimate conduct.[149]

The International Committee of Medical Journal Editors has acknowledged that redundant or duplicate content may be justifiable in certain circumstances as long as the author makes full disclosure to the editor and repetition is referenced in the new paper.[150] In today's enormous and often highly specialised body of scientific publications, repetition in different specialist publication areas may actually prove useful to bring valuable research ideas and findings to a wider scientific audience.[151]

To avoid the linguistic challenges which arise from the terms 'self' and 'plagiarism' being used together and to manage some of the significant diversity of opinions, a less loaded term, for example, 'inappropriate reuse of ideas, text or data,' might better ensure that legitimate concerns can still be addressed, while also separating this form of behaviour from other, arguably more serious, areas of research misconduct.[152]

Plagiarism compared to intellectual property protection

From a criminological perspective, plagiarists could be categorised as white-collar offenders,[153] but in formal legal terms plagiarism norms are ethical rather than legal principles 'created by social groups [to] give authors certain

148 See, for example, Helgesson, G., & Eriksson, S. (2014). Plagiarism in research. *Medicine, Health Care, and Philosophy,* 18, 91–101, 95. doi: 10.1007/s11019-014-9583-8.

149 Berlin, L. (2009). Plagiarism, salami slicing, and Lobachevsky. *Skeletal Radiology*, 38, 1–4. https://doi.org/10.1007/s00256-008-0599-0 citing David, D. Duplication spreads the word to a wider audience. *Nature* 452, 29 (2008). https://doi.org/10.1038/452029b

150 Recommendations for the Conduct, Reporting, Editing, and Publication of Scholarly Work in Medical Journals Updated December 2019, 19, www.icmje.org/icmje-recommendations.pdf (accessed 3 January 2021)

151 Andreescu, L. (2012). Self-plagiarism in academic publishing: The anatomy of a misnomer. *Science and Engineering Ethics,* 19, 790. doi: 10.1007/s11948-012-9416-1. Changes to the ways in which research outputs are disseminated and engaged with may also influence other aspects of researcher behaviour. See, for example, Nuffield Council on Bioethics, *The Culture of Scientific Research in the UK*, December 2014, Foreword

152 Andreescu, L. (2012). Self-plagiarism in academic publishing: The anatomy of a misnomer. *Science and Engineering Ethics,* 19, 796. doi: 10.1007/s11948-012-9416-1

153 Payne, B. K. (2012). *White-Collar Crime, A Text/Reader* (p. 203). Thousand Oaks, CA: Sage.

attribution rights.'[154] This contrasts with the formal legal protections of intellectual property rights.[155] Scientific authorship has been described as construing credit by means of attribution – peer recognition in the form of citations.[156] Such professional recognition can translate into financial rewards in the form of career advancement or grants, but this is different in nature from the potential financial benefits accruing to the ownership associated with copyright.[157] Copyright infringement can result in penalties imposed by law, and proven allegations of plagiarism can result in career damage, even career ruination at the hands of the research community social group.[158] Copyright issues and plagiarism can, but usually do not, overlap. Copyright infringement focuses on the reproduction and distribution of the original work, but does not address failure to attribute.[159]

Copyright protection rests solely with the owner of the copyright, and if that owner does not object, no one else can intervene. In contrast, concerns about plagiarism can become an issue for the research community as a whole. Authors cannot disclaim attribution as if it were a right which belonged to them individually, and the research community can address plagiarism as misconduct even if the authors who are subject to the misattribution are unaware or are aware but unconcerned.[160]

Publication bias

It has been argued that 'publication bias' – the preferential publishing of positive research results and a tendency to keep negative or inconclusive findings out of the publication record – is of greater significance than many other forms of research misconduct. A culture of incomplete and inaccurate reporting, for example, in the field of medical research, may have significant societal impact

154 Frye, B. L. (2020). Plagiarize this paper (October 1, 2019). *IDEA: The IP Law Review*, 60(294). Available at SSRN: https://ssrn.com/abstract=3462144

155 See for example IP offences in the UK, https://www.gov.uk/government/organisations/intellectual-property-office (accessed 1st December 2021)

156 Biagioli, M. (2012). Recycling texts or stealing time? Plagiarism, authorship, and credit in science. *International Journal of Cultural Property*, 19, 453–476, 458

157 Biagioli, M. (2012). Recycling texts or stealing time? Plagiarism, authorship, and credit in science. *International Journal of Cultural Property*, 19, 453–476, 458.

158 Dames, K. M. (2007). Understanding plagiarism and how it differs from copyright infringement. *Computers in Libraries*, 27(6) (June), 25–27.

159 Frye, B. L. (2020). Plagiarize this paper (October 1, 2019). *IDEA: The IP Law Review*, 60(294). Available at SSRN: https://ssrn.com/abstract=3462144

160 Frye, B. L. (2020). Plagiarize this paper (October 1, 2019). *IDEA: The IP Law Review*, 60(294), 319. Available at SSRN: https://ssrn.com/abstract=3462144. This reflects the observation that discursivity is central to the academic projects, with continuous 'paraphrasing, repeating, glossing [and] recombining or parodying the words of others' being key features. Absolute ownership of ideas and concepts is, therefore, problematic. Zwart, H. (2017). *Tales of Research Misconduct. Library of Ethics and Applied Philosophy* (Vol 36, p. 181). Cham: Springer

by distorting the research base underpinning medical practice.[161] Systematic reviews and meta-analyses are similarly exposed to distortion if the research record is incomplete.[162]

Publication bias has been identified in many scientific fields.[163] In the field of ecology, for example, it has been argued that rigid expectations from journals coupled with publish-or-perish pressures can encourage questionable research practices from researchers who feel under pressure to:

> [P]resent a short, cohesive story with statistically significant results that confirm a priori hypotheses, rather than a full (and likely messy) account of the research as it was conceptualised and conducted.[164]

In the biomedical field, commercial pressures and the status afforded to 'flashy breakthrough-type results' have been identified as pressure points.[165]

One way forward is the greater use of pre-registering studies in advance of research being undertaken, for example, the acceptance of 'Registered Reports' in which the hypotheses, methods and proposed methods of analysis of a research project, including an indication of how sample size and data exclusion will be determined, are peer reviewed and pre-registered before the research.[166]

161 Dr Ben Goldacre, giving evidence to House of Commons Science and Technology Committee, Research integrity, Sixth Report of Session 2017–19, 11 July 2018 HC 350

162 AMA Council of Scientific Affairs, *Influence of Funding Source on Outcome, Validity, and Reliability of Pharmaceutical Research* (2004) 4, cited by Edmond, G. (2008). Judging the scientific and medical literature: Some legal implications of changes to biomedical research and publication. *Oxford Journal of Legal Studies*, 28(3), 523, at 529. doi: 10.1093/ojls/gqn021.

163 Fraser, H., Parker, T., Nakagawa, S., Barnett, A., & Fidler, F. (2018). Questionable research practices in ecology and evolution. *PLoS ONE*, 13(7), e0200303. https://doi.org/10.1371/journal.pone.0200303, citing Fanelli, D. (2010). "Positive" results increase down the hierarchy of the sciences. *PLoS One*, 5. https://doi. org/10.1371/journal.pone.0010068 PMID: 20383332; Sterling, T. D. (1959). Publication decisions and their possible effects on inferences drawn from tests of significance – or vice versa. *Journal of the American Statistical Association*, 54, 30–34. https://doi.org/10.1080/01621459.1959. 10501497; Fanelli, D. (2012). Negative results are disappearing from most disciplines and countries. *Scientometrics*, 90, 891–904. https://doi.org/10.1007/s11192-011-0494-7

164 Fraser, H., Parker, T., Nakagawa, S., Barnett, A., & Fidler, F. (2018). Questionable research practices in ecology and evolution. *PLoS ONE*, 13(7), e0200303. https://doi.org/10.1371/journal.pone.0200303

165 Professor Dame Ottoline Leyser, giving evidence to House of Commons Science and Technology Committee, Research integrity, Sixth Report of Session 2017–19, 11 July 2018 HC 350

166 Centre for Open Science. *Registered Reports,* www.cos.io/initiatives/registered-reports; Kretser, A., Murphy, D., Bertuzzi, S., Abraham, T., Allison, D., Boor, K., Dwyer, J., Grantham, A., Harris, L., Hollander, R., Jacobs-Young, C., Rovito, S., Vafiadis, D., Woteki, C., Wyndham, J., & Yada, R. (2019). Scientific integrity principles and best practices: Recommendations from a scientific integrity consortium. *Science and Engineering Ethics*, 25. doi: 10.1007/s11948-019-00094-3.; BA Nosek, CR Ebersole, AC DeHaven, DT Mellor, The preregistration revolution, Proceedings of

Such pre-notice of the research activity gives rise to the anticipation that findings will be published, whatever the results, and that selective reporting will be minimised.[167] This is a model already used in some research fields, for example, clinical trials, and which could be extended more broadly,[168] although significant safeguards may be needed to persuade those members of research communities who fear potential restrictions to research creativity and research exploration.[169]

Borderlines of misconduct

Inadequately designed experiments or problematic handling of data can harm the integrity of the scientific record, yet don't necessarily cross the line into misconduct.[170] As previously noted, even established areas of misconduct can be subject to different interpretations by members of the scientific community. For example, Johnson and Ecklund, drawing from interviews with 171

the National Academy of Sciences 115 (11), 2600–2606; Fraser, H., Parker, T., Nakagawa, S., Barnett, A., & Fidler, F. (2018). Questionable research practices in ecology and evolution. *PLoS ONE*, 13(7), e0200303. https://doi.org/10.1371/journal. pone.0200303

167 Lerouge, I., & Hol, A. (2020). *Towards a Research Integrity Culture at Universities: From Recommendations to Implementation*. Advice Paper no. 26 – January 2020, League of European Research Universities, 12, www.leru.org/files/Towards-a-Research-Integrity-Culture-at-Universities-full-paper.pdf (accessed 11 February 2020); Commons Select Committee (2018, October 30th) Failing to publish results from clinical trials presents risk to human health; Kretser, A., Murphy, D., Bertuzzi, S., Abraham, T., Allison, D., Boor, K., Dwyer, J., Grantham, A., Harris, L., Hollander, R., Jacobs-Young, C., Rovito, S., Vafiadis, D., Woteki, C., Wyndham, J., & Yada, R. (2019). Scientific integrity principles and best practices: Recommendations from a scientific integrity consortium. *Science and Engineering Ethics*, 25. doi: 10.1007/s11948-019-00094-3; House of Commons Science and Technology Committee, Research integrity: clinical trials transparency, Tenth Report of Session 2017–19, 23 October 2018 HC 1480

168 Lerouge, I., & Hol, A. (2020). *Towards a Research Integrity Culture at Universities: From Recommendations to Implementation*. Advice Paper no. 26 – January 2020, League of European Research Universities, 12; House of Commons Science and Technology Committee, Research integrity: clinical trials transparency, Tenth Report of Session 2017–19, 23 October 2018 HC 1480

169 Nosek, B. A., Ebersole, C. R., DeHaven, A. C., & Mellor, D. T. (2018). The preregistration revolution. *Proceedings of the National Academy of Sciences*, 115(11), 2600–2606; Fraser, H., Parker, T., Nakagawa, S., Barnett, A., & Fidler, F. (2018). Questionable research practices in ecology and evolution. *PLoS ONE*, 13(7), e0200303. https://doi.org/10.1371/journal. pone.0200303.

170 See, for example, John, L. K., Loewenstein, G., & Prelec, D. (2012). Measuring the prevalence of questionable research practices with incentives for truth telling. *Psychological Science*, 23(5), 524–532. Members of the scientific community recognise that breaches of research integrity which undermine results have the potential ultimately to corrupt the overall body of scientific knowledge. Breaches of research integrity can, therefore, be intrinsically harmful, as well as being ethically problematic for the individual scientists involved. Shaw, D., & Satalkar, P. (2018). Researchers' interpretations of research integrity: A qualitative study. *Accountability in Research*, 25(2), 79–93, 89. doi: 10.1080/08989621.2017.1413940

physicists about the concept of ethical ambiguity, at universities in the United States and the UK, cite one associate professor as saying:

> There are a lot of flowing boundaries having to do with plagiarism. So for instance, if you compare all the papers that I have written, we certainly have cut and pasted generic descriptions of apparatus and methods from one to the other . . . I think a lot of it is portrayed in the media as a very black and white issue, and I think there is actually a pretty big gray area.[171]

A similar example arose when the editors of *General Relativity and Gravitation* were asked to check three papers against allegations of plagiarism. The editors acknowledged that there was considerable repetition in the introductory material, where cut and paste approaches had been adopted. However, they did not consider authors using cutting and pasting from their own papers for introductory material as a serious problem. Even though writing material anew each time would be preferable, it was a matter of taste how much introductory material is repeated in each paper. The amount of overlap in the papers under scrutiny exceeded what was desirable, but not to an extent to constitute plagiarism.[172]

Ethical ambiguity may also arise from altruistic motivations. An example from the Johnson and Ecklund study is that of a US professor of physics who used elements of grant funding for purposes and projects distinct from the aims and outcomes identified in the funding proposal. The professor justified this as follows:

> There's a gray area where somebody gets a large grant for some activity and they use those funds to support another activity. . . . [Y]our students have got to eat and when the government can't produce a budget and the agencies can't disperse funds and you've got no money coming in the door. . . . I think it's – it's reasonable to, to use what resources one has to try and – try and keep them.[173]

Similar examples of grey areas were recounted by UK respondents. Johnson and Ecklund conclude that in environments of ethical ambiguity, the physicists

171 Johnson, D. R., & Ecklund, E. H. (2016). Ethical ambiguity in science. *Science and Engineering Ethics,* 22(4), 989–1005, 990. doi: 10.1007/s11948-015-9682-9, citing De Vries, R., Anderson, M. S., & Martinson, B. C. (2006). Normal misbehavior: Scientists talk about the ethics of research. *Journal of Empirical Research on Human Research Ethics*, 1(1), 43–50.

172 Ellis, G., & Nicolai, H. (2007). Editorial note: The issue of plagiarism. *General Relativity and Gravitation*, 39, 1969–1970. doi: 10.1007/s10714-007-0531-2.

173 Johnson, D. R., & Ecklund, E. H. (2016). Ethical ambiguity in science. *Science and Engineering Ethics,* 22(4), 989–1005, 990. doi: 10.1007/s11948-015-9682-9

who contributed to their study distinguished matters of ethics from approaches which promote the collective interests of science. This mindset underpinned the redrawing of ethical boundary lines, or at least the extensions of unclear boundaries.[174]

Suggestions have also been made that attempts to challenge established scientific orthodoxy, to challenge prevailing paradigms, may be perceived to encounter obstacles, such as a reduced likelihood of securing research grants, opportunities for publication or even reduced opportunities in some quarters for promotion or lab space.[175] Malicious rumours may even be circulated.[176] This, it has been argued, should be categorised as scientific misconduct – disseminating falsely negative conclusions about research by another – contrasting with the more readily recognised misconduct of disseminating falsely positive conclusions about one's own research.[177] Examples might include a referee 'falsely and with blatant disregard for the ethics of scientific discourse reaching the conclusion that a work is of insufficient scientific quality.'[178] However, great care is needed to avoid stifling legitimate, even heated, debate. The differences between legitimate critique and illegitimate smear can be subtle. Pejorative language and an absence of carefully considered scientific norms such as cross checking and the balanced inclusion of evidence may be indicators that a line has been crossed.[179]

Another concern at the borderline of potential misconduct is the position where the underlying science may be appropriate in ethical terms but the scientific record remains incomplete because, for example, a commercial funder resists publication if the findings are not in its interests. Academic researchers

174 Johnson, D. R., & Ecklund, E. H. (2016). Ethical ambiguity in science. *Science and Engineering Ethics,* 22(4), 989–1005, 990. doi: 10.1007/s11948-015-9682-9

175 Campanario, J. M., & Martin, B. (2004). Challenging dominant physics paradigms. *Journal of Scientific Exploration*, 18(3), 421–438, 422; Cabbolet, M. J. T. F. (2014). Scientific misconduct: Three forms that directly harm others as the modus operandi of Mill's Tyranny of the prevailing opinion. *Science and Engineering Ethics,* 20(1), 41–54. https://doi.org/10.1007/s11948-013-9433-8

176 Campanario, J. M., & Martin, B. (2004). Challenging dominant physics paradigms. *Journal of Scientific Exploration*, 18(3), 421–438, 422; Cabbolet, M. J. T. F. (2014). Scientific misconduct: Three forms that directly harm others as the modus operandi of Mill's Tyranny of the prevailing opinion. *Science and Engineering Ethics,* 20(1), 41–54. https://doi.org/10.1007/s11948-013-9433-8

177 Cabbolet, M. J. T. F. (2014). Scientific misconduct: Three forms that directly harm others as the modus operandi of Mill's Tyranny of the prevailing opinion. *Science and Engineering Ethics,* 20(1), 41–54. doi: 10.1007/s11948-013-9433-8

178 Cabbolet, M. J. T. F. (2014). Scientific misconduct: Three forms that directly harm others as the modus operandi of Mill's Tyranny of the prevailing opinion. *Science and Engineering Ethics,* 20(1), 41–54. doi: 10.1007/s11948-013-9433-8

179 Cabbolet, M. J. T. F. (2014). Scientific misconduct: Three forms that directly harm others as the modus operandi of Mill's Tyranny of the prevailing opinion. *Science and Engineering Ethics,* 20(1), 41–54. doi: 10.1007/s11948-013-9433, citing Brown, C. L. (2005). Overcoming barriers to use of promising research among elite Middle East policy groups. *Journal of Social Behavior and Personality,* 17(1), 489–544.

may succumb to such pressures if they fear that future funding from the same, or another commercial source, may be at risk.[180]

Potential explanations for integrity failures and research misconduct

In December 2014 the Nuffield Council on Bioethics published a report, *The Culture of Scientific Research in the UK*. Twenty-nine per cent of respondents expressed concerns that competitive pressures influenced ethical behaviours, for example, tempting researchers to adopt less rigorous methodologies and to complete and publish prematurely.[181] Key factors identified in the report as contributing to these concerns were:

- Significant competition for jobs, promotion and research funding
- The impact of short-term funding and the capacity to plan research and to undertake it in a timeframe which is manageable
- A culture of short-termism in other respects, for example, with regard to career security, progression and associated stress-inducing workload issues
- The overall 'publish or perish' culture and disproportionate pressure on researchers to publish in high-impact journals[182]

Similar findings have emerged from other studies. For example, almost 60 per cent of UK researchers surveyed reported career promotion requirements as having at least some negative impact on research integrity.[183] Appointment and promotion often focus upon quantitative metrics, such as publications and grant capture, as opposed to qualitative measures of research integrity associated with good research practice.[184] In the words of one research survey respondent:

180 See, for example, Kondro, W et al. (2004). Drug company experts advised staff to withhold data about SSRI use in children. *CAMJ*, 170(8), 1211; Friedberg, M., Saffran, B., Stinson, T. J., Nelson, W., & Bennett, C. L. (1999). Evaluation of conflict of interest in economic analyses of new drugs used in oncology. *Journal of American Medical Association*, 282(15), 1453–1457. doi: 10.1001/jama.282.15.1453. Findings drawn from the latter study involved the examination of research into new drugs that had been funded by pharmaceutical companies compared to research funded by not-for-profit organisations. The findings indicated that unfavourable conclusions were published in 38 per cent of studies funded by the not-for-profit organisations compared to 5 per cent of those funded by pharmaceutical companies.

181 Nuffield Council on Bioethics, *The Culture of Scientific Research in the UK*, December 2014.

182 Nuffield Council on Bioethics, *The Culture of Scientific Research in the UK*, December 2014.

183 Metcalfe, J., Wheat, K., Munafò. M., Parry, J. (2020). *Research Integrity: A Landscape Study* (p. 29). Vitae/UK Research Integrity Office/UK Reproducibility Network, www.ukri.org/files/legacy/documents/research-integrity-main-report/, citing McKiernan, E. C., Schimanski, L. A., Muñoz Nieves, C., Matthias, L., Niles, M. T., & Alperin, J. P. (2019). Use of the Journal Impact Factor in academic review, promotion, and tenure evaluations. *eLife*, 8, e47338. https://doi.org/10.7554/eLife.47338

184 Metcalfe, J., Wheat, K., Munafò. M., Parry, J. (2020). *Research Integrity: A Landscape Study* (p. 29). Vitae/UK Research Integrity Office/UK Reproducibility Network, www.ukri.org/files/

> Research has become a zero-sum game whereby opportunities to secure funding, publications and sustained work are pitifully small and ridiculously competitive. This kind of environment, where it is all about the metrics and not the substance or legacy, encourages the cutting of corners.[185]

Giving evidence to the House of Commons Science and Technology Committee, Professor Dame Ottoline Leyser, representing the Nuffield Council on Bioethics, argued that a hyper-competitiveness and the rules for 'winning' have detracted from 'what science actually is':

> Science is a method. It is a way of building models of the world that have both explanatory and predictive power. It is not about the ultimate quest for 'Truth'. It is not about correct and incorrect; it is a progressive method for proposing, testing and rejecting or refining models of the world. . . . It moves forward extensively by being wrong. . . . The way things have gone in the research system, we have developed a culture where people are rewarded for being 'right' and being 'exciting' in some way. Those things have nothing to do with science.[186]

Furthermore, misdirected competition among researchers may affect scientific progress through secrecy, undermining relationships between researchers and interference with peer review systems.[187] Rather than leading to optimal levels of innovation and discovery, certain forms of competition may lead to the opposite by manifesting as 'unguided, evolutionary forces than . . . rational planning.'[188]

legacy/documents/research-integrity-main-report/, citing McKiernan, E. C., Schimanski, L. A., Muñoz Nieves, C., Matthias, L., Niles, M. T., & Alperin, J. P. (2019). Use of the Journal Impact Factor in academic review, promotion, and tenure evaluations. *eLife*, 8, e47338. https://doi.org/10.7554/eLife.47338

185 Metcalfe, J., Wheat, K., Munafò. M., Parry, J. (2020). *Research Integrity: A Landscape Study* (p. 35). Vitae/UK Research Integrity Office/UK Reproducibility Network, www.ukri.org/files/legacy/documents/research-integrity-main-report/

186 House of Commons Science and Technology Committee, Research integrity, Sixth Report of Session 2017–19, 11 July 2018 HC 350, para 52.

187 Anderson, M., Ronning, E., De Vries, R., & Martinson, B. (2008). The perverse effect of competition on scientists' work and relationships. *Science and Engineering Ethics*, 13, 437–461, 458–459. doi: 10.1007/s11948-007-9042-5, citing Cech, T. R. (2005). Fostering innovation and discovery in biomedical research. *The Journal of the American Medical Association*, 294, 1390–1393.

188 Anderson, M., Ronning, E., De Vries, R., & Martinson, B. (2008). The perverse effect of competition on scientists' work and relationships. *Science and Engineering Ethics*, 13, 437–461, 458–459. doi: 10.1007/s11948-007-9042-5, citing Cech, T. R. (2005). Fostering innovation and discovery in biomedical research. *The Journal of the American Medical Association*, 294, 1390–1393; Brazil, R. (2021). What's wrong with research culture. *Chemistry World*, September 28, 2021, www.chemistryworld.com/features/whats-wrong-with-research-culture/4014361.article

At an extreme, scientists starting out motivated by pursuit of knowledge may become demoralised 'if they see rewards going to those who adopt dubious practices to get ahead.'[189]

What has been described as 'academic greed' may manifest in almost 'pathological publishing,' driven by the assumption that a 'vast' publication list is necessary for career advancement.[190] It has also been argued that some journals exacerbate the problems by expecting data to fit hypotheses near perfectly for an article to be accepted. Initial successes in this regard may even encourage fraudulent behaviour among a small minority of researchers if they feel that subsequent findings are insufficient and they fear harm to their reputation. In extreme cases, initial manipulation of good data to turn it into apparently excellent data may gradually morph into the abandonment entirely of data collection to be replaced by its invention.[191]

Significant cultural change further in the direction of ethics rather than harmful levels of competition will be challenging to achieve, but a relatively straightforward starting point would be the adoption by institutions of promotion procedures which require applicants to discuss their research papers without identifying the source of the publication, to focus upon research substance rather than source reputation.[192]

The boundary between methodological disagreement and research misconduct

In 2006 Geoffrey Chang, Department of Molecular Biology, The Scripps Research Institute, and five other authors retracted a number of papers published between 2001 and 2005.[193] This provides a useful example from which

189 Professor Lewandowsky and Professor Bishop giving evidence to the House of Commons Science and Technology Committee, Research integrity, Sixth Report of Session 2017–19, 11 July 2018 HC 350, para 53. The House of Commons Science and Technology Committee further recommended that research be undertaken to better understand the implications for researcher behaviour of different incentive models, para 58.

190 Martin, B. R. (2013). Whither research integrity? Plagiarism, self-plagiarism and coercive citation in an age of research assessment. *Research Policy*, 42(5) (June), 1005–1014, 1012. doi: 10.1016/j.respol.2013.03.011

191 Stroebe, W., Postmes, T., & Spears, R. (2012). Scientific misconduct and the myth of self-correction in science. *Perspect Psychol Sci.*, 7(6), 670–688. doi: 10.1177/1745691612460687. What is far less clear is what leads a small minority of researchers to succumb to such temptations while the majority do not.

192 Strech, D., Weissgerber, T., & Dirnagl, U., on behalf of QUEST Group (2020). Improving the trustworthiness, usefulness, and ethics of biomedical research through an innovative and comprehensive institutional initiative. *PLoS Biol*, 18(2), e3000576. https://doi.org/10.1371/journal.pbio.3000576

193 Penders, B., Horstman, K., & Vos, R. (2007). Proper science in moist biology. *EMBO Reports*, 8(7), 613; Penders, B., Horstman, K., & Vos, R. (2008). Walking the line between biology and computation: The 'moist' zone. *BioScience*, 58(8), 747–755.

to consider discussion within scientific communities about the distinction between methodological disputes and research misconduct.

In a letter published in *Science* Chang and his fellow researchers explained that

> An in-house data reduction program introduced a change in sign for anomalous differences. This program, which was not part of a conventional data processing package, converted the anomalous pairs (I+ and I-) to (F- and F+), thereby introducing a sign change. . . . We very sincerely regret the confusion that these papers have caused and, in particular, subsequent research efforts that were unproductive as a result of our original findings.[194]

Challenges to the underlying science arose from an article in *Nature* in September 2006.[195] This led the original research team to investigate and discover the software fault. The software had been designed by Chang. Reaction from the scientific community was mixed, with some defenders and some detractors. One, for example, argued for the essentiality of knowing 'what your software is actually doing' if such computer modelling is to be used.[196] Another questioned the responsibility of the journals which published the papers, expressing concerns that publishers and referees were operating in an environment where:

> [E]xperimental details are relegated to 'Supplemental material' . . . and when canned software makes it easy for people without a deep understanding of the method to determine structures and to referee the structure papers of others, it may be too much to expect that technical errors can be caught reliably.[197]

When considering methodology versus misconduct, the case provides a useful example of discussions surrounding different ideas about 'proper science' and 'proper methodological conduct and norms for integrity.'[198] The specific

194 Chang, G., Roth, C. B., Reyes, C. L., Pornillos, O., Chen, Y-J., & Chen, A. P. (2006). Retraction. *Science*, New Series, 314(5807) (December 22), 1875.

195 Dawson, R. J. P., & Locher, K. P. (2006). Structure of a bacterial multidrug ABC transporter. *Nature*, 443, 180–185.

196 Miller, C. (2007). Pretty structures, but what about the data? *Science*, 315(5811), 459–459. Retrieved from www.jstor.org/stable/20038816

197 Petsko, G. A. (2007). And the second shall be first. *Genome Biology*, 8, 103. https://doi.org/10.1186/gb-2007-8-2-103. The risk is that some leading journals place such importance on being the first to publish what is perceived to be important new research that they create a culture where researchers feel under significant pressure to rush to publication.

198 Penders, B., Vos, R., & Horstman, K. (2009). A question of style: Method, integrity and the meaning of proper science. *Endeavour*, 33(3).

group with which a scientist identifies results in differing responses to these questions. Such group identity can also become so entrenched that it closes off alternative viewpoints, which can have consequences when research collaboration arises between members of different groupings.[199] For example, data collected by experimental scientists but needing to pass through tools created by specialists in computation and statistics may present significant challenges for each to check the methodology and quality of the work of the other.[200] At the extreme, different methodological expectations may become connected to different norms for professional integrity, such that what is categorised as proper science in one could be viewed as improper, even misconduct, in another.[201] The Chang et al retractions illustrate the difficult line which may need to be walked when two scientific traditions meet and the problems which can arise if research quality is assessed predominantly on outcomes and impact at the expense of the subtleties of research design and integrity.[202]

Markers of success from the integrity perspective

A pervasive culture of scientific integrity within research communities and institutions offers the best prospect as effective instruments for change.[203] Institutions supporting and rewarding scientists who undertake solid, as opposed to 'just flashy,' research while holding to account members of the research community whose methods are questionable provide a solid basis for such integrity.[204] A connected argument is that as research integrity is central to undertaking the researcher role in an appropriately professional way, no greater reward than the salary for the job should be needed. However, such arguments tend to be ineffective if accompanied by countervailing measures of perceived success and status chasing. At least with some members of the research community,

199 Penders, B., Vos, R., & Horstman, K. (2009). A question of style: Method, integrity and the meaning of proper science. *Endeavour*, 33(3).

200 Penders, B., Vos, R., & Horstman, K. (2009). A question of style: Method, integrity and the meaning of proper science. *Endeavour*, 33(3).

201 Penders, B., Vos, R., & Horstman, K. (2009). A question of style: Method, integrity and the meaning of proper science. *Endeavour*, 33(3).

202 Miller, C. (2007). Pretty structures, but what about the data? *Science*, 315(5811), 459–459. Retrieved from www.jstor.org/stable/20038816; Penders, B., Vos, R., & Horstman, K. (2009). A question of style: Method, integrity and the meaning of proper science. *Endeavour*, 33(3); Metcalfe, J., Wheat, K., Munafò. M., Parry, J. (2020). *Research Integrity: A Landscape Study* (p. 43). Vitae/UK Research Integrity Office/UK Reproducibility Network, www.ukri.org/files/legacy/documents/research-integrity-main-report/

203 Kretser, A., Murphy, D., Bertuzzi, S., Abraham, T., Allison, D., Boor, K., Dwyer, J., Grantham, A., Harris, L., Hollander, R., Jacobs-Young, C., Rovito, S., Vafiadis, D., Woteki, C., Wyndham, J., & Yada, R. (2019). Scientific integrity principles and best practices: Recommendations from a scientific integrity consortium. *Science and Engineering Ethics*, 25. doi: 10.1007/s11948-019-00094-3.

204 Begley, C. G., Buchan, A. M., & Dirnagl, U. (2015). Robust research: Institutions must do their part for reproducibility. *Nature*, 525(7567), 25–27.

these may incentivise the taking of shortcuts or even outright cheating. In other professions, equivalent inappropriate success chasing which could lead to integrity breaches may be addressed by appropriate regulatory models, which include character checking for honesty and integrity prior to admission to the profession and post-admission approaches which encourage reflection and the avoidance of risky behaviour.

Peer review

Research findings are usually communicated to the wider scientific community by means of the publication of peer-reviewed outputs, usually journal articles. Peer review in one form or another dates back a number of centuries, although the systematic form recognised today mainly dates back to the latter half of the twentieth century.[205] Peer review is the mechanism by which journal editors assess whether or not a piece warrants publication, with the principles underpinning review usually seeking to assess the rigour of the research in terms of its methodology and findings and the contribution it makes to knowledge in the field.[206]

Peer review can be linked to ideas of professional self-regulation. The scientific community has been imbued with authority to speak on behalf of society with regard to esoteric scientific knowledge, and with this authority comes a responsibility 'as the guardian for the integrity of science.'[207] Each individual member of the scientific community enjoys the freedom to pursue knowledge, but the community as a whole is obliged 'to provide the normative processes for research activity through peer evaluation.'[208]

Surveys suggest that significant numbers within scientific communities have confidence in peer review. For example, in one such survey 71 per cent of

205 Squazzoni, F., Bravo, G., & Takacs, K. (2013). Does incentive provision increase the quality of peer review? An experimental study. *Research Policy*, 42, 287–294. doi: 10.1016/j.respol.2012.04.014; Edmond, G. (2008). Judging the scientific and medical literature: Some legal implications of changes to biomedical research and publication. *Oxford Journal of Legal Studies*, 28(3), 523, at 529. doi: 10.1093/ojls/gqn021, citing Kronick, D. (1990). Peer review in 18th-century scientific journalism. *JAMA*, 263, 1321–1322; Burnham, J. (1990). The evolution of editorial peer review. *JAMA*, 263, 1323–1329.

206 Squazzoni, F., Bravo, G., & Takacs, K. (2013). Does incentive provision increase the quality of peer review? An experimental study. *Research Policy*, 42, 287–294. doi: 10.1016/j.respol.2012.04.014; Edmond, G. (2008). Judging the scientific and medical literature: Some legal implications of changes to biomedical research and publication. *Oxford Journal of Legal Studies*, 28(3), 523, at 529. doi: 10.1093/ojls/gqn021, citing Kronick, D. (1990). Peer review in 18th-century scientific journalism. *JAMA*, 263, 1321–1322; Burnham, J. (1990). The evolution of editorial peer review. *JAMA*, 263, 1323–1329.

207 Jones, N. (2007). A code of ethics for the life sciences. *Science and Engineering Ethics*, 13, 25–43, 39. doi: 10.1007/s11948-006-0007-x.

208 Jones, N. (2007). A code of ethics for the life sciences. *Science and Engineering Ethics*, 13, 25–43, 39. doi: 10.1007/s11948-006-0007-x.

UK scientists reported that they considered the peer review system to have a positive or very positive effect in terms of encouraging the production of high-quality science.[209]

The nature of peer review is not always clearly formulated or subject to an agreed definition but may be compared to, for example, the role of expert witnesses in English and Welsh court proceedings. An expert witness is usually appointed by one of the parties in litigation, but despite being retained and paid for by a party, the expert's primary duty is to the court and the interests of justice. Along similar lines, peer reviewers, while usually appointed by a journal editor or funding body, should be viewed as acting neither for the appointing party nor the author but for the broader interests of science.

The nature of scientific debate and disagreement is such that passing peer review cannot be expected to certify the 'correctness' of the research findings, nor can peer reviewers be expected, in terms of the time and resources available to them, to seek to replicate the research results. Data falsification and manipulation are also relatively unlikely to be detected as part of peer review, as review does not generally engage with the scrutiny of raw data.[210] What may reasonably be expected is that peer reviewers check the internal consistency of papers.[211] Other than this, the main benefit of peer review is likely to be to seek to ensure that authors are communicating clearly and reviewers are providing feedback to help authors improve contributions, rather than differentiating legitimate from illegitimate research.[212]

A further complicating factor is that as funding resources and space in prestigious journals have become scarcer, peer reviewers have become participants in a rationing process. As such, role demarcation has become blurred. Unlike expert witnesses in a courtroom, with the aim of bringing a single-minded focus to truth and justice, peer reviewers may place obstacles in the way of a scientific advancement not because it is unsound, but because they deem a particular proposed publication or research project to be less exciting or less deserving than a competitor's. In terms of the balance between functions, peer reviewers may find themselves more involved in market rationing than autonomous protection of science.[213] Along connected lines, peer

209 Nuffield Council on Bioethics, *The Culture of Scientific Research in the UK*, December 2014

210 It has been suggested that this issue could be addressed in part if at least one reviewer was specifically assigned the task of scrutinising data. Martin, B. (2007). Keeping plagiarism at bay – A salutary tale. *Research Policy*, 36(7), 905–911, 910. In the absence of payment to reviewers at an appropriate level to reflect the time involved, this may be difficult to apply in practice.

211 See, for example, Oreskes, N., & Conway, E. M. (2010). *Merchants of Doubt: How a Handful of Scientists Obscured the Truth on Issues from Tobacco Smoke to Global Warming* (pp. 3–4). New York: Bloomsbury.

212 See, for example, Smith, R. (1999). Opening up BMJ peer review. *BMJ (Clinical research ed.)*, 318, 4–5. doi: 10.1136/bmj.318.7175.4.

213 See, for example, Anon. (2020). Reviewers should stop doing the market's dirty work, *Times Higher Education*, February, 6. www.timeshighereducation.com/opinion/reviewers-should-stop-doing-markets-dirty-work

review may occupy a significant role in preserving established paradigms, but at the expense of research challenging these. Proportionally, the highest rates of rejection at review or editorial stages have been found among some of the most innovative work, measured in terms of high levels of citation when eventually finding an outlet for publication.[214] Rationing may therefore be viewed in terms of numerical control but also in terms of hierarchical and, to some extent, status quo control.[215]

As well as critiquing the functions of peer review, its effectiveness in other respects has come under scrutiny. Some studies suggest that peer review demonstrates significant levels of subjectivity, such that there can be major differences in the conclusions from different reviewers of the same submission.[216] It has even been suggested that rates of agreement and disagreement between different peer reviewers can be little more than chance.[217] Peer review has also been found to be a poor mechanism for detecting scientific misconduct and is ill suited for detecting plausible and internally consistent fabrication.[218] In the words of one observer: 'If peer review was a drug it would never be allowed onto the market . . . because we have no convincing evidence of its benefits but a lot of evidence of its flaws.'[219] The *British Medical Journal* undertook studies involving the insertion of major errors into papers then sent for review. No reviewer spotted all of the errors, and some spotted none. On average reviewers

214 Siler, K., Lee, K., & Bero, L. (2014). Measuring the effectiveness of scientific gatekeeping. *Proceedings of the National Academy of Sciences of the United States of America*, 112. doi: 10.1073/pnas.1418218112.

215 Hatton, L., & Warr, G. (2017). Scientific peer review: An ineffective and unworthy institution. *Times Higher Education*, December 9, 2017, www.timeshighereducation.com/blog/scientific-peer-review-ineffective-and-unworthy-institution

216 Cole, S., Cole, J. R., & Simon, G. A. (1981). Chance and consensus in peer review. *Science*, 214(4523) (November 20), 881–886. doi: 10.1126/science.7302566. PMID: 7302566; Smith R. (2006). Peer review: A flawed process at the heart of science and journals. *Journal of the Royal Society of Medicine*, 99(4), 178–182. https://doi.org/10.1258/jrsm.99.4.178; Schroter, S., Black, N., Evans, S., Godlee, F., Osorio, L., & Smith, R. (2008). What errors do peer reviewers detect, and does training improve their ability to detect them? *Journal of the Royal Society of Medicine*, 101(10), 507–514. https://doi.org/10.1258/jrsm.2008.080062

217 Rothwell, P. M., & Martyn, C. (2000). Reproducibility of peer review in clinical neuroscience – is agreement between reviewers any greater than would be expected by chance alone? *Brain*, 123, 1964–1969. doi: 10.1093/brain/123.9.1964, cited by Smith, R. (2010). Classical peer review: an empty gun. *Breast Cancer Res*, 12, S13. https://doi.org/10.1186/bcr2742

218 Hardwig, J. (1991). The role of trust in knowledge. *Journal of Philosophy*, 88(12), 693–708, 706. For example, in this investigation of alleged misconduct the peer reviewers had not identified the problems, which were eventually brought to light by an anonymous whistle-blower. Allegation of research misconduct in respect of 32 papers published between 1990 and 2013 by researchers based at the UCL Institute of Child Health: Report of the Investigation Panel, www.documentcloud.org/documents/6178710-UCL-FOIA-Latchman-Lab-Investigations.html (accessed 6 July 2019).

219 Smith, R. (2010). Classical peer review: An empty gun. *Breast Cancer Res*, 12, S13. https://doi.org/10.1186/bcr2742

spotted a quarter of the errors.[220] Some of the most noteworthy examples of scientific fraud have not been detected through peer review but rather:

> [S]uspicious competitors, aggrieved post-graduate students, incredulous promotion committees and jilted lovers have often played more prominent roles in the identification of anomalies deemed worthy of further investigation.[221]

Reviewers may fail to identify potential warning signs in some articles; in others they may risk the distortion of research findings by favouring the telling of a compelling story, potentially at the expense of scientific diligence.[222] Such focus carries the risk of crossing the boundary between selectivity in the publication process and more outright manipulation of research findings. For example, in the Diederik Stapel case, investigations indicated that on occasions editors and reviewers had requested that certain variables be omitted to 'better support the reasoning and flow of the narrative' with the outcome also that 'unwelcome results' would be omitted.[223] It was also said that reviewers sometimes requested retrospective pilots, to be discussed in the article as if performed in advance, thereby appearing to justify the experimental parameters.[224]

It may also be argued that in an environment of 'hyper-specialisation' within science, peer reviewers 'are rarely true peers in the sense of having equal expertise.'[225] For example, in the case of Diederik Stapel, certain issues, which hadn't been identified at peer review, only came to light because of expert statistical analysis within and across publications.[226] One possible response is the selection of highly specialist reviewers who review only those

220 Smith R. (2006). Peer review: A flawed process at the heart of science and journals. *Journal of the Royal Society of Medicine*, 99(4), 178–182. https://doi.org/10.1258/jrsm.99.4.178 Citing Godlee, F., Gale, C. R., & Martyn, C. N. (1998). Effect on the quality of peer review of blinding reviewers and asking them to sign their reports: A randomized controlled trial. *JAMA*, 280, 237–240; Schroter, S., Black, N., Evans, S., Carpenter, J., Godlee, F., & Smith, R. (2004). Effects of training on quality of peer review: Randomised controlled trial. *BMJ*, 328, 673.

221 Edmond, G. (2008). Judging the scientific and medical literature: Some legal implications of changes to biomedical research and publication. *Oxford Journal of Legal Studies*, 28(3), 523, at 529. doi: 10.1093/ojls/gqn021, citing Broad, W., & Wade, N. (1982). *Betrayers of the Truth: Fraud and Deceit in Science* (pp. 79–82, 203–211). New York: Simon and Schusterx.

222 Levelt Committee, Noort Committee, Drenth Committee. *Flawed Science: The Fraudulent Research Practices of Social Psychologist Diederik Stapel*, November 28, 2012; Nuffield Council on Bioethics, *The Culture of Scientific Research in the UK*, December 2014

223 Levelt Committee, Noort Committee, Drenth Committee. *Flawed Science: The Fraudulent Research Practices of Social Psychologist Diederik Stapel*, November 28, 2012

224 Levelt Committee, Noort Committee, Drenth Committee. *Flawed Science: The Fraudulent Research Practices of Social Psychologist Diederik Stapel*, November 28, 2012

225 Huang, S. (2017). Bland peer review needs a pinch of salt. *Times Higher Education*, August 31, 2017, www.timeshighereducation.com/opinion/bland-peer-review-needs-a-pinch-of-salt

226 Levelt Committee, Noort Committee, Drenth Committee. *Flawed Science: The Fraudulent Research Practices of Social Psychologist Diederik Stapel*, November 28, 2012, 21

parts of a paper relevant to their expertise, with other reviewers engaging with the parts they have expertise in.[227] However, for such an approach to work, the reward and career recognition system for peer review has to be such that reviewers with the appropriate expertise are motivated to fully engage with the process.[228]

Experiments with alternatives to traditional peer review have included open-access journals with review tracks which involve authors working with reviewers directly, names of reviewers being published with the paper and in some instances publication of the reviews. The reviewer moves from being an anonymous critic to a collaborator with the author and editor in a transparent process.[229] Such approaches may offer promising alternative models as long as reviewers remain appropriately independent and offer informed critique.

Post-publication peer review has also grown in use in recent years. This may involve publishing reviews alongside an article and may also facilitate ongoing comment from the wider research community.[230]

Peer reviewers may not consider a key, or even any, aspect of their role to detect misconduct. Also, as discussed earlier, they may lack the time and diagnostic tools to interrogate a submission for this purpose.[231] Even if a reviewer

227 Kretser, A., Murphy, D., Bertuzzi, S., Abraham, T., Allison, D., Boor, K., Dwyer, J., Grantham, A., Harris, L., Hollander, R., Jacobs-Young, C., Rovito, S., Vafiadis, D., Woteki, C., Wyndham, J., & Yada, R. (2019). Scientific integrity principles and best practices: Recommendations from a scientific integrity consortium. *Science and Engineering Ethics*, 25. doi: 10.1007/s11948-019-00094-3.

228 Kretser, A., Murphy, D., Bertuzzi, S., Abraham, T., Allison, D., Boor, K., Dwyer, J., Grantham, A., Harris, L., Hollander, R., Jacobs-Young, C., Rovito, S., Vafiadis, D., Woteki, C., Wyndham, J., & Yada, R. (2019). Scientific integrity principles and best practices: Recommendations from a scientific integrity consortium. *Science and Engineering Ethics*, 25. doi: 10.1007/s11948-019-00094-3; Moher, D., Bouter, L., Kleinert, S., Glasziou, P., Sham, M. H., Barbour, V., et al. (2020). The Hong Kong principles for assessing researchers: Fostering research integrity. *PLoS Biol*, 18(7), e3000737. https://doi.org/10.1371/journal.pbio.3000737. Exceptions are cited, for example academic promotion criteria at the University of Glasgow explicitly acknowledge participation in peer review www.gla.ac.uk/media/Media_498056_smxx.pdf (accessed 25 July 2020); Nuffield Council on Bioethics, *The Culture of Scientific Research in the UK*, December 2014

229 Kretser, A., Murphy, D., Bertuzzi, S., Abraham, T., Allison, D., Boor, K., Dwyer, J., Grantham, A., Harris, L., Hollander, R., Jacobs-Young, C., Rovito, S., Vafiadis, D., Woteki, C., Wyndham, J., & Yada, R. (2019). Scientific integrity principles and best practices: Recommendations from a scientific integrity consortium. *Science and Engineering Ethics*, 25. doi: 10.1007/s11948-019-00094-3, discussing an experiment by the American Society for Microbiology with a review track called *m-Sphere Direct* within its open-access journal *m-Sphere*.

230 Nuffield Council on Bioethics, *The Culture of Scientific Research in the UK*, December 2014

231 See, for example, Bornmann, L., Nast, I., & Daniel, H. (2008). Do editors and referees look for signs of scientific misconduct when reviewing manuscripts? A quantitative content analysis of studies that examined review criteria and reasons for accepting and rejecting manuscripts for publication. *Scientometrics*, 77, 415. https://doi.org/10.1007/s11192-007-1950-2; Stroebe, W., Postmes, T., & Spears, R. (2012). Scientific misconduct and the myth of self-correction in science. *Perspect Psychol Sci.*, 7(6), 670–688. doi: 10.1177/1745691612460687

has suspicions about an experimental outcome, with the time and resources available, such suspicions cannot be readily followed up.[232]

Only occasionally will peer review identify a suspicious case.[233] Close reading and careful re-analysis of the results can give rise to concerns,[234] but the current model of peer reviewing as an unpaid contribution to the scientific endeavour and one for which time has to be found alongside competing demands may not be best suited to ensuring this level of scrutiny. Peer reviewers may be alert for plagiarism if suspicious text stands out or if modern technological scanning is utilised. Historically, instances of plagiarism could easily slip through the net. Martin, for example, discusses an example of plagiarism only detected after 14 years by a keen-eyed reader.[235]

An inherent tendency within research communities towards trust rather than suspicion may also explain why reviewers tend not to place detecting misconduct as an expectation of their role. Nor, given assumptions of trustworthiness, may reviewers consider misconduct as a likely explanation for data or other anomalies. Peer review has been built upon assumptions that authors are researching and writing in good faith.[236] If reviewers are not looking for fraud, they are unlikely to discover fraud.[237] Were peer reviewers to be tasked with actively looking for fraud, this could change their role substantially.[238] Also, in the absence of clear-cut indications of misconduct, if a peer reviewer spots an issue which gives rise to concerns, recommending rejection may be seen as a sufficient response. However, this leaves the author free to submit the piece elsewhere. An example can be drawn from the Paolo Macchiarini case. Macchiarini was found to have committed misconduct by his employer, the

232 Stroebe, W., Postmes, T., & Spears, R. (2012). Scientific misconduct and the myth of self-correction in science. *Perspect Psychol Sci.*, 7(6), 670–688. doi: 10.1177/1745691612460687

233 Science and Technology Committee, Eighth Report of Session 2010–12, *Peer review in scientific publications*, HC 856, para 244

234 For example, early criticisms of some of the work of Grossarth-Maticek, a co-researcher of Hans Eysenck, were 'based solely on a close reading and careful re-analysis of the reported results.' Pelosi, A. J. (2019). Personality and fatal diseases: Revisiting a scientific scandal. *Journal of Health Psychology*, 24(4), 421–439, citing Fox, B. H. (1991). Quandaries created by unlikely numbers in some of Grossarth-Maticek's studies. *Psychological Inquiry*, 2, 242–247; Schuler, G., & Fox, B. H. (1991). Questions about Grossarth-Maticek's procedures and results. *Psychological Inquiry*, 2, 257–261.

235 Martin, B. (2007) Keeping plagiarism at bay – A salutary tale. *Research Policy*, 36(7), 905–911, 908.

236 Levi, B. G. (2002). Investigation finds that one lucent physicist engaged in scientific misconduct. *Physics Today*, 55(11) (November 1). https://doi.org/10.1063/1.1534995, quoting Donald Levy (University of Chicago), editor of the Journal of Chemical Physics, and chair of the American Institute of Physics journal editors' panel.

237 Stroebe, W., Postmes, T., & Spears, R. (2012). Scientific misconduct and the myth of self-correction in science. *Perspect Psychol Sci.*, 7(6), 670–688. doi: 10.1177/1745691612460687

238 Levi, B. G. (2002). Investigation finds that one lucent physicist engaged in scientific misconduct. *Physics Today*, 55(11) (November 1). https://doi.org/10.1063/1.1534995, quoting Donald Levy (University of Chicago), editor of the Journal of Chemical Physics, and chair of the American Institute of Physics journal editors' panel.

Karolinska Institute in Sweden. By investigating email correspondence the inquiry discovered that an article published in the *Lancet* and subsequently retracted had previously been rejected by another journal, the reviewer having raised questions about some of the datasets.[239] To address the risk of this type of journal shopping, the *COPE Code of Conduct* states that editors are ethically obliged to further investigate suspicions, rather than simply rejecting papers that raise concerns about possible misconduct.[240] To be effective, such an approach relies on reviewers understanding and complying with their obligations to raise suspicions in an appropriate and effective manner.

While peer review in social science and humanities publications is often double-blind, the identities of author and reviewer being hidden from each other, in science disciplines, single-blind, where the identity of the reviewer is hidden from the author but the author is known to the reviewer, has been more common.[241] It has been found that knowledge of author identity by reviewers can result in scores for papers exhibiting bias, for example, higher scores for papers with male-first authors and lower scores for papers with female-first authors. In medical fields, reviewers in the United States were found to be more favourable towards papers from authors in US institutions.[242] Reviewers were over one and a half times more likely to favour papers from 'famous' authors or 'top' institutions.[243] Double-blind review can help to address this, although it has also been found that some reviewers may be able to guess the identity of an author, although more thorough anonymisation procedures can help to reduce successful guessing – for example, blinding references in papers to the author's previous work.[244]

239 *Suspected Scientific Misconduct*, Karolinska Institute Summary Report (English translation), p. 18 (accessed 20 November 2020)

240 COPE Code of conduct and best practice guidelines for journal editors, para 11.2, http://publicationethics.org/files/Code_of_conduct_for_journal_editors_Mar11.pdf

241 Nuffield Council on Bioethics, *The Culture of Scientific Research in the UK*, December 2014

242 Le Goues, C., Brun, Y., Apel, S., Berger, E., Khurshid, S., & Smaragdakis, Y. (2018). Effectiveness of anonymization in double-blind review. *Communications of the ACM*, 61(6) (June), 30–33. doi: 10.1145/3208157, citing Link, A. M. (1998). U.S. and non-U.S. submissions: An analysis of reviewer bias. *JAMA* 280(3) (July), 246–247.

243 Le Goues, C., Brun, Y., Apel, S., Berger, E., Khurshid, S., & Smaragdakis, Y. (2018). Effectiveness of anonymization in double-blind review. *Communications of the ACM*, 61(6) (June), 30–33. doi: 10.1145/3208157, citing Tomkins, A., Zhang, M., & Heavlin, W. D. (2017). Single versus double-blind reviewing at WSDM 2017. *CoRR*, abs/1702.00502.

244 CLe Goues, C., Brun, Y., Apel, S., Berger, E., Khurshid, S., & Smaragdakis, Y. (2018). Effectiveness of anonymization in double-blind review. *Communications of the ACM*, 61(6) (June), 30–33. doi: 10.1145/3208157. In contrast, Huang argues, in the context of reviewing grant proposals, that anonymity weakens accountability and the pressure on reviewers to exercise due diligence, Huang, S. (2017). Bland peer review needs a pinch of salt. *Times Higher Education*, August 31, 2017, www.timeshighereducation.com/opinion/bland-peer-review-needs-a-pinch-of-salt Anonymity may also increase the likelihood of some reviewers behaving inappropriately, for example, rudeness or,

From a lawyer's perspective, anonymity of a reviewer is peculiar. Anonymity in judicial and governmental processes in democratic societies is rare – transparent justice and decision-making accountability are of central importance.

Anonymous peer review may also reduce the opportunity for peer reviewers to identify misconduct which may only be detectable if more than one paper by the same author is read. For example, although not an example of reviewer detection, in the case of Robert A. Slutsky fraud was only detected because two of his papers were 'read in quick succession by an astute reader' and otherwise could have remained undetected for years if each fraudulent publication had only been read independently.[245] The investigation of research fraud by Diederik Stapel found a number of publications which included replications, identical up to four decimal places, of the same experimental control conditions. These had identical 'mean values of the dependent variables (and/or of their standard deviations).' Such evidence of potential fraud can only come to light by close comparison of different publications.[246] This is one strand supporting the observation that, on balance, anonymity may not improve the quality of a review.[247]

In practical terms, in the absence of reviewer anonymity in a field where it has been the norm, there may be an increase in the likelihood of reviewers declining to review.[248] A compromise is the removal of reviewer anonymity in cases of 'pseudoskeptical attack,'[249] for example, if after a lengthy delay a referee responds with a clearly hastily written report, perhaps abusive in tone, which rejects the submitted paper without engaging with the specific content. The justification of loss of anonymity is that such an 'attack' departs from the core

---

more seriously, providing an unfavourable review of research which competes with or challenges that of the reviewer, Nuffield Council on Bioethics, *The Culture of Scientific Research in the UK*, December 2014.

245 See, for example, Hardwig, J. (1991). The role of trust in knowledge. *Journal of Philosophy*, 88(12), 693–708, 703.

246 Levelt Committee, Noort Committee, Drenth Committee, *Flawed Science: The Fraudulent Research Practices of Social Psychologist Diederik Stapel*, November 28, 2012, 21 (accessed 5 April 2020)

247 Smith R. (2006). Peer review: A flawed process at the heart of science and journals. *Journal of the Royal Society of Medicine*, 99(4), 178–182. citing Justice, A. C., Cho, M. K., Winker, M. A., Berlin, J. A., & Rennie D. (1998). Does masking author identity improve peer review quality? A randomized controlled trial. *PEER Investigators. JAMA*, 280(3) (July 15), 240–242. doi: 10.1001/jama.280.3.240. Erratum in: *JAMA*, 280(11)(September 16), 968. PMID: 9676668; van Rooyen, S., Godlee, F., Evans, S., Smith, R., & Black, N. (1998). Effect of blinding and unmasking on the quality of peer review: a randomized trial. *JAMA*, 280(3) (July 15), 234–237. doi: 10.1001/jama.280.3.234. PMID: 9676666.

248 Van Rooyen, S., Godlee, F., Evans, S., Black, N., & Smith R. (1999). Effect of open peer review on quality of reviews and on reviewers' recommendations: A randomised trial. *British Medical Journal*, 318, 23–27.

249 Cabbolet, M. J. T. F. (2014). Scientific misconduct: Three forms that directly harm others as the modus operandi of Mill's Tyranny of the prevailing opinion. *Science and Engineering Ethics*, 20(1), 41–54. doi: 10.1007/s11948-013-9433

principles of good scientific practice.[250] The sentiment behind such a suggestion is likely to be shared by many authors who have been on the receiving end of a review which exhibits some or all of these features. However, it would be challenging to reach consensus within scientific communities about a list of characteristics essential to triggering such a response and applying the criteria consistently. Even if such a list and application criteria could be agreed, the threat these posed might deter even conscientious prospective reviewers from undertaking the work.

Misconduct by peer reviewers

Peer reviewers largely rely upon the honesty of researchers in their recording of the experimental process and reporting of results. Researchers also place trust in reviewers not to misuse information which comes into their possession as part of the review process. Some researchers report experiencing ethical transgressions by reviewers, such as breaching confidentiality or misusing ideas from papers they reviewed.[251] From a legal perspective, the peer review process lacks formal legal protections which lawyers are used to in their own professional spheres in terms of conflicts of interest and the protection of confidential information. Rigorous peer review is credited with contributing significantly to the success of science, yet it also presents threats to individual scientists if reviewers misappropriate text or ideas.[252] In the words of one commentator:

> Scientific peer-review resembles a bizarre version of poker in which competitors show each other their cards for analysis and comment but expect that everyone will continue to play their own cards unaffected by what has been seen.[253]

In 2019 Netherlands-based publisher Elsevier investigated a significant number of researchers suspected of deliberately manipulating the peer-review process to boost their own citation numbers.[254] The investigation was prompted following research by Elsevier analytics experts, Jeroen Baas and Catriona Fennell,

250 Cabbolet, M. J. T. F. (2014). Scientific misconduct: Three forms that directly harm others as the modus operandi of Mill's Tyranny of the prevailing opinion. *Science and Engineering Ethics,* 20(1), 41–54. doi: 10.1007/s11948-013-9433

251 Resnik, D., Gutierrez-Ford, C., & Peddada, S. (2008). Perceptions of ethical problems with scientific journal peer review: An exploratory study. *Resources,* 14. doi: 10.1007/s11948-008-9059-4.

252 Grinnell, F. (2013). Research integrity and everyday practice of science. *Science and Engineering Ethics*, 19, 685–701. doi: 10.1007/s11948-012-9376-5.

253 Grinnell, F. (2013). Research integrity and everyday practice of science. *Science and Engineering Ethics*, 19, 685–701. doi: 10.1007/s11948-012-9376-5.

254 Chawla, D. S. (2019). Elsevier investigates hundreds of peer reviewers for manipulating citations. *Nature,* 573, 174. doi: 10.1038/d41586-019-02639-9

who looked at the peer-review activity of over 50,000 academic reviewers for Elsevier journals. Baas and Fennell were interested in identifying how often the work of reviewers is cited by the papers they review, considering the risk of 'coercive citation,' where an author is encouraged or feels obliged to cite the reviewer's work in return for a more positive review.[255]

Baas and Fennell found that the number of instances were not large. Out of almost 55,000 cases examined, around 98.5 per cent of the reviewers were found to have been cited in less than 10 per cent of the papers they reviewed. Given the likelihood that a reviewer will work in the same field as authors under review, some cross citing is to be expected in the normal course of events. However, a small number – under 1 per cent – consistently had their own work referenced in studies they have reviewed.[256] Among this small proportion there were some extreme cases. For example, one reviewer had submitted 120 reviewer reports which contained requests to include numerous irrelevant citations. In only four instances did authors refuse to accede to these requests.[257]

A poll of over 4,300 *Nature* readers indicated much higher levels of coercive citation than found in the Elsevier investigation, with around two-thirds of respondents reporting that they had 'felt pressured by peer reviewers to cite seemingly superfluous studies.'[258] By way of a specific example, a reviewer for *Bioinformatics* was found to have requested an average of 35 citations be added to papers reviewed, with around nine out of ten of the additional citations relating to research outputs of the reviewer. The reviewer was banned from

255 Baas, J., & Fennell, C. (2019). When peer reviewers go rogue – Estimated prevalence of citation manipulation by reviewers based on the citation patterns of 69,000 reviewers (May 22, 2019). ISSI 2019, September 2–5, 2019, Rome, Italy, www.issi2019.org/. Available at SSRN: https://ssrn.com/abstract=3339568 (accessed 17 September 2019 and not itself peer reviewed at that time). In terms of methodology the authors recognise that journal editors may use citations in an article to identify possible reviewers. So the fact that a reviewer is cited in an article doesn't in itself indicate any problematic issue. A more sophisticated approach is needed to ensure that only citations which may have arisen following the review process are considered.

256 Chawla, D. S. (2019). Elsevier investigates hundreds of peer reviewers for manipulating citations. *Nature,* 573, 174. doi: 10.1038/d41586-019-02639-9; Baas, J., & Fennell, C. (2019). When peer reviewers go rogue – estimated prevalence of citation manipulation by reviewers based on the citation patterns of 69,000 reviewers (May 22, 2019). ISSI 2019, September 2–5, 2019, Rome, Italy, www.issi2019.org/. Available at SSRN: https://ssrn.com/abstract=3339568 (accessed 17 September 2019 and not itself peer reviewed at that time)

257 Baas, J., & Fennell, C. (2019). When peer reviewers go rogue – estimated prevalence of citation manipulation by reviewers based on the citation patterns of 69,000 reviewers (May 22, 2019). ISSI 2019, September 2–5, 2019, Rome, Italy www.issi2019.org/. Available at SSRN: https://ssrn.com/abstract=3339568 (accessed 17 September 2019 and not itself peer reviewed at that time)

258 Chawla, D. S. (2019). Two-thirds of researchers report 'pressure to cite'. *Nature*, NEWS, October 1, 2019, www.nature.com/articles/d41586-019-02922-9?sf220470438=1. Limitations of the *Nature* poll included the self-selecting nature of respondents, some of who may have had particular interests in coercive citation

further reviewing for *Bioinformatics*, although the investigation also found evidence to suggest that the reviewer's behaviour extended to other journals.[259]

The Elsevier review also uncovered examples of reviewers engaging in other questionable practices in their own research – notably 'publishing the same studies more than once.' The latter is likely to give grounds for retractions by Elsevier, but not the submissions involving coercive citation, given that the reviewed authors were not at fault and the additional citations did not affect the integrity of the reported research.[260] Slipping in one or more additional citations at the suggestion of a reviewer, and which the author may or may not suspect includes those of the (anonymous) reviewer, may be unlikely to impact on key underpinnings of the research. However, in some instances there will be a tipping point where an anonymous reviewer may be seeking to nudge the author in the direction of modifying conclusions drawn from research findings to support the reviewer's own research agenda. Both the Elsevier investigation and the specific example from *Bioinformatics* give publishers and editors pause for thought to consider vulnerabilities of the peer-review system, the trust placed in it and the extent to which publisher or journal policies and approaches might be modified to improve the detection of reviewer manipulation, including whether technological enhancements would aid detection.[261] Publication of reviews is a possible way forward.[262] Engaging institutional regulatory mechanisms where a reviewer is employed or broader national or international codes of scientific conduct may also help to discourage reviewer misbehaviour.[263] At present, responses rest at the discretion of individual journals or publishers. As in the *Bioinformatics* example, excluding a reviewer removes the risk of reoffending, at least on a journal-by-journal basis, while retraction of individual

259 Wren, J. D., Valencia, A., & Kelso, J. (2019). Reviewer-coerced citation: Case report, update on journal policy and suggestions for future prevention. *Bioinformatics*, 35(18) (September 15), 3217–3218. https://doi.org/10.1093/bioinformatics/btz071

260 Chawla, D. S. (2019). Elsevier investigates hundreds of peer reviewers for manipulating citations. *Nature*, 573, 174. doi: 10.1038/d41586-019-02639-9

261 Wren, J. D., Valencia, A., & Kelso, J. (2019). Reviewer-coerced citation: Case report, update on journal policy and suggestions for future prevention. *Bioinformatics*, 35(18) (September 15), 3217–3218. https://doi.org/10.1093/bioinformatics/btz071

262 van Groenigen, J. W., Agnelli, A., Bai, J., Capowiez, Y., Cayuela, M., Kögel-Knabner, I., . . . Vepraskas, M. (2018). Citation stacking in soil science articles: our response to the open letter by concerned early-career soil scientists. *Geoderma*, 328, 119–120. https://doi.org/10.1016/j.geoderma.2018.03.023

263 Baas, J., & Fennell, C. (2019). When peer reviewers go rogue – estimated prevalence of citation manipulation by reviewers based on the citation patterns of 69,000 reviewers (May 22, 2019). ISSI 2019, September 2–5, 2019, Rome, Italy www.issi2019.org/. Available at SSRN: https://ssrn.com/abstract=3339568 (accessed 17 September 2019 and not itself peer reviewed at that time). Citing by way of example The Netherlands Code of Conduct for Research Integrity 2018, section 3.5.48: "*Do not use the system of peer review to generate additional citations for no apparent reason, with the aim of increasing your own or other people's citation scores ('citation pushing').*" (https://www.nwo.nl/en/netherlands-code-conduct-research-integrity).

references or issuing corrections ensures that the reviewer does not benefit from their misbehaviour.[264]

The findings discussed earlier raise important questions about reviewer trustworthiness and associated ethics, but also raise questions about the ethical responsibilities of editors and authors to maintain trust. Drawing from other professional regulatory fields such as medicine and law, there are well-established principles that practitioners not only have obligations to report concerns about fellow practitioners but also that it is each practitioner's professional responsibility to resist pressure from others in positions of power, authority or influence to act in inappropriate ways. In essence, the interests of patients or clients and the integrity of the professions is paramount. From the equivalent perspective, that the integrity of the research process and research record are paramount, it may be argued that an author knowing or having reasonable cause to suspect that reviewer suggestions or requirements will improperly affect the integrity of the process should have an ethical duty to report that. The circumstances in which an author may be expected to have reasonable suspicions will be limited if the review process is blind and reviewer demands are not excessive. Editors know the identity of reviewers and should be alert for attempts to coerce citation and also attempts to disguise this behaviour, for example, if citation recommendations are presented in the review by means of title but not author names and full references.[265]

Trust breaches on the part of peer reviewers can also manifest in other ways. In an anonymous survey of over 1,100 participants in science, technology, engineering and mathematics (STEM) fields from 46 countries, the investigators considered perceptions of long-term implications of receiving unprofessional reviewer comments.[266] Over half of the study participants recounted reviews which contained harsh and cruel comments and unprofessional personal attacks directed at the author.[267] These findings build upon other research evidence which indicates bias in the peer review process arising from factors

264 Chawla, D. S. (2019). Elsevier investigates hundreds of peer reviewers for manipulating citations. *Nature*, 573, 174. doi: 10.1038/d41586-019-02639-9

265 Baas, J., & Fennell, C. (2019). When peer reviewers go rogue – estimated prevalence of citation manipulation by reviewers based on the citation patterns of 69,000 reviewers (May 22, 2019). ISSI 2019, September 2–5, 2019, Rome, Italy www.issi2019.org/. Available at SSRN: https://ssrn.com/abstract=3339568 (accessed 17 September 2019 and not itself peer reviewed at that time)

266 Silbiger, N. J., & Stubler, A. D. (2019). Unprofessional peer reviews disproportionately harm underrepresented groups in STEM. *PeerJ*, 7, e8247. https://doi.org/10.7717/peerj.8247

267 Silbiger, N. J., & Stubler, A. D. (2019). Unprofessional peer reviews disproportionately harm underrepresented groups in STEM. *PeerJ*, 7, e8247. https://doi.org/10.7717/peerj.8247. Unprofessional peer review comments were defined for the purposes of the study as 'any statement that is unethical or irrelevant to the nature of the work; this includes comments that: (1) lack constructive criticism, (2) are directed at the author(s) rather than the nature or quality of the work, (3) use personal opinions of the author(s)/work rather than evidence-based criticism, or (4) are "mean-spirited" or cruel.'

such as author nationality or gender.[268] As well as presenting a risk to the scientific record in terms of the potential blocking of important research findings,[269] such behaviour may exacerbate self-doubt in individual authors and more broadly undermine trust within the scientific community. Traditionally underrepresented groups in STEM fields, while not found to be more likely to receive unprofessional reviews, were most likely to perceive negative impacts on self-confidence, potentially impacting productivity in terms of writing output.[270] Education and codes of best practice in the ethics and appropriate trust relationships for peer reviewers might help to address these issues,[271] as might the publication of peer reviews alongside papers. Evidence from open review journals which take this approach indicates that it significantly reduces the incidence of unprofessional reviews.[272] Less than 3 per cent of participants who reported receipt of an unprofessional peer review indicated that the review was from an open review journal.[273]

268 Lee, C. J., Sugimoto, C. R., Zhang, G., & Cronin, B. (2013). Bias in peer review. *Journal of the American Society for Information Science and Technology*, 64(1), 2–17. https://doi.org/10.1002/asi.227; Silbiger, N. J., & Stubler, A. D. (2019). Unprofessional peer reviews disproportionately harm underrepresented groups in STEM. *PeerJ*, 7, e8247. https://doi.org/10.7717/peerj.8247

269 See, for example, Fox, C. W., & Paine, C. E. T. (2019). Gender differences in peer review outcomes and manuscript impact at six journals of ecology and evolution. *Ecol Evol.*, 9, 3599–3619. https://doi.org/10.1002/ece3.4993

270 Silbiger, N. J., & Stubler, A. D. (2019). Unprofessional peer reviews disproportionately harm underrepresented groups in STEM. *PeerJ*, 7, e8247. https://doi.org/10.7717/peerj.8247. The authors acknowledge that the findings of a study of this type, reporting participant perceptions, cannot be used to confer causality, leading to diminished productivity, but nevertheless argue that 'the results show that unprofessional reviews reinforce bias that is already being encountered by underrepresented groups on a daily basis.' See also, Howe-Walsh, L., & Turnbull, S. (2016). Barriers to women leaders in academia: Tales from science and technology. *Studies in Higher Education*, 41(3), 415–428. doi: 10.1080/03075079.2014.929102

271 Other connected responses include education for students and scientists more broadly about appropriate approaches to peer reviewing; published guidelines for best practices from learned societies; and journal-, institutional- and learned society–level sanctions for inappropriate reviewing. Silbiger, N. J., & Stubler, A. D. (2019). Unprofessional peer reviews disproportionately harm underrepresented groups in STEM. *PeerJ*, 7, e8247. https://doi.org/10.7717/peerj.8247; Resnik, D. B., & Elmore, S. A. (2016). Ensuring the quality, fairness, and integrity of journal peer review: A possible role of editors. *Science and Engineering Ethics*, 22(1), 169–188. https://doi.org/10.1007/s11948-015-9625-5

272 Pulverer, B. (2010). Transparency showcases strength of peer review. *Nature*, 468, 29–31. doi: 10.1038/468029a

273 Silbiger, N. J., & Stubler, A. D. (2019). Unprofessional peer reviews disproportionately harm underrepresented groups in STEM. *PeerJ*, 7, e8247. https://doi.org/10.7717/peerj.8247, although the overall conclusion was that more research was required in this regard. There are notes of caution in terms of identifying reviewers more generally, as this may place more junior researchers acting as reviewers at risk from retaliation by more senior members of the research community if unhappy with the reviews they receive. Double-blind review would be preferable in that regard. Wilcox, C. (2019). Rude paper reviews are pervasive and sometimes harmful, study finds. December 12, 2019 www.sciencemag.org/news/2019/12/rude-paper-reviews-are-pervasive-and-sometimes-harmful-study-finds

General guidance by journals to reviewers should clearly indicate that in the event of suspected misconduct on their part, a report to the reviewer's employing institution may be necessary.[274] It is advisable for journals to retain peer-review records for significant periods of time, at least ten years has been recommended, to ensure the meaningful prospect of investigating allegations of inappropriate behaviour by reviewers.[275]

However, sanction-based approaches are likely to face the overarching problem that peer review, as a voluntary activity with limited measurable career benefit, is easy to step away from if additional deterrents are added. Even those committed to behaving with the utmost integrity may fear false accusations or may review unduly leniently to minimise the risk of author accusations, to the detriment of the research process and the scientific record. Sanction-based approaches may bring with them greater pressure for reviewing to be remunerated and thereby becoming a professionalised role in its own right, perhaps akin to scientists taking on a paid role when acting as an expert witnesses in the litigation process. With regard to the various issues which can arise in the context of peer review, the remuneration and professionalisation of the process, with associated legal obligations, may offer a way forward.

Bogus peer reviewers

As well as misconduct by otherwise legitimate peer reviewers, the peer review process itself can be manipulated by bogus reviews. Electronic systems can be vulnerable to manipulation, and so editors need to be alert the risks of, for example, non-institutional email addresses for reviewers, glowing reviews often returned unduly swiftly and systematised 'business' models for the creation of bogus peer reviews for those authors willing to pay for this service.[276] For example, in 2012 the editor of *The Journal of Enzyme Inhibition and Medicinal Chemistry* became suspicious when reviews for manuscripts by a medicinal-plant researcher based in South Korea were returned unusually quickly, sometimes within 24 hours. When challenged, the author admitted that he had written a number of the reviews himself. The journal operated a practice of requesting author suggestions for prospective reviews, and this particular author had provided names, some real and some fabricated, with email contact details which would lead to review requests coming to him or to his colleagues. As a result of

274 Wager, E., Kleinert, S., Garfinkel, M., Volker Bahr, C., et al. (2017). Cooperation & Liaison between Universities & Editors (CLUE): Recommendations on best practice. *bioRxiv*. doi: https://doi.org/10.1101/139170.

275 Wager, E., Kleinert, S., Garfinkel, M., Volker Bahr, C., et al. (2017). Cooperation & Liaison between Universities & Editors (CLUE): Recommendations on best practice. *bioRxiv*. doi: https://doi.org/10.1101/139170.

276 Haug, C. (2015). Peer-review fraud – hacking the scientific publication process. *The New England Journal of Medicine*, 373. doi: 10.1056/NEJMp1512330, 2394.

the fraud, 28 papers were subsequently retracted by a number of journals and an editorial resignation also resulted.[277]

The practice by some journals to ask authors to suggest reviewers is time saving for editors, but exacerbates the risks of inappropriate reviewer behaviour.[278] It has even been suggested that editors may rule out reviewers recommended by authors to minimise the risks, including those of authors seeking to nominate friends or close colleagues.[279] The COPE guidelines accept the practice of author-suggested reviewers but note that editors retain ultimate decision-making power and should always carefully check reviewer credentials and independence.[280] Some journals which previously utilised the approach of author-suggested reviewers have moved away from this. However, challenges remain, for example, if reviewers have to be chosen from jurisdictions unfamiliar to an editor.[281]

Other examples of peer review manipulation include an engineering researcher in Taiwan who created a relatively sophisticated scheme – a 'peer review and citation ring' involving 130 fake email addresses and fabricated reviewer identities.[282] The fraud was detected after a suspicious editor instigated a comprehensive investigation, which resulted in the retraction of 60 articles.[283] In December 2020, *The Journal of Nanoparticle Research* reported being subject to a relatively sophisticated fraud relating to the publication of a special edition. The fraudsters were knowledgeable about the research field, such that the proposed special edition targeted an area of topical interest. The fraudsters created false email addresses to imitate eminent academics and fabricated domain names to give the impression that communications came from respected universities. Once the accepted special edition was in place, a large number of submissions were received, including numerous poor-quality papers which would not have satisfied the journal's usual quality control processes.[284] The

277 Ferguson, C., Marcus, A., & Oransky, I. (2014). Publishing: The peer-review scam. *Nature*, 515 (November 27), 480–482. doi: 10.1038/515480

278 Ferguson, C., Marcus, A., & Oransky, I. (2014). Publishing: The peer-review scam. *Nature*, 515 (November 27), 480–482. doi: 10.1038/515480

279 Ferguson, C., Marcus, A., & Oransky, I. (2014). Publishing: The peer-review scam. *Nature*, 515 (November 27), 480–482. doi: 10.1038/515480; Haug, C. (2015). Peer-review fraud – hacking the scientific publication process. *The New England Journal of Medicine*, 373. doi: 10.1056/NEJMp1512330, 2394.

280 Committee on Publication Ethics (COPE). *Guidelines on Good Publication Practice*, p. 44, https://publicationethics.org/files/u7141/1999pdf13.pdf

281 Ferguson, C., Marcus, A., & Oransky, I. (2014). Publishing: The peer-review scam. *Nature*, 515 (November 27), 480–482. doi: 10.1038/515480

282 Haug, C. (2015). Peer-review fraud – hacking the scientific publication process. *The New England Journal of Medicine*, 373. doi: 10.1056/NEJMp1512330, 2394.

283 Haug, C. (2015). Peer-review fraud – hacking the scientific publication process. *The New England Journal of Medicine*, 373. doi: 10.1056/NEJMp1512330, 2394.

284 Pinna, N., Clavel, G., & Roco, M. C. (2020). The victim of an organized rogue editor network! *Journal of Nanoparticle Research*, 22, 376. https://doi.org/10.1007/s11051-020-05094-0

rogue network was detected by the editorial team after they began to check individual papers, although 19 had already been published electronically.[285] A particularly sophisticated element of the fraud was utilising a special edition model which gave the fraudulent special edition editors greater control over the refereeing process, in the knowledge that the usual journal editors would not have the resources to double-check a large number of submissions.[286]

As long as researcher recognition and reward largely revolve around publishing a high number of articles and journal editors are encouraged to publish them rapidly, approaches to gaming or cheating the system, with bogus peer reviewing being one example, are incentivised to evolve more quickly than mechanisms aimed at preventing this behaviour.[287]

Illegitimate journals and 'industrialised cheating'

It has been estimated that worldwide there are over 8,000 predatory journals publishing over 400,000 pieces annually.[288] These journals do not aim at transparent and rigorous scientific outputs, but rather have profit as their primary focus. They seek to extract fees from authors, often by means of questionable, even misleading, marketing schemes.[289] Some may seek to mimic legitimate journals online (or even acquire the titles), utilising reputation to attract fees.[290] Peer review procedures tend to be lax or even non-existent, such that flawed papers are unlikely to be rejected. Appointment practices for editors and editorial board membership tend to be suspect.[291] Recent years have witnessed rapid growth in the outputs of such journals, for example, from around 50,000

285 Pinna, N., Clavel, G., & Roco, M. C. (2020). The victim of an organized rogue editor network! *Journal of Nanoparticle Research,* 22, 376. https://doi.org/10.1007/s11051-020-05094-0

286 It is to the credit of the editors that they were open about the attempted fraud to alert others within the scientific publishing community of the lengths to which some fraudsters will go, Pinna, N., Clavel, G., & Roco, M. C. (2020). The victim of an organized rogue editor network! *Journal of Nanoparticle Research,* 22, 376. https://doi.org/10.1007/s11051-020-05094-0

287 Haug, C. (2015). Peer-review fraud – hacking the scientific publication process. *The New England Journal of Medicine*, 373. doi: 10.1056/NEJMp1512330, 2394.

288 Patwardhan, B. (2019). Why India is striking back against predatory journals. *Nature,* 571, 7. doi: 10.1038/d41586-019-02023-7; Chawla, D. (2021). Hundreds of 'predatory' journals indexed on leading scholarly database. *Nature*. February 8, 2021. doi: 10.1038/d41586-021-00239-0.

289 Sorokowski, P., Kulczycki, E., Sorokowska, A., & Pisanski, K. (2017). Predatory journals recruit fake editor. *Nature*, 543, 481–483, 481. doi: 10.1038/543481a.

290 Siler, K., Larivière, V., Vincent-Lamarre, P., & Sugimoto, C. (2021). Predatory publishers' latest scam: Bootlegged and rebranded papers. *Nature*, 598, 563–565. doi: 10.1038/d41586-021-02906-8, citing Moussa, S. (2021). Journal hijacking: Challenges and potential solutions. *Learned Publishing,* 34(4), 688–695.

291 Sorokowski, P., Kulczycki, E., Sorokowska, A., & Pisanski, K. (2017). Predatory journals recruit fake editor. *Nature*, 543, 481–483, 481. doi: 10.1038/543481a; Chawla, D. S. (2013). Predatory-journal papers have little scientific impact Analysis of hundreds of articles in predatory titles shows that 60% have never been cited. *Nature*, January 13, 2013. doi: https://doi.org/10.1038/d41586-020-00031-6

articles in 2010 to over 400,000 in 2014.[292] Predatory journals also pose a potential threat to the reputations of the growing number of legitimate open-access journals.[293]

Predatory journals pose a particular risk to unsuspecting researchers, for example, some in the early stages of their careers being tempted by what they are misled into thinking are legitimate outlets.[294] Unsuspecting researchers may also be misled into reviewing for such journals.[295] Predatory journals may also tempt into poor practices researchers seeking to game the system.[296] Assumptions that predatory journals are mainly a problem affecting researchers in the developing world have been shown to be unjustified, with ample evidence of involvement by researchers based in countries the World Bank defines as high-income or upper-middle-income.[297]

The risk from predatory journals to the scientific record arises from it being compromised by publications which have not been subject to full quality assurance.[298] There is debate about the actual impact on the scientific record of articles in predatory journals, with 'only' 60 per cent never being citied.[299] However, given the numbers of articles in predatory journals, the 40 per cent being cited amounts to around 160,000. When multiple citations are considered, over a million citations may be circulating in the research record.[300]

Attempts have begun to emerge to address predatory publishing practices by means of established legal and institutional mechanisms. For example, a federal court in the United States imposed a fine in excess of $50 million in

292 Shen, C., & Björk, B. (2015). 'Predatory' open access: A longitudinal study of article volumes and market characteristics. *BMC Med,* 13, 230. doi: 10.1186/s12916–015–0469–2

293 Chawla, D. S. (2013). Predatory-journal papers have little scientific impact Analysis of hundreds of articles in predatory titles shows that 60% have never been cited. *Nature*, January 13, 2013, doi: https://doi.org/10.1038/d41586-020-00031-6. Quoting Matt Hodgkinson, head of research integrity at the open-access publisher Hindawi in London.

294 Patwardhan, B. (2019). Why India is striking back against predatory journals. *Nature,* 571, 7. doi: 10.1038/d41586-019-02023-7

295 Van Noorden, R. (2020). Hundreds of scientists have peer-reviewed for predatory journals. *Nature*. doi: 10.1038/d41586-020-00709-x. It is also observed that some may not be unsuspecting, but instead be seeking to enhance their CV with an extended list of review titles.

296 Patwardhan, B. (2019). Why India is striking back against predatory journals. *Nature,* 571, 7. doi: 10.1038/d41586-019-02023-7

297 Moher, D., Shamseer, L., Cobey, K. D. et al. (2017). Stop this waste of people, animals and money. *Nature,* 549 (September 7), 23–25. doi: 10.1038/549023a; Cobey, K. (2017). Illegitimate journals scam even senior scientists. *Nature,* 549 (September 7), 7. doi: 10.1038/549007a

298 See, for example, Patwardhan, B. (2019). Why India is striking back against predatory journals. *Nature,* 571, 7. doi: 10.1038/d41586-019-02023-7

299 Chawla, D. S. (2013). Predatory-journal papers have little scientific impact Analysis of hundreds of articles in predatory titles shows that 60% have never been cited. *Nature*, January 13, 2013, doi: https://doi.org/10.1038/d41586-020-00031-6.

300 Chawla, D. S. (2013). Predatory-journal papers have little scientific impact Analysis of hundreds of articles in predatory titles shows that 60% have never been cited. *Nature*, January 13, doi: https://doi.org/10.1038/d41586-020-00031-6.

a case brought by the Federal Trade Commission against a major publisher based in India accused of making deceptive claims relating to the publishing process, hiding the requirement for steep publication fees and other misleading practices.[301]

Another response to the challenge of predatory journals is a quality assurance system for legitimate peer-reviewed journals which follow internationally accepted guidelines for the publication process. A suggested title for such a system is publication process quality assurance (PPQA).[302] Institutions, libraries, funding bodies and other interested parties can then seek to ensure publication in and subscription to only PPQA-compliant journals.

Mass-produced misconduct: paper mills

The systematic creation of falsified articles by so-called 'paper mills,' businesses churning out fake manuscripts to order, are providing challenges to legitimate journals.[303] Such papers will often reproduce key components of legitimate publications and then find their way into print under the names of different, unconnected authors and institutions. Work by scientists determined to reveal the extent of such fraudulent activity has resulted in the recent flagging of over 1,000 studies, although the extent of the problem could be much larger.[304]

Improved detection procedures may include using the ScholarOne manuscript-processing system to identify submissions from the same computer.[305]

301 Federal Trade Commission v. OMICS Group Inc. FTC Matter/File Number 152 3113; Civil Action Number 2:16-cv-02022. (accessed 23 July 2021). Calls have also been made in the UK for legal action to be brought by Universities UK, the representative body for the university sector, to curb predatory publishing, Grove, J. (2021). UUK 'should sue predatory publishers over tsunami of spam'. *Times Higher Education*, July 23, 2021, www.timeshighereducation.com/news/uuk-should-sue-predatory-publishers-over-tsunami-spam, quoting Douglas Kell, a former chief executive officer of the Biotechnology and Biological Sciences Research Council.

302 Finkel, A., Office of the Chief Scientist (2019). 'There is a problem': Australia's top scientist Alan Finkel pushes to eradicate bad science, September 12, 2019, https://theconversation.com/there-is-a-problem-australias-top-scientist-alan-finkel-pushes-to-eradicate-bad-science-123374 (accessed 14 September 2019)

303 RSC Advances retractions, 20 January 2021 RSC Advances retractions; Else, H., & Van Noorden, R. (2021). The fight against fake-paper factories that churn out sham science. *Nature,* 591, 516–519. doi: https://doi.org/10.1038/d41586-021-00733-5

304 Else, H., & Van Noorden, R. (2021). The fight against fake-paper factories that churn out sham science. *Nature,* 591, 516–519. doi: https://doi.org/10.1038/d41586-021-00733-5; Byrne, J. A., & Christopher, J. (2020). Digital magic, or the dark arts of the 21st century – how can journals and peer reviewers detect manuscripts and publications from paper mills? *FEBS Lett*, 594, 583–589. https://doi.org/10.1002/1873-3468.13747. Concerns have arisen to the extent that the Committee on Publication Ethics held a forum specifically about the issue, COPE, Systematic manipulation of the publishing process via 'paper mills', September 2020 https://publicationethics.org/resources/forum-discussions/publishing-manipulation-paper-mills (accessed 1 September 2021)

305 Else, Holly, & Van Noorden, Richard (2021). The fight against fake-paper factories that churn out sham science. *Nature,* 591, 516–519. doi: https://doi.org/10.1038/d41586-021-00733-5

Upgraded review processes might include greater scrutinisation of raw data, although the faking of data remains a risk; use of specialists with expertise in checking images; and remaining alert for email addresses which don't link to author names. An obstacle highlighted by some publishers may arise from editorial independence and concerns about sharing information, which could breach data protection provisions or even be defamatory.[306]

Misbehaviour within research hierarchies

'Shameless chicanery' and 'skulduggery' have been descriptors applied to the behaviour of some senior scientists towards their junior colleagues.[307] The focus on metrics as measures of career success is described by some commentators as being largely to blame – moral behaviour of researchers is somehow 'being overshadowed by the performance against metrics.'[308]

Some senior researchers may be tempted to use for their own benefit information and ideas shared with them in confidence by their junior colleagues. The victims may be reluctant to jeopardise their careers by complaining or even raising the issue. This is particularly reprehensible, as it is a betrayal of trust and abuse of academic authority:

> [It] expresses and reinforces the toxic power dynamics of the academic hierarchy. Junior scholars are robbed of credit for their ideas and often find themselves obligated to abandon entire research projects, which suddenly 'belong' to the plagiaristic senior scholar.[309]

Building upon this, unjustified claims of authorship have also been described as a form of scientific misconduct within research hierarchies.[310] The position is complicated by the fact that, historically, many journals have lacked clarity about the eligibility for authorship in multi-author pieces. Authorship abuse includes senior scientists insisting on authorship attribution, sometimes lead authorship, on work to which they have made little or no contribution,

306 Else, Holly, & Van Noorden, Richard (2021). The fight against fake-paper factories that churn out sham science. *Nature,* 591, 516–519. doi: https://doi.org/10.1038/d41586-021-00733-5

307 Gill, J. (2017). Collaboration and competition: Essential for research. *Times Higher Education,* November 30, 2017, quoting Trisha Greenhalgh, Professor of primary healthcare sciences, University of Oxford.

308 Gill, J. (2017). Collaboration and competition: Essential for research. *Times Higher Education,* November 30, 2017, quoting Trisha Greenhalgh, Professor of primary healthcare sciences, University of Oxford.

309 Frye, B. L. (2020). Plagiarize this paper (October 1, 2019). *IDEA: The IP Law Review,* 60(294), 323. Available at SSRN: https://ssrn.com/abstract=3462144

310 Scientific Integrity Committee of Swiss Academies of Arts and Sciences, Hess, C. W., Brückner, C., et al. (2015). Authorship in scientific publications: Analysis and recommendations. *Swiss Med Wkly.,* 145, w14108. Published 2015 Feb 21. doi: 10.4414/smw.2015.14108

on papers produced by members of their team or department.[311] From the opposite perspective, senior scientists with an established reputation may be offered 'gift' authorship to enhance the status of a paper and perhaps even to curry favour in terms of junior scientist career development.[312] Some academic fraudsters have even exploited offering gift authorship to draw unsuspecting fellow researchers into their ambit, perhaps to deflect suspicion by giving the impression of team-based research with associated mutual oversight.

The dangers of accepting authorship without sufficient involvement in the research and writing processes is illustrated by the Paolo Macchiarini case. An inquiry by the Karolinska Institute in Sweden initially concluded that a number of co-authors also shared some culpability, having accepted co-authorship and the responsibilities associated with this without appropriate engagement with the research.[313] On the specific facts of the case, aspects of this decision were revisited,[314] but the risks the matter highlights of agreeing to be named as a co-author without sufficient control over the content of the publication remain pertinent. The value that named co-authors can bring to legitimising fraudulent research can, in extreme cases, lead to names being added as authors to papers with the supposed co-author totally unaware.[315] For example, a sometime collaborator of Yoshihiro Sato, Jun Iwamoto claimed that he was not aware of Sato's misconduct nor that his name had been included on certain papers. Because of Sato's reputation, Dr Iwamoto claimed to have felt honoured to have his name included on those of Dr Sato's papers where he

311 The survey is indicative only, comprising a poll of 364 self-selecting respondents from across the globe. It does, however, provide a useful snapshot of issues which would benefit from further exploration. Else, H. (2017). Authorship wars: Academics outline the rules for recognition. *Times Higher Education*, November 30, 2017

312 Flanagin, A., and others (1998). Prevalence of articles with honorary authors and ghost authors in peer-reviewed medical journals. *JAMA*, 280, 222–224. In some parts of the World gift authorship may be seen as more of a cultural norm. In the context of the humanities and social sciences see, for example, Macfarlane, B. *Co-authorship in the Humanities and Social Sciences a Global View,* A white paper from Taylor & Francis, http://authorservices.taylorandfrancis.com/custom/uploads/2017/09/Coauthorship-white-paper.pdf (accessed 5 December 2017). It is also of note that such gifting can be directed upwards to demonstrate respect and thanks towards, for example, a doctoral supervisor and also directed downwards in the form of over-crediting, to boost the career chances of a more junior researcher.

313 *Suspected Scientific Misconduct*, Karolinska Institute Summary Report (English translation), p. 27 (accessed 20 November 2020)

314 Karolinska Institutet News (2022). *Karolinska Institutet Announces New Decision: Researcher Was Not Careless*, Published: 2017–03–22. https://news.ki.se/karolinska-institutet-announces-new-decision-researcher-was-not-careless (accessed 22 November 2020)

315 See, for example, claims by Evan Ekman that Scott Reuben added him as a co-author without his knowledge or consent to one of his fraudulent research papers. Borrell, B. (2009). A medical Madoff: Anesthesiologist faked data in 21 studies. *Sci. Am.*, www.scientificamerican.com/article/a-medical-madoff-anesthestesiologist-faked-data/ (10 March 2009).

was aware of this occurring, 'even though he did not know much about the content.'[316]

Determining authorship

During the twentieth and early twenty-first centuries multi-author publications have increasingly become the norm. Time commitments necessary for complex research have increasingly exceeded the capacity of sole researchers, or even small research teams, as have the complexity of individual component elements of larger research programmes – in essence, no single person knows enough to undertake the research alone.[317]

In misconduct terms, a positive observation regarding multi-authored work is that with larger numbers of researchers involved, in terms of incentives to commit misconduct, a larger number of people involved in a project minimises any benefit to any one individual, reducing or removing personal reward as a motivating factor.[318] However, unjustified authorship has also increased in prominence as an issue, and attempts are emerging which seek to control this.[319] Determining legitimate authorship can pose challenges. A complex research project may involve numerous stages: the generation and refinement of ideas; the designing and undertaking of experiments; analysis and interpretation of the data; the writing up of the findings. Tens, hundreds and in some areas such as contributors to particle physics research at CERN, even a thousand or more contributors can be involved.[320] For example, in relation to the case of Viktor

316 Kupferschmidt, K. (2018). Researcher at the center of an epic fraud remains an enigma to those who exposed him. *Science*, August 17, 2018, Inexperience was thought to be the most likely explanation in this situation.

317 de Solla Price, D. J. (1963). *Little Science, Big Science*. New York: Columbia University Press; Hardwig, J. (1991). The role of trust in knowledge. *The Journal of Philosophy*, 88(12), (December), 693–708, 695. www.jstor.org/stable/2027007; Hussinger, K., & Pellens, M. (2019). Scientific misconduct and accountability in teams. *PLoS ONE*, 14(5), e0215962. https://doi.org/10.1371/journal. pone.0215962

318 Hartgerink, C. H. J., Voelkel, J. G., Wicherts, J. M., van Assen, M. A. L. M. (2019). Detection of data fabrication using statistical tools. August 19, 2019 (pre-print)

319 See, for example, the Swiss Academy of Arts and Sciences (2021). *Code of Conduct for Scientific Integrity*, p. 23

320 See, for example, Else, H. (2017). Authorship wars: Academics outline the rules for recognition. *Times Higher Education*, November 30, 2017, quoting "Brian Nosek, a professor in the department of psychology at the University of Virginia." One, 9 page, publication referred to, arising from work undertaken with the Large Hadron Collider at the European Organisation for Nuclear Research (Cern), included a 24 page list of 5,154 authors. The position contrasts with the humanities and social sciences where co-authorship, while not insignificant, was far less common and large research teams very uncommon. See, for example, Macfarlane, B. *Co-authorship in the Humanities and Social Sciences a Global View*, A white paper from Taylor & Francis, http://authorservices.taylorandfrancis.com/custom/uploads/2017/09/Coauthorship-white-paper.pdf (accessed 5 December 2017)

Ninov and the purported discovery of element 118, the following observation has been made:

> Anyone involved was included as a co-author, down to the graduate students. One of them . . . remembers the excitement that rushed through the team. If you worked a shift [at the cyclotron] your name went on the paper. I worked a few shifts, so my name was on it.[321]

Across a range of organisational and research body definitions of authorship, there is a lack of consistency. For example, some definitional approaches omit the need for an 'author' to be directly involved in writing the published piece.[322]

The National Ethical Charter for the research professions, developed in 2015 by a number of research bodies and universities, provides that attribution of authorship must be based on explicit input into the research project and should be attributed to all who deserve it in accordance with international criteria.[323] The International Committee of Medical Journal Editors (ICMJE) recommends that authorship be based on the following four criteria:

- Substantial contributions to the conception or design of the work; or the acquisition, analysis, or interpretation of data for the work
- Drafting the work or revising it critically for important intellectual content
- Final approval of the version to be published
- Agreement to be accountable for all aspects of the work in ensuring that questions related to the accuracy or integrity of any part of the work are appropriately investigated and resolved[324]

These criteria are intended to ensure that authorship status is attributed only to those who deserve that level of credit and, of particular relevance when considering research misconduct, who can be held responsible for the work.[325]

321 Chapman, K. (2019). The element that never was. *Chemistry World*, June 10, 2019, www.chemistryworld.com/features/victor-ninov-and-the-element-that-never-was/3010596.article; Dalton, R. (2002). The stars who fell to Earth. *Nature,* 420, 728–729. https://doi.org/10.1038/420728a

322 Adeney, E. (2016). Research collaborations and 'authorship': Differentiating legal from management norms. *Australian Business Law Review*, 44(2), 132–143.

323 ETINED Council of Europe Platform on Ethics (2016). *Transparency and Integrity in Education Volume 1–7th Session of the Prague Forum*, 149–150, https://rm.coe.int/volume-1-7th-session-of-the-prague-forum/168074427a (accessed 18 June 2019)

324 ICMJE. *Defining the Role of Authors and Contributors,* www.icmje.org/recommendations/browse/roles-and-responsibilities/defining-the-role-of-authors-and-contributors.html (accessed 5 December 2017)

325 If all four criteria are not met, contributors should be acknowledged as such, subject to their agreement given that acknowledgment may be taken to imply endorsement by those acknowledged of

The ICMJE guidance further states that knowing that they take public responsibility for the work, each author should be confident in the integrity of all co-authors and the accuracy of the completed project. In the latter respect, each author should also be clear about the specific contributions of each co-author.[326] The corresponding author is responsible for communication with the journal during the submission, peer review and other aspects of the publication process. However, each author should have the opportunity to participate in drafting, reviewing and final approval of the manuscript. The ICMJE recommends that all listed authors receive copies of all correspondence from journal editors. Those who are involved in the work are collectively responsible for determining authorship, rather than this being the role of journal editors.[327]

The COPE has also engaged with the definition and categorisation of authorship and explored principles allowing for transparency regarding who contributed to the work and a process for managing potential disputes.[328] Detail of the type produced by the ICMJE is not provided by COPE, but various guidance documents and an advice provision service for specific case examples are offered.

From a different perspective, Consortia Advancing Standards in Research Administration Information (CASRAI), an international non-profit body, developed CRediT (Contributor Roles Taxonomy) as a means of assigning roles to reflect more accurately the roles typically played by contributors to scientific scholarly output. The approach is not intended to define authorship

the accuracy of data and the conclusions drawn. Such acknowledgement may be on an individual basis or under group headings, for example, 'served as scientific advisors,' 'collected data' or 'critically reviewed the study proposal.' ICMJE. *Defining the Role of Authors and Contributors*, www.icmje.org/recommendations/browse/roles-and-responsibilities/defining-the-role-of-authors-and-contributors.html (accessed 5 December 2017)

326 In broader terms it has been observed that comparative status and responsibility of each author is not clear-cut – for example, the question 'who should be the first named author on a manuscript?' is likely to elicit different responses from different researchers and different research fields. Kalichman, M., Sweet, M., & Plemmons, D. (2014). Standards of scientific conduct: Are there any? *Sci Eng Ethics*, 20, 885–896. doi: 10.1007/s11948-013-9500-1

327 ICMJE. *Defining the Role of Authors and Contributors*. In the absence of agreement between the research team, employing institutions should investigate www.icmje.org/recommendations/browse/roles-and-responsibilities/defining-the-role-of-authors-and-contributors.html (accessed 5 December 2017). The criteria are far from universally agreed. For example, in a Times Higher survey 180 respondents (almost 50 per cent of the total) indicated that they saw securing research funding as a legitimate criterion for authorship, Else, H. (2017). Authorship wars: Academics outline the rules for recognition. *Times Higher Education*, November 30, 2017

328 COPE Council (2014). *What Constitutes Authorship? COPE Discussion Document*, June 9, 2014, https://publicationethics.org/files/Authorship_DiscussionDocument.pdf (accessed 22 March 2021)

and is not restricted to traditional authorship roles. The aim is to capture all the work that allows research publications to be produced.[329]

Other attempts at defining authorship are less detailed. For example, the American Physical Society states that authorship should be limited to 'those who have made a significant contribution to the concept, design, execution or interpretation of the research study.'[330] Those who have contributed but don't meet these criteria should be acknowledged, but not be named as authors.[331]

From the perspective of intellectual property law, the legal position regarding authorship in some jurisdictions is very different from the position taken by some research institutions or organisations. For example, in English copyright law authorship is a question of fact and law. Copyright becomes relevant when work is reduced to 'material form,' such as the drafting of a scientific article. Authorship establishes commercial and moral rights – which protect an author's connection with the work by enabling the author to control the treatment of the work.[332] Authorship is attributed to 'the person who creates' the work and as such usually requires expression, rather than just, or even absent, the ideas behind the work.[333] As copyright law does not necessitate an author to have contributed to or even to fully understand the underlying research beyond what

329 CRediT - Contributor Roles Taxonomy (https://casrai.org/credit/ (accessed 1 December 2021)). The full list of roles are: '*Conceptualization* – Ideas; formulation or evolution of overarching research goals and aims; *Data curation* – Management activities to annotate (produce metadata), scrub data and maintain research data (including software code, where it is necessary for interpreting the data itself) for initial use and later re-use; *Formal analysis* – Application of statistical, mathematical, computational, or other formal techniques to analyze or synthesize study data; *Funding acquisition* - Acquisition of the financial support for the project leading to this publication; Investigation – Conducting a research and investigation process, specifically performing the experiments, or data/evidence collection; *Methodology* – Development or design of methodology; creation of models; *Project administration* – Management and coordination responsibility for the research activity planning and execution; *Resources* – Provision of study materials, reagents, materials, patients, laboratory samples, animals, instrumentation, computing resources, or other analysis tools; *Software* – Programming, software development; designing computer programs; implementation of the computer code and supporting algorithms; testing of existing code components; *Supervision* – Oversight and leadership responsibility for the research activity planning and execution, including mentorship external to the core team; *Validation* – Verification, whether as a part of the activity or separate, of the overall replication/reproducibility of results/experiments and other research outputs; *Visualization* – Preparation, creation and/or presentation of the published work, specifically visualization/data presentation; *Writing* – original draft – Preparation, creation and/or presentation of the published work, specifically writing the initial draft (including substantive translation); *Writing* – review & editing – Preparation, creation and/or presentation of the published work by those from the original research group, specifically critical review, commentary or revision – including pre- or post-publication stages.'

330 APS. *02.2 APS Guidelines for Professional Conduct*, www.aps.org/policy/statements/02_2.cfm

331 APS. 02.2 APS Guidelines for Professional Conduct, www.aps.org/policy/statements/02_2.cfm

332 Adeney, E. (2016). Research Collaborations and 'Authorship': Differentiating Legal from Management Norms. *Australian Business Law Review*, 44(2).

333 Copyright, Designs and Patents Act 1988, section 9

is communicated by the researchers, the legal position can be very different from norms within the scientific community. It is possible that a writer who writes up the results of a research project but who has had no involvement in the actual research would, in law, be the only author.[334] There is a presumption of authorship by those named as authors on published work, unless the contrary is proved.[335] 'Joint authorship' arises where two or more authors collaborate in a manner where the contribution of each author is not distinct from that of the other author(s) and each author's contribution is 'significant' and 'original.'[336] Contributory proportions need not be equal, but having ideas alone would not usually be sufficient. For example, architectural drawings can be jointly authored by a draftsperson creating the drawings and the person instructing and so directing the activities of the draftsperson. Both individuals have contributed to the expression of the ideas, rather than just contributing the ideas themselves, and in so doing each has a direct involvement in producing what appears on paper.[337]

An added complication when considering authorship and misconduct are what have been referred to as hyper-prolific authors. Ioannidis, Klavans and Boyack identify individuals who, between the years 2000 and 2016, had each published more than 72 papers in any one calendar year, the equivalent of one paper every 5 days. In some cases this rate of output continued beyond a single calendar year.[338] While alleging no inappropriate behaviour, Ioannidis et al note that many would consider this to be 'implausibly prolific.' The numbers of such authors (after certain exclusions) were not large, 265, but had increased by a factor of around 20 between 2001 and 2014, compared with an overall increase in authorship numbers during this period of under three-fold.[339] The 265 were drawn from 37 countries, with the highest numbers from the United States, Germany and Japan.[340] Around half of these hyper-prolific authors were researchers in the fields of medicine and life sciences. Even though the ICMJE does not count supervision, mentoring or obtaining funding as sufficient for authorship, it was observed that hyper-prolific status coincided with achieving full professorial, department chair or director status.[341] Despite increased

334 Adeney, E. (2016). Research collaborations and 'authorship': Differentiating legal from management norms. *Australian Business Law Review*, 44(2).

335 Copyright, Designs and Patents Act 1988, section 104

336 Copyright, Designs and Patents Act 1988, section 10(1)

337 *Cala Homes v Alfred McAlpine Homes East Ltd* [1995] *Fleet Street Reports* 818; Lightman J in *Ray v Classic FM plc* [1998] FSR 622, 636.

338 Ioannidis, J. P. A., Klavans, R., & Boyack, K. W. (2018). Thousands of scientists publish a paper every five days. *Nature*, 561, 167–169.

339 Ioannidis, J. P. A., Klavans, R., & Boyack, K. W. (2018). Thousands of scientists publish a paper every five days. *Nature*, 561, 167–169.

340 Ioannidis, J. P. A., Klavans, R., & Boyack, K. W. (2018). Thousands of scientists publish a paper every five days. *Nature*, 561, 167–169.

341 Ioannidis, J. P. A., Klavans, R., & Boyack, K. W. (2018). Thousands of scientists publish a paper every five days. *Nature*, 561, 167–169.

administrative obligations, in some research fields examples of 'stunning' acceleration in outputs can be found, at the extreme seeing between 10 and 80 times more papers in one year compared with earlier annual productivity. To complete the loop, a sharp decrease was often observed after the chair role was passed to a successor.[342]

Some journals require the submission of author contribution statements. *Nature*, for example, has had this as a mandatory requirement since 2009, voluntary for the 10 years preceding this, to discourage inappropriate practices such as gift or ghost authorship.[343] Ghost authorship may typically arise when researchers with a conflict of interest, for example, employees of a pharmaceutical company, seek to disguise their involvement in a project by 'invoking the credibility of an apparently independent, and usually eminent, researcher.'[344] It has been argued that in recent decades commercial bodies have increasingly sought to pay eminent researchers to attach their name to research undertaken and written by others, typically company employees, whose involvement is not acknowledged.[345]

Selective non-publication

So far, discussion has focused upon regulating positive act misconduct. However, issues can also arise from omissions, for example, a failure to disclose research findings, leaving potentially problematic gaps in the research record, undermining public trust and, in the case of human-based research, breaking the ethical pact between scientists and the research participants.[346] When the findings relate to clinical trials, information on the efficacy of treatments also has associated risks to health.[347] Gaps of this type in the research record may

342 Ioannidis, J. P. A., Klavans, R., & Boyack, K. W. (2018). Thousands of scientists publish a paper every five days. *Nature,* 561, 167–169.; J.J. Drenth, Multiple Authorship: The Contribution of Senior Authors, *Am. Med. Assoc.* 280, 219–221 (1998).

343 Ghost authorship is defined to cover those who have done enough to earn an authorship credit but are not listed. Gift authorship is attributed to those who have not contributed enough to warrant inclusion. Else, H. (2017). Authorship wars: Academics outline the rules for recognition. *Times Higher Education*, November 30, 2017. While 77 per cent of respondents to the *THE* survey agreed with this stance, a number were sceptical of its effectiveness. Dishonesty among some senior scientists (or even a genuine belief within their own mind that their contribution is greater than can be evidenced) coupled with power structures within institutions can readily undermine the approach in practice.

344 Edmond, G. (2008). Judging the scientific and medical literature: Some legal implications of changes to biomedical research and publication. *Oxford Journal of Legal Studies*, 28(3), 523, at 529. doi: 10.1093/ojls/gqn021.

345 Edmond, G. (2008). Judging the scientific and medical literature: Some legal implications of changes to biomedical research and publication. *Oxford Journal of Legal Studies*, 28(3), 523, at 529. doi: 10.1093/ojls/gqn021.

346 Science and Technology Committee, Third Report of Session 2013–14, *Clinical trials*, HC 104, para 4

347 House of Commons Science and Technology Committee, *Research integrity: clinical trials transparency*, Tenth Report of Session 2017–19, 30 October 2018, HC 1480

also fuel allegations from those who seek to deny scientific ideas, for example, 'anti-vaccination conspiracy theorists, and climate change denialists.'[348]

The World Medical Association (WMA) in its Declaration of Helsinki requires that every research study involving human subjects is registered in a publicly accessible database before recruiting research subjects, and researchers must make publicly available all research results – whether positive, negative or inconclusive.[349] The United Nations also calls for the publication of all clinical trial results, positive and negative, and recommends that national governments ensure that these requirements are implemented.[350] The World Health Organization has issued timeframe expectations for the publication of clinical trial results, including calling for a catch-up process for older but still unpublished trials.[351]

In terms of examples from individual jurisdictions, in the United States the enactment of the Food and Drug (FDA) Amendments Act 2007 required sponsors to post results of certain types of trials within 12 months of completion, although historically compliance has not been high.[352]

In the European Union any medicinal product trials undertaken since 2004 are required to be registered on the European Union Clinical Trials Register (EUCTR) and results to be disclosed to the European Medicines Agency (EMA) within 12 months of trial completion.[353] However, compliance within the 12-month requirement has been found to be less than 50 per cent.[354]

In the UK moves towards full transparency in reporting the outcome of clinical trials have also only been partially successful.[355] Around half of clinical

348 House of Commons Science and Technology Committee, *Research integrity: clinical trials transparency*, Tenth Report of Session 2017–19, 30 October 2018, HC 1480, citing evidence from Dr Ben Goldacre, University of Oxford

349 WMA Declaration of Helsinki – Ethical Principles for Medical Research Involving Human Subjects, 9th July 2018, para 36, www.wma.net/policies-post/wma-declaration-of-helsinki-ethical-principles-for-medical-research-involving-human-subjects/ (accessed 30 November 2018)

350 Report of United Nations Secretary-General's High-Level Panel on Access to Medicines, 2016, 4.3.5 www.unsgaccessmeds.org/#homepage-1 (accessed 1 December 2018)

351 WHO Statement on Public Disclosure of Clinical Trial Results, April 2015, www.who.int/ictrp/results/reporting/en/ (accessed 30 November 2018)

352 Prayle, A. P., Hurley, M. N., & Smyth, A. R. (2012). Compliance with mandatory reporting of clinical trial results on ClinicalTrials.gov. Cross sectional study. *BMJ*, 344, d7373. doi: 10.1136/bmj.d7373

353 Commission Guideline – Guidance on posting and publication of result-related information on clinical trials in relation to the implementation of Article 57(2) of Regulation (EC) No 726/2004 and Article 41(2) of Regulation (EC) No 1901/2006. Official Journal of the European Union C 302/7, 6.10.2012 (accessed 1 December 2021)

354 House of Commons Science and Technology Committee, Research integrity: clinical trials transparency, Tenth Report of Session 2017–19, 30 October 2018, HC 1480, citing Goldacre, B. (2018). Compliance with requirement to report results on the EU Clinical Trials Register: Cohort study and web resource. *BMJ*, 362, doi: https://doi.org/10.1136/bmj.k3218.

355 This is despite political assurances to the contrary, see, for example, the commitment in the Universities UK Concordat to Support Research Integrity to recognise that failure to publish negative research findings is 'harmful to the reputation and quality of UK research, and to the research record,' Universities UK, *The Concordat to Support Research Integrity* (July 2012), p. 17

trials have been found to be unreported, with trials achieving positive results being twice as likely to be published.[356] The House of Commons Science and Technology Committee called for the UK Concordat to Support Research Integrity to be strengthened to require that all trials are reported.[357]

In the UK a body with the name the Health Research Authority (HRA) was established in December 2011 to protect and promote 'the interests of patients and the public in health research.'[358] In 2014 that body was replaced with a new body of the same name,[359] which has responsibility for 'promoting research transparency' and describes itself as 'champion for transparency in research.'[360] This includes promoting 'the publication and dissemination of research findings and conclusions' and 'the provision of access to data on which research findings or conclusions are based.'[361] In essence, to drive improvements in transparency, rather than merely promoting transparency as a virtue.[362] The access the HRA has to confidential research protocols also places it in a strong position to support research ethics committees to compare outcomes reported in publications with the objectives specified in the original research proposals.[363] In practice, the HRA has tended to focus on negotiation with the research community, including seeking to enhance awareness and working with funders to align expectations of researchers.[364] The House of Commons Science and Technology Committee reported in 2018 that the HRA appeared to be reluctant to engage in enforcement or to make legislative compliance in terms of transparency a prerequisite for ethical approval of future trials. The outcome was that sponsors or investigators who failed to comply with HRA rules could escape without sanction.[365] The committee recommended that rigour in this

356 House of Commons Science and Technology Committee, *Research Integrity: Clinical Trials Transparency*, Tenth Report of Session 2017–19, 30 October 2018, HC 1480

357 House of Commons Science and Technology Committee, *Research Integrity: Clinical Trials Transparency*, Tenth Report of Session 2017–19, 30 October 2018, HC 1480. See also the UK Government response, *Government Response to the House of Commons Science and Technology Committee Report on Research Integrity: Clinical Trials Transparency*, CP 24, February 2019, 5

358 The Health Research Authority (Establishment and Constitution) Order 2011 (S.I. 2011/2323) and the Health Research Authority Regulations 2011 (S.I. 2011/2341).

359 Care Act 2014

360 Health Research Authority Annual Report and Accounts 2017/18, p. 7, www.hra.nhs.uk/

361 Care Act 2014, s110(7)

362 House of Commons Science and Technology Committee, *Research integrity: clinical trials transparency*, Tenth Report of Session 2017–19, 30 October 2018, HC 1480

363 House of Commons Science and Technology Committee, *Research integrity: clinical trials transparency*, Tenth Report of Session 2017–19, 30 October 2018, HC 1480, drawing from the evidence of Dr Simon Kolstoe, University of Portsmouth

364 The Health Research Authority, Statement in response to 'Failing to publish data from clinical trials presents risk to human health' (Science and Technology Select Committee), 29 Oct 2018 (accessed 1 December 2021)

365 House of Commons Science and Technology Committee, *Research Integrity: Clinical Trials Transparency*, Tenth Report of Session 2017–19, 30 October 2018, HC 1480

regard be improved, including the development of an audit programme to list published and overdue results.[366]

Pharmaceutical companies have higher rates of reporting compliance than organisations in or associated with the public sector, such as Public Health England, various National Health Service (NHS) Foundation trusts and universities. This is problematic in terms of public bodies occupying an important position with regard to the maintenance of public trust.[367] While neither private nor public sector is close to a 100 per cent reporting rate, the existing differences discussed by the House of Commons Science and Technology Committee were significant – commercially sponsored trials were reported in 68 per cent of cases compared with 11 per cent for non-commercially sponsored trials, with significant disparities within these figures between, for example, different universities.[368] In the opinion of one commentator giving evidence to the House of Commons Committee, improvements may be stifled by attitudes from within the research community. Undertaking an audit indicating which institutions in the UK are best and worst at reporting their clinical trial results can be met with responses from some within the research community which give the impression that such findings are 'transgressive or confrontational,' rather than providing valuable comparative insights to help to facilitate improvement.[369]

The extent of research misconduct

Accurately estimating the extent of misconduct is problematic – coupled with the fact that historical comparisons must take into account changing attitudes over time regarding acceptable and unacceptable research practices.[370] Some commentators argue that misconduct is quite rare; others that it is less so or that detected examples are only the tip of an iceberg.[371] Studies indicate that

366 House of Commons Science and Technology Committee, *Research Integrity: Clinical Trials Transparency*, Tenth Report of Session 2017–19, 30 October 2018, HC 1480

367 House of Commons Science and Technology Committee, *Research Integrity: Clinical Trials Transparency*, Tenth Report of Session 2017–19, 30 October 2018, HC 1480, citing Goldacre, B. (2018). Compliance with requirement to report results on the EU Clinical Trials Register: Cohort study and web resource. *BMJ*, 362, doi: https://doi.org/10.1136/bmj.k3218.

368 House of Commons Science and Technology Committee, *Research integrity: clinical trials transparency*, Tenth Report of Session 2017–19, 30 October 2018, HC 1480

369 House of Commons Science and Technology Committee, *Research integrity: clinical trials transparency*, Tenth Report of Session 2017–19, 30 October 2018, HC 1480, referring to the evidence of Dr Ben Goldacre. See also the AllTrials initiative, www.alltrials.net/ (accessed 1 December 2018).

370 See, for example, Zuckerman, H. (2020). Is "the time ripe" for quantitative research on misconduct in science? *Quantitative Science Studies*, 1(3), 945–958. doi: https://doi.org/10.1162/qss_a_00065

371 For example, Goodstein, D. (2010). *On Fact and Fraud* (p. 4). Princeton: Princeton University Press; Armstrong, J. S. (1983). The ombudsman: Cheating in management science. *Interfaces*, 13(4) (August), 20–29, 20. For an example of research identifying relatively high levels of false data in

retractions increased ten-fold between 2001 and 2010, even after adjusting for the overall growth in journal outputs. A majority of these retractions were attributed to unacceptable research practices rather than accidental errors.[372] There is some correlation between the impact factor of a journal and the frequency of retraction, although this may be explained to some extent by high-impact journals having better-developed procedures for detecting and dealing with misconduct.[373] However, the possibility also remains open that those scientists who are motivated to commit misconduct for the purposes of self-advancement, or even career preservation in the face of intense pressure to secure tenure or promotion, may be tempted to seek to place papers in the highest-status journals possible. In the words of one researcher:

> Anything which incentivises publication in high-profile journals (which typically require big, splashy results), especially in a metrics-driven way, incentivises bad scientific practice and publication bias.[374]

Meta-analysis of international surveys suggests that globally around 2 per cent of scientists had falsified data at least once in their career. A third of scientists admitted to other questionable research practices.[375] The Nuffield Council on Bioethics in 2014 found that 26 per cent of UK researchers admitted temptation or pressure to compromise research integrity, with a higher proportion of respondents aged under 35 years falling into this category. Thirty-eight per cent of respondents blamed 'pressure to publish' as incentivising data altering, 'cherry-picking' results or outright fabrication. More benign but still problematic, a rush to publish risked researchers failing adequately to replicate or otherwise scrutinize their work. In the same study 58 per cent of UK researchers reported that they were aware of scientists feeling tempted to compromise on research integrity.[376]

---

one medical field, see Carlisle, J. B. (2021). False individual patient data and zombie randomised controlled trials submitted to Anaesthesia. *Anaesthesia*, 76, 472–479.

372 Fang, F. C., & Casadevall, A. (2011). Retracted science and the retraction index. *Infection and Immunity*, 79, 3855–3859.

373 Martin, B. R. (2013). Whither research integrity? Plagiarism, self-plagiarism and coercive citation in an age of research assessment. *Research Policy*, 42(5) (June), 1005–1014, 1012. doi: 10.1016/j.respol.2013.03.011; Fang, F. C., & Casadevall, A. (2011). Retracted science and the retraction index. *Infection and Immunity*, 79, 3855–3859.

374 Metcalfe, J., Wheat, K., Munafò. M., Parry, J. (2020). *Research Integrity: A Landscape Study* (p. 35). Vitae/UK Research Integrity Office/UK Reproducibility Network, www.ukri.org/files/legacy/documents/research-integrity-main-report/

375 House of Commons Science and Technology Committee, Research integrity, Sixth Report of Session 2017–19, 11 July 2018 HC 350, p. 12

376 Nuffield Council on Bioethics, *The Culture of Scientific Research in the UK*, December 2014, 3

Chapter 4

Research conduct and professional regulation

Historically, with limited exceptions, research has not been subject to significant formal regulation. This has changed to some extent in more recent years, with researchers increasingly subject to regulation and professionalised to some extent by means of professional scientific organisations and 'soft law instruments' such as codes of ethics and conduct.[1] However, such approaches are fragmented and lack uniformity between different research groupings.[2] Codes set out expectations of researchers in encouraging appropriate behaviour within their community. The effectiveness of a code relies both on its content and on how many of those it seeks to influence are familiar with it. Codes and professional regulatory mechanisms underpinning them can also support practical aspects of effective regulation, such as requiring that original documents such as laboratory notebooks, electronic records and supervision records relating to members of the research team are available for independent review, systematic or even random audits.[3]

There are some indications that researchers may at best have a general awareness of codes, regulations or guidelines governing their areas of research activity, and some have little more than a vague sense that standards exist but have no knowledge of detail.[4] For example, Gullifer and Tyson found that half of

1 Jacob, M.-A. (2017). The strikethrough: An approach to regulatory writing and professional discipline. *Legal Studies*, 37(7), 137–161. doi: 10.1111/lest.12142.

2 Jacob, M.-A. (2017). The strikethrough: An approach to regulatory writing and professional discipline. *Legal Studies*, 37(7), 137–161. doi: 10.1111/lest.12142, citing Lafollette, M. (1992). Stealing into print: Fraud, plagiarism and misconduct in scientific publishing. Berkeley, CA: University of California Press; Dixon-Woods, M. (2010). Regulating research, regulating professionals. *J R Soc Med*, 103(4), 125–126; Alghrani, A., & Chan, S. (2013). "Scientists in the dock": Regulating science. In A. Alghrani, R. Bennett, & S. Ost (Eds.), *The Criminal Law and Bioethical Conflict: Walking the Tightrope* (pp. 121–139). Cambridge: Cambridge University Press at 132.

3 See, for example, discussion in Begley, C. G., Buchan, A. M., & Dirnagl, U. (2015). Robust research: Institutions must do their part for reproducibility. *Nature*, 525, 25–27. https://doi.org/10.1038/525025a

4 Kalichman, M., Sweet, M., & Plemmons, D. Standards of scientific conduct: Are there any? *Sci Eng Ethics*, 20, 885–896. doi: 10.1007/s11948-013-9500-1; Gullifer, J. M., & Tyson, G. A. (2014).

DOI: 10.4324/9780429492129-4

students may not read the code which applies to their discipline area, and a significant proportion of those who do read it may not fully understand it.[5] However, other studies have reported much greater awareness amongst student research communities, although do not determine levels of engagement or understanding beyond this.[6]

In terms of the content of codes, there may be a significant lack of consensus among researchers from different fields, with standards varying widely.[7] However, there may be no agreed basis for making ethical distinctions between these standards, a finding which is of particular relevance to research collaborations between disciplines and the potential for misunderstandings.[8] Discipline-specific approaches may each have their own validity, and seeking to develop a one-size-fits-all model would create its own challenges, although discussion among researchers from different fields provides the opportunity for at least some points of commonality to be identified.[9]

Hanson provides an example of the division between the ethical requirements imposed upon researchers compared with some other occupations in the same or associated environment.[10] A researcher working on a commercial trawler selects a small number of fish to briefly measure or otherwise study and then releases these unharmed in accordance with his institutional ethical approval. At the same time members of a different occupation, the trawler crew, can stand by while the remainder of the catch dies on deck.[11] Another example is that of clinical practitioners who may be relatively free to undertake informal research by trying out new treatments on a patient incrementally, whereas medical researchers must have appropriate ethical approval for what may be broadly similar investigations but by their nature are more formalised research.[12]

Who has read the policy on plagiarism? Unpacking students' understanding of plagiarism. *Studies in Higher Education*, 39(7), 1202–1218. doi: 10.1080/03075079.2013.777412.

5 Gullifer, J. M., & Tyson, G. A. (2014). Who has read the policy on plagiarism? Unpacking students' understanding of plagiarism. *Studies in Higher Education*, 39(7), 1202–1218. doi: 10.1080/03075079.2013.777412.

6 Leonard, M., Schwieder, D. Buhler, A., Bennett, D. B., & Royster, M. (2015). Perceptions of plagiarism by STEM graduate students: A case study. *Science and Engineering Ethics,* 21(6), 1587–1608.

7 Kalichman, M., Sweet, M., & Plemmons, D. (2014). Standards of scientific conduct: Are there any? *Sci Eng Ethics*, 20, 885–896. doi: 10.1007/s11948-013-9500-1

8 Kalichman, M., Sweet, M., & Plemmons, D. (2014). Standards of scientific conduct: Are there any? *Sci Eng Ethics*, 20, 885–896. doi: 10.1007/s11948-013-9500-1. For example, of questions asked about code content, only 16 per cent of such questions resulted in substantial agreement among all respondents.

9 Kalichman, M., Sweet, M., & Plemmons, D. (2014). Standards of scientific conduct: Are there any? *Sci Eng Ethics*, 20, 885–896. doi: 10.1007/s11948-013-9500-1

10 Hansson, S. O. (2009). Do We Need a Special Ethics for Research? *Science and Engineering Ethics,* 17, 21–9, 24. doi: 10.1007/s11948–009–9186–6.

11 Hansson, S. O. (2009). Do We Need a Special Ethics for Research? *Science and Engineering Ethics,* 17, 21–9, 24. doi: 10.1007/s11948–009–9186–6.

12 Hansson, S. O. (2009). Do We Need a Special Ethics for Research? *Science and Engineering Ethics,* 17, 21–9, 24. doi: 10.1007/s11948–009–9186–6.

To be effective, professional regulation must be acceptable to researchers who are subject to it as well as to the wider public.[13] Prospective professional bodies face challenges in placing themselves at the forefront of research integrity and regulation. For example, in a survey of UK researchers asked to rank a list of participants in terms of greatest responsibility for increasing research integrity, professional bodies, learned societies and disciplinary networks were ranked lowest.[14] Individual researchers have been ranked highest as having responsibility for research integrity, followed, inter alia, by supervisors and principal investigators, department heads, ethics committees, research funders and publishers.[15]

Past failures at attempts to develop professional self-regulatory models can, in part, be attributed to failures to secure scientific and public support and consensus.[16] For example, some researchers argue that codes or aspects of them hamper research.[17] Effective self-regulation encompasses creating an appropriate ethical culture by means of education, the career-long reinforcement of ethical behaviour and breadth of coverage necessary to encompass the regulated field.[18] Self-regulatory models have a number of arguments presented in their favour.[19] One is the greater adaptability and appropriate speed a well-functioning self-regulatory process can offer. Science can develop very quickly, and so adaptability in the regulatory process is of importance. Legislating and re-legislating for regulatory processes can be extremely slow in comparison. The common law, judge-made law, in jurisdictions which operate it, has been praised for its adaptability, but for complex cases can also be slow.

It has been suggested that the scientific community has implicitly appealed to professional standards and self-regulation.[20] However, this has not been

13 Taylor, P. (2009). Scientific self-regulation – so good, how can it fail? Commentary on "the problems with forbidding science". *Science and Engineering Ethics,* 15, 395–406. doi: 10.1007/s11948-009-9123-8.

14 Metcalfe, J., Wheat, K., Munafò. M., Parry, J. (2020). *Research Integrity: A Landscape Study* (p. 43). Vitae/UK Research Integrity Office/UK Reproducibility Network, www.ukri.org/files/legacy/documents/research-integrity-main-report/

15 Metcalfe, J., Wheat, K., Munafò. M., Parry, J. (2020). *Research Integrity: A Landscape Study* (p. 43). Vitae/UK Research Integrity Office/UK Reproducibility Network, www.ukri.org/files/legacy/documents/research-integrity-main-report/

16 Taylor, P. (2009). Scientific self-regulation – so good, how can it fail? Commentary on "the problems with forbidding science". *Science and Engineering Ethics,* 15, 395–406. doi: 10.1007/s11948-009-9123-8.

17 Jacob, M.-A. (2017). The strikethrough: An approach to regulatory writing and professional discipline. *Legal Studies*, 37(1), 137–161. doi: 10.1111/lest.12142

18 Taylor, P. (2009). Scientific self-regulation – so good, how can it fail? Commentary on "the problems with forbidding science". *Science and Engineering Ethics,* 15, 395–406. doi: 10.1007/s11948-009-9123-8.

19 In the latter context see, for example, Taylor, P. (2009). Scientific self-regulation – so good, how can it fail? Commentary on "the problems with forbidding science". *Science and Engineering Ethics,* 15, 395–406. doi: 10.1007/s11948-009-9123-8.

20 Jones, N. (2007). A code of ethics for the life sciences. *Science and Engineering Ethics,* 13, 25–43, 28. doi: 10.1007/s11948-006-0007-x.

translated into explicit regulatory norms necessary to ensure high professional standards, to identify inappropriate conduct and, overall, in common with other professional regulatory models, to define the basis for the social contract between science and society.[21] In the absence of a developed formal professional regulatory model, less formal regulation has emerged within scientific communities, and this can involve significant voluntary dedication to the task and commitment of time. For example, the researchers who identified the fraudulent activity of Yoshihiro Sato were described as spending 'thousands of hours combing through Sato's papers' to identify fabricated data for numerous clinical trials published in international journals.[22] The importance of this dedication by a small group of fellow researchers is illustrated by the observation that Sato's misconduct went undetected for a significant period, despite warning flags arising from his prolific output.[23] Other examples include German anaesthetist Joachim Boldt, who had more than 90 papers retracted. Boldt's behaviour was initially uncovered by an expert reader of *Anesthesia & Analgesia* who wrote to the journal editor that the pattern of data in one of Boldt's papers was implausibly perfect, leading to an investigation.[24] John Carlisle, whose main occupation was that of a hospital anaesthetist in the UK, was featured in *Nature* as having identified in his spare time statistical errors in numerous research papers.[25] A number of retractions and corrections, including some described as 'large-scale fakers' and others innocent mistakes, have followed.[26]

Admiration from within research communities for such voluntary policing from within is not universal. Hostility has arisen in some quarters when suspicions have been raised. As one commentator observed 'trying to find flaws in other people's work . . . is not something that will make you very popular.'[27] For example, one peer reviewer is reported to have commented 'drop [your] crusade

21 Jones, N. (2007). A code of ethics for the life sciences. *Science and Engineering Ethics,* 13, 25–43, 28. doi: 10.1007/s11948-006-0007-x.

22 Kupferschmidt, K. (2018). Researcher at the center of an epic fraud remains an enigma to those who exposed him. *Science*, August 17, 2018, www.sciencemag.org/news/2018/08/researcher-center-epic-fraud-remains-enigma-those-who-exposed-him

23 Kupferschmidt, K. (2018). Researcher at the center of an epic fraud remains an enigma to those who exposed him. *Science*, August 17, 2018, www.sciencemag.org/news/2018/08/researcher-center-epic-fraud-remains-enigma-those-who-exposed-him. These flags included the fact that some extensive studies purported to have been undertaken by Sato would have taken most researchers significantly more years to complete.

24 Stroebe, W., Postmes, T., & Spears, R. (2012). Scientific misconduct and the myth of self-correction in science. *Perspect Psychol Sci.*, 7(6), 670–688. doi: 10.1177/1745691612460687

25 Adam, D. (2019). How a data detective exposed suspicious medical trials. *Nature*, 571, 462–464. doi: 10.1038/d41586-019-02241-z

26 Adam, D. (2019). How a data detective exposed suspicious medical trials. *Nature*, 571, 462–464. doi: 10.1038/d41586-019-02241-z. Carlise reported that he had identified suspect data in at least 90 of over 5,000 trials published over a 16 year period.

27 Michèle Nuijten cited in Adam, D. (2019). How a data detective exposed suspicious medical trials. *Nature*, 571, 462–464. doi: 10.1038/d41586-019-02241-z

against [named researcher] and his colleagues and pursue more worthwhile scientific endeavours,' while another reviewer is said to have described the exercise as a 'considerable waste of time.'[28] Another scientist, committed to exposing image and data manipulation, plagiarism and methodological issues in research papers, has commented: 'Unfortunately, as I have experienced in the past years, being critical about scientific papers can lead to online harassment, doxxing and threats of lawsuits and jail time.'[29] Although there is also evidence that integrity-focused members of the scientific community are pushing back in a more organised and formalised manner with, for example, the John Maddox Prize for standing up for science recognising commitment to pursuing integrity in the face of hostility from some within the scientific community.[30]

There is some evidence of opposition, even hostility, from within the scientific community towards the idea of professional-style registration. For example, faced with the prospect of professional registration, one senior scientist in the UK is quoted as saying:

> This is an utterly demented idea by some functionary or functionaries who have far too much spare time, little imagination, and the desire to thwart the progress of science and regulate creativity. . . . If I had wanted chartered status, I would have become an accountant or surveyor.[31]

With established professions such as medicine and law, self-regulation underpinned by appropriate professional codes and overseen by professional bodies aims to offer society efficiency and expertise in terms of maintaining standards. In common with traditional ideas of professionalism, many areas of scientific knowledge, including 'tacit knowledge,' involve a level of complexity such that only other experts in the same field can readily assess and evaluate it.[32] Tacit knowledge plays a central role in acquiring deep understanding. Unlike express

28 Kranke, P. (2012). Putting the record straight: Granisetron's efficacy as an antiemetic 'post-Fujii'. *Anaesthesia*, 67, 1063–1067. https://doi.org/10.1111/j.1365-2044.2012.07318.x

29 Bik, E., quoted by Upton, B. (2021). Research detective wins standing up for science prize. *Times Higher Education*, December 1, 2021, www.timeshighereducation.com/news/research-detective-wins-standing-science-prize

30 Sense about Science, John Maddox Prize, https://senseaboutscience.org/john-maddox-prize/; Upton, B. (2021). Research detective wins standing up for science prize. *Times Higher Education*, December 1, 2021, www.timeshighereducation.com/news/research-detective-wins-standing-science-prize

31 Else, H. (2017). Drive to register all UK scientists: Benchmark or bureaucracy? *Times Higher Education*, April 20, 2017, www.timeshighereducation.com/news/drive-register-all-uk-scientists-benchmark-or-bureaucracy

32 Priaulx, N. M., & Weinel, M. (2014). Behavior on a beer mat: Law, interdisciplinarity & expertise. *Journal of Law, Technology & Policy*, (2), 361–391, 365, discussing Collins, H. M., & Evans, R. J. (2007). *Rethinking Expertise* (pp. 85, 238). Chicago: The University of Chicago Press. Also citing Nonaka, I. et al. (2000). SECI, Ba and leadership: A unified model of dynamic knowledge creation. *Long Range Plan*, 33(5), 7.

knowledge, contained in the guides and other texts of the field of expertise, tacit knowledge consists of unformalised approaches and unwritten conventions and can only be acquired through immersion in the requisite expert domain.[33] In the context of scientific expertise, engaging with the literature without the benefit of engagement with the field of research risks giving a partial understanding or even a false impression of the area of science. Knowing which sources to focus on, the relative importance of different sources and the plausibility of technical arguments all deepen understanding.[34]

Professions benefit from self-regulation by minimising government intervention and its associated risks of stifling intellectual freedoms and professional creativity.[35] Society benefits from higher-quality, expert-led regulation, the financial cost of which is largely borne from within the profession. Professional regulatory bodies also offer some scope towards satisfying a more critical starting assumption – that unless the regulated community knows that somebody is watching them in a policing role, they cannot be fully trusted to behave in an appropriate manner.[36]

Certain hallmarks for professional self-regulation may already be established within research communities. For example, a survey of UK scientists suggested that high levels of personal integrity were imposed by researchers upon themselves and equivalent standards expected of others. Disciplinary norms and the influence of learned societies and professional bodies were perceived to be important to the maintenance of research integrity.[37] However, such self-validation has to be treated with some caution in terms of the reliability of individuals' perceptions of their own behaviour and even the analysis of the

33 Priaulx, N. M., & Weinel, M. (2014). Behavior on a beer mat: Law, interdisciplinarity & expertise. *Journal of Law, Technology & Policy*, (2), 361–391, 365, discussing Collins, H. M., & Evans, R. J. (2007). *Rethinking Expertise* (pp. 85, 238). Chicago: The University of Chicago Press. Also citing Nonaka, I. et al. (2000). SECI, Ba and leadership: A unified model of dynamic knowledge creation. *Long Range Plan*, 33(5), 7.

34 Collins, H. M., & Evans, R. J. (2007). *Rethinking Expertise* (p. 22). Chicago: The University of Chicago Press; Weinel, M. (2007). Primary source knowledge and technical decision-making: Mbeki and the AZT debate. *Stud. Hist. & Phil. Sci.*, 38, 748, cited in Priaulx, N. M., & Weinel, M. (2014). Behavior on a beer mat: Law, interdisciplinarity & expertise. *Journal of Law, Technology & Policy*, (2), 361–391, 386.

35 Jones, N. (2007). A code of ethics for the life sciences. *Science and Engineering Ethics*, 13, 25–43, 28. doi: 10.1007/s11948-006-0007-x, citing Heitman, E. (2000). Ethical values in the education of biomedical researchers. *Hastings Center Report*, 30, S40–S44. Perceived failures on the part of self-regulating professions can result in threats to remove self-regulatory capacity. See, for example, Davies, M. (2007). *Medical Self-regulation, Crisis and Change*. London and New York: Routledge.

36 Biagioli, M. (2012). Recycling texts or stealing time? Plagiarism, authorship, and credit in science. *International Journal of Cultural Property*, 19, 466.

37 Metcalfe, J., Wheat, K., Munafò. M., Parry, J. (2020). *Research Integrity: A Landscape Study*, Vitae/UK Research Integrity Office/UK Reproducibility Network, www.ukri.org/files/legacy/documents/research-integrity-main-report/

behaviour of other members of their disciplinary community.[38] In this respect, the desire to preserve a positive self- and group image can distort more objective ethical analyses.[39]

Existing professional bodies and learned societies play important roles in reviewing research integrity and ethical approval processes within their specialist areas.[40] In essence, this may be viewed as an embryonic professional model – a system built on trust which relies upon individuals and the wider professional community to self-regulate aspects of their working environment.[41] An example can be identified in the case of Jan Hendrik Schön. Suspicions arose regarding the unduly perfect precision of some of Schön's purported findings. Such suspicions can realistically only come from within a community of fellow experts. These and other traits – for example, standardised developments in education and training, certification of expertise and the articulation of best practices – represent examples of developmental markers of the professionalisation process.[42] However, in the field of scientific research, developments are far from complete in terms of ideas that a scientific field which effectively self-regulates is key to maintaining ethical integrity.[43] Researchers may experience inconsistent approaches to misconduct, given that there is no single formal registration mechanism or overarching professional governing body for scientific research. Those researchers with more formal professional qualifications, for example, as registered medical practitioners, may find themselves treated differently, potentially more harshly, because of this professional status which brings with it well-developed regulatory and disciplinary processes.[44] For example,

38 Valdesolo, P., & DeSteno, D. (2007). Moral hypocrisy: Social groups and the flexibility of virtue. *Psychological Science*, 18(8), 689–690 690 doi: 10.1111/j.1467–9280.2007.01961.x. For example, there are also indications that individuals may have greater propensity to excuse problematic behaviour on the part of others if they belong to the same disciplinary groups.

39 Valdesolo, P., & DeSteno, D. (2007). Moral hypocrisy: Social groups and the flexibility of virtue. *Psychological Science*, 18(8), 689–690 690 doi: 10.1111/j.1467-9280.2007.01961.x

40 Metcalfe, J., Wheat, K., Munafò. M., Parry, J. (2020). *Research Integrity: A Landscape Study* (p. 46). Vitae/UK Research Integrity Office/UK Reproducibility Network, www.ukri.org/files/legacy/documents/research-integrity-main-report/

41 Metcalfe, J., Wheat, K., Munafò. M., Parry, J. (2020). *Research Integrity: A Landscape Study*. Vitae/UK Research Integrity Office/UK Reproducibility Network, www.ukri.org/files/legacy/documents/research-integrity-main-report/

42 Biagioli, M. (2012). Recycling texts or stealing time? Plagiarism, authorship, and credit in science. *International Journal of Cultural Property*, 19, 468.

43 See, for example, Kretser, A., Murphy, D., Bertuzzi, S., Abraham, T., Allison, D., Boor, K., Dwyer, J., Grantham, A., Harris, L., Hollander, R., Jacobs-Young, C., Rovito, S., Vafiadis, D., Woteki, C., Wyndham, J., & Yada, R. (2019). Scientific integrity principles and best practices: Recommendations from a scientific integrity consortium. *Science and Engineering Ethics*, 25. doi: 10.1007/s11948-019-00094-3.

44 A newsworthy example of this involved Consultant Psychiatrist Raj Persaud, who having admitted to a number of instances of plagiarism, was disciplined by the General Medical Council,

a researcher committing plagiarism may risk being frowned upon within the wider research community and may even lose their job, but there is no formal sanction mechanism. In contrast, established professions may treat misconduct such as plagiarism as a form of dishonesty – seeking to gain unfair advantage by deception.[45] An example from the UK is the case of *Dr Fazal Hussain v General Medical Council.*[46] At first instance before a Fitness to Practise Panel of the Medical Practitioners' Tribunal Service, Dr Hussain's fitness to practise was found to be impaired and an order made that his name should be erased from the Medical Register, the most severe penalty available to the tribunal. This decision was upheld on appeal to the Administrative Court and then the Court of Appeal. Dr Hussain had plagiarised a reflective learning log and portfolio content submitted as part of a General Practitioner training course, as well as including misleading information regarding qualifications details on his curriculum vitae. This behaviour was found to be dishonest and as such constituted serious misconduct.[47] The outcome was career ending for Dr Hussain, but the Court of Appeal confirmed that protecting the reputation of the profession is more important than the impact upon the individual member.[48]

Owen, D. (2008). Psychiatrist is suspended for three months for plagiarism. *BMJ*, 336, 1457. doi: https://doi.org/10.1136/bmj.a487 (Published 26 June 2008), Disgraced Raj Persaud quits as consultant at leading hospital, *The Guardian*, 24th October 2008. www.theguardian.com/lifeandstyle/2008/oct/24/raj-persaud-psychiatry-maudsley

45 See, for example, the study by David, T. J., & Bray, S. A. (2009). Healthcare student fitness to practise cases: Reasons for referral and outcomes. *Education Law Journal*, 10(3), 196–203, 201–202. The authors also note that in some cases a student may compound certain types of misconduct by further deceit or fabrication – for example, falsifying supervisors' assessments and/or forging supervisors' signatures.

46 [2014] EWCA Civ 2246

47 The Court of Appeal reviewed the allegations in the context of the legal meaning of 'dishonest' applicable at the time and any differentiation between falsity and dishonesty, concluding that the panel was entitled to decide that Dr Hussain's behaviour in relation to the curriculum vitae (CV) entries and the plagiarism had been dishonest. With regard to the CV entries, the Court of Appeal disagreed with the reasoning of the first-instance appeal judge who had questioned the dishonest finding, although the General Medical Council, as prosecutorial body, had not sought to cross-appeal this aspect of the decision. [2014] EWCA Civ 2246 Paras 30–31

48 Para 44, citing *Gupta v GMC* [2002] 1 WLR 1699 at 1702; *Bolton v Law Society* [1994] 1 WLR 512. Even at the student stage of career development, matters such as plagiarism may imperil career progress for those studying for professional qualifications, such as medicine, in a manner not shared by students in other scientific fields. David, T. J., & Bray, S. A. (2009). Healthcare student fitness to practise cases: Reasons for referral and outcomes. *Education Law Journal*, 10(3), 196–203, 202, citing Papadakis, M. A. et al. (2004). Unprofessional behavior in medical schools is associated with subsequent disciplinary action by a state medical board. *Acad Med*, 244; Papadakis, M. A. et al. (2005). Disciplinary action by medical boards and prior behavior in medical school. *N Engl J Med*, 2673; M. A. Papadakis et al. (2008). Performance during internal medicine residency training and subsequent disciplinary action by state licensing boards. *Ann Intern Med*, 869. Evidence also indicates that some students who are permitted to continue in the face of dishonest conduct exhibit unprofessional behaviour in their post-qualification careers.

Focusing on another example relating to the UK General Medical Council (GMC), when considering the high-profile case of Andrew Wakefield, the GMC made clear that it did not concern itself when dealing with the pros and cons of the underlying research: 'this case is not concerned with whether there is or might be any link between the MMR vaccination and autism.' Rather, the focus was upon Wakefield's honesty and integrity when undertaking his research.[49] It is also important to note that while the GMC procedures may impact upon future registration and practising status as medical practitioner, they have no direct impact on the status as a researcher in other contexts.[50] In that respect, researchers who are also qualified in established professional fields such as medicine can only be formally controlled in relation to future research activity if regulatory processes exist within the wider research community. These latter points may constitute contributing factors to the decision of the Investigatory Committee of the British Psychological Society (BPS) in 1995 not to refer concerns about the influential psychologist, Hans Eysenck, to a full disciplinary hearing.[51] The Code of Ethics and Conduct published at the time by the society's Ethics Committee confined discussion of professional misconduct largely to behaviour focused upon harming clients or behaviour that brought the reputation of the profession into disrepute. While research misconduct, if proven, will be harmful to the reputation of the profession, it is possible that the Investigatory Committee, being used to dealing with practitioner-focused complaints and allegation of harm to patients, downplayed the potential seriousness of allegations of academic-focused misconduct.[52] If professional disciplinary panel members find themselves adjudicating alleged research misconduct by a leading or pioneering member in their field, they may find this particularly challenging, providing a further incentive to leave such matters to universities or other research employers. The BPS acknowledged the importance of research integrity, but the overarching assumption was that the locus of overseeing the conduct of research lies with the academic institutions.[53] A further observation arising from this example is that elements of the research and publishing communities, such

49 Jacob, M.-A. (2017). The strikethrough: An approach to regulatory writing and professional discipline. *Legal Studies*, 37(1), 137–161. doi: 10.1111/lest.12142

50 Jacob, M.-A. (2017). The strikethrough: An approach to regulatory writing and professional discipline. *Legal Studies*, 37(1), 137–161. doi: 10.1111/lest.12142

51 Craig, R., Pelosi, T., & Tourish, D. (2020). Research misconduct complaints and institutional logics: The case of Hans Eysenck and the British Psychological Society. *Journal of Health Psychology*. (pre-print)

52 Craig, R., Pelosi, T., & Tourish, D. (2020). Research misconduct complaints and institutional logics: The case of Hans Eysenck and the British Psychological Society. *Journal of Health Psychology*. (pre-print)

53 Craig, R., Pelosi, T., & Tourish, D. (2020). Research misconduct complaints and institutional logics: The case of Hans Eysenck and the British Psychological Society. *Journal of Health Psychology*. (pre-print)

as employing institutions and journal editors, should not be unduly influenced by external professional body decisions, as the regulations of such bodies may not particularly be designed to map onto the interests of regulating the research process.[54]

In the absence of an organised and refined regulatory model, members of the research community can find themselves talking rather than acting:

> Gossip about, rather than action on, fraud allows people to vent indignation or dissatisfaction yet avoid the due process and accountability of investigation.[55]

Such informal regulatory approaches have been found to operate within occupational groupings – accepted community practices 'enforced' by, for example, gossip based community shaming.[56] Gossip can have an effect as a social sanction in at least three ways: by leading others in the field to take a suspected transgressor's work less seriously, to discourage collaboration with them or to discourage employing them.[57] Some members of the scientific community may welcome such ideas of community control and view them as a mechanism for addressing certain transgressions.[58] However, shunning someone within the scientific community on the basis of perceived but unproven misbehaviour is highly problematic.[59] Not only does the subject of such behaviour lack the benefit of due process, but those within the community who feel uncomfortable condemning a colleague without proven liability, or at all, may feel bullied into doing so, perhaps fearing being shunned themselves.[60] Such approaches can also exacerbate issues of hierarchy if the target of gossip is junior or otherwise less powerful than their accusers.[61] Informal approaches can extend

54 Craig, R., Pelosi, T., & Tourish, D. (2020). Research misconduct complaints and institutional logics: The case of Hans Eysenck and the British Psychological Society. *Journal of Health Psychology*. (pre-print)

55 Fox, M. F. (1994). Scientific misconduct and editorial and peer review processes. *The Journal of Higher Education*, 65, 298–309, 302. For further discussion, see Martin, B. (2007) Keeping plagiarism at bay – A salutary tale. *Research Policy*, 36(7), 905–911, 909.

56 Haller, L. (2018). Regulating the professions. In *The Oxford Handbook of Empirical Research* (pp. 216–234). Oxford: Oxford University Press, at pp. 230–231.

57 Vaidyanathan, B., Khalsa, S., & Ecklund, E. (2016). Gossip as social control: Informal sanctions on ethical violations in scientific workplaces. *Social Problems*, 63(4), 554–572, https://doi.org/10.1093/socpro/spw022.

58 Vaidyanathan, B., Khalsa, S., & Ecklund, E. (2016). Gossip as social control: Informal sanctions on ethical violations in scientific workplaces. *Social Problems*, 63(4), 554–572, https://doi.org/10.1093/socpro/spw022.

59 Kuhar, M. (2008). On blacklisting in science. *Science and Engineering Ethics,* 14, 301–303. doi: 10.1007/s11948-008-9082-5.

60 Kuhar, M. (2008). On blacklisting in science. *Science and Engineering Ethics,* 14, 301–303. doi: 10.1007/s11948-008-9082-5.

61 Vaidyanathan, B., Khalsa, S., & Ecklund, E. (2016). Gossip as social control: Informal sanctions on ethical violations in scientific workplaces. *Social Problems*, 63(4), 554–572, https://doi.org/10.1093/

to addressing perceived errors in the research record. As Sanders observes, informal statements of the type 'everyone knows that paper is wrong' can in some contexts be favoured over the formal raising of concerns, investigations incorporating appropriate due process and correction of the research record if necessary.[62]

As a structured and transparent alternative to informal approaches, professional bodies can take a lead role in setting standards and disciplining members and act as moral agents of a self-regulatory community, influencing the moral judgments of that community and compliance with research integrity principles.[63] Setting up regulatory and disciplinary processes in advance to address integrity failings maximises consistency and should better instil confidence in the regulated community and wider public.[64] The cost of professional self-regulation is not insignificant, and the model of the so-called state-profession bargain sees funding for such regulation coming from the regulated community, so it is important that members of the regulated community are informed about the benefits of such a regulatory approach. Examples of statements by existing organisations can be found broadly in support of this approach. For example, the National Academy of Sciences, Engineering, and Medicine has stated that to address threats to scientific integrity requires an understanding of the research system and challenges to the integrity of that system.[65] The Interacademy Partnership has emphasised that every researcher has an obligation not only to personally meet the highest ethical and regulatory standards but also to contribute to their development and dissemination.[66]

socpro/spw022, citing Kurland, N. B., & Pelled, L. H. (2000). Passing the word: Toward a model of gossip and power in the workplace. *Academy of Management Review*, 25(2), 428–438.

62 Sanders, D. A. (2020). Each scientist must stand up, at all costs, for the truth. *Times Higher Education* July 9, 2020, www.timeshighereducation.com/features/each-scientist-must-stand-all-costs-truth

63 Komić, D., Marušić, S. L., & Marušić, A. (2015). Research integrity and research ethics in professional codes of ethics: Survey of terminology used by professional organizations across research disciplines. *PLoS ONE*, 10(7), e0133662. doi: 10.1371/journal.pone.0133662, citing Sama, L. M., & Shoaf, V. (2008). Ethical leadership for the professions: Fostering a moral community. *J Bus Ethics*, 78, 39–46.

64 Kretser, A., Murphy, D., Bertuzzi, S., Abraham, T., Allison, D., Boor, K., Dwyer, J., Grantham, A., Harris, L., Hollander, R., Jacobs-Young, C., Rovito, S., Vafiadis, D., Woteki, C., Wyndham, J., & Yada, R. (2019). Scientific integrity principles and best practices: Recommendations from a scientific integrity consortium. *Science and Engineering Ethics*, 25. doi: 10.1007/s11948-019-00094-3.

65 National Academy of Sciences. (2017). *Reproducibility of Research: Issues and Proposed Remedies*, cited by Kretser, A., Murphy, D., Bertuzzi, S., Abraham, T., Allison, D., Boor, K., Dwyer, J., Grantham, A., Harris, L., Hollander, R., Jacobs-Young, C., Rovito, S., Vafiadis, D., Woteki, C., Wyndham, J., & Yada, R. (2019). Scientific integrity principles and best practices: Recommendations from a scientific integrity consortium. *Science and Engineering Ethics*, 25. doi: 10.1007/s11948-019-00094-3.

66 Partnership, Interacademy. (2016). *Doing Global Science* (p. 4). Princeton, NJ: Princeton University Press.

Professional societies and foundations already play a role in developing and implementing training standards in their scientific fields; such training may include aspects of scientific integrity and broader principles around scientific integrity policies.[67] However, such approaches are not consistent across scientific fields, nor do they constitute the extent of input more usual among established professions. Within the scientific research community more broadly there is nothing in regulatory terms akin to traditional professional models covering the whole professional sphere.

The gaps in the development of a comprehensive regulatory model for scientific research have become more prominent as the visibility of misconduct and comment about it have increased with the rapid development of electronic communications.[68] Whether or not failures of scientific integrity are more common now than in the past, they are far more visible with proliferation of news sources and social media discussion. This increases the pressure to the scientific community to police itself effectively in order to mitigate reputational damage and associated weakening of public trust.[69] The numerous stakeholders, notably individual researchers, principal investigators, department heads, ethics committees, research funders, publishers, professional bodies and learned societies, who feed into the ethics process must be considered in the context of a bigger systemic picture, with necessary synergies for all elements to work together as effectively as possible.[70] To achieve this, consideration should be

67 Kretser, A., Murphy, D., Bertuzzi, S., Abraham, T., Allison, D., Boor, K., Dwyer, J., Grantham, A., Harris, L., Hollander, R., Jacobs-Young, C., Rovito, S., Vafiadis, D., Woteki, C., Wyndham, J., & Yada, R. (2019). Scientific integrity principles and best practices: Recommendations from a scientific integrity consortium. *Science and Engineering Ethics*, 25. doi: 10.1007/s11948-019-00094-3.

68 Kretser, A., Murphy, D., Bertuzzi, S., Abraham, T., Allison, D., Boor, K., Dwyer, J., Grantham, A., Harris, L., Hollander, R., Jacobs-Young, C., Rovito, S., Vafiadis, D., Woteki, C., Wyndham, J., & Yada, R. (2019). Scientific integrity principles and best practices: Recommendations from a scientific integrity consortium. *Science and Engineering Ethics*, 25. doi: 10.1007/s11948-019-00094-3.

69 Kretser, A., Murphy, D., Bertuzzi, S., Abraham, T., Allison, D., Boor, K., Dwyer, J., Grantham, A., Harris, L., Hollander, R., Jacobs-Young, C., Rovito, S., Vafiadis, D., Woteki, C., Wyndham, J., & Yada, R. (2019). Scientific integrity principles and best practices: Recommendations from a scientific integrity consortium. *Science and Engineering Ethics*, 25. doi: 10.1007/s11948-019-00094-3.

70 Metcalfe, J., Wheat, K., Munafò. M., Parry, J. (2020). *Research Integrity: A Landscape Study* (p. 43). Vitae/UK Research Integrity Office/UK Reproducibility Network, www.ukri.org/files/legacy/documents/research-integrity-main-report/; Wager, L. (2015). Why we need a journal on research integrity and peer review. *BioMed Central Blog*, https://blogs.biomedcentral.com/bmcblog/2015/09/28/journal-research-integrity-peer-review/; Kretser, A., Murphy, D., Bertuzzi, S., Abraham, T., Allison, D., Boor, K., Dwyer, J., Grantham, A., Harris, L., Hollander, R., Jacobs-Young, C., Rovito, S., Vafiadis, D., Woteki, C., Wyndham, J., & Yada, R. (2019). Scientific integrity principles and best practices: Recommendations from a scientific integrity consortium. *Science and Engineering Ethics*, 25. doi: 10.1007/s11948-019-00094-3.

given to ideas of 'ecosystems' of scientific integrity, incorporating responsibility for ensuring integrity among these various stakeholders.[71]

Incremental developments building upon what already exists could see the utilisation within the scientific community of checklists incorporating a set of standard procedures for scientific integrity, offering guides to best practice in research design, research conduct and the reporting of research findings.[72] 'Accreditation badges' accompanying satisfactory compliance present an embryonic development towards more comprehensive ethical and regulatory codes, seeking to create social contracts within research communities, with the aim of instigating moral standards and encouraging ethical behaviour.[73]

Professional codes have to be carefully crafted to ensure effectiveness, although no code will be effective in all circumstances.[74] Ineffective elements in a code will fail to prevent the behaviour that it was designed to prevent, or the focus of the code may inadequately address areas which should be addressed.[75] For example, for organisations with a research focus, the expectation may be

71 Wager, L. (2015). Why we need a journal on research integrity and peer review. *BioMed Central Blog*, https://blogs.biomedcentral.com/bmcblog/2015/09/28/journal-research-integrity-peer-review/; Kretser, A., Murphy, D., Bertuzzi, S., Abraham, T., Allison, D., Boor, K., Dwyer, J., Grantham, A., Harris, L., Hollander, R., Jacobs-Young, C., Rovito, S., Vafiadis, D., Woteki, C., Wyndham, J., & Yada, R. (2019). Scientific integrity principles and best practices: Recommendations from a scientific integrity consortium. *Science and Engineering Ethics*, 25. doi: 10.1007/s11948-019-00094-3.

72 Kretser, A., Murphy, D., Bertuzzi, S., Abraham, T., Allison, D., Boor, K., Dwyer, J., Grantham, A., Harris, L., Hollander, R., Jacobs-Young, C., Rovito, S., Vafiadis, D., Woteki, C., Wyndham, J., & Yada, R. (2019). Scientific integrity principles and best practices: Recommendations from a scientific integrity consortium. *Science and Engineering Ethics*, 25. doi: 10.1007/s11948-019-00094-3.

73 Kretser, A., Murphy, D., Bertuzzi, S., Abraham, T., Allison, D., Boor, K., Dwyer, J., Grantham, A., Harris, L., Hollander, R., Jacobs-Young, C., Rovito, S., Vafiadis, D., Woteki, C., Wyndham, J., & Yada, R. (2019). Scientific integrity principles and best practices: Recommendations from a scientific integrity consortium. *Science and Engineering Ethics*, 25. doi: 10.1007/s11948-019-00094-3, citing Rowhani-Farid, A., Allen, M., & Barnett, A. G. (2017). What incentives increase data sharing in health and medical research? A systematic review. *Research Integrity and Peer Review*, *2*(1), 4; Komić, D., Marušić, S. L., & Marušić, A. (2015). Research integrity and research ethics in professional codes of ethics: Survey of terminology used by professional organizations across research disciplines. *PLoS ONE*, 10(7), e0133662. doi: 10.1371/journal.pone.0133662; (2012). Professional ethical standards: The journey toward effective codes of ethics. In N. P. Reilly, M. J. Sirgy, & C. A. Gorman (Eds.), *Work and Quality of Life. Ethical Practices in Organizations* (pp. 21–34). Amsterdam: Springer Netherlands.

74 Komić, D., Marušić, S. L., & Marušić, A. (2015). Research integrity and research ethics in professional codes of ethics: Survey of terminology used by professional organizations across research disciplines. *PLoS ONE*, 10(7), e0133662. doi: 10.1371/journal.pone.0133662, citing Fanelli, D. (2009). How many scientists fabricate and falsify research? A systematic review and meta-analysis of survey data. *PLoS One*, 4, e5738. doi: 10.1371/journal.pone.0005738 PMID: 19478950 3; Marušić, A., Bošnjak, L., & Jerončić, A. (2011). A systematic review of research on the meaning, ethics and practices of authorship across scholarly disciplines. *PLoS One*, 6, e23477. doi: 10.1371/journal. pone. 0023477 PMID: 21931600

75 Schwartz, M. S. (2003). Effective corporate codes of ethics: Perceptions of code users. *J Bus Ethics*, 55, 323–343.

that terms such as 'honesty,' 'malpractice,' 'misconduct,' 'fraud,' 'fabrication' and 'falsification' will be present in codes. Yet in practice terms such as these have been found to appear in a relatively small number of codes.[76] It appears that important concepts in the area of research ethics and research integrity have not been key points of focus by many existing research communities.[77]

Self-correction in science is a logical starting point to consider ideas of self-regulation. While structures and approaches vary, all major scientific jurisdictions have approaches which rely on self-corrective models.[78] From one perspective the 'self' in self-correction reflects a collective enterprise within the scientific community – reviewers, readers or other researchers seeking to replicate results, identify errors and methodological weaknesses.[79] The speed and effectiveness of this can be problematic – at the extreme, examples of a century passing before the inappropriate alteration of data is discovered.[80] The 'self' in self-correction can also represent individuals who identify errors in their own contributions to the body of scientific knowledge. This is a less common conceptualisation of scientific self-correction and often not deemed essential to the overall self-correcting enterprise. However, it can be valuable in terms of providing a speedy and efficient route to correction, with researchers usually being better placed to identify errors and weaknesses in their own work.[81] Individual self-correction also offers the prospect of de-stressing what otherwise can become a hostile environment if misunderstandings occur and offense is taken during the process of one scientist

76 Komić, D., Marušić, S. L., & Marušić, A. (2015). Research integrity and research ethics in professional codes of ethics: Survey of terminology used by professional organizations across research disciplines. *PLoS ONE*, 10(7), e0133662. doi: 10.1371/journal.pone.0133662; Steneck, N. H. (2006). Fostering integrity in research: Definitions, current knowledge, and future directions. *Science and Engineering Ethics*, 12, 53–74.

77 Only 23 per cent of professional organizations were found to have included in their code one or more key research integrity/ethics terms. Of those, typically only 2 or 3 important provisions were included. Komić, D., Marušić, S. L., & Marušić, A. (2015). Research integrity and research ethics in professional codes of ethics: Survey of terminology used by professional organizations across research disciplines. *PLoS ONE*, 10(7), e0133662. doi: 10.1371/journal.pone.0133662, citing Fanelli, D. (2009). How many scientists fabricate and falsify research? A systematic review and meta-analysis of survey data. *PLoS One*, 4, e5738. doi: 10.1371/journal.pone.0005738 PMID: 19478950; Joseph, A., Koehlmoos, T., Smith, R., & Yan, L. L. (2013). Research misconduct in low- and middle-income countries. *PLoS Medicine*, 10, e1001315. doi: 10.1371/journal.pmed.1001315 PMID: 23555197

78 House of Commons Science and Technology Committee, Research integrity, Sixth Report of Session 2017–19, 11 July 2018 HC 350, para 114

79 Mayo-Wilson, C., Zollman, K. J. S., & Danks, D. (2011). The independence thesis: When individual and social epistemology diverge. *Philos. Sci.*, 78(4), 653–677, cited in Rohrer, J. M., DeBruine, L. M., Heyman, T., Jones, B. C., Schmukle, S. C., Silberzahn, R., . . . Yarkoni, T. (2018). *Putting the Self in Self-Correction*. December 12. osf.io/ps8nt

80 Kornfeld, D. S. (2012). Perspective: Research misconduct: The search for a remedy. *Acad Med*, 87, 877–882, 877

81 Mayo-Wilson, C., Zollman, K. J. S., & Danks, D. (2011). The independence thesis: When individual and social epistemology diverge. *Philos. Sci.* 78(4), 653–677, cited in Rohrer, J. M., DeBruine, L. M., Heyman, T., Jones, B. C., Schmukle, S. C., Silberzahn, R., . . . Yarkoni, T. (2018). *Putting the Self in Self-Correction*. December 12. osf.io/ps8nt

criticising the work of another.[82] Notwithstanding these advantages, individual self-correction remains relatively rare. Reasons for this are unclear, but contributing factors are likely to include opportunity cost considerations – correcting past mistakes takes time away from new research in an environment where quantity of new research output is highly valued. Some researchers may also be concerned about the reputational impact of the correction of their work.[83] This is unfortunate, as speedy correction by an author is likely to do more to instil public trust in science than delayed corrections or prolonged arguments between authors and their critics.[84] An ideal situation would see individual self-correction signalling that a researcher is diligent and concerned for the accuracy of the scientific record, with publishers helping in this regard by adopting different terminology for enforced retractions compared with publications withdrawn at the request of the authors.[85] Alternatively, utilising more fully the opportunities offered by online publication, an article could be corrected, with the uncorrected version remaining available in archived form.[86] Calls for the scientific community to seek to create an environment that incentivises self-correction has parallels with established professions which in regulatory codes impose obligations on each member of the profession to declare certain matters which may give rise to regulatory concerns – seeking to ensure that professional self-regulation operates at the level of each individual member.

Integrity and assessing character

As well as placing trust in regulatory mechanisms, trust in individual members of a regulated community not to overstep the boundaries of appropriate behaviour

82 Rohrer, J. M., DeBruine, L. M., Heyman, T., Jones, B. C., Schmukle, S. C., Silberzahn, R., . . . Yarkoni, T. (2018). *Putting the Self in Self-Correction*. December 12. osf.io/ps8nt, citing Bohannon, J. (2014, May). Replication effort provokes praise – and 'bullying' charges. *Science*, *344*(6186), 788–789.

83 Rohrer, J. M., DeBruine, L. M., Heyman, T., Jones, B. C., Schmukle, S. C., Silberzahn, R., . . . Yarkoni, T. (2018). *Putting the Self in Self-Correction*. December 12. osf.io/ps8nt; Rohrer J.M., Tierney W., Uhlmann E. L, et al. (2021) Putting the Self in Self-Correction: Findings From the Loss-of-Confidence Project. *Perspectives on Psychological Science*. 16(6):1255–1269. doi:10.1177/1745691620964106

84 Rohrer, J. M., DeBruine, L. M., Heyman, T., Jones, B. C., Schmukle, S. C., Silberzahn, R., . . . Yarkoni, T. (2018). *Putting the Self in Self-Correction*. December 12. osf.io/ps8nt; Rohrer J.M., Tierney W., Uhlmann E. L, et al. (2021) Putting the Self in Self-Correction: Findings From the Loss-of-Confidence Project. *Perspectives on Psychological Science*. 16(6):1255–1269. doi:10.1177/1745691620964106

85 Rohrer, J. M., DeBruine, L. M., Heyman, T., Jones, B. C., Schmukle, S. C., Silberzahn, R., . . . Yarkoni, T. (2018). *Putting the Self in Self-Correction*. December 12. osf.io/ps8nt, citing Alberts, B., Cicerone, R. J., Fienberg, S. E., Kamb, A., McNutt, M., Nerem, R. M., . . . Jamieson, K. H. (2015). Self-correction in science at work. *Science*, 348(6242), 1420–1422.

86 Rohrer, J. M., DeBruine, L. M., Heyman, T., Jones, B. C., Schmukle, S. C., Silberzahn, R., . . . Yarkoni, T. (2018). *Putting the Self in Self-Correction*. December 12. osf.io/ps8nt, citing Nosek, B. A. & Bar-Anan, Y. (2012). Scientific utopia: i. opening scientific communication. *Psychol. Inq.* *23*(3), 217–243.

can also play an important role.[87] It is challenging to satisfactorily define 'integrity' as it applies to research, although ideas of honesty and collegiality occupy a central place within many definitions.[88] National and international guidelines have proliferated in recent years but lack definitional consensus.[89] Definitions which focus upon adherence to standards set by professional bodies or research institutions may lack solid theoretical underpinnings.[90]

Established professional regulatory models in areas such as medicine or law look to address integrity via mechanisms seeking to determine the suitability of character of those requesting admission. Similar observations have been made in relation to science: trust in the character and associated integrity of the individual scientist is essential to the effectiveness of regulation:

> The reliability of scientific testimony, like the reliability of most other testimony, ultimately depends on the reliability of the testifier, or on the reliability of those charged with ensuring the reliability of the testifier.[91]

In established professions, suitability of character at the point of admission is assessed in the negative, for example, the absence of criminal convictions and the absence of cheating or other academic misconduct.

Established professional bodies not only check identity and relevant background issues at the point of admission but also maintain some ongoing oversight of their members via, for example, employment records. The potential benefit of such an approach within the research field is illustrated by a case study presented by Martin encountered in his role as a journal editor. The case involved a professor of managerial and industrial economics and the discovery of evidence which gave rise to suspicions regarding a number of instances of plagiarism spread over a considerable period of time. The professor's curriculum vitae indicated employment at a number of prestigious institutions. Martin notes that the usual procedure as journal editor, once suspicion of misconduct

87 Hardwig, J. (1991). The role of trust in knowledge. *Journal of Philosophy,* 88(12), 693–708, 707.

88 Haack, S. (2007). The integrity of science: What it means, why it matters. *Contrastes: Revista Internacional de Filosofia (Spain),* XII, 5–26. Available at SSRN: https://ssrn.com/abstract=1105831; Resnik, D. B. (2011). Scientific research and the public trust. *Science and Engineering Ethics.,* 17(3), 399–409; Komić, D., Marušić, S. L., & Marušić, A. (2015). Research integrity and research ethics in professional codes of ethics: Survey of terminology used by professional organizations across research disciplines. *PLoS One.* doi: 10.1371/journal.pone.0133662.

89 See, for example, Resnik, D. B. (2011). Scientific research and the public trust. *Science and Engineering Ethics.,* 17(3), 399–409; Komić, D., Marušić, S. L., & Marušić, A. (2015). Research integrity and research ethics in professional codes of ethics: Survey of terminology used by professional organizations across research disciplines. *PLoS One.* doi: 10.1371/journal.pone.0133662.

90 See, for example, observations by Steneck, N. H. (2006). Fostering integrity in research: Definitions, current knowledge, and future directions. *Science and Engineering Ethics,* 12(1), 53–74 and critique by Winter, J. D., & Kosolosky, L. (2013). The epistemic integrity of scientific research. *Sci Eng Ethics,* 19, 757–774. doi: 10.1007/s11948-012-9394-3

91 Hardwig, J. (1991). The role of trust in knowledge. *Journal of Philosophy,* 88(12), 693–708, 707.

arose, would have been to inform the current employing institution of an investigation and to hand over the results to enable that institution to investigate further. It was at this stage that it was discovered that the researcher's stated current employer, Maastricht University, did not employ the researcher and had never had an Institute of Management Science, to which he purported to belong. No actual current employer could be ascertained.[92] In the context of professions where a professional body maintains an employment record, the likelihood of being able to maintain a deceit of the type encountered in this case should be significantly reduced. Furthermore, a professional body offers the prospect of a mechanism to deal with allegations of misconduct outside of the context of any particular employer. With regard to this particular case, Martin decided to take the unusual step of writing an explanatory editorial, in addition to the usual retraction notice, to more fully alert the wider research community to the investigation and the alleged behaviour of this particular researcher.[93] However, as Martin acknowledges, allegations – some anonymous – and disjointed investigations are 'surely not an appropriate way to raise such a serious matter.'[94]

Dishonesty

A number of approaches to research integrity focus on the idea of honesty but often lack sufficient definitional clarity. Recent considerations of dishonesty in English law have focused on objective standards of ordinary reasonable and honest people, having moved away from a two-element approach, the second element considering whether the accused realised that ordinary honest people would regard their behaviour as dishonest.[95] Attempts at definitions within the research community have tended towards relatively imprecise terms such as 'good faith.'[96] There is scope for the regulation of research to learn lessons from the many years of deliberation within the legal sphere regarding the pros and cons of different definitions of dishonesty.

Potential deceit and dishonesty can manifest in numerous ways in the research context. Bias in research can sit alongside misbehaviours such as fabrication, falsification, plagiarism and misrepresentation.[97] For example, a scientist may subtly mislead if observations are presented in a manner which may lead to inappropriate inferences.[98] In the context of clinical trials, if a new drug is

92 Martin, B. (2007) Keeping plagiarism at bay – A salutary tale. *Research Policy*, 36(7), 905–911.
93 Martin, B. (2007) Keeping plagiarism at bay – A salutary tale. *Research Policy*, 36(7), 905–911.
94 Martin, B. (2007) Keeping plagiarism at bay – A salutary tale. *Research Policy*, 36(7), 905–911, 909.
95 *Ivey v Genting Casinos (UK) Ltd t/a Crockfords* [2017] UKSC 67, discussed in paras 52–59
96 Winter, J. D., & Kosolosky, L. (2013). The epistemic integrity of scientific research. *Sci Eng Ethics*, 19, 757–774. doi: 10.1007/s11948-012-9394-3
97 Steneck, N. H. (2006). Fostering integrity in research: Definitions, current knowledge, and future directions. *Science and Engineering Ethics*, 12(1), 53–74.
98 Winter, J. D., & Kosolosky, L. (2013). The epistemic integrity of scientific research. *Sci Eng Ethics*, 19, 757–774. doi: 10.1007/s11948-012-9394-3

administered in appropriate dosages while the comparison drug is administered in inadequate dosages, reporting that a significantly higher percentage of patients in receipt of the new drug recovered compared with the competing product group without highlighting the dosage irregularities is deceptive if recipients of the information are unaware of the discrepancy.[99] An alternative example would be if an abundance of data points in a particular direction, yet a scientist states that the research is inconclusive. Such a statement may be deemed to be deceptive.[100]

Integrating dishonesty with the epistemic integrity of research can be problematic.[101] For example, De Winter and Kosolosky define the epistemic integrity of a practice as 'a function of the degree to which the statements resulting from this practice are deceptive. The more deceptive these statements, the lower the epistemic integrity of the practice.'[102] Epistemic integrity and honesty have a complex interrelationship – epistemic integrity can be low because research has been undertaken dishonestly and results intentionally misstated, but also equally low if misreporting is accidental.[103] It can take a skilled and determined data checker to spot problems and further skill to differentiate between deceit and accident.[104]

99 Winter, J. D., & Kosolosky, L. (2013). The epistemic integrity of scientific research. *Sci Eng Ethics*, 19, 757–774. doi: 10.1007/s11948-012-9394-3, citing Rochon, P. A., Gurwitz, J. H., Simms, R. W., Fortin, P. R., Felson, D. T., Minaker, K. L. et al. (1994). A study of manufacturer-supported trials of nonsteroidal anti-inflammatory drugs in the treatment of arthritis. *Archives of Internal Medicine*, 154(2), 157–163; Johansen, H. K., & Gøtzsche, P. C. (1999). Problems in the design and reporting of trials of antifungal agents encountered during meta-analysis. *Journal of the American Medical Association*, 282(18), 1752–1759; Tandon, R., & Fleischhacker, W. W. (2005). Comparative efficacy of antipsychotics in the treatment of schizophrenia: A critical assessment. *Schizophrenia Research*, 79(2–3), 145–155; Reiss, J. (2010). In favour of a Millian proposal to reform biomedical research. *Synthese*, 177(3), 427–447.

100 Winter, J. D., & Kosolosky, L. (2013). The epistemic integrity of scientific research. *Sci Eng Ethics*, 19, 757–774. doi: 10.1007/s11948-012-9394-3

101 Winter, J. D., & Kosolosky, L. (2013). The epistemic integrity of scientific research. *Sci Eng Ethics*, 19, 757–774. doi: 10.1007/s11948-012-9394-3, considering, inter alia, the place of 'honesty' in approaches by Resnik, D. B. (1998). *The Ethics of Science: An Introduction*. London: Routledge; National Academy of Sciences. (1992). *Responsible Science: Ensuring the Integrity of the Research Process* (Vol. I). Washington, DC: National Academies Press; Office of Research Integrity (2007). *Research on Research Integrity*. (accessed 25 October 2020).

102 Winter, J. D., & Kosolosky, L. (2013). The epistemic integrity of scientific research. *Sci Eng Ethics*, 19, 757–774. doi: 10.1007/s11948-012-9394-3

103 Winter, J. D., & Kosolosky, L. (2013). The epistemic integrity of scientific research. *Sci Eng Ethics*, 19, 757–774. doi: 10.1007/s11948-012-9394-3, considering, inter alia, the place of 'honesty' in approaches by Resnik, D. B. (1998). *The Ethics of Science: An Introduction*. London: Routledge; National Academy of Sciences. (1992). *Responsible Science: Ensuring the Integrity of the Research Process* (Vol. I). Washington, DC: National Academies Press; Office of Research Integrity. (2007). *Research on Research Integrity*. (accessed 25 October 2020).

104 See, for example, Adam, D. (2019). How a data detective exposed suspicious medical trials. *Nature*, 571, 462–464. doi: 10.1038/d41586-019-02241-z

Self-regulation in action

At a local level, well-organised research teams can scrutinise the data and research methods within a team, but to achieve consistency across scientific communities requires a more organised structure, to provide opportunities for critique and to nurture robustness in matters of research integrity and research practice.[105] The creation and funding of centres of research integrity present opportunities to display models of excellence and, if imbued with appropriate authority, can enable the investigation, detection and sanctioning of researchers who fall short of expected standards.[106]

Alongside structural considerations, self-regulation is likely to be most effective if all members of the profession are the eyes and ears of the regulatory process. With long-standing professions such as medicine and law, this was a key factor when embryonic professional bodies were giving assurances to the state that self-regulation was the best way to regulate complex professional practice. Only members of the professions could meaningfully detect concerns and adjudicate within the complex professional environment. An example may be drawn from the case of Yoshihiro Sato, who in 2016 admitted to fabricating data, which subsequently led to numerous retractions.[107] In 2003 Sato published an article which assessed a very rare complication from treatment of Parkinson's disease.[108] Concerns were raised about the improbability that the researchers had been able to identify 40 research subjects with this complication from a single institution within the timeframe of the study.[109] Other concerns related to ethical oversight and randomisation failures.[110] Observations

105 Begley, C. G., Buchan, A. M., & Dirnagl, U. (2015). Robust research: Institutions must do their part for reproducibility. *Nature,* 525, 25–27. https://doi.org/10.1038/525025a

106 Begley, C. G., Buchan, A. M., & Dirnagl, U. (2015). Robust research: Institutions must do their part for reproducibility. *Nature,* 525, 25–27. https://doi.org/10.1038/525025a. As part of this model of infractions which are not sufficiently serious to warrant formal disciplinary action, researchers could face loss of laboratory space and even demotion. In contrast, for those who excel, this should be picked up by appropriate metrics to feed into reward and promotion processes.

107 Bolland, M. J., Avenell, A., Gamble, G. D., & Grey, A. (2016). Systematic review and statistical analysis of the integrity of 33 randomized controlled trials. *Neurology,* 87(23) (December), 2391–2402. doi: 10.1212/WNL.0000000000003387; Gross, R. A. Editor-in-Chief (2016). Statistics and the detection of scientific misconduct. *Neurology,* 87(23) (December), 2388. doi: 10.1212/WNL.0000000000003390

108 Sato, Y., Asoh, T., Metoki, N., & Satoh, K. J. (2003). Efficacy of methylprednisolone pulse therapy on neuroleptic malignant syndrome in Parkinson's disease. *Neurol. Neurosurg. Psychiatry,* 74, 574–576; retraction 89, e3 (2018). https://jnnp.bmj.com/content/74/5/574

109 Clarke, C. E. (2004). Efficacy of methyprednisolone pulse therapy on neuroleptic malignant syndrome in Parkinson's disease. *J. Neurol. Neurosurg. Psychiatry,* 75, 510–511, cited by Grey, A., Avenell, A., Klein, A. A., & Gunsalus, C.K. (2020). Check for publication integrity before misconduct. *Nature,* 577, 167–169 doi: https://doi.org/10.1038/d41586-019-03959-6

110 Grey, A., Avenell, A., Klein, A. A., & Gunsalus, C.K. (2020). Check for publication integrity before misconduct. *Nature,* 577, 167–169 doi: https://doi.org/10.1038/d41586-019-03959-6

of this type require high levels of expertise, likely only to be found within the research community.

Self-regulatory proactivity requires engagement by all relevant participants in the research and publication process. The impact when this is not the position is illustrated by the case of Luk Van Parijs, a former associate professor of immunology at the Massachusetts Institute of Technology (MIT), who was initially investigated for suspected research misconduct in 2004 and found to be responsible for more than 11 incidents of data fabrication in grant applications and papers submitted between 1997 and 2004.[111] Later, in 2011, he was convicted of grant fraud, criminal charges having been filed in the US District Court in Boston, citing Van Parijs' use of fake data in a 2003 $2 million grant application to the National Institutes of Health.[112] Fourteen years earlier David Baker, a neuroimmunologist at Queen Mary, University of London, had raised concerns in an email to a journal in which Van Parijs had published. No response was received from the journal.[113] Baker and members of his team subsequently noticed apparently manipulated data in three further papers published by Van Parijs, all three later retracted. However, Baker did not raise further concerns. In part because the editor of the journal he had originally emailed, as part of the extended professional research community, had given no indication of taking seriously his attempts to raise concerns. He said that 'I felt I'd done my bit,' although he also stated that he regretted not having done more once the full extent of the misconduct came to light.[114]

Issues which may arise in the absence of a professional regulatory body

The powers of a traditional professional regulatory body apply across employing organisations, helping to bring consistency between cases and clarity to employers when a disciplinary sanction is imposed. Clarity is also present for the person disciplined, including a reasonable expectation of resuming their professional life once a sanction comes to an end. Such consistency and

111 Reich, S. E. (2011). Biologist spared jail for grant fraud. *Nature*, 474, 552. https://doi.org/10.1038/474552a

112 Reich, S. E. (2011). Biologist spared jail for grant fraud. *Nature*, 474, 552. https://doi.org/10.1038/474552a

113 Follow-up with the journal some years later, with a different editorial team in place, resulted in an apology for the lack of response but otherwise shed no light on the position. At the time the journal lacked professional editors, and the two scientists who had served as editors around that time did not recall reading the original email, which was sent to a communal email address. Reich, E. S. (2011). Fraud case we might have seen coming. *Nature*, 474, 552. www.nature.com/news/2011/110628/full/474552a.html

114 Reich, S. E. (2011). Fraud case we might have seen coming. *Nature*, 474, 552. www.nature.com/news/2011/110628/full/474552a.html

clarity are currently lacking within the research field. An example of this is illustrated by a news article relating to Italian surgeon Paolo Macchiarini, who was disciplined for scientific misconduct by an employer, the Karolinska Institute in Stockholm, dismissed and had a number of publications retracted. As the article points out, he was soon able to publish again as senior author in a peer-reviewed journal. The publication was described as being 'strikingly similar to the plastic trachea transplants that ultimately left most of his patients dead.' The editor of the journal was unaware of Macchiarini's history.[115] Macchiarini is reported to have undertaken the work for that article while employed at Kazan Federal University in Russia, a post from which he was later dismissed.[116]

For the purposes of this work no observations are made regarding the scientific credibility of Macchiarini's later published work, but it is clear that the absence of an overarching professional regulatory body with multi-national reach, the decision of which could have settled the matter, means that the position remains confused and unsatisfactory. Quoted comments from a number of scientists familiar with Macchiarini's conduct history indicate disquiet at his prompt return to research.[117] Had the journal editor been aware of Macchiarini's history, a different approach may have been taken. Whether that would have been further peer review by way of additional checking or outright rejection to avoid the journal being associated with the Macchiarini name can only be speculated upon. This may be seen as unfair because of the lack of consistency, clear procedural fairness and other attributes of due process.[118] A regulatory body, as long as respected and trusted within the community it oversees, offers the prospect of significantly alleviating these difficulties. For example, had a scientist in Macchiarini's position been permanently excluded

115 Warren, M. (2018). Disgraced surgeon is still publishing on stem cell therapies. *Science*, April 27, 2018, www.sciencemag.org/news/2018/04/disgraced-surgeon-still-publishing-stem-cell-therapies. The editor of the journal said that the peer review of the submission was 'rigorous,' but that he would, however, have found it helpful to have known about Macchiarini's history.

116 Warren, M. (2018). Disgraced surgeon is still publishing on stem cell therapies. *Science*, April 27, 2018, www.sciencemag.org/news/2018/04/disgraced-surgeon-still-publishing-stem-cell-therapies

117 Warren, M. (2018). Disgraced surgeon is still publishing on stem cell therapies. *Science*, April 27, 2018, www.sciencemag.org/news/2018/04/disgraced-surgeon-still-publishing-stem-cell-therapies

118 An example of the due process point can also be drawn from the protracted considerations of the Macchiarini case. An editorial in *The Lancet* noted the importance of the presumption of innocence until guilt is proven in observing 'dragging the professional reputation of a scientist through the gutter of bad publicity before a final outcome of any investigation had been reached was indefensible.' Editorial, Paolo Macchiarini is not guilty of scientific misconduct. *The Lancet*, 386 (9997) (September 5, 2015), 932. https://doi.org/10.1016/S0140-6736(15)00118-X. An overarching professional regulatory body can address this. In well-developed areas of professional regulation, such bodies will typically have the power to suspend from or otherwise restrict practice if the nature of the allegations warrants that, but otherwise the accused person remains free to practise and benefits from a presumption of innocence until guilt is established.

from professional practice by such a body, then subsequent professional activity would have been in breach of that, with further sanction potentially following. In contrast, had such a scientist been dealt with in a different way, for example, suspended from practice for a period of time, then a return to practice would be justified and whatever the personal opinions of others within the scientific community, there should be acceptance that justice had been served and that further public criticism was inappropriate.

Embryonic external oversight bodies

Central oversight bodies which take direct control or oversee institutional regulatory activities have yet to emerge to a significant extent, but there are a limited number of examples offering some semblance of parts of the forward-looking control powers traditional professional bodies possess.[119] The United States has been a lead jurisdiction in this regard, with developments in Europe much slower in comparison.[120] For example, the US Office of Research Integrity (ORI) has powers to prohibit researchers from receiving federal grants either for a specified period or indefinitely, although the ORI cannot directly investigate suspected fraud or misconduct. The origins of the ORI can be traced back to the early 1980s, following a number of cases of research misconduct and concerns that research institutions were not responding sufficiently robustly.[121]

In the case of University of Vermont researcher Eric Poehlman, who was sentenced to a period of imprisonment for defrauding the federal government of grant funding as a result of fabricating or falsifying data on 15 grant applications, the ruling included barring Poehlman for life from participation in US government procurement programmes – described by one commentator as a restriction which 'effectively forever removed [Poehlman] from the community of researchers who once held him in such high esteem.'[122] In 2015

119 See, for example, Gunsalus, C. K., McNutt, M. K. et al. (2019). Overdue: A US advisory board for research integrity. *Nature*, 566, 173–175 doi: https://doi.org/10.1038/d41586-019-00519-w

120 Stroebe, W., Postmes, T., & Spears, R. (2012). Scientific misconduct and the myth of self-correction in science. *Perspect Psychol Sci.*, 7(6), 670–688. doi: 10.1177/1745691612460687

121 ORI - The Office of Research Integrity | ORI - The Office of Research Integrity (hhs.gov); for discussion about the development of the ORI see https://ori.hhs.gov/historical-background

122 Souder, L. (2009). A rhetorical analysis of apologies for scientific misconduct: Do they really mean it? *Science and Engineering Ethics,* 16, 175–184. doi: 10.1007/s11948-009-9149-y; Shamoo, A. S., & Resnik, D. B. (2009). *Responsible Conduct of Research* (2nd ed.). New York: Oxford University Press; The Office of Research Integrity. *Case Summary – Eric T. Poehlman*, https://ori.hhs.gov/case-summary-eric-t-poehlman (accessed 16 January 2021). See also, Dahlberg, J. E., & Mahler, C. C. (2006). The Poehlman case: Running away from the truth. *Sci Eng Ethics.*, 12(1) (January),157–173. doi: 10.1007/s11948-006-0016-9. PMID: 16501657; Tilden, S. J. (2010). Incarceration, restitution, and lifetime debarment: Legal consequences of scientific misconduct in the

Dong-Pyou Han, formerly a researcher at Iowa State University, was sentenced to 57 months imprisonment and fined US$7.2 million for fabricating and falsifying data in HIV vaccine trials.[123] Han was prohibited by the ORI from receiving federal grants for three years.[124]

UK Research and Innovation (UKRI) has proposed the creation of an oversight body with the responsibility to 'champion research integrity in the UK and independently examine whether research institutions have followed appropriate processes to investigate misconduct' and to ensure the creation of a vibrant and responsible research environment.[125] The commissioning by UKRI of a research integrity landscape study and the creation of the UKRI Research Integrity Committee are steps intended to champion research integrity in the UK and to independently examine the adherence by research institutions to appropriate processes to investigate misconduct.[126] A UKRI ethics statement and framework will further underpin these developments.[127]

The UK Research Integrity Office (UKRIO) is an independent charity and was established in 2006 with the purpose of offering advice and support on issues of research integrity in the fields of science and medicine. Support and advice are available to researchers, research organisations and members of the public. UKRIO has no direct investigatory role or any legally underpinned regulatory powers, but may advise others on investigating allegations of fraud and misconduct. UKRIO describes its aims as including the provision of a confidential advice role in support of individual researchers, employers and funding bodies, encouraging a professional ethos and the sharing of experience and expertise across discipline boundaries. Guidance is not mandatory, but UKRIO aims to encourage best practice in the conduct of research and addressing research misconduct. At the time of writing over 100 research

---

Eric Poehlman case: Commentary on: "Scientific forensics: How the office of research integrity can assist institutional investigations of research misconduct during oversight review". *Science and Engineering Ethics,* 16(4), 737–741.

123 Department of Justice U.S. Attorney's Office, Southern District of Iowa, Former Iowa State Researcher Sentenced for Making False Statements, www.justice.gov/usao-sdia/pr/former-iowa-state-researcher-sentenced-making-false-statements; Reardon, S. (2015). US vaccine researcher sentenced to prison for fraud. *Nature,* 523, 138–139. doi: 10.1038/nature.2015.17660

124 Reardon, S. (2015). US vaccine researcher sentenced to prison for fraud. *Nature,* 523, 138–139. doi: 10.1038/nature.2015.17660

125 UKRI to create Research Integrity Committee by Summer 2020, www.ukri.org/news/ukri-to-create-research-integrity-committee-by-summer-2020/ (accessed 10 October 2020)

126 *UK Research and Innovation Delivery Plan 2019,* www.ukri.org/about-us/delivery-plans/ (accessed 14 June 2019), pp. 28–29; Metcalfe, J., Wheat, K., Munafò. M., Parry, J. (2020). *Research Integrity: A Landscape Study.* Vitae in partnership with the UK Research Integrity Office (UKRIO) and the UK Reproducibility Network (UKRN), June 2020, www.vitae.ac.uk/vitae-publications/research-integrity-a-landscape-study

127 *UK Research and Innovation Delivery Plan 2019,* www.ukri.org/about-us/delivery-plans/ (accessed 14 June 2019), pp. 28–29.

organisations subscribe to UKRIO, including a significant number of UK universities, and various UK academies and institutes such as the Royal Society and the British Academy. Research organisations from outside the UK have also begun to subscribe.[128] A concern is that some of those universities and other bodies which have not engaged may be the ones in greatest need of support.[129] The UK House of Commons Science and Technology Committee has recommended that the default assumption should be subscription to UKRIO, unless non-subscribing institutions could satisfactorily explain why they were not in need of UKRIO's advisory services.

However, questions have been raised about the independence of UKRIO, given its reliance on funding from research organisations. In response, UKRIO has emphasised that subscriptions from individual organisations are modest (under £3,000 pa) and as such present little or no danger that UKRIO will be swayed to favour any particular institution, although it is more challenging to determine whether, in an overarching collective sense, a body with regulatory-style functions may be swayed towards treading more gently in order to minimise the risk of alienating the community on which its continued existence depends.[130] Funding of professional regulators by the regulated community is a common aspect of self-regulation and generally works satisfactorily, so even though the nature of UKRIO is somewhat different from a traditional professional regulator, the approach to funding should not be seen as unduly problematic, unless evidence to the contrary was to emerge.

In Canada, a Panel on Responsible Conduct of Research (PRCR) and a Tri-Agency Framework: Responsible Conduct of Research were established in 2011 by Canada's federal research agencies with the aim of ensuring a coherent approach to dealing with allegations of research misconduct and the promotion of responsible research conduct to enhance public trust and the quality of research.[131] The role of the PRCR was intended, inter alia, to review institutional investigation reports and to provide advice to the agencies on matters related to the responsible conduct of research.[132] Evidence indicates that in its first five years of operation, 43 per cent of cases considered involved at least one breach of the PRCR Framework, although with regard to the accuracy of data,

128 For the current list, see UKRIO » Our subscribers

129 House of Commons Science and Technology Committee, Research integrity, Sixth Report of Session 2017–19, 11 July 2018 HC 350, para 49

130 House of Commons Science and Technology Committee, Research integrity, Sixth Report of Session 2017–19, 11 July 2018 HC 350, para 49

131 The Canadian Institutes of Health Research; the Natural Sciences and Engineering Research Council; and the Social Sciences and Humanities Research Council.

132 Government of Canada, Panel on Responsible Conduct of Research, https://rcr.ethics.gc.ca/eng/home.html (accessed 12 March 2019)

it has been suggested that transparency, in terms of public disclosure of details regarding investigations, remains an issue.[133]

The Australian government established the Australian Research Integrity Committee (ARIC) in 2011 to undertake reviews of institutional processes used to manage and investigate potential breaches of the Australian Code for the Responsible Conduct of Research.[134] One requirement of the code is that research institutions have timely and effective processes for investigating complaints or suspicions of misconduct. The ARIC can be called upon to conduct an independent review of the processes an institution followed when managing or investigating a potential breach of the code. Any individual or organisation may request that the ARIC undertake a review. The ARIC therefore plays an important part in the quality assurance process and associated maintenance of public confidence. Scope of the ARIC role does not extend to certain matters, for example: consideration of breach of the code, rather than institutional processes in response to a suspected breach; the merits of any institutional findings, unless relating to an error in the institution's processes; matters of misconduct unrelated to the code; and institutional sanctions having found a breach of the code.[135]

Following a review, the ARIC may provide advice to the institution on improving future practice, advise the institution to offer an apology to the complainant, advise that the institution appoint an independent party to review the institution decision on finding of a breach of the code or advise that the institution undertake a new investigation.[136]

Authorship and responsibility for research misconduct

Determining liability for misconduct in multi-author papers gives rise to a number of considerations. Approaches which cast the liability net so wide that individuals who, on other measures, could not be said to have any direct involvement in the misconduct risk undermining the willingness of scientists to collaborate in larger projects.[137] Professional responsibility on the part of co-authors requires balancing the trust which is important to research collaboration

133 Stueck, W. (2017). Questions raised about disclosure of Canadian research-policy breaches. *The Globe and Mail British Columbia*, October 19, 2017, www.theglobeandmail.com/news/british-columbia/questions-raised-about-disclosure-of-canadian-research-policy-breaches/article36674314/ (accessed 12 March 2019); Government of Canada, Panel on Responsible Conduct of Research, resources (accessed 12 March_2019)

134 The Australian Code for the Responsible Conduct of Research (2018) www.nhmrc.gov.au/about-us/publications/australian-code-responsible-conduct-research-2018 (accessed 14 March 2019)

135 Australian Government, *Australian Research Integrity Committee Framework, 2019,* 4.

136 Australian Government, *Australian Research Integrity Committee Framework, 2019,* 4–5.

137 Hussinger, K., & Pellens, M. (2017). *Guilt by Association: How Scientific Misconduct Harms Prior Collaborators*. ZEW – Centre for European Economic Research Discussion Paper No. 17-051. Available at SSRN: https://ssrn.com/abstract=3072290 or http://dx.doi.org/10.2139/ssrn.3072290

with the responsibility researchers bear regarding the veracity of findings in publications which carry their name.[138]

Co-authors who are innocent of misbehaviour may find themselves being viewed as guilty by association. An example arose from the case of Robert A. Slutsky, a former member of the Departments of Medicine and Radiology at the University of California at San Diego, who in the 1980s was found to have produced 13 fraudulent papers with a further 55 categorised as questionable. A number of co-authors, even though not accused of participating knowingly in misconduct, were caught up in the scandal, resulting in implications for their professional careers. One co-author is quoted as saying:

> I worry that it will hurt me in looking for a job or applying for grants. There are certain people on the faculty that think less of me for my association with Slutsky.[139]

Another co-author said:

> Basically, three years of effort were wiped out. It has an effect on my brain, my psyche and my soul.[140]

Another co-author explained that the stain of being associated with fraudulent research carried over into a private practice medical career and the ability to secure employment:

> I knew it would hurt me in the academic world, but I never thought it would make a difference for a [private practice] job. . . . When I saw this could hurt me to the tune of $250,000 per year, I realized it was no game.[141]

For more junior co-authors in particular, with papers which were of particular importance to their career development, the loss of these papers and the reputational damage may be particularly striking.[142]

138 Report of the Investigation Committee on the Possibility of Scientific Misconduct in the Work of Hendrik Schön and Co-authors, September 2002, 3, http://w.astro.berkeley.edu/~kalas/ethics/documents/schoen.pdf (accessed 11 November 2020)

139 Dalton, R. (1987). Fraudulent papers stain co-authors fraudulent papers stain co-authors. *The Scientist*, May 1987, www.the-scientist.com/news/fraudulent-papers-stain-co-authors-63762 (accessed 4 March 2020)

140 Dalton, R. (1987). Fraudulent papers stain co-authors fraudulent papers stain co-authors. *The Scientist*, May 1987, www.the-scientist.com/news/fraudulent-papers-stain-co-authors-63762 (accessed 4 March 2020)

141 Dalton, R. (1987). Fraudulent papers stain co-authors fraudulent papers stain co-authors. *The Scientist*, May 1987, www.the-scientist.com/news/fraudulent-papers-stain-co-authors-63762 (accessed 4 March 2020)

142 Stroebe, W., Postmes, T., & Spears, R. (2012). Scientific misconduct and the myth of self-correction in science. *Perspect Psychol Sci.*, 7(6), 670–688. doi: 10.1177/1745691612460687

Co-authors may also face questions about their role in self-regulation within an author team. For example, the committee investigating misconduct by Dutch social psychologist Diederik Alexander Stapel, while finding no evidence of deliberate misconduct by co-authors, concluded that some of these authors should have adopted a more critical attitude and better ensured compliance with fundamental principles of scientific practice.[143] The manner in which Stapel was able to manipulate data without being detected by co-authors suggested that the culture was not one in which scientific integrity was sufficiently prioritised or 'held in high esteem.'[144] In particular, the committee observed that:

> It is almost inconceivable that co-authors who analysed the data intensively, or reviewers of the international 'leading journals', who are deemed to be experts in their field, could have failed to see that a reported experiment would have been almost infeasible in practice, did not notice the reporting of impossible statistical results . . . and did not spot values identical to many decimal places in entire series of means in the published tables. Virtually nothing of all the impossibilities, peculiarities and sloppiness mentioned in this report was observed by all these local, national and international members of the field, and no suspicion of fraud whatsoever arose.[145]

The committee which investigated the misconduct of Hendrik Schön also considered the potential obligations of co-authors. The committee cleared all co-authors of scientific misconduct, but also considered whether they exercised appropriate professional responsibility with regard to the validity of data and the claims made in published papers.[146] Co-authors provide implicit endorsement to work on which their names appear and so, the committee observed, issues of professional responsibility can remain even in the absence of personal misconduct.[147] More experienced co-authors with an established reputation are particularly valuable to fraudsters in a non-anonymous peer review environment if their names lead some reviewers to presume certain levels of quality and integrity.[148]

143 Levelt Committee, Noort Committee, Drenth Committee. *Flawed Science: The Fraudulent Research Practices of Social Psychologist Diederik Stapel*, November 28, 2012, 33

144 Levelt Committee, Noort Committee, Drenth Committee. *Flawed Science: The Fraudulent Research Practices of Social Psychologist Diederik Stapel*, November 28, 2012, 33

145 Levelt Committee, Noort Committee, Drenth Committee. *Flawed Science: The Fraudulent Research Practices of Social Psychologist Diederik Stapel*, November 28, 2012, 53

146 Report of the Investigation Committee on the Possibility of Scientific Misconduct in the Work of Hendrik Schön and Co-authors, September 2002, 4, http://w.astro.berkeley.edu/~kalas/ethics/documents/schoen.pdf

147 Report of the Investigation Committee on the Possibility of Scientific Misconduct in the Work of Hendrik Schön and Co-authors, September 2002, 4, http://w.astro.berkeley.edu/~kalas/ethics/documents/schoen.pdf

148 Cassuto, L. (2002). Big trouble in the world of 'Big Physics'. *The Guardian*, Wednesday, September 18, 2002, www.theguardian.com/education/2002/sep/18/science.highereducation;

Negative impact may even extend to researchers uninvolved in a project involving misconduct but who have been prior collaborators of the scientists committing misconduct.[149] This has implications for scientists who are in a position to blow the whistle but are fearful of doing so, even though entirely innocent, because they have some current or prior association with the suspected misbehaving scientists.[150]

It is important that the approach adopted attributes liability as accurately as possible, utilising a system which has the confidence of the scientific community and society more broadly – such that any scientists to whom no liability is attached are viewed as entirely innocent.

In practical terms the responsibility of each co-author, and thereby degrees of innocence or guilt relating to misconduct, is dependent upon input to the published piece and factors such as experience, expertise and seniority.[151] However, it has been argued that a researcher who is insufficiently informed about the research underpinnings of a paper, or otherwise unwilling to accept responsibility for the paper, should not accept co-authorship.[152]

In recent years attempts have been made to more precisely identify and attribute each author's contribution to the research and publication processes.[153] Recent organisational approaches to determining author accountability include the International Committee of Medical Editors (ICMJE) and the Council of Science Editors (CSE), who base accountability on the actual contribution of each author, and the Committee on Publication Ethics (COPE) and ALL European Academies (ALLEA), who provide that all authors are accountable for the whole piece, unless a different approach is specified.[154] The ICMJE

Levi, B. G. (2002). Investigation finds that one lucent physicist engaged in scientific misconduct. *Physics Today*, 55(11) (November 1). https://doi.org/10.1063/1.1534995

149 Hussinger, K., & Pellens, M. (2017). *Guilt by Association: How Scientific Misconduct Harms Prior Collaborators*. ZEW – Centre for European Economic Research Discussion Paper No. 17-051. Available at SSRN: https://ssrn.com/abstract=3072290 or http://dx.doi.org/10.2139/ssrn.3072290

150 Hussinger, K., & Pellens, M. (2017). *Guilt by Association: How Scientific Misconduct Harms Prior Collaborators*. ZEW – Centre for European Economic Research Discussion Paper No. 17-051. Available at SSRN: https://ssrn.com/abstract=3072290 or http://dx.doi.org/10.2139/ssrn.3072290

151 Report of the Investigation Committee on the Possibility of Scientific Misconduct in the Work of Hendrik Schön and Co-authors, September 2002, 3, http://w.astro.berkeley.edu/~kalas/ethics/documents/schoen.pdf (accessed 11 November 2020)

152 Their contributions could, alternatively, be recognised by means of an appropriate acknowledgement. Report of the Investigation Committee on the Possibility of Scientific Misconduct in the Work of Hendrik Schön and Co-authors, September 2002, 3, http://w.astro.berkeley.edu/~kalas/ethics/documents/schoen.pdf (accessed 11 November 2020)

153 Brand, A., Allen, L., Altman, M., Hlava, M., & Scott, J. (2015). Beyond authorship: Attribution, contribution, collaboration, and credit. *Learned Publishing*, 28(2), 151–155, cited by Moher, D., Bouter, L., Kleinert, S., Glasziou, P., Sham, M. H., Barbour, V., et al. (2020). The Hong Kong principles for assessing researchers: Fostering research integrity. *PLoS Biol*, 18(7), e3000737. https://doi.org/10.1371/journal.pbio.3000737

154 Hussinger, K., & Pellens, M. (2019). Scientific misconduct and accountability in teams. *PLoS ONE*, 14(5), e0215962. https://doi.org/10.1371/journal. pone.0215962 citing, inter alia,

requires authors to be accountable for answering questions aimed at identifying which author was responsible for each aspect of the research if clarification is needed.[155] It has also been recommended that authors should be willing to identify where each element of a research project was undertaken to facilitate which employing institution should undertake investigations if matters of concern arise.[156] From the limited data available, it has been suggested that for biomedical journals, the ICMJE guidelines are used by approximately half, approximately a quarter use other criteria and the remaining quarter require all authors to approve the manuscript.[157]

Other approaches include 'guarantor' models – a single principal author who acts as guarantor for the integrity of the whole work. This would move principal authorship on the part of one author from general oversight responsibility for the whole manuscript to guarantor of the integrity of the entire project.[158] A risk faced by guarantor models is that they can confuse responsibility (who committed the misconduct and is morally responsible) and accountability (the one to whom blame is attached) and place unrealistic and unreasonable

Jones, A. H. (2003). Can authorship policies help prevent scientific misconduct? What role for scientific societies? *Sci Eng Ethics*, 9, 243–256. https://doi.org/10.1007/s11948-003-0011-3; Helgesson, G., & Eriksson, S. (2017). Responsibility for scientific misconduct in collaborative papers. *Medicine, Health Care and Philosophy*, 21, 423–430. https://doi.org/10.1007/s11019-017-9817-7; Wager, E., & Kleinert, S. (2011). Responsible research publication: International standards for authors. A position statement developed at the 2nd world conference on research integrity, Singapore, July 22–24, 2010. In T. Mayer & N. Steneck (Eds,), *Promoting Research Integrity in a Global Environment* (pp. 309–316). Imperial College Press/World Science Publishing.

155 International Committee of Medical Journal Editors. Recommendations for the conduct, reporting, editing, and publication of scholarly work in medical journals. www.icmje.org/recommendations

156 Wager, E., Kleinert, S., Garfinkel, M., Volker Bahr, C., et al. (2017). Cooperation & Liaison between Universities & Editors (CLUE): Recommendations on best practice. *bioRxiv*. doi: https://doi.org/10.1101/139170. Wager, E., Kleinert, S. & on behalf of the CLUE Working Group (2021). Cooperation & Liaison between Universities & Editors (CLUE): recommendations on best practice. Res Integr Peer Rev 6, 6. https://doi.org/10.1186/s41073-021-00109-3

157 Hussinger, K., & Pellens, M. (2019). Scientific misconduct and accountability in teams. *PLoS ONE*, 14(5), e0215962. https://doi.org/10.1371/journal. pone.0215962 citing Wager E. Do medical journals provide clear and consistent guidelines on authorship? MedGenMed. 2007; 9: 16. In terms of the number of high-ranking, peer-reviewed journals which provide any guidance for handling allegations of misconduct, that number has been placed at 'less than half,' Bosch, X., Herna´ndez, C., Pericas, J. M., Doti, P., & Marusˇić, A. (2012). Misconduct policies in high-impact biomedical journals. *PLoS One*, 7. https://doi.org/10.1371/journal.pone.0051928.

158 Hussinger, K., & Pellens, M. (2019). Scientific misconduct and accountability in teams. *PLoS ONE*, 14(5), e0215962. https://doi.org/10.1371/journal. pone.0215962 citing by way of example the approach of the American Psychological Association, American Psychological Association. Publication Practices & Responsible Authorship [Internet]. 2018 www.apa.org/research/responsible/publication/index.aspx (accessed 27 May 2019) and the British Medical Journal BMJ. Authorship & contributorship: www.bmj.com/about-bmj/resources-authors/article-submission/authorship-contributorship (accessed 27 May 2019). Also, for further consideration of co-authorship and journal disclosure requirements see, for example, Sauermann, H., & Haeussler, C. (2017). Authorship and contribution disclosures. *Sci Adv.*, 3. https://doi.org/10.1126/sciadv.1700404

expectations upon one or a small number of members of large, complex research collaborations with numerous specialists.[159] As one commentator observes:

> [T]he clinician who stages the cancer and collects the specimens cannot vouch for the analysis by the molecular biologist nor for the analysis of the data by the statistician.[160]

Research collaborators are chosen because they can offer input beyond the capacity of the other team members. There may arise a moral unjustness to expecting researchers to be responsible for tasks in the project that they did not and could not perform.[161]

Empirical findings indicate that first authors and corresponding authors are more likely to be found responsible for scientific misconduct than middle authors – 65 per cent of first authors, 45 per cent for corresponding authors but under 20 per cent for lower listed authors.[162] Focusing accountability on senior authors has, therefore, some confluence with data relating to actual findings of responsibility, suggesting that certain versions of a guarantor model could be best placed to attach accountability in a manner which reflects empirical reality.[163] The position may be further complicated by a diversity of accounts presented by senior scientists who appear as named authors but have no personal involvement in preparing data which appears in publications or in directly or supervising researchers. For example, a department head at a leading English university justified his name appearing on publications because of his 'advisory' role and the help he gave more junior staff in his department 'in their applications for grant funding and promotion.'[164]

159 Hussinger, K., & Pellens, M. (2019). Scientific misconduct and accountability in teams. *PLoS ONE*, 14(5), e0215962. https://doi.org/10.1371/journal. pone.0215962 citing Helgesson G, Eriksson S. Responsibility for scientific misconduct in collaborative papers. Medicine, Health Care and Philosophy. Springer Netherlands; 2017. pp. 1–8. https://doi.org/10.1007/s11019-0179817-7. Hussinger and Pellens suggest that COPE and ALLEA guidelines may unfairly place accountability with contributing authors who are less likely to have been involved in misconduct, whereas the ICMJE and CSE policies are less problematic in that regard.

160 Kempers, R. D. (2002). Ethical issues in biomedical publications. *Fertil Steril.*, 77, 883–888. https://doi.org/10.1016/S0015–0282(02)03076–5 cited by Hussinger, K., & Pellens, M. (2019). Scientific misconduct and accountability in teams. *PLoS ONE*, 14(5), e0215962. https://doi.org/10.1371/journal. pone.0215962

161 Rennie, D. (2001). Who did what? Authorship and contribution in 2001. *Muscle and Nerve* 24, 1274–1277. https://doi.org/10.1002/mus.1144 cited by Hussinger, K., & Pellens, M. (2019). Scientific misconduct and accountability in teams. *PLoS ONE*, 14(5), e0215962. https://doi.org/10.1371/journal. pone.0215962

162 Hussinger, K., & Pellens, M. (2019). Scientific misconduct and accountability in teams. *PLoS ONE*, 14(5), e0215962. https://doi.org/10.1371/journal. pone.0215962

163 Hussinger, K., & Pellens, M. (2019). Scientific misconduct and accountability in teams. *PLoS ONE*, 14(5), e0215962. https://doi.org/10.1371/journal. pone.0215962

164 Allegation of research misconduct in respect of 32 papers published between 1990 and 2013 by researchers based at the UCL Institute of Child Health: Report of the Investigation Panel,

Whistleblowing

In common with other professions, the complexity of scientific research and the opaque nature of some aspects of practice make whistle-blowers central to the reporting of suspicions about research misconduct.[165] Whistle-blowers are often far better placed than other participants in the research process, such as journal editors and peer reviewers, to detect and report misconduct.[166]

The virtues or vices exhibited by individual scientists not only impact upon their own perceived trustworthiness and credibility but also impact upon the credibility of scientific communities as a whole. Scientific communities should, therefore, appeal to the consciences of scientists to ensure the highest possible standards of research integrity.[167] Expressed more robustly:

> Those who bear witness to scientific misconduct and do nothing are themselves culpable. Taking no action aids and abets perpetrators and the harms committed as a consequence.[168]

Robust challenge and disagreement among scientists have a greater chance of leading to greater trust than timid conformity – the perception that a community of scientists has only reached a consensus position on a particular point

www.documentcloud.org/documents/6178710-UCL-FOIA-Latchman-Lab-Investigations.html (accessed 6 July 2019)

165 For further discussion, see Thomas, J. (2015). So you want to be a whistleblower? A lawyer explains the process. *Retraction Watch*, March 18, 2015, https://retractionwatch.com/2015/03/18/so-you-want-to-be-a-whistleblower-a-lawyer-explains-the-process/#more-26683 (accessed 1 April 2019)

166 Breen, K. J. (2016). Research misconduct: Time for a re-think? *Internal Medicine Journal*, 46, 728–733. doi: 10.1111/imj.13075, 729; Kleinert, S. (2008). The role of the whistleblower. In F. Wells & M. Farthing (Eds.), *Fraud and Misconduct in Biomedical Research* (4th ed., pp. 121–134). London: The Royal Society of Medicine Press; Marusic, A. (2008). The role of the peer review process. In F. Wells & M. Farthing (Eds.), *Fraud and Misconduct in Biomedical Research* (4th ed., pp. 135–160). London: The Royal Society of Medicine Press. A somewhat oblique example can be found in the case of Luk Van Parijs. Concerns about potential misconduct in an article he had authored were raised with the journal in 1997 but received no response. Investigations were only initiated seven years later by Van Parijs' employer when concerns were raised by members of his lab. Reich, E. S. (2011). Fraud case we might have seen coming. *Nature*. https://doi.org/10.1038/news.2011.437

167 Board on Health Sciences Policy. Institute of Medicine. Integrity in Scientific Research: Creating an Environment That Promotes Responsible Conduct. Executive Summary. Washington, DC: National Academies Press; 2002. Cited by Kornfeld, D. S. (2012). Perspective: Research misconduct: The search for a remedy. *Acad Med*, 87, 877–882, 878; Gunsalus, C. K., & Rennie, D. (2008). Handling whistleblowers: Bane and boon. In F. Wells & M. Farthing (Eds.), *Fraud and Misconduct in Biomedical Research* (4th ed., pp. 227–259). London: The Royal Society of Medicine Press; Breen, K. J. (2016). Research misconduct: Time for a re-think? *Internal Medicine Journal*, 46, 728–733. doi: 10.1111/imj.13075, 730

168 Marks, D. F. (2019). The Hans Eysenck affair: Time to correct the scientific record, Editorial. *Journal of Health Psychology*, 24(4), 409–420. https://doi.org/10.1177/1359105318820931

after robust argument, 'rather than being attributable to groupthink or bias or interest.'[169] In the words of one senior researcher:

> I want people to speak up their minds. I want people to have an opinion. I mean they don't have to be argumentative about everything, but honesty is very important.[170]

Instilling a willingness on the part of individual scientists to report suspected misconduct may be viewed as an offshoot of this important aspect of scientific method. The importance of whistleblowing becomes embedded as an integral aspect of ensuring the robustness of the scientific record and as a means to achieve prompt exposure of misconduct and to serve as a deterrent within the scientific community.[171]

Those who choose to blow the whistle exhibit a range of motivations. For example, some are following an idealistic path when reporting matters about which they have concerns. For some, analysing data or scrutinising other information which has given rise to suspicions and blowing the whistle if such suspicions are deemed to be well founded can become something of a calling.[172] However, while whistle-blowers are of significant importance to the raising of concerns, whistleblowing within a research community may come with a significant risk of retribution if the identities of whistle-blowers are known.[173] Accusations of misconduct against fellow researchers may be deemed to be so serious that unambiguous proof is likely to be needed to support the suspicion before concerns are raised: 'the well-known "smoking gun."'[174] Perhaps the most significant challenge for researchers in terms of maintaining honesty and

169 Ranalli, B. (2013). Science communication as communication about persons. In J. Goodwin, M. F. Dahlstrom, & S. Priest (Eds.). *Ethical Issues in Science Communication: A Theory-Based Approach*. https://doi.org/10.31274/sciencecommunication-180809–46

170 Shaw, D., & Satalkar, P. (2018). Researchers' interpretations of research integrity: A qualitative study. *Accountability in Research*, 25(2), 79–93. doi: 10.1080/08989621.2017.1413940

171 Kornfeld, D. S. (2012). Perspective: Research misconduct: The search for a remedy. *Acad Med,* 87, 877–882

172 See, for example, discussion in Yong, E., Ledford, H., & Van Noorden, R. (2013). Research ethics: 3 ways to blow the whistle. *Nature*, 503. 454–457. doi: 10.1038/503454a.

173 See, for example, Lubalin, J. S., & Matheson, J. L. (1999). The fallout: What happens to whistle-blowers and those accused but exonerated of scientific misconduct? *Sci Eng Ethics,* 5, 229–250. https://doi.org/10.1007/s11948-999-0014-9. One report indicated that 68 per cent of whistle-blowers were damaged by making a claim of misconduct, Frankel, M. (2000). Scientific societies as sentinels of responsible research conduct. *Proceedings of the Society for Experimental Biology and Medicine*, 224(4), 216–219. doi: 10.1111/jel.1525-1373.2000.22424.x., cited by Sovacool, B. (2008). Exploring scientific misconduct: Isolated individuals, impure institutions, or an inevitable idiom of modern science? *Journal of Bioethical Inquiry*, 5, 271–282, 277. doi: 10.1007/s11673-008-9113-6.

174 Stroebe, W., Postmes, T., & Spears, R. (2012). Scientific misconduct and the myth of self-correction in science. *Perspect Psychol Sci.*, 7(6), 670–688. doi: 10.1177/1745691612460687

transparency is raising concerns about potential breaches of research integrity by close colleagues.[175] Group norms may also stand in the way of effective whistleblowing. For example, such norms can tend towards viewing misconduct as virtually unthinkable among one's team, which may result in suspicions of misconduct being displaced with more innocent explanations.[176] Furthermore, group norms may discourage open discussion of suspected misbehaviour – misconduct within a peer group tending towards being a taboo topic.[177] Contravening such norms risks, or at least gives rise to the perception of risks, being ostracised.[178]

Legal and employer protections have been found to be inadequate in a number of cases, with almost 25 per cent of whistle-blowers reporting career damage.[179] Significant numbers of whistle-blowers have also reported harm to their physical and/or mental health and to feeling stigmatised.[180] Clear and supportive institutional policies are required if the central importance of whistleblowers in maintaining research integrity is to be acknowledged.[181] Effective protection from reprisals should be provided, along with institutional reassurances that swift action will result if needed.[182] Acknowledgment and gratitude by institutional leaderships for the courage shown by whistle-blowers and the

175 Shaw, D., & Satalkar, P. (2018). Researchers' interpretations of research integrity: A qualitative study. *Accountability in Research*, 25(2), 79–93, 88 doi: 10.1080/08989621.2017.1413940

176 Stroebe, W., Postmes, T., & Spears, R. (2012). Scientific misconduct and the myth of self-correction in science. *Perspect Psychol Sci.*, 7(6), 670–688. doi: 10.1177/1745691612460687

177 Stroebe, W., Postmes, T., & Spears, R. (2012). Scientific misconduct and the myth of self-correction in science. *Perspect Psychol Sci.*, 7(6), 670–688. doi: 10.1177/1745691612460687

178 Breen, K. J. (2016). Research misconduct: Time for a re-think? *Internal Medicine Journal,* 46, 728–733. doi: 10.1111/imj.13075, 729; Lubalin, J. S., & Matheson, J. L. (1999). The fallout: What happens to whistleblowers and those accused but exonerated of scientific misconduct? *Sci Eng Ethics,* 5, 229–250

179 Redman, B., & Caplan, A. (2014). No One Likes a Snitch. *Science and Engineering Ethics,* 21. doi: 10.1007/s11948-014-9570-8, 814. Other studies have reported even higher figures, for example in the USA an ORI study found that over two-thirds of whistleblowers experienced adverse consequences, notwithstanding regulatory prohibition against such retaliation, Kornfeld, D. S. (2012). Perspective: Research misconduct: The search for a remedy. *Acad Med,* 87, 877–882, 880, citing Research Triangle Institute (1995). *Consequences of Whistleblowing for the Whistleblower in Misconduct in Science Cases.* Washington, DC: Office of Research Integrity; Department of Health and Human Services. Public health service standards for the protection of research misconduct whistleblowers. 42 CFR Part 94. 65 Fed Reg 70830 and 65 Fed Reg 82972.

180 Redman, B., & Caplan, A. (2014). No One Likes a Snitch. *Science and Engineering Ethics,* 21. doi: 10.1007/s11948-014-9570-8, 814.

181 Breen, K. J. (2016). Research misconduct: Time for a re-think? *Internal Medicine Journal,* 46, 728–733. doi: 10.1111/imj.13075, 730; Kornfeld, D. S. (2012). Perspective: Research misconduct: The search for a remedy. *Acad Med,* 87, 877–882.

182 Breen, K. J. (2016). Research misconduct: Time for a re-think? *Internal Medicine Journal,* 46, 728–733. doi: 10.1111/imj.13075, 730; Kornfeld, D. S. (2012). Perspective: Research misconduct: The search for a remedy. *Acad Med,* 87, 877–882, 880

significant contributions made to the scientific community and the integrity of the institution are important.[183] Even with such assurances in place, a level of moral courage is needed to translate moral intentions into effective actions.[184] For some prospective whistle-blowers only the promise of anonymity will be sufficient to persuade them to report suspicions.[185] An associated recommendation is that research institutions and journal editors do not automatically dismiss or treat less seriously anonymous or pseudonymous allegations, but rather all expressions of concern should be fully assessed on their merits.[186]

The timing of whistleblowing can also be significant if, for example, the whistle-blower is part of the research team involved in the alleged misconduct. The misconduct case involving surgeon Paolo Macchiarini provides an example of this. An inquiry by his employing organisation, the Karolinska Institute in Sweden, included on the list of those to be investigated one of Macchiarini's co-workers, Karl-Henrik Grinnemo, who had alerted the institute to defects in published research outputs. The president of the institute expressed the view that whistleblowing after the event could not absolve from responsibility or criticism a co-author of the work drawn into question.[187] Grinnemo is reported to have said in response:

> [The Karolinska Institute] and its leadership has throughout all these years tried to harass me and my whistleblowing colleagues. We have been very critical of the way KI has handled the Macchiarini case and it is ridiculous that KI should have the final word in this case, they are so biased. Me and my colleagues have done fantastic work to uncover the Macchiarini scandal, while KI has always tried to stop us.[188]

183 Kornfeld, D. S. (2012). Perspective: Research misconduct: The search for a remedy. *Acad Med,* 87, 877–882, 880.

184 May, D. R., Chan, A. Y. L., Hodges, T. D., & Avolio, B. J. (2003). Developing the moral component of authentic leadership. *Organizational Dynamics*, 32, 247–260, 255; May, D. R., & Luth, M. T. (2013). The effectiveness of ethics education: A quasi-experimental field study. *Science and Engineering Ethics,* 19, 545–568. doi: 10.1007/s11948-011-9349-0

185 See, for example, discussion in Yong, E., Ledford, H., & Van Noorden, R. (2013). Research ethics: 3 ways to blow the whistle. *Nature*, 503. 454–457. doi: 10.1038/503454a.

186 Wager, E., Kleinert, S., Garfinkel, M., Volker Bahr, C., et al. (2017). Cooperation & Liaison between Universities & Editors (CLUE): Recommendations on best practice. *bioRxiv*. doi: https://doi.org/10.1101/139170; Wager, E., Kleinert, S. & on behalf of the CLUE Working Group (2021). Cooperation & Liaison between Universities & Editors (CLUE): recommendations on best practice. Res Integr Peer Rev 6, 6. https://doi.org/10.1186/s41073-021-00109-3

187 Hawkes, N. (2018). Macchiarini case: Seven researchers are guilty of scientific misconduct, rules Karolinska's president. *BMJ,* 361, k2816 doi: 10.1136/bmj.k2816

188 Hawkes, N. (2018). Macchiarini case: Seven researchers are guilty of scientific misconduct, rules Karolinska's president. *BMJ,* 361, k2816 doi: 10.1136/bmj.k2816

This institute's finding of misconduct against Karl-Henrik Grinnemo was subsequently reversed, but reputational harm and some negative career impact had already occurred.[189] There also remains the potential that other prospective whistle-blowers in similar circumstances will be deterred from reporting concerns as a result of the tribulations encountered by Grinnemo.

For those members of a research community who do demonstrate commitment and perseverance in the uncovering of research misconduct, disillusionment may be a challenge to be addressed. For example, in the case of immunologist Luk Van Parijs who falsified data and committed grant fraud, a researcher in an associated field had noticed inconsistencies at what turned out to be very early stages of Van Parijs' misconduct, but attempts to alert the relevant journal editors met with silence.[190] In the case of Yoshihiro Sato, the four researchers, one based in the UK and three in New Zealand, worked over a considerable period to reveal Sato's misconduct. At best, initially lukewarm responses from journals led to demoralisation and even despondency. One of the four is reported to have described the situation as being so pressured that sometimes they would 'just sit in a corner of [their] open floor plan office and cry.'[191] Such experiences and the reporting of them to the wider scientific community are likely to deter others from investigating further if matters of concern come to their attention.

Senior scientists, secure in their careers, should be first in line to blow the whistle on suspected misconduct. However, such leadership is not always in evidence, and the task may instead fall to more junior members of the scientific community. For example, fraud committed by Diederik Alexander Stapel came to light following the observations of three young researchers in the same department as Stapel. Having gathered sufficient evidence to support their concerns, in August 2011 they raised these with the head of department.[192] The committee which subsequently investigated Stapel's activities noted that the 'three young whistleblowers showed more courage, vigilance and inquisitiveness than

189 Karolinska Institutet announces new decision: researcher was not careless, Published: 2017-03-22, https://news.ki.se/karolinska-institutet-announces-new-decision-researcher-was-not-careless (accessed 15 November 2020); For an account from Grinnemo himself see Retraction Watch. "It's been three tough years:" Macchiarini whistleblower cleared of previous charges. March 24, 2017, https://retractionwatch.com/2017/03/24/three-toughyears-macchiarini-whistleblower-cleared-previous-charges/ (accessed 15 November 2020).

190 Reich, E. (2011). Fraud case we might have seen coming. *Nature*. https://doi.org/10.1038/news.2011.437; Reich, S. E. (2011). Biologist spared jail for grant fraud. *Nature,* 474, 552. https://doi.org/10.1038/474552a

191 Kupferschmidt, K. (2018). Researcher at the center of an epic fraud remains an enigma to those who exposed him. *Science*, August 17, 2018, www.sciencemag.org/news/2018/08/researcher-center-epic-fraud-remains-enigma-those-who-exposed-him (accessed 14 September 2020)

192 Levelt Committee, Noort Committee, Drenth Committee. *Flawed Science: The Fraudulent Research Practices of Social Psychologist Diederik Stapel*, November 28, 2012, 9. Previous attempts by other researchers to raise concerns to senior faculty members had not been acted upon. https://pure.mpg.de/rest/items/item_1569964_8/component/file_1569966/content (accessed 5 April 2020

incumbent full professors.'[193] Whistleblowing was particularly important in this case. It was noted that compared to medical research, detailed patient record keeping was not as essential or well developed for participants in psychology experiments. As a result, after the completion of the experiment, falsification of data by a fraudulent researcher in the field of psychology may be more difficult to detect, adding to the importance of fellow researchers being willing to blow the whistle.[194] Similarly, in cases such as those involving Luk Van Parijs, Eric Poehlman and Niels Birbaumer, junior researchers were instrumental in raising concerns.[195]

In terms of financial incentives to whistle blow, although historically rarely used to tackle research fraud arising from the submission of falsified research data to secure federal grants, the False Claims Act in the United States offers potentially lucrative financial rewards to whistle-blowers. In the United States some practising lawyers offer their services to prospective whistle-blowers to maximise the chances that they will succeed in such a claim.[196] Whether more widely applicable material reward-based incentives would be desirable as a mechanism to encourage blowing the whistle on suspected research misconduct is debatable. Such moves could undermine attempts to build a professional regulatory model for scientific research based upon ethics and the greater good, rather than personal self-interest.

Fear or threats of defamation

Concerns about potential legal proceedings may inhibit the willingness to expose suspected misconduct, with some prospective whistle-blowers being

193 Levelt Committee, Noort Committee, Drenth Committee. *Flawed Science: The Fraudulent Research Practices of Social Psychologist Diederik Stapel*, November 28, 2012, 46 https://pure.mpg.de/rest/items/item_1569964_8/component/file_1569966/content (accessed 5 April 2020)

194 Stroebe, W., Postmes, T., & Spears, R. (2012). Scientific misconduct and the myth of self-correction in science. *Perspect Psychol Sci.*, 7(6), 670–688. doi: 10.1177/1745691612460687

195 MIT News. MIT professor dismissed for research misconduct, October 27, 2005, https://news.mit.edu/2005/misconduct (accessed 19 January 2022); Reich, S. E. (2011). Biologist spared jail for grant fraud. *Nature,* 474, 552. https://doi.org/10.1038/474552a; Reich, E. (2011). Fraud case we might have seen coming. *Nature*. https://doi.org/10.1038/news.2011.437; The Office of Research Integrity. *Case Summary – Eric T. Poehlman*, https://ori.hhs.gov/case-summary-eric-t-poehlman (accessed 16 January 2021). See also, Dahlberg, J. E., & Mahler, C. C. (2006). The Poehlman case: Running away from the truth. *Sci Eng Ethics.*, 12(1) (January),157–173. doi: 10.1007/s11948-006-0016-9. PMID: 16501657; Tilden, S. J. (2010). Incarceration, restitution, and lifetime debarment: Legal consequences of scientific misconduct in the Eric Poehlman case: Commentary on: "Scientific forensics: How the office of research integrity can assist institutional investigations of research misconduct during oversight review". *Science and Engineering Ethics,* 16(4), 737–741; Abbott, A. (2019). Prominent German neuroscientist committed misconduct in 'brain-reading' research. *Nature*, September 21, 2019. doi: 10.1038/d41586-019-02862-4

196 See, for example, Phillips and Cohen, Choosing a Whistleblower Lawyer https://www.phillipsandcohen.com/whistleblower-resources/tips-for-choosing-whistleblower-lawyer/ (accessed 6 February 2021)

deterred by the fear of being sued by those they accuse.[197] Those who are willing to raise issues may do so online behind a cloak of anonymity. Even though such a cloak may not be impenetrable in the event of legal proceedings, it is concerning that those willing to reveal violations feel the need to seek to protect themselves in this way.[198] One potential way to address the latter is for universities and other research employers, in addition to safeguards discussed earlier in this chapter, to appoint confidential advisors to help to encourage the discussion of concerns and to explore openness in reporting.[199]

In English law, the Defamation Act 2013 is the latest statutory attempt to modify aspects of the common law rules which were considered to be unduly favourable to protecting reputation at the expense of freedom of expression.[200] The 2013 Act increases the protection for peer reviewers, a development which came about after a significant campaign to highlight the dangers of defamation being able to stifle or even silence some aspects of scientific debate.[201] Section 6 of the Act provides protection by way of qualified privilege for peer-reviewed statements published in scientific or academic journals. To qualify, the statement must relate to 'a scientific or academic matter' and prior to publication 'an independent review of the statement's scientific or academic merit was carried out by (a) the editor of the journal, and (b) one or more persons with expertise in the scientific or academic matter concerned.'[202] However, until a sufficient body of interpretive case law emerges, it remains uncertain where the boundaries of what constitutes 'peer review' will be drawn in terms of those engaging in scientific critique.[203]

197 Grove, J. (2019). Are legal concerns stifling scientific debate? *Times Higher Education*, November 7, 2019, www.timeshighereducation.com/features/are-legal-concerns-stifling-scientific-debate

198 Grove, J. (2019). Are legal concerns stifling scientific debate? *Times Higher Education*, November 7, 2019, www.timeshighereducation.com/features/are-legal-concerns-stifling-scientific-debate

199 Lerouge, I., & Hol, A. (2020). *Towards a Research Integrity Culture at Universities: From Recommendations to Implementation*. Advice Paper no. 26–January 2020, League of European Research Universities, www.leru.org/files/Towards-a-Research-Integrity-Culture-at-Universities-full-paper.pdf (accessed 8 February 2020)

200 See observations by Lord Sumption in *Lachaux v Independent Pty Ltd* [2019] UKSC 27 at [1]

201 *British Chiropractic Association v Singh* [2010] EWCA Civ 350 was a catalyst case with regard to this debate. See also Cressey, D. (2012). Nature Publishing Group wins long-running libel trial. *Nature*, July 6, 2012. doi: 10.1038/nature.2012.10965 in which it is observed that, prior to the legislative change, 'Campaigners pushing for a reform of libel laws in England and Wales say that *Nature*'s win provides more evidence that only those with deep pockets can afford to defend themselves under existing laws. "It's not really a 'win' [for *Nature*] if it took three years and cost enough money to bankrupt a normal person," says Síle Lane, campaigns manager at Sense About Science in London, one of a number of non-governmental organizations running the Libel Reform Campaign.'

202 Section 6(3)

203 For example, a case of the type discussed in Cressey, D. (2012). Nature Publishing Group wins long-running libel trial. *Nature*, July 6, 2012. doi: 10.1038/nature.2012.10965 may not fall within the new protections, so the litigation battle *Nature* faced to determine the defences of: truth (the 'justification' defence); 'honest comment' on the matter, and; publication in the public interest may still be faced, appropriately adapted by changes introduced

Other jurisdictions have seen the scientific community itself reacting directly against threats of defamation. For example, in late 2017 an online discussion arose relating to an alleged $10 million defamation lawsuit brought by a senior academic scientist working in a prestigious US university.[204] The lawsuit was brought against fellow scientists who allegedly questioned aspects of the validity of the plaintiff's research findings. Reactions from within the scientific community were swift – condemning an attack against scientific method and free speech.[205]

Varieties of litigation or the threat of it from some quarters continues to 'attempt to intimidate critics into silence,' resulting in the 'chilling [of] debate that is vital for scientific progress.'[206] For example, the courts have become venues for challenging decisions to retract papers.[207] Counter-arguments to those who view litigation as a threat to the freedom of scientific discourse focus upon legalistic approaches becoming necessary to protect reputations of researchers, especially in an era where social media and other online sources have proliferated and given rise to otherwise unchecked critical commentary, often behind a cloak of anonymity, free from traditional restraints of publication quality control.[208]

Replicating or reproducing research

Self-correction, discussed earlier, plays an important role on an individual basis, but at the level of the scientific community, a central and long-standing self-regulatory aspect of scientific method is the replication or reproducibility of research findings. Replication and reproducibility underpin research quality and research integrity, a prerequisite for making science trustworthy.[209]

---

in the 2013 Act. The hope may be that the modification of the defamation landscape by the 2013 Act provides additional discouragement against unfounded complaints.

204 Mooney, C. (2017). Stanford professor files $10 million lawsuit against scientific journal over clean energy claims. *The Washington Post*, November 1, 2017, www.washingtonpost.com/news/energy-environment/wp/2017/11/01/stanford-professor-files-libel-suit-against-leading-scientific-journal-over-clean-energy-claims/?utm_term=.b703a8dcbfb0 (accessed 2 November 2017)

205 See, for example, Shellenberger, M., Stanford University Professor Mark Z. Jacobson Sues Prestigious Team of Scientists for Debunking 100% Renewables, *Environmental Progress*, November 1, 2017 (accessed 20 November 2017); Rhodes, J, Helman, C., Stanford Scientist Sues Critics Of His 100% Green Energy Dogma, *Forbes*, November 7, 2017 (accessed 20 November 2017)

206 Grove, J. (2019). Are legal concerns stifling scientific debate? *Times Higher Education*, November 7, 2019, www.timeshighereducation.com/features/are-legal-concerns-stifling-scientific-debate

207 See, for example, Johns, M., University of Pittsburgh researchers file lawsuit against journal that retracted their pulmonary disease article, *Pennsylvania Record*, September 24, 2019 (accessed 1 September 2020); Pitt researchers sue journal for defamation following retraction, *Retraction Watch*, https://retractionwatch.com/2019/12/02/pitt-researchers-sue-journal-for-defamation-following-retraction/ (accessed 1 September 2020)

208 Grove, J. (2019). Are legal concerns stifling scientific debate? *Times Higher Education*, November 7, 2019, www.timeshighereducation.com/features/are-legal-concerns-stifling-scientific-debate

209 See, for example, Pérignon, C., & Hurlin, C. (2019). Data police force will help clean up research. *Times Higher Education*, August 26, 2019, www.timeshighereducation.com/science/data-police-force-will-help-clean-research

In definitional terms, there is a certain amount of linguistic inconsistency.[210] For the purposes of this work the term replication will be used to mean the process where other researchers seek to achieve the same findings by undertaking research from scratch – data, analytical methods, laboratories and instruments are specific to each study.[211] In contrast, the term reproducibility does not involve independent investigators attempting to rerun a whole study, but instead other researchers subject the original data to their own analyses and interpretations.[212] Replication and reproducibility are not perfect solutions to the challenges of ensuring high-quality science, and the practicalities vary between different types of studies. For example, replicating basic laboratory research studies should be more straightforward, whereas very large and expensive studies which extend over significant timescales will present far more challenges.[213] It has also been found that papers with findings which could not readily be replicated or reproduced have been cited more frequently than those subject to replication or reproduction. This remained the case even after the failure to replicate or reproduce was made public.[214]

It has been suggested that original studies which have not yet been reproduced or replicated should be valued less.[215] A more nuanced version of this suggestion is to assign a numerical measure to the replication of published findings: the 'R-factor.'[216] The R-factor of a researcher would be the average of the R-factors of the claims they reported and would rise or fall subject to whether subsequent work corroborates their research findings.[217] A significant challenge to developing such an approach is the task of assessing replication studies, unless this could be automated in a manner acceptable to the scientific community.

210 For further discussion, see Goodman, S. N., Fanelli, D., & Ioannidis, J. P. A. (2016). What does research reproducibility mean? *Science Translational Medicine*, 8(341), 341ps12.

211 House of Commons Science and Technology Committee, Research integrity, Sixth Report of Session 2017–19, 11 July 2018 HC 350, para 23, citing evidence submitted by the British Medical Journal.

212 House of Commons Science and Technology Committee, Research integrity, Sixth Report of Session 2017–19, 11 July 2018 HC 350, para 23, citing evidence submitted by the British Medical Journal.

213 Ioannidis, J. (2014). How to make more published research true. *PLoS Medicine*, 11, e1001747. doi: 10.1371/journal.pmed.1001747.

214 Some citation of a failed attempt to replicate is to be expected, but in this study that only account for small proportion, 12 per cent. Serra-Garcia, M., & Gneezy, U. (2021). Nonreplicable publications are cited more than replicable ones. *Science Advances*, 7(21) (May 21), eabd1705. doi: 10.1126/sciadv.abd1705

215 See, for example, observations by Lerouge, I., & Hol, A. (2020). *Towards a Research Integrity Culture at Universities: From Recommendations to Implementation*. Advice Paper no. 26 – January 2020, League of European Research Universities, 12, www.leru.org/files/Towards-a-Research-Integrity-Culture-at-Universities-full-paper.pdf (accessed 11 February 2020)

216 Grabitz, P., Lazebnik, Y., Nicholson, J., & Rife, S. (2017). Science with no fiction: Measuring the veracity of scientific reports by citation analysis. *bioRxiv*, 172940. doi: 10.1101/172940

217 Grabitz, P., Lazebnik, Y., Nicholson, J., & Rife, S. (2017). Science with no fiction: Measuring the veracity of scientific reports by citation analysis. *bioRxiv*, 172940. doi: 10.1101/172940

Fully documented research protocols are vital to enable other scientists to replicate the original study.[218] Institutional proactivity could see universities encouraging, even compelling, researchers to publish such information – either in supplementary data sections of journals or, if such sections are unavailable, in institutional repositories.[219] This may also be one way to slow down an inappropriate rush to publication by ensuring that researchers are focused upon the fact that any inappropriate shortcuts are likely to be visible to the wider scientific community.[220]

Editors and publishers can also play a key role if they require raw data to be submitted with draft publications, or at the very latest before publication.[221] The Transparency and Openness Promotion (TOP) guidelines propose requiring, as part of journal policies, authors to indicate 'whether the data, methods used in the analysis, and materials used to conduct the research will be made available to any researcher for purposes of reproducing the results or replicating the procedure.'[222] Authors would indicate in acknowledgments or the first footnote if they will or will not make their data, analytic methods and study materials available to other researchers and if they will, specify where that material will be made available.[223] In some circumstances researchers may be reluctant to provide raw data because of the work involved in gathering and uploading it for this purpose, or because it is data which they hope to mine further for future publications.[224]

Researchers are encouraged to consider right at the beginning of a project the need to share data and to develop and write up the project on that basis.

218 See, for example, observations by Lerouge, I., & Hol, A. (2020). *Towards a Research Integrity Culture at Universities: From Recommendations to Implementation*. Advice Paper no. 26 – January 2020, League of European Research Universities, 12, www.leru.org/files/Towards-a-Research-Integrity-Culture-at-Universities-full-paper.pdf (accessed 11 February 2020)

219 Matosin, N., Frank, E., Engel, M., Lum, J. S., & Newell, K. A. (2014). Negativity towards negative results: a discussion of the disconnect between scientific worth and scientific culture. *Disease Models & Mechanisms*, 7(2), 171–173. https://doi.org/10.1242/dmm.015123

220 Matosin, N., Frank, E., Engel, M., Lum, J. S., & Newell, K. A. (2014). Negativity towards negative results: a discussion of the disconnect between scientific worth and scientific culture. *Disease Models & Mechanisms*, 7(2), 171–173. https://doi.org/10.1242/dmm.015123

221 Miyakawa, T. (2020). No raw data, no science: Another possible source of the reproducibility crisis. *Molecular Brain*, 13, 24. https://doi.org/10.1186/s13041-020-0552-2. There will be necessary exceptions, for example, ethical or legal reasons for non-disclosure (e.g. the data consist of confidential personal information or proprietary data from a third party). It is also acknowledged that the meaning of 'raw data' should be considered within each field of science in an attempt to achieve some consensus.

222 Guidelines for Transparency and Openness Promotion (TOP) in Journal Policies and Practices "The TOP Guidelines" Version 1.0.1, www.cos.io/our-services/top-guidelines (accessed 12 September 2020)

223 Guidelines for Transparency and Openness Promotion (TOP) in Journal Policies and Practices "The TOP Guidelines" Version 1.0.1, www.cos.io/our-services/top-guidelines (accessed 12 September 2020)

224 Miyakawa, T. (2020). No raw data, no science: Another possible source of the reproducibility crisis. *Molecular Brain*, 13, 24. https://doi.org/10.1186/s13041-020-0552-2

Research design should include consideration of approaches which maximise transparency regarding the research process and minimise the likelihood of vague or incomplete reporting of the methodology.[225] Preregistration of the study design in an independent or institutional registry, including variables and treatment conditions, prior to conducting the research is the most fully developed version of this approach and should be noted in the first footnote of an article.[226] Preregistration also presents the opportunity for research to be more easily discoverable even if it does not result in publication.[227] Institutional repositories of all manuscripts submitted for publication could also be used to check changes between resubmissions in order to map the research process.[228]

In a similar way that sources are cited to avoid plagiarism, a set of standards developed and applied to the citation of data may be of value to reproducibility and to discouraging sloppy or fraudulent research practices.[229] Once established as a standard practice, researchers should also benefit from citations reflecting their original intellectual contributions to data gathering when reproduction of their research is undertaken.[230]

The keeping of raw data securely and for an appropriate period is also important if checking of research integrity becomes necessary. As illustrated by some of the case studies discussed in this work, the loss or deletion of raw data

225 Guidelines for Transparency and Openness Promotion (TOP) in Journal Policies and Practices "The TOP Guidelines" Version 1.0.1, www.cos.io/our-services/top-guidelines (accessed 12 September 2020)

226 Guidelines for Transparency and Openness Promotion (TOP) in Journal Policies and Practices "The TOP Guidelines" Version 1.0.1, www.cos.io/our-services/top-guidelines (accessed 12 September 2020)

227 Guidelines for Transparency and Openness Promotion (TOP) in Journal Policies and Practices "The TOP Guidelines" Version 1.0.1, www.cos.io/our-services/top-guidelines (accessed 12 September 2020)

228 Wager, E., Kleinert, S., Garfinkel, M., Volker Bahr, C., et al. (2017). Cooperation & Liaison between Universities & Editors (CLUE): Recommendations on best practice. *bioRxiv*. doi: https://doi.org/10.1101/139170. To encourage compliance, researchers would need to be confident that such databases would not be misused, for example, by employers drawing unfounded conclusions about the quality of research if it happens to meet with rejection before ultimately being published, there being numerous examples of what ultimately turns out to be ground-breaking research being rejected by one or more journals before eventually being accepted – see, for example, Campanario, J. M. (2009). Rejecting and resisting Nobel class discoveries: Accounts by Nobel Laureates. *Scientometrics,* 81, 549–565. https://doi.org/10.1007/s11192-008-2141-5; Katz, Y. (2016). Why are scientists so fascinated by rejection? *Scientific American*, August 25, 2016. https://blogs.scientificamerican.com/guest-blog/why-are-scientists-so-fascinated-by-rejection1/ (accessed 1 August 2021)

229 Guidelines for Transparency and Openness Promotion (TOP) in Journal Policies and Practices "The TOP Guidelines" Version 1.0.1, www.cos.io/our-services/top-guidelines (accessed 12 September 2020)

230 Guidelines for Transparency and Openness Promotion (TOP) in Journal Policies and Practices "The TOP Guidelines" Version 1.0.1, www.cos.io/our-services/top-guidelines (accessed 12 September 2020)

can thwart full investigation. Subject to compliance with jurisdictional data protection laws, institutions and funders should have clear policies aimed at the retention of raw data for at least 10 years and ideally permanently.[231] Data in repositories accessible by other researchers increase the chances that errors or fraudulent activity will be detected.[232] Journals should retain peer review and other records for appropriate time periods, should these become part of any misconduct investigations relating to authors or reviewers.[233]

In terms of the specific focus of this work, replication and reproducibility are not in themselves mechanisms for detecting misconduct, but problems may raise suspicions which lead to further investigation. Attempting to replicate or reproduce research is a valuable means to ensure that the scientific community engages with and closely analyses the detail of the data presented in research papers. Busy researchers, when reading scientific papers, may find themselves focusing on the text of a paper, paying less attention to the data presented to support the findings. Such data often hold valuable information should anything be amiss. Researchers seeking to replicate or reproduce a study have greater incentives to examine the data from the original study more thoroughly and with a critical mindset.[234] For example, Robert Gullis, a postdoctoral biochemist, admitted in 1977 that his published work on the concentration of cyclic guanosine monophosphate in neuroblastoma cells was not based on experiments but derived from fabricated data. Gullis admitted to faking his data after co-authors on four of his articles attempted but failed to replicate Gullis' findings. Gullis was asked to replicate his experiments himself. When he failed in his replication attempts, Gullis finally admitted fabricating the data.[235] Caution should be exercised if replication initially fails – premature suspicion that fraud may be an explanation could detract from continued attempts at replication and potentially the discovery of new theoretical insights.[236]

231 Wager, E., Kleinert, S., Garfinkel, M., Volker Bahr, C., et al. (2017). Cooperation & Liaison between Universities & Editors (CLUE): Recommendations on best practice. *bioRxiv*. doi: https://doi.org/10.1101/139170.

232 Stroebe, W., Postmes, T., & Spears, R. (2012). Scientific misconduct and the myth of self-correction in science. *Perspect Psychol Sci.*, 7(6), 670–688. doi: 10.1177/1745691612460687, citing Crocker, J., Cooper, L. (2011). Editorial: Addressing scientific fraud. Science, 334, 1182. doi: 10.1126/science.1216775.

233 Wager, E., Kleinert, S., Garfinkel, M., Volker Bahr, C., et al. (2017). Cooperation & Liaison between Universities & Editors (CLUE): Recommendations on best practice. *bioRxiv*. doi: https://doi.org/10.1101/139170.

234 Reich, S. E. (2011). Fraud case we might have seen coming. *Nature*, 474, 552. www.nature.com/news/2011/110628/full/474552a.html

235 Stroebe, W., Postmes, T., & Spears, R. (2012). Scientific misconduct and the myth of self-correction in science. *Perspect Psychol Sci.*, 7(6), 670–688. doi: 10.1177/1745691612460687; Tharyan P. (2012). Criminals in the Citadel and Deceit all along the Watchtower: Irresponsibility, Fraud, and Complicity in the Search for Scientific Truth. *Mens sana monographs*, *10*(1), 158–180. https://doi.org/10.4103/0973-1229.91426

236 Stroebe, W., Postmes, T., & Spears, R. (2012). Scientific misconduct and the myth of self-correction in science. *Perspect Psychol Sci.*, 7(6), 670–688. doi: 10.1177/1745691612460687 citing

The theory and the reality of replication and reproducibility diverge in significant respects. In excess of 30 million scientific articles have been published in the last 50 years, and so there are significant practical obstacles to replicating anything beyond a small proportion of these.[237] Pressure to produce original high-quality research and the career advantages this brings also acts as a disincentive to researchers spending time seeking to replicate existing findings, notwithstanding the critical importance replication plays in underpinning the research process.[238] A further disincentive is the low success rate in some areas of research when attempts are made to replicate or reproduce findings. For example, a study of 53 key articles in oncology reported that only 6 could be reproduced.[239] An American Society for Cell Biology survey found significant evidence of irreproducibility, and biomedical researchers from the pharmaceutical industry have reported that 75 per cent or more of high-profile papers are not reproducible.[240] In 2016 *Nature* reported that over 70 per cent of researchers failed to reproduce experiments recorded by other scientists. Over 50 per cent failed to reproduce their own experiments. However, while 52 per cent expressed a belief in 'a significant reproducibility crisis' and another 38 per cent a 'slight crisis,' less than 31 per cent thought that a failure to reproduce published results inevitably meant that the results are probably wrong or that it undermined the trustworthiness in the published literature. Seventy-three per cent said that they thought at least half of the papers in their field can be trusted.[241] Concerns about non-reproducibility in some scientific fields extend to potential direct implications for the wider public. For example:

> Some non-reproducible preclinical [cancer] papers had spawned an entire field, with hundreds of secondary publications that expanded on elements of the original observation, but did not actually seek to confirm or falsify

Festinger, L., Carlsmith, J. M. (1959). Cognitive consequences of forced compliance. *Journal of Abnormal and Social Psychology*, 59, 203–210; Linder, D. E., Cooper, J., Jones, E. E. (1967). Decision freedom as a determinant of the role of incentive magnitude in attitude change. *Journal of Personality and Social Psychology*, 6, 245–254.

237 Pan, R. K., Petersen, A. M., Pammolli, F., & Fortunato, S. (2018). The memory of science: Inflation, myopia, and the knowledge network. *J. Informetr.*, 12(3), 656–678.

238 Moher, D., Bouter, L., Kleinert, S., Glasziou, P., Sham, M. H., Barbour, V., et al. (2020). The Hong Kong principles for assessing researchers: Fostering research integrity. *PLoS Biol*, 18(7), e3000737. https://doi.org/10.1371/journal.pbio.3000737; Ioannidis, J. (2014). How to make more published research true. *PLoS Medicine*, 11, e1001747. doi: 10.1371/journal.pmed.1001747.

239 Begley, C., & Ellis, L. (2012). Raise standards for preclinical cancer research. *Nature*, 483, 531–533. https://doi.org/10.1038/483531a

240 Begley, C. G., Buchan, A. M., & Dirnagl, U. (2015). Robust research: Institutions must do their part for reproducibility. *Nature*, 525, 25–27. https://doi.org/10.1038/525025a, citing Begley, C. G. & Ellis, L. M. (2012). Raise standards for preclinical cancer research. *Nature*, 483, 531–533; Prinz, F., Schlange, T., & Asadullah, K. (2011). Believe it or not: How much can we rely on published data on potential drug targets? *Nature Rev. Drug Discov.*, 10, 712–713.

241 Baker, M. (2016). 1,500 scientists lift the lid on reproducibility. *Nature*, 533(7604) (May 26), 452–454. doi: 10.1038/533452a.

> its fundamental basis. More troubling, some of the research has triggered a series of clinical studies – suggesting that many patients had subjected themselves to a trial of a regimen or agent that probably wouldn't work.[242]

The Center for Open Science in the United States began an initiative in 2013 considering the replication of experiments from a significant number of influential cancer studies. A number of such attempts failed to get off the ground due to the absence of key methodological data either in the paper or obtainable from the authors. A reluctance to share data to facilitate attempts to replicate is of particular concern. Fewer than one-third of experiments could be re-run, with a significant reason being methodological data gaps.[243]

As previously noted, researchers may have legitimate reasons for being reluctant to share data if, for example, they plan to mine it for additional publications. However, misbehaviour – for example, the invention or manipulation of data or cherry-picking of results – may also fuel a reluctance to disclose data.[244] Alternatively, honest researchers may produce irreproducible findings due to inadequate training and lack of understanding of the methodology they adopt, or simply bad luck if an element of the research is unstable.[245]

Selective reporting of findings, unclear protocols and inadequately described research methodology also present obstacles. For example, a Center of Open Science project seeking to replicate studies in psychology succeeded in 36 per cent of attempts, compared with 97 per cent of the original studies reporting statistically significant findings.[246] The case of Diederik Alexander Stapel demonstrates that verification bias – use of various mechanisms to repress results unhelpful to the verification of his hypothesis – undermines the possibility of replication by other researchers.[247] Also illustrated by the Stapel case, if the original researcher has high status within their research community, if other

242 Begley, C., & Ellis, L. (2012). Raise standards for preclinical cancer research. *Nature,* 483, 531–533. https://doi.org/10.1038/483531a

243 Mullard, A. (2021). Half of top cancer studies fail high-profile reproducibility effort. *Nature,* December 9, 2021. doi: 10.1038/d41586-021-03691-0; Reproducibility Project, https://osf.io/p7ayb/

244 House of Commons Science and Technology Committee, Research integrity, Sixth Report of Session 2017–19, 11 July 2018 HC 350 at para 25, citing evidence from Professor Stephan Lewandowsky and Professor Dorothy Bishop

245 House of Commons Science and Technology Committee, Research integrity, Sixth Report of Session 2017–19, 11 July 2018 HC 350 at para 25, citing evidence from Catriona Fennell, representing the Publishers Association

246 Van Rossum, J. (2017). *Blockchain for Research.* Digital Science Report, November 2017, https://figshare.com/articles/_/5607778, citing Editorial (2016). Reality check on reproducibility. *Nature,* 533 (May 26), 437. doi: 10.1038/533437a; https://digest.bps.org.uk/2015/08/27/this-is-what-happened-when-psychologists-tried-to-replicate-100-previously-published-findings/

247 Levelt Committee, Noort Committee, Drenth Committee. *Flawed Science: The Fraudulent Research Practices of Social Psychologist Diederik Stapel,* November 28, 2012, 48–50

researchers attempt but fail to replicate findings, they may attribute this to their own insufficient experience and expertise.[248] The repeated failure by other researchers to replicate the findings of Jan Hendrik Schön were for a significant time attributed to differences in equipment or to the belief that Schön had superior technical skills.[249] If researchers also conclude that the outcomes are not publishable, these and perhaps other failed replication attempts will not be revealed, and any patterns of such failures will remain hidden from view.[250]

Compounding disincentives faced by scientists to seek to reproduce or replicate research is the reluctance of some journal editors to publish such studies, especially those with negative findings. In the *Nature* study discussed earlier, only 24 per cent of respondents had been able to publish a successful replication study and 13 per cent had published a failed replication study. Several respondents also reported that in order to publish failed replications, editors and reviewers had required them to play down comparisons with the original study.[251] As one commentator observed:

> [I]n science what we are supposed to value above all else is reproducibility. The report that confirms a finding should, therefore, be considered of equal value to the one that first announces it, but somehow we have either forgotten that fact or succumbed to a collective frenzy for high-profile [first] publications.[252]

This 'frenzy' to be first with high-profile findings and the associated reward system undermines the idea that embracing the sharing of null results is a valuable component of the scientific method.[253] An example can be drawn from the Berlin Institute of Health (BIH) which in 2017 founded the QUEST (Quality-Ethics-Open Science-Translation) Center to improve the quality and ethics of

248 Levelt Committee, Noort Committee, Drenth Committee. *Flawed Science: The Fraudulent Research Practices of Social Psychologist Diederik Stapel*, November 28, 2012, 54

249 Stroebe, W., Postmes, T., & Spears, R. (2012). Scientific misconduct and the myth of self-correction in science. *Perspect Psychol Sci.*, 7(6), 670–688. doi: 10.1177/1745691612460687, citing Reich, E. S. (2009). Plastic fantastic. New York, NY: Palgrave Macmillan.

250 Levelt Committee, Noort Committee, Drenth Committee. *Flawed Science: The Fraudulent Research Practices of Social Psychologist Diederik Stapel*, November 28, 2012, 54.

251 Baker, M. (2016). 1,500 scientists lift the lid on reproducibility. *Nature*, 533(7604) (May 26), 452–454. doi: 10.1038/533452a.

252 Petsko, G. A. (2007). And the second shall be first, *Genome Biology*, 8, 103. https://doi.org/10.1186/gb-2007-8-2-103

253 Matosin, N., Frank, E., Engel, M., Lum, J. S., & Newell, K. A. (2014). Negativity towards negative results: A discussion of the disconnect between scientific worth and scientific culture. *Disease Models & Mechanisms*, 7(2), 171–173. https://doi.org/10.1242/dmm.015123; Metcalfe, J., Wheat, K., Munafò. M., Parry, J. (2020). *Research Integrity: A Landscape Study* (pp. 43–44). Vitae/UK Research Integrity Office/UK Reproducibility Network, www.ukri.org/files/legacy/documents/research-integrity-main-report/

research conducted at the institution. The incentives included a €1,000 research fund bonus if scientists publish null results or a replication study. Also, financial incentives for the publication of the raw data associated with experiments are provided.[254] It is acknowledged that the fund levels are modest in research terms, but sufficient to start discussions about neglected areas of research practice and the potential to refocus certain existing performance incentives.[255]

Dedicated space within at least some journals for the publication of replicated research would boost opportunities to publish such studies.[256] Or, more proactively, editors should encourage the submission of studies attempting to replicate previous research, especially research published in the same journal.[257] If reports of repeated failure to replicate come to light, journal editors should demonstrate a willingness to publish this information.[258] Journal editors also have a key role to play in initiating a cultural change by providing more effective mechanisms to report negative data and facilitating the creation of links to other published sources in which investigators have reported alternative findings.[259] Utilising technological opportunities, for example, websites focusing upon the posting of results from replication attempts, would help to indicate which research findings are proving to be most problematic to replicate.[260]

There is also a lack of consensus regarding the appropriate response when attempts at replication fail. For example, in 2019 the journal *Science* decided to correct rather than retract a 2016 paper on a potential HIV treatment after three replication studies had failed to reproduce the results of the original study. It had also come to light that one of the co-authors had used a slightly different strain of virus from that stated in the paper, and this had not been reported to

254 Strech, D., Weissgerber, T., & Dirnagl, U., on behalf of QUEST Group (2020). Improving the trustworthiness, usefulness, and ethics of biomedical research through an innovative and comprehensive institutional initiative. *PLoS Biol*, 18(2), e3000576. https://doi.org/10.1371/journal.pbio.3000576

255 Strech, D., Weissgerber, T., & Dirnagl, U., on behalf of QUEST Group (2020). Improving the trustworthiness, usefulness, and ethics of biomedical research through an innovative and comprehensive institutional initiative. *PLoS Biol*, 18(2), e3000576. https://doi.org/10.1371/journal.pbio.3000576

256 Levelt Committee, Noort Committee, Drenth Committee. *Flawed Science: The Fraudulent Research Practices of Social Psychologist Diederik Stapel*, November 28, 2012, 58

257 Guidelines for Transparency and Openness Promotion (TOP) in Journal Policies and Practices "The TOP Guidelines" Version 1.0.1, www.cos.io/our-services/top-guidelines (accessed 12 September 2020)

258 Van Lange, P. A. M. et al. (2012). *Sharpening Scientific Policy after Stapel.* Internal Report, September 2012, 10, https://kli.sites.uu.nl/wp-content/uploads/sites/426/2019/09/Sharpening-Scientific-Policy-After-Stapel.pdf (accessed 1 May 2020)

259 Begley, C., & Ellis, L. (2012). Raise standards for preclinical cancer research. *Nature,* 483, 531–533. https://doi.org/10.1038/483531a

260 Stroebe, W., Postmes, T., & Spears, R. (2012). Scientific misconduct and the myth of self-correction in science. *Perspect Psychol Sci.*, 7(6), 670–688. doi: 10.1177/1745691612460687

the co-researchers.[261] Debate within the relevant scientific community ensued about the closeness of the replication attempts to the original study methodology. The ultimate conclusion by *Science* was that in the absence of evidence of malfeasance, there were insufficient grounds to warrant retraction. In the words of the editors:

> We are maintaining an Editorial Expression of Concern . . . to alert readers that current evidence suggests that the reported result is not robust and therefore does not provide a good basis for guiding work on therapies for HIV. *Science* is not moving beyond an Editorial Expression of Concern because neither the [original] authors, the authors of the attempted replication studies, nor the editors can account for the differences in results.[262]

The editor-in-chief of *Molecular Brain* has argued that the current system, largely based upon a 'trust me' assumption that all researchers are entirely honest, should be replaced by an approach which adopts a greater degree of scepticism. This observation is underpinned by a small study in 2017 in which the editor requested raw data for 41 submitted manuscripts, on the basis that the purported research results were, for example, 'too beautiful to be true.'[263] Twenty-one manuscripts were withdrawn by the authors without providing the data.[264] A further 19 out of the remaining 20 manuscripts were rejected because insufficient raw data were provided or the raw data provided by the authors did not match the data presented in the results.[265] In two cases, evidence of image duplications and inappropriate cuts and pastes in the images provided was identified.[266] Overall, more than 97 per cent of the 41 manuscripts did not present

261 Grove, J. (2019). Three failed replication attempts but no retraction for HIV study. *Times Higher Education*, September 6, 2019, www.timeshighereducation.com/news/three-failed-replication-attempts-no-retraction-hiv-study

262 Berg, J. Editor-in-Chief (2019). Editorial expression of concern. *Science*, 365(6457) (September 6), 991. doi: 10.1126/science.aaz2722

263 In accordance with the editorial policy of *Molecular Brain* which required authors to be aware that submission of a manuscript implies that materials described in the manuscript, including all relevant raw data, will be freely available to any scientist wishing to use them for non-commercial purposes. It has been noted that a fraudulent researcher seeking to reduce the risk of detection is likely to avoid presenting findings which look too close to perfection, instead aiming to make results look more realistic and less suspicious. Miyakawa, T. (2020). No raw data, no science: Another possible source of the reproducibility crisis. *Molecular Brain*, 13, 24. https://doi.org/10.1186/s13041-020-0552-2

264 Miyakawa, T. (2020). No raw data, no science: Another possible source of the reproducibility crisis. *Molecular Brain*, 13, 24. https://doi.org/10.1186/s13041-020-0552-2

265 Miyakawa, T. (2020). No raw data, no science: Another possible source of the reproducibility crisis. *Molecular Brain*, 13, 24. https://doi.org/10.1186/s13041-020-0552-2

266 Miyakawa, T. (2020). No raw data, no science: Another possible source of the reproducibility crisis. *Molecular Brain*, 13, 24. https://doi.org/10.1186/s13041-020-0552-2

the raw data supporting their results, giving rise to a possibility that in some of these cases at least the raw data did not exist.[267] Alerting authors' employing institutions may be the only way to address such matters, as institutions should have the capacity to draw together any patterns emerging if concerns emanate from more than one source.[268] Drawing concerns to the attention of the employing institution should also reduce the likelihood, if the institutional response is sufficient to address concerns, of a submission questioned by one journal being submitted afresh elsewhere.[269]

Professionalisation of researchers

An erroneous assumption is that completion of a doctorate alone equips scientists with the ability to plan and execute good research in full compliance with ethical principles.[270] Extending training and assessment should fill these knowledge gaps, with certification of compliance playing an important role in confirming that an individual has the necessary expertise in ethics and conduct to undertake scientific research, and if overseen by a professional regulatory body, this would bring the ethical aspect of research practice into line with many other established professions.[271]

Established professions have centralised mechanisms to control entry, monitor and control practitioner practice and, at the extreme, compel exit. There is no equivalent in the field of scientific research. One challenge to adapting such approaches to the research field are instances of a lack of career linearity. While established professions experience examples of particularly high-flying individuals, employment structures tend to be such that these individuals still have to undergo some period of supervised post-qualification work experience as they advance their careers within organisational structures. In contrast, examples of 'young superstars' emerge from within the research community

267 Miyakawa, T. (2020). No raw data, no science: Another possible source of the reproducibility crisis. *Molecular Brain*, 13, 24. https://doi.org/10.1186/s13041-020-0552-2. Fourteen of the manuscripts were subsequently published elsewhere. Twelve of these were in journals which required or recommend that the authors provide raw data if requested.

268 Wager, E., Kleinert, S., Garfinkel, M., Volker Bahr, C., et al. (2017). Cooperation & Liaison between Universities & Editors (CLUE): Recommendations on best practice. *bioRxiv*. doi: https://doi.org/10.1101/139170.

269 Wager, E., Kleinert, S., Garfinkel, M., Volker Bahr, C., et al. (2017). Cooperation & Liaison between Universities & Editors (CLUE): Recommendations on best practice. *bioRxiv*. doi: https://doi.org/10.1101/139170.

270 Sumpter, J. (2019). Licence to publish will restore trust in science. *Times Higher Education*, August 29, 2019, www.timeshighereducation.com/opinion/licence-publish-will-restore-trust-science

271 Sumpter, J. (2019). Licence to publish will restore trust in science. *Times Higher Education*, August 29, 2019, www.timeshighereducation.com/opinion/licence-publish-will-restore-trust-science

who may undertake research without supervision at an early stage in their careers.[272] Whereas researcher misconduct may typically begin later in careers when sufficient autonomy has been secured, 'young superstars,' if prone to misconduct, may engage in this from early in their careers. Until detected, such behaviour may continue to underpin the perceived outstanding status which allowed such early autonomy in the first place.[273] Examples of such researchers include Diederik Stapel, John Darsee and Jan Hendrik Schön, who were each viewed for a time as outstandingly productive superstars, publishing at a phenomenal rate – as it ultimately turned out because the time-consuming research stages of collecting and analysing data were being omitted in favour of fabrication.[274]

The absence of overarching professional control mechanisms can also be problematic in the context of misconduct by a researcher without an identifiable employer. For example, as discussed earlier, Martin recounts the case of a researcher who had engaged in multiple acts of misconduct – fabricating institutional affiliations for over 20 years and engaging in numerous acts of plagiarism. In the absence of a suitable institutional employer to investigate, investigations were undertaken by the editors of two journals – *Research Policy* and *Nature* – and the findings published in August 2007. Notwithstanding this scrutiny and public revelation, the subject of the investigation continued to perpetrate misconduct for several more years.[275] *Research Policy* also identified an author who had used others' databases without acknowledgement and had plagiarised. Papers were rejected and the author informed that no further submissions would be considered for the following three years. The editor of *Research Policy* also reserved the option to notify the editors of other journals if similar issues were to arise with papers submitted elsewhere.

From legal and procedural perspectives, the need for such ad hoc approaches is problematic. Risks simultaneously involve less-than-complete protection

272 Stroebe, W., Postmes, T., & Spears, R. (2012). Scientific misconduct and the myth of self-correction in science. *Perspect Psychol Sci.*, 7(6), 670–688. doi: 10.1177/1745691612460687

273 Stroebe, W., Postmes, T., & Spears, R. (2012). Scientific misconduct and the myth of self-correction in science. *Perspect Psychol Sci.*, 7(6), 670–688. doi: 10.1177/1745691612460687

274 Stroebe, W., Postmes, T., & Spears, R. (2012). Scientific misconduct and the myth of self-correction in science. *Perspect Psychol Sci.*, 7(6), 670–688. doi: 10.1177/1745691612460687; Reich, E. S. (2009). *Plastic fantastic*. New York, NY: Palgrave Macmillan

275 Martin, B. R. (2013). Whither research integrity? Plagiarism, self-plagiarism and coercive citation in an age of research assessment. *Research Policy*, 42(5) (June), 1005–1014, 1012. doi: 10.1016/j.respol.2013.03.011, citing: Abbott, A. (2007). Academic accused of living on borrowed lines. *Nature*, 448, 6320633; Martin, B. R. et al. (2007). Keeping plagiarism at bay – a salutary tale. *Research Policy*, 36, 905–911; Abbott, A. (2008). The fraudster returns. *Nature*, 452, 672; Martin, B. R. (2012). Does peer review work as a self-policing mechanism in preventing misconduct: A case study of a serial plagiarist. In T. Mayer & N. Steneck (Eds.), *Promoting Research Integrity in a Global Environment* (pp. 97–114). London and Singapore: World Scientific Publishing/Imperial College Press

against further misconduct and, depending upon the detailed circumstances of each case, allegations by authors that due process has not been followed, for example, in the context of gathering evidence or with regard to the standard of proof applied, and that their careers have been harmed as a result.[276]

Examples of the types noted earlier illustrate the challenges facing journal editors. Following the raising of concerns, significant effort is needed to determine whether a prima facie case of misconduct exists. If it does, then evidence has to be collected and the authors presented with it and provided with the opportunity to respond – with a presumption of innocence being maintained during this process.[277] The editor then moves from being an investigator to being a judge in terms of the publication or retraction decision and any further action, such as notifying the author's employing institution. In Martin's words, 'All this requires very great care, not least because of the high costs involved if one were to arrive at an incorrect decision.'[278] Some editors will be willing to spend the time and effort, but others may be content to 'pass by on the other side.'[279] Even the most ethical of editors may struggle to distance themselves and be fully objective. Lessons regarding the risks can be drawn from mistakes made in the past by established professional regulators. For example, the GMC regulating registered medical practitioners in the UK was subject to sustained criticism because of a lack of role demarcation – at certain points in the history of the GMC some senior individuals held multiple roles with regard to the investigation, prosecution and adjudication of cases.[280] However well-intentioned and ethically careful such office holders were, the appearance of unfairness could not be avoided.

Even when genuinely employed, researchers suspected of or even found to have committed misconduct may move from employer to employer.[281] The

276 Martin, B. R. (2013). Whither research integrity? Plagiarism, self-plagiarism and coercive citation in an age of research assessment. *Research Policy,* 42(5) (June), 1005–1014, 1012. doi: 10.1016/j.respol.2013.03.011.

277 Martin, B. R. (2013). Whither research integrity? Plagiarism, self-plagiarism and coercive citation in an age of research assessment. *Research Policy,* 42(5) (June), 1005–1014, 1012. doi: 10.1016/j.respol.2013.03.011.

278 Martin, B. R. (2013). Whither research integrity? Plagiarism, self-plagiarism and coercive citation in an age of research assessment. *Research Policy,* 42(5) (June), 1005–1014, 1012. doi: 10.1016/j.respol.2013.03.011.

279 Martin, B. R. (2013). Whither research integrity? Plagiarism, self-plagiarism and coercive citation in an age of research assessment. *Research Policy,* 42(5) (June), 1005–1014, 1012. doi: 10.1016/j.respol.2013.03.011.

280 Davies, M. (2007). *Medical Self-regulation, Crisis and Change.* London and New York: Routledge.

281 An example involving UCL illustrates that internal investigatory procedures have little or no impact if the employee in question has left the institution and so is outside of its disciplinary reach. A further point in this case was that records of investigatory proceedings were only released after a somewhat protected freedom of information dispute with a national newspaper, and the records eventually released had key information, including the name of this particular researcher redacted, thus preventing the wider scientific community knowing their identity. UCL Institute of Child

potential impact of this can be exacerbated if university or other employers seek to discourage publicity and encourage such employee moves in the perceived interests of institutional reputation management. Positive or neutral employment references and non-disclosure agreements to facilitate such moves further add to the problems.[282] Investigatory journalists may seek to uncover detail by means of freedom of information requests, but there is evidence to suggest that some institutions may be reluctant to comply unless compelled.[283] The UK House of Commons Science and Technology Committee described the hiding of misconduct through non-disclosure agreements as unacceptable, effectively making the institution 'complicit in future misconduct by that individual.'[284] For institutions in receipt of public funds, the committee called upon the government to consider banning the practice.[285] The committee also recommended that employers, research funders and publishers seek to develop legally compliant protocols for information sharing about researchers suspected of research integrity breaches.[286] However, such approaches could be problematic

Health: Report of the Investigation Panel www.documentcloud.org/documents/6178710-UCL-FOIA-Latchman-Lab-Investigations.html (accessed 6 July 2019). For further discussion see, for example, Sample, I. (2019). Research misconduct claim upheld against former head of UCL lab. *The Guardian*, July 1, 2019, www.theguardian.com/science/2019/jul/01/research-misconduct-claim-upheld-against-former-head-of-ucl-lab; Aldhous, P. *Documents Reveal Widespread Data Fraud in a Leading UK Scientist's Lab,* www.buzzfeednews.com/article/peteraldhous/david-latchman-scientific-misconduct (accessed 10 July 2019)

282 In the UK in recent years the use of non-disclosure agreements by universities for a variety of purposes has been subject to critical scrutiny. See, for example, Murphy, S. (2019). UK universities pay out £90m on staff 'gagging orders' in past two years. *The Guardian*, April 17, 2019; UK Parliamentary Question Universities: Disclosure of Information, 12 February 2020 Written questions and answers - Written questions, answers and statements - UK Parliament (accessed 25 April 2021)

283 See, for example, Sample, I. (2019). Research misconduct claim upheld against former head of UCL lab. *The Guardian*, July 1, 2019, www.theguardian.com/science/2019/jul/01/research-misconduct-claim-upheld-against-former-head-of-ucl-lab. The institution itself explains the position as following 'guidance sought from the ICO' and the redaction of personal data relating to individuals involved in the investigations the reports were released. The reporting newspaper's account is 'The Guardian had requested the documents under the Freedom of Information Act 2000 in January and, after a lengthy delay, referred the case to the Information Commissioner's Office.'

284 House of Commons Science and Technology Committee, Research integrity, Sixth Report of Session 2017–19, 11 July 2018 HC 350, para 99, citing evidence from Dr Elizabeth Wager and Dr Tony Peatfield.

285 House of Commons Science and Technology Committee, Research integrity, Sixth Report of Session 2017–19, 11 July 2018 HC 350, para 99, citing evidence from Dr Elizabeth Wager and Dr Tony Peatfield.

286 House of Commons Science and Technology Committee, Research integrity, Sixth Report of Session 2017–19, 11 July 2018 HC 350, para 106. Early-stage voluntary steps in this direction can be found in the Russell Group Research Integrity Forum 'Statement of cooperation in respect of cross institutional research misconduct allegations' which commits Russell Group members to contacting associated parties with whom a researcher is connected. The self-described purpose of

legally.[287] Approaches of this type should be far less problematic if appropriate models of professional regulation were utilised, including the incorporation of a renewable or revocable licence to practise. A move in this direction would formalise the process, ensure that researchers can benefit from due process and appeal procedures and ensure that sanctions are proportionate to the misconduct. It would also address the problems associated with sharing of confidential information if more than one body is involved.[288]

The UK House of Commons Science and Technology Committee recommended the creation of an independent national committee to check first-line action by employers and formal responsibility for promoting research integrity. This constitutes a bold proposal, as it is rare for the handling of research misconduct to be taken entirely out of the hands of employers, notably universities.[289] The committee would have its own secretariat to ensure independence and the authority to recommend that funding be restricted or reclaimed if an employer has not followed appropriate processes in responding to research misconduct. At the time of writing the UK government had resisted calls for the creation of an external regulatory framework on the basis that any new regulatory body would increase regulatory burden on research employers, as well as potentially overlapping with existing provision with the associated risk of causing confusion.[290]

In the longer term, if the research community wishes to minimise the risk of losing control, the onus rests upon it to support the creation of a body which will be sympathetic to the challenges of regulating research, understand the subtleties of the research community and being robust in investigating and adjudicating suspicions of misconduct.[291] The likelihood of such a development

the Russell Group is to provide strategic direction, policy development and communications for 24 major research-intensive universities in the UK. Established in 2013, the forum is a network of the professionals with lead research responsibilities within their universities designed to support their researcher communities in fostering research integrity. *Russell Group Statement of Cooperation in Respect of Cross Institutional Research Misconduct Allegations*, May 2018, https://russellgroup.ac.uk/policy/policy-documents/research-integrity-statement-of-cooperation/ (accessed 25 April 2021)

287 House of Commons Science and Technology Committee, Research integrity, Sixth Report of Session 2017–19, 11 July 2018 HC 350, para 99, citing evidence from Dr Elizabeth Wager and Dr Tony Peatfield.

288 House of Commons Science and Technology Committee, Research integrity, Sixth Report of Session 2017–19, 11 July 2018 HC 350, para 106.

289 House of Commons Science and Technology Committee, Research integrity, Sixth Report of Session 2017–19, 11 July 2018 HC 350. UKRIO would play a key role in creating the new committee, as well as continuing in its role to provide advice on research integrity and to share best practices.

290 House of Commons Science and Technology Committee, Research integrity, Sixth Report of Session 2017–19, 11 July 2018 HC 350, para 115. The government response noted that it will expect employers of researchers to deal with research integrity in an open and transparent manner, in accordance with the Research Integrity Concordat.

291 House of Commons Science and Technology Committee, Research integrity, Sixth Report of Session 2017–19, 11 July 2018 HC 350, paras 122–123.

must be weighed in the context of universities and other research institutions being protective of their powers to deal with alleged misconduct, even though they can be poorly equipped to exercise these powers due, for example, to limited opportunities to acquire in-depth experience with investigation and adjudication.[292] Attitudes within institutions can also undermine confidence – as one commentator has suggested, institutions are 'autonomous and secretive, and there the matter ends.'[293] Current institutional approaches can also present an inherent risk of conflicts of interest on the part of members of panels, other challenges associated with administrative law as it applies to tribunals and limited or no access to a body of precedent extending beyond a single institution.[294] In contrast, a national or international professional regulatory body can collate precedent findings and other data across a range of institutions.[295] Furthermore, investigating research integrity can be an unpleasant experience, not only for those accused but also for those involved in investigation and adjudication – in essence, it can be a 'stressful, difficult, time-consuming and thankless' task.[296] The latter is likely especially to be the case for members of academic and research communities who find themselves sitting in judgement in a legalistic context alien to their normal day-to-day working experience.[297] Individual institutional structures are also likely to lack the wide-ranging expertise and experience to provide the type of education and training that a national or international professional body can offer.

In terms of institutional concerns about losing regulatory autonomy, such concerns may be assuaged if lessons are learned from established professions which have centralised regulatory structures but have enjoyed high levels of self-regulatory autonomy.[298] This offers the scope for such professions to develop regulatory approaches deemed to be most suitable for the regulated community. For example, the Solicitors Regulation Authority in England and Wales

292 The House of Commons Science and Technology Committee, Research integrity, Sixth Report of Session 2017–19, 11 July 2018 HC 350, para 116; Breen, K. J. (2016). Research misconduct: Time for a re-think? *Internal Medicine Journal,* 46, 728–733. doi: 10.1111/imj.13075, 730.

293 Dr Elizabeth Wager, in evidence to the House of Commons Science and Technology Committee, Research integrity, Sixth Report of Session 2017–19, 11 July 2018 HC 350, para 118.

294 Breen, K. J. (2016). Research misconduct: Time for a re think? *Internal Medicine Journal,* 46, 728–733. doi: 10.1111/imj.13075, 731, citing Forbes JRS. *Justice in Tribunals*, 4th edn. Sydney: Federation Press; 2014.

295 Brooks, P. M., Vaux, D. L., & Williamson, R. (2016). Australia needs an ombudsman or office for research integrity. *Internal Medicine Journal,* 46(10) (October),1233–1235. doi: 10.1111/imj.13211

296 Brooks, P. M., Vaux, D. L., & Williamson, R. (2016). Australia needs an ombudsman or office for research integrity. *Internal Medicine Journal,* 46(10) (October),1233–1235. doi: 10.1111/imj.13211

297 Brooks, P. M., Vaux, D. L., & Williamson, R. (2016). Australia needs an ombudsman or office for research integrity. *Internal Medicine Journal,* 46(10) (October),1233–1235. doi: 10.1111/imj.13211

298 Only if failures to ensure significant rigour have emerged have challenges arisen to dilute or even remove such autonomy. See, for example, Davies, M. (2007). *Medical Self-regulation, Crisis and Change.* London and New York: Routledge; Case, P. (2013). Doctoring Confidence and Soliciting Trust: Models of Professional Discipline in Law and Medicine. *Journal of Professional Negligence,* 29(2), 87–107.

has in recent years moved away from an overly legalistic rule-based approach, favouring instead outcomes-focused, risk-based regulation. The onus rests with members of the profession to apply ethical considerations to broadly drafted rules in a manner which best protects clients and the wider public.[299] Lessons may also be learned from the financial accounting approaches, to be adopted by professional external auditors, developed after the Enron and other financial scandals in the United States in the late 2000s.[300] Key practices could include internal controls requiring research organisations to implement sampling and audit protocols in relation to research activity and the requirement that a senior officer review and certify the integrity of research activities.[301]

If universities and other research bodies collectively grasp the initiative, they may simultaneously develop a more effective regulatory model which lies at a level beyond individual organisations, whilst also creating a buffer against future state intervention. Some jurisdictions are further ahead than others in terms of developments.

In Australia, primary responsibility to investigate research misconduct remains with individual universities, but since 2011 a government-established independent ARIC, jointly administered by the Australian Research Council and the National Health and Medical Research Council, has been in place and can act as a form of appellate body.[302] The Research Integrity Committee provides an avenue for redress if individuals or groups consider that an institution has not acted appropriately in internally investigating alleged research misconduct.[303] Institutions have incentives to ensure that internal investigations are conducted rigorously and transparently and to minimise referrals to the Integrity Committee, and should it be needed, whistle-blowers have a route for redress. The approach is not faultless, for example, researchers have identified

299 In the field of research ethics, similar avoidance of unduly mechanistic approaches has been recommended when providing ethics education, Lerouge, I., & Hol, A. (2020). *Towards a Research Integrity Culture at Universities: From Recommendations to Implementation*. Advice Paper no. 26 – January 2020, League of European Research Universities, 12, www.leru.org/files/Towards-a-Research-Integrity-Culture-at-Universities-full-paper.pdf (accessed 11 February 2020)

300 Richman, V., & Richman, A. (2011). A tale of two perspectives: Regulation versus self-regulation. A financial reporting approach (from Sarbanes-Oxley) for research ethics. *Science and Engineering Ethics*, 18, 241–246. doi: 10.1007/s11948-011-9260-8.

301 Richman, V., & Richman, A. (2011). A tale of two perspectives: Regulation versus self-regulation. A financial reporting approach (from Sarbanes-Oxley) for research ethics. *Science and Engineering Ethics*, 18, 241–246. doi: 10.1007/s11948-011-9260-8.

302 The Australian government was motivated to protect its reputation by ensuring that the public funding invested in research was utilised properly and ethically and that all concerns about research misconduct were thoroughly investigated. Australian Government/Australian Research Council, New independent Committee to assure research integrity, Medial release, 1 February 2011 https://www.arc.gov.au/news-publications/media/media-releases/new-independent-committee-assure-research-integrity (accessed 1 March 2021)

303 Australian Government/Australian Research Council, New independent Committee to assure research integrity, Medial release, 1 February 2011 https://www.arc.gov.au/news-publications/media/media-releases/new-independent-committee-assure-research-integrity (accessed 1 March 2021)

concerns around transparency, and it has also been noted that the Integrity Committee lacks the wider role of proactively promoting research integrity.[304]

In Canada, the PRCR reviews institutional investigation reports and provides advice about the responsible conduct of research and educational outreach. The overall aim of the PRCR is to help to foster an ethical research environment in the hope of enhancing public trust in the research community. The panel also encourages a level of transparency by publishing anonymised summaries of every confirmed breach of the framework agreed by the three federal research agencies.[305]

In the United States the ORI has the power to demand institutional accountability if suspected research misconduct arises from projects in receipt of federal funding.[306]

In Denmark, the Danish Committee on Research Misconduct (DCRM), described as an independent body under the Danish Ministry of Higher Education, has the task to strengthen the credibility of Danish research and prevent research misconduct. Since 2017 it has taken the form of a single research misconduct committee chaired by a High Court judge and consisting of eight to ten researchers drawn from different scientific areas. Approaches to research integrity divide into three parts: self-regulation by the research community using shared guidelines and practices; the first line of engagement against questionable research behaviour rests with individual institutions; and all suspected research misconduct, legally defined as fabrication, falsification and plagiarism, are referred to the DCRM. Institutions report to the DCRM with regard to their activities, which in turn publishes an annual report.[307] The DCRM is interested in research misconduct, rather than with scientific disagreements, research quality or research practices per se, but as discussed previously, clear demarcation lines at the boundaries of misconduct can be difficult to draw.

In Sweden, in 2020 following a number of scientific misconduct cases, new procedures for promoting good practice and handling research misconduct were introduced, with central investigation of serious research misconduct being intended to go some way to restoring public trust damaged by, for example, the case of trachea surgeon Paolo Macchiarini.[308] The stated aims of the Swedish

304 House of Commons Science and Technology Committee, Research integrity, Sixth Report of Session 2017–19, 11 July 2018 HC 350, para 119.

305 House of Commons Science and Technology Committee, Research integrity, Sixth Report of Session 2017–19, 11 July 2018 HC 350, para 119.

306 US Department of Health and Human Services: The Office of Research Integrity, https://ori.hhs.gov/

307 https://ufm.dk/en/research-and-innovation/councils-and-commissions/The-Danish-Committee-on-Research-Misconduct. See also discussion by the House of Commons Science and Technology Committee, Research integrity, Sixth Report of Session 2017–19, 11 July 2018 HC 350, para 121

308 Else, H. (2019). Scandal-weary Swedish government takes over research-fraud investigations. *Nature,* 571, 158. doi: 10.1038/d41586-018-05493-3; Lönnstedt, O., & Eklöv, P. (2016). *Science,*

government included the desire to remove the potential conflicts of interest faced by institutions when required to deal with allegations of research misconduct, including the problematic situation that institutions may be tempted to prioritise their reputational interests, or at least give that appearance. In the words of the Swedish Minister for Higher Education and Research:

> Even if such an investigation is conducted impeccably, the clash of interests may result in reduced confidence in both the investigation and the higher education institution.[309]

The new system also aims to achieve greater clarity and legal certainty, with a uniform body of rules to address alleged research misconduct.[310] Along similar lines to the position in Denmark, the law in Sweden requires all cases of alleged serious research misconduct, defined as fabrication, falsification or plagiarism, at publicly funded research institutes to be investigated by the National Board for Assessment of Research Misconduct.[311] Findings will be public and legally binding for universities, although the latter will be allowed to determine the consequences for the researcher.[312] Beyond fabrication, falsification and plagiarism, other matters continue to be dealt with locally. Concerns have been expressed that the centralised approach for 'serious' misconduct may come at the expense of resources being diverted away from breaches of acceptable research practice which individually are less serious but which cumulatively cause more harm to the research community and to the research record.[313]

352, 1213–1216; retraction 356, 812 (2017); New procedures for promoting good practice and handling research misconduct (SOU 2017:10), cited at www.government.se/press-releases/2018/06/new-procedure-for-handling-alleged-research-misconduct/ (accessed 19 July 2019)

309 Government Offices of Sweden. (2018). New procedure for handling alleged research misconduct, 25 June. www.government.se/press-releases/2018/06/new-procedure-for-handling-alleged-research-misconduct/ (accessed 19 July 2019)

310 Government Offices of Sweden. (2018). New procedure for handling alleged research misconduct, 25 June. www.government.se/press-releases/2018/06/new-procedure-for-handling-alleged-research-misconduct/ (accessed 19 July 2019)

311 It had been recommended that the board should be chaired by a judge and consist of up to ten scientists with an appropriate range of expertise. The system will include public higher education institutions, central government agencies, municipalities, county councils and private education providers. Government Offices of Sweden. (2018). New procedure for handling alleged research misconduct, 25 June. www.government.se/press-releases/2018/06/new-procedure-for-handling-alleged-research-misconduct/ (accessed 19 July 2019)

312 Else, H. (2019). Scandal-weary Swedish government takes over research-fraud investigations. *Nature,* 571, 158. doi: 10.1038/d41586-018-05493-3

313 It is also suggested that unless funding of the National Board keeps pace with demand, there is a risk that it becomes overwhelmed, Else, H. (2019). Scandal-weary Swedish government takes over research-fraud investigations. *Nature,* 571, 158. doi: 10.1038/d41586-018-05493-3, quoting Alan Price, a consultant in Lago Vista, Texas. In the same piece it is noted that a similar centralised investigatory body investigated nine cases over a period of months after its creation. A floodgates risk may, therefore, not be great, although an effective central body in which those with concerns

Also, in some cases matters to be dealt with by the National Board and matters which remain subject to local jurisdiction may be intertwined.[314]

Trust is also complex in that the implied message to the public may be that universities cannot be trusted to properly investigate suspected misconduct, yet the same universities continue to be trusted with large sums of public money for the research itself.[315]

An ethical oath

Medical doctors who hold human life in their hands take the Hippocratic oath or equivalent. The oath, dating back more than two millennia, acts as a moral compass pointing towards the standards expected of medical professionals.[316] In contrast, scientists who may also hold life in their hands, at the extreme in the context of technologies capable of mass destruction, are subject to no equivalent or indeed any oath.[317] Medical practitioners who engage in academic research and become tempted to take ethical shortcuts breach the spirit and possibly the letter of their oath.[318] There is no equivalent for other areas of scientific research, and while current structures underpinning research incentivise various behaviours, adherence to an oath as an incentive for ethical behaviour is not currently among them.[319] The question arises, why not?

The Hippocratic oath is often, but not always, taken at the point of graduation, and the wording has developed over time and varied between diffident jurisdictions. Initially relatively short, the oath has been supplemented by more detailed, nuanced and adaptable professional codes, such as the UK General Medical Council's *Good Medical Practice*. Pledging an oath in public before

have confidence may initiate greater numbers of reports from those with concerns but who might have been less inclined to report to university-level investigation if they lacked confidence in such an investigation being satisfactory or appropriate. the latter, for example, in the context of local breaches of confidentiality and retaliation.

314 Else, H. (2019). Scandal-weary Swedish government takes over research-fraud investigations. *Nature,* 571, 158. doi: 10.1038/d41586-018-05493-3

315 Else, H. (2019). Scandal-weary Swedish government takes over research-fraud investigations. *Nature,* 571, 158. doi: 10.1038/d41586-018-05493-3

316 Oxtoby, K. (2016). Is the Hippocratic oath still relevant to practising doctors today? *BMJ*, 355. doi: 10.1136/bmj.i6629

317 Do scientists need an equivalent of the Hippocratic Oath to ensure ethical conduct?, Lindau Nobel Laureate Meetings, Posted on 29/06/2012 by Lou Woodley www.lindau-nobel.org/do-scientists-need-an-equivalent-of-the-hippocratic-oath-to-ensure-ethical-conduct/ (accessed 10 May 2020)

318 Diokno, A. C. (2010). Editorial comment: Hippocratic Oath and plagiarism. *International Urology and Nephrology*, 42, 709. doi: 10.1007/s11255-010-9776-x

319 Iverson, M. (2001). Should there be an oath for scientists and engineers? *AAAS*, April, www.aaas.org/programs/scientific-responsibility-human-rights-law/should-there-be-oath-scientists-and-engineers (accessed 8 May 2020), quoting Karen Davis, a design engineer at Siemens Building Technologies

family, friends and colleagues emphasises the magnitude of the responsibility placed in the hands of the medical professional role.[320]

The idea of an ethical pledge, a form of Hippocratic oath for scientists, has long been mooted.[321] Popper, for example, argued that just as the medical practitioners owe an overriding loyalty to their patients, scientists should remain alert to the potential that their work may produce results which detrimentally impact upon people. Therefore, they should 'constantly try to foresee, and guard against, any possible danger, or possible misuse of . . . results.'[322] More recently, Nobel Prize–winning biologist Sir John Sulston and chemist Sir David King have each called for an 'oath' or 'code' requiring scientists to promise to do no harm and to be wholly truthful in their pronouncements.[323] An oath can help to signal an 'ethics of professional practice' and can represent a symbolic public commitment to something beyond the individual, which helps to enlist the individual into a moral community.[324] Ideally, an oath would constitute 'the magnetic core that can help to create a moral community' and a belief in collective responsibility within the scientific community.[325]

320 www.gmc-uk.org/ethical-guidance/ethical-guidance-for-doctors/good-medical-practice; Oxtoby, K. (2016). Is the Hippocratic oath still relevant to practising doctors today? *BMJ*, 355. doi: 10.1136/bmj.i6629

321 See, for example, Popper, K. (1970). The moral responsibility of the scientist. In P. Weingartner & G. Zecha (Eds.), *Induction, Physics and Ethics. Proceedings and Discussions of the 1968 Salzburg Colloquium in the Philosophy of Science* (pp. 329–336). Dordrecht: Reidel;Popper, K. R. (1994). *The Myth of the Framework: In Defence of Science and Rationality*. London and New York: Routledge, edited by M.A. Notturno, 123; Rotblat, Sir J. (1999). A Hippocratic oath for scientists. *Science*, 286(5444) (November 19), 1475. doi: 10.1126/science.286.5444.1475; Trisha Greenhalgh, Professor of primary healthcare sciences, University of Oxford, cited in Else, H. (2017). Authorship wars: Academics outline the rules for recognition. *Times Higher Education*, November 30, 2017

322 Popper, K. R. (1994). *The Myth of the Framework: In Defence of Science and Rationality*. London and New York: Routledge, edited by M.A. Notturno, 123

323 Briggs, H. (2001). An oath for scientists. March 30, 2001, http://news.bbc.co.uk/1/hi/sci/tech/1250331.stm; Ghosh, P. (2007). UK science head backs ethics code, September 12. 2007, http://news.bbc.co.uk/1/hi/sci/tech/6990868.stm (accessed 8 May 2020)

324 Greenhalgh, T. (2017). Do we need a Hippocratic oath for academics? *Times Higher Education*, August 24, 2017, www.timeshighereducation.com/opinion/do-we-need-a-hippocratic-oath-for-academics; Iverson, M. (2001). Should there be an oath for scientists and engineers? *AAAS*, April, www.aaas.org/programs/scientific-responsibility-human-rights-law/should-there-be-oath-scientists-and-engineers (accessed 8 May 2020), quoting Edmund Pellegrino, John Caroll Professor of Medicine and Medical Ethics at the Center for Clinical Bioethics at Georgetown University Medical Center

325 Iverson, M. (2001). Should there be an oath for scientists and engineers? *AAAS*, April, www.aaas.org/programs/scientific-responsibility-human-rights-law/should-there-be-oath-scientists-and-engineers (accessed 8 May 2020), quoting Edmund Pellegrino, John Caroll Professor of Medicine and Medical Ethics at the Center for Clinical Bioethics at Georgetown University Medical Center. For example, it has been suggested that mathematicians, computer engineers and others in related fields should engage with ethics training early in their education and take an appropriate oath in order to encourage deep reflection about potential applications of their work and the need to ensure societal protection from powerful new technologies, Sample, I. (2019). Maths and tech

An oath would encourage students and scientists to maintain an awareness to be self-critical, reflecting on the wider consequences of their work, and also to be appropriately critical of others, including teachers and colleagues, and to resist succumbing to intellectual fashions.[326] For example, self-reflective honesty and openness could see the concluding sections of papers containing 'limitations' sections in which the authors would reflect on the weaknesses in their work.[327] An oath may also offer some protection against those employers who might be tempted to pressure researchers to behave in ways which cross ethical boundaries.[328]

Some elements of the discussions about a prospective oath for scientific researchers sit in opposition to arguments which focus upon ideas of scientific neutrality and a clear divide between scientific ideas and their application – the moral obligation of scientists being only to ensure that the results of research are released into the public domain. The use to which they are put then becomes a matter for society, not scientists.[329] Such reasoning seeks to categorise scientists as amoral, but there is a fine line between this and immorality arising from the neglect of personal responsibility.[330] Fry provides an example of an ethical blind spot drawn from presenting to an academic conference about computer modelling of riots undertaken for the metropolitan police. Academics from countries which had experienced 'the realities of a police state' reacted strongly to the ethical underpinnings of this type or research.[331]

The benefits of a researcher oath have also been mooted as a possible mechanism to address academic bullying – for example, in the context of power being used to acquire 'gift' authorship – although an oath alone will not remedy the

specialists need Hippocratic oath, says academic. *The Guardian*, Friday, August 16, 2019, https://www.theguardian.com/science/2019/aug/16/mathematicians-need-doctor-style-hippocratic-oath-says-academic-hannah-fry

326 Popper, K. R. (1994). *The Myth of the Framework: In Defence of Science and Rationality*. London and New York: Routledge, edited by M.A. Notturno, 123–124. Popper adds a note of caution: that there can be a growth of misguided assumptions that the oath underpins 'special ethical obligations' towards professional colleagues, leading to a form of 'guild morality.' Rotblat, Sir J. (1999). A Hippocratic oath for scientists. *Science*, 286(5444) (November 19), 1475. doi: 10.1126/science.286.5444.1475

327 Sumpter, J. (2019). Licence to publish will restore trust in science. *Times Higher Education*, August 29, 2019, www.timeshighereducation.com/opinion/licence-publish-will-restore-trust-science

328 Do scientists need an equivalent of the Hippocratic Oath to ensure ethical conduct? Lindau Nobel Laureate Meetings, Posted on 29/06/2012 by Lou Woodley, www.lindau-nobel.org/do-scientists-need-an-equivalent-of-the-hippocratic-oath-to-ensure-ethical-conduct/ (accessed 10 May 2020), citing John Sulston.

329 Rotblat, Sir J. (1999). A Hippocratic oath for scientists. *Science*, 286(5444) (November 19), 1475. doi: 10.1126/science.286.5444.1475

330 Rotblat, Sir J. (1999). A Hippocratic oath for scientists. *Science*, 286(5444) (November 19), 1475. doi: 10.1126/science.286.5444.1475

331 Sample, I. (2019). Maths and tech specialists need Hippocratic oath, says academic. *The Guardian*, Friday, August 16, 2019, https://www.theguardian.com/science/2019/aug/16/mathematicians-need-doctor-style-hippocratic-oath-says-academic-hannah-fry (accessed 18 August 2019)

misuse of status and power.[332] Such an approach can provide no guarantees, and it could even 'serve as a moral curtain behind which academia's bullies and cowards can better hide.'[333]

As well as discussions about the desirability of an oath for scientists, attempts have been made to formulate suggested content for such an oath. For example, Sir David King suggests a seven-point code:

- Act with skill and care in all scientific work. Maintain up to date skills and assist their development in others.
- Take steps to prevent corrupt practices and professional misconduct. Declare conflicts of interest.
- Be alert to the ways in which research derives from and affects the work of other people, and respect the rights and reputations of others.
- Ensure that your work is lawful and justified.
- Minimise and justify any adverse effect your work may have on people, animals and the natural environment.
- Seek to discuss the issues that science raises for society. Listen to the aspirations and concerns of others.
- Do not knowingly mislead, or allow others to be misled, about scientific matters. Present and review scientific evidence, theory or interpretation honestly and accurately.[334]

Given the extremely broad scope of scientific research, the likelihood of even specialist sub-areas agreeing to the wording of an oath, let alone the research community as a whole, is low. However, the process of attempting to formulate an oath, even with a small chance of success, still offers the potential to raise awareness of research ethics and aid in the guiding of ethics education.[335]

Professional sanctions

Sanctions play a number of roles within the context of professional regulation. A primary one is public protection and the maintenance of public confidence.[336]

332 Greenhalgh, T. (2017). Do we need a Hippocratic oath for academics? *Times Higher Education*, August 24, 2017, www.timeshighereducation.com/opinion/do-we-need-a-hippocratic-oath-for-academics

333 Greenhalgh, T. (2017). Do we need a Hippocratic oath for academics? *Times Higher Education*, August 24, 2017, www.timeshighereducation.com/opinion/do-we-need-a-hippocratic-oath-for-academics

334 Cressey, D. (2007). Hippocratic oath for scientists. *Nature* news blog, September 12, 2007, http://blogs.nature.com/news/2007/09/hippocratic_oath_for_scientist.html

335 Iverson, M. (2001). Should there be an oath for scientists and engineers? *AAAS*, April, www.aaas.org/programs/scientific-responsibility-human-rights-law/should-there-be-oath-scientists-and-engineers (accessed 8 May 2020), quoting Kathinka Evers, executive director of ICSU's Standing Committee on Responsibility and Ethics in Science

336 Breen, K. J. (2016). Research misconduct: Time for a re-think? *Internal Medicine Journal*, 46, 728–733. doi: 10.1111/imj.13075, 731; Dresser, R. (1993). Sanctions for research misconduct: A legal perspective. *Acad Med*, 68, S39–43.

Deterrence, both specific to the individual perpetrators of misconduct and general deterrence directed at the wider researcher community, also has value, subject to misconduct hearings being transparent and their findings appropriately disseminated in order for the research community to gain an awareness of the misconduct process and the potential sanctions for particular types of misbehaviour.[337]

While not intended as a sanction in itself, there is debate within scientific communities regarding the disclosing of names of those accused of misconduct, especially if ultimately exonerated, and those found guilty of misconduct.[338] One line of argument is that it is sufficient to publish, without names, the salient features of each case to provide a 'teachable moment' for others.[339] A counter-argument is that the disclosure of names is important to ensure that prospective employers and other researchers are aware of the professional history of a potential employee or research collaborator.[340] Furthermore, 'teachable moments' may be enhanced if case studies involve identified individuals, better enabling other members of the research community to identify with the consequences of misdeeds by those who they know, or at least may have heard of, and encouraging vigilance amongst the wider professional community.[341] With limited exceptions, the courts and the self-regulatory mechanisms of well-established professions such as medicine and law adopt transparency, which includes the names of those accused. The overarching assumption is that in mature legal and regulatory processes adherence to the presumption of innocence will prevail until guilt is proven.

Researcher rehabilitation

A hallmark of established professions is that members of the profession who find themselves subject to disciplinary action usually, in all but the most serious of cases, have a time-limited sanction or otherwise have the opportunity to demonstrate rehabilitation and to be readmitted into the professional fold.

Even though the research community does not yet have a fully developed professional regulatory model, there are examples of approaches to rehabilitation in place. One example from the United States is a training programme

337 Breen, K. J. (2016). Research misconduct: Time for a re-think? *Internal Medicine Journal*, 46, 728–733. doi: 10.1111/imj.13075, 731.

338 See, for example, Bird, S. J. (2004). Publicizing scientific misconduct and its consequences. *Science and Engineering Ethics*, 10, 435–436. https://doi.org/10.1007/s11948-004-0001-0; Lubalin, J. S., & Matheson, J. L. (1999). The fallout: What happens to whistleblowers and those accused but exonerated of scientific misconduct? *Sci Eng Ethics*, 5, 229–250.

339 Bird, S. J. (2004). Publicizing scientific misconduct and its consequences. *Science and Engineering Ethics*, 10, 435–436. https://doi.org/10.1007/s11948-004-0001-0.

340 Bird, S. J. (2004). Publicizing scientific misconduct and its consequences. *Science and Engineering Ethics*, 10, 435–436. https://doi.org/10.1007/s11948-004-0001-0.

341 Bird, S. J. (2004). Publicizing scientific misconduct and its consequences. *Science and Engineering Ethics*, 10, 435–436. https://doi.org/10.1007/s11948-004-0001-0.

launched in 2013, the Professionalism and Integrity Program (PIP), to which participants can be referred by their employing institutions. Developed with funding from the US National Institutes of Health, PIP aims to prepare participants for regaining their institutional research privileges.[342] Enrolees have included researchers who, among other things, have plagiarised, committed data fabrication or engaged in data falsification.[343] Remedial strategies include additional training about compliance with rules and profiling participants using the Clifton StrengthsFinder to reveal issues related to 'compliance-related talents, such as focus, discipline and consistency.'[344] Participants rarely intended to commit misconduct, mislead or breach rules, but as one participant is quoted as saying: 'Prior to this situation, I tried to follow the spirit of the law – now I try to follow the letter of the law.'[345]

342 DuBois, J., Chibnall, J., Tait, R., & Vander Wal, J. (2016). Misconduct: Lessons from researcher rehab. *Nature,* 534, 173–175. doi: 10.1038/534173a. www.nature.com/news/misconduct-lessons-from-researcher-rehab-1.20029; DuBois, J. M., Chibnall, J. T., Tait, R., & Vander Wal, J. S. (2018). The professionalism and integrity in research program: Description and preliminary outcomes. *Acad Med.,* 93(4) (April), 586–592. doi: 10.1097/ACM.0000000000001804. PMID: 28640035; PMCID: PMC5738297.

343 DuBois, J., Chibnall, J., Tait, R., & Vander Wal, J. (2016). Misconduct: Lessons from researcher rehab. *Nature,* 534, 173–175. doi: 10.1038/534173a. www.nature.com/news/misconduct-lessons-from-researcher-rehab-1.20029; DuBois, J. M., Chibnall, J. T., Tait, R., & Vander Wal, J. S. (2018). The professionalism and integrity in research program: Description and preliminary outcomes. *Acad Med.,* 93(4) (April), 586–592. doi: 10.1097/ACM.0000000000001804. PMID: 28640035; PMCID: PMC5738297.

344 DuBois, J., Chibnall, J., Tait, R., & Vander Wal, J. (2016). Misconduct: Lessons from researcher rehab. *Nature,* 534, 173–175. doi: 10.1038/534173a. www.nature.com/news/misconduct-lessons-from-researcher-rehab-1.20029, citing Asplund, J., Lopez, S. J., Hodges, T. & Harter, J. (2009). *The Clifton StrengthsFinder 2.0 Technical Report: Development and Validation.* The Gallup Organization; Hodges, T. D., & Harter, J. K. (2005). A review of the theory and research underlying the StrengthsQuest program for students. *Educational Horizons,* 83(3), 190–201. www.jstor.org/stable/42926536.

345 DuBois, J., Chibnall, J., Tait, R., & Vander Wal, J. (2016). Misconduct: Lessons from researcher rehab. *Nature,* 534, 173–175. doi: 10.1038/534173a. www.nature.com/news/misconduct-lessons-from-researcher-rehab-1.20029.

Chapter 5

Educating for ethical behaviour

Avoiding misconduct is preferable to addressing it after it has arisen, and the ability of researchers to readily invoke ethical standards may have a positive influence in this regard.[1]

Bourdieu argues that tradition within scientific research is continually recreated and deviance punished. The scientific habitus results from scientific education and the experiences of scientists doing science and observing the work of others.[2] Adapting this idea to the cultivation of a research environment in which ethics is integral and central may be seen as a key element of researcher education.[3] Conversely, cultural norms within a scientific community which point towards poor practice, even fraud, rather than a principled ethical climate are likely to encourage at least some students in that direction.[4] A culture where honesty and integrity feature strongly in all aspects of scientific research starts with appropriate education, such that educators do a disservice both to the scientific community and society as a whole if students are not appropriately educated to understand the ethical underpinnings of their work.[5] Integrating ethics and research integrity education into core curricula at undergraduate and master levels – tailor-making it to suit specific disciplines,

1 Quandt, R. (2012). Some models of academic corruption. *European Journal of Law and Economics*, 72, 29. doi: 10.1007/s10657-010-9162-2, citing Ariely, D. (2009). *Predictably Irrational*. London: HarperCollins Publishers

2 Bourdieu, P. (1990). *The Logic of Practice* (p. 53). Stanford, CA: Stanford University Press, cited by Foster, J. G., Rzhetsky, A., & Evans, J. A. (2013). Tradition and innovation in scientists' research strategies. *American Sociological Review*, 80(5) (February). doi: 10.1177/0003122415601618

3 See, for example, Nuffield Council on Bioethics, *The Culture of Scientific Research in the UK*, December 2014, 4.

4 Stroebe, W., Postmes, T., & Spears, R. (2012). Scientific misconduct and the myth of self-correction in science. *Perspect Psychol Sci.*, 7(6), 670–688. doi: 10.1177/1745691612460687; Whitley, B. E. (1998). Factors associated with cheating among college students: A review. *Research in Higher Education*, 39, 235–274. https://doi.org/10.1023/A:1018724900565

5 Roach, S., & Simon, J. (2008). Teaching and assessing graduate ethics in engineering, science, and technology. In M. Iskander (Ed.), Innovative techniques in instruction, technology, e-learning, e-assessment, and education (pp. 509–513). Netherlands: Springer.

DOI: 10.4324/9780429492129-5

using appropriately challenging case studies and tying it to other core aspects of scientific education such as conducting research replication – helps to ensure that future scientists are well versed in the area before undertaking research at the doctorate level and above.[6] In terms of university commitments, a focus on continuous development and improvement in ethics and integrity by all researchers irrespective of experience and seniority should be as much a part of facilitating and supporting research excellence as focuses on securing funding, publication and commercial exploitation.[7]

For less experienced researchers ethics education offers a crucial opportunity to inculcate core traits of ethical understanding and honesty, upon which more specialist understanding from the perspective of research integrity can then be built.[8] Challenges may be greater for experienced researchers if they are used to certain approaches acquired from experience or who may even be aware of the problematic nature of certain behaviours but nevertheless engage in them.[9] However, formal ethics education is of value to experienced researchers who recognise that experience can be a problematic teacher and that learning from hindsight can be costly.[10]

Formal ethics education also provides the opportunity for researchers in narrow specialist areas to learn from ethical challenges drawn from other research areas.[11] Such education can help to counter poor ethical training where, for

6 See, for example, observations by Lerouge, I., & Hol, A. (2020). *Towards a Research Integrity Culture at Universities: From Recommendations to Implementation*. Advice Paper no. 26 – January 2020, League of European Research Universities, 12, www.leru.org/files/Towards-a-Research-Integrity-Culture-at-Universities-full-paper.pdf (accessed 11 February 2020) and recommendations by Levelt Committee, Noort Committee, Drenth Committee. *Flawed Science: The Fraudulent Research Practices of Social Psychologist Diederik Stapel*, November 28, 2012, 58

7 Lerouge, I., & Hol, A. (2020). *Towards a Research Integrity Culture at Universities: From Recommendations to Implementation*. Advice Paper no. 26 – January 2020, League of European Research Universities, 12, www.leru.org/files/Towards-a-Research-Integrity-Culture-at-Universities-full-paper.pdf (accessed 11 February 2020). Lerouge and Hol draw inspiration from *Kaizen* (Japanese for Continuous Improvement) – employees at all levels of an organisation proactively working together to achieve regular, incremental improvements to a process.

8 Breen, K. J. (2016). Research misconduct: Time for a re-think? *Internal Medicine Journal*, 46, 728–733. doi: 10.1111/imj.13075, 728.

9 Riis, P. (2008). The concept of scientific dishonesty: Ethics, values, systems, and research. In F. Wells & M. Farthing (Eds.), *Fraud and misconduct in biomedical research* (4th ed., pp. 3–13). London: The Royal Society of Medicine Press; Marusic, A., Wager, E., Utrobicic, A., Rothstein, H. R., & Sambunjak, D. (2016). Interventions to prevent misconduct and promote integrity in research and publication. *Cochrane Database of Systematic Reviews*, (4), Art. No.: MR000038. doi: 10.1002/14651858.MR000038.pub2; Kornfeld, D. S. (2012). Perspective: Research misconduct: The search for a remedy. *Acad Med*, 87, 877–882; Riis, P. (2008). The concept of scientific dishonesty: Ethics, values, systems, and research. In F. Wells & M. Farthing (Eds.), *Fraud and misconduct in biomedical research* (4th ed., pp. 3–13). London: The Royal Society of Medicine Press.

10 Davis, M., & Keefer, M. (2011). Getting started: Helping a new profession develop an ethics program. *Science and Engineering Ethics*, 261, 19. doi: 10.1007/s11948-011-9279-x.

11 Davis, M., & Keefer, M. (2011). Getting started: Helping a new profession develop an ethics program. *Science and Engineering Ethics*, 262, 19. doi: 10.1007/s11948-011-9279-x.

example, students have limited access to positive role models. For example, the joint committee investigating research fraud by Diederik Alexander Stapel identified a research environment in which 'the diligent and critical handling of research and data were not held in high esteem, and were not part of the practical research education of PhD students.'[12] In evidence to the UK House of Commons Science and Technology Committee, a representative from the Wellcome Trust and also the chief executive of the UK Research Integrity Office (UKRIO) noted the risk that, in the absence of formal educational provision, bad habits regarding research design, practice and ethics could be passed down from more experienced researchers to junior counterparts.[13] Studies of student perceptions of research misconduct reveal inconsistency in responses, also suggesting that education in this area may be inadequate or at least inconsistent.[14]

Once graduate students become postdoctoral researchers they are expected to be fully educated in matters of ethics, demonstrating independence and a critical ethical mindset.[15] Effective ethics education prior to this point is vital, with the local research environment being receptive to and capable of putting it into practice.[16] It may be expected that PhD students who find themselves inculcated in improper research practices perpetrated by more senior colleagues may be treated as still learning and therefore having lower levels of culpability. However, when accused of misconduct, graduate students are more likely to be found guilty than their more senior and experienced counterparts.[17]

12 Levelt Committee, Noort Committee, Drenth Committee. *Flawed Science: The Fraudulent Research Practices of Social Psychologist Diederik Stapel*, November 28, 2012, 52

13 House of Commons Science and Technology Committee, Research integrity, Sixth Report of Session 2017–19, 11 July 2018 HC 350, para 60

14 Compare, for example: Sowden, C. (2005). Plagiarism and the culture of multilingual students in higher education abroad. *ELT Journal: English Language Teachers Journal,* 59(3), 226–233; Walker, J. (2010). Measuring plagiarism: Researching what students do, not what they say they do. *Studies in Higher Education*, 35(1), 41–59; Leonard, M., Schwieder, D. Buhler, A., Bennett, D. B., & Royster, M. (2015). Perceptions of plagiarism by STEM graduate students: A case study. *Science and Engineering Ethics,* 21(6), 1587–1608.

15 Levelt Committee, Noort Committee, Drenth Committee. *Flawed Science: The Fraudulent Research Practices of Social Psychologist Diederik Stapel,* November 28, 2012, 32; Metcalfe, J., Wheat, K., Munafò. M., Parry, J. (2020). *Research Integrity: A Landscape Study* (p. 31). Vitae/UK Research Integrity Office/UK Reproducibility Network, www.ukri.org/files/legacy/documents/research-integrity-main-report/

16 Metcalfe, J., Wheat, K., Munafò. M., Parry, J. (2020). *Research Integrity: A Landscape Study* (p. 31). Vitae/UK Research Integrity Office/UK Reproducibility Network, www.ukri.org/files/legacy/documents/research-integrity-main-report/

17 Parrish, D. (2004). Scientific misconduct and findings against graduate and medical students. *Science and Engineering Ethics,* 10, 483–491. doi: 10.1007/s11948-004-0006-8; McCabe, D. L. (1997). Classroom cheating among natural science and engineering majors. *Science and Engineering Ethics,* 3(4), 433–445. doi: 10.1007/s11948-997-0046-y; McCabe, D. L. (2005). Cheating among college and university students: A North American perspective. *International Journal for Educational Integrity,* 1(1), 2/16/2010, cited by Leonard, M., Schwieder, D. Buhler, A., Bennett, D. B., & Royster, M.

In educating for professional ethics, the meaning of ethics focuses upon those particular standards of conduct applying to members of a profession solely because of their membership of that profession.[18] Ethics in this context sits apart from ordinary morality (to be truthful, keep promises, etc.), even though aspects of it will play a role in professional models. Drawing from legal and other spheres, a starting point for ethical education is the intellectual and emotional disengagement from one's own work and the evaluation of the work of others to benefit from an outsider's viewpoint, fostering integrity and instilling the virtue of professional self-awareness.[19] Objectives of ethical education include knowledge of ethical standards and good ethical judgment, preparation for dealing with ethically ambiguous situations and developing courage and robust willpower to underpin this.[20] In this latter regard, confidence by scientists in their ethical abilities and their willingness to engage proactively in seeking to develop and implement ethical solutions is vital.[21] Development of such 'moral efficacy' can then influence an individual's willingness in the workplace to raise ethical issues with management and to aid in the seeking of solutions.[22]

(2015). Perceptions of plagiarism by STEM graduate students: A case study. *Science and Engineering Ethics,* 21(6), 1587–1608.

18 Davis, M., & Keefer, M. (2011). Getting started: Helping a new profession develop an ethics program. *Science and Engineering Ethics*, 260, 19. doi: 10.1007/s11948-011-9279-x.

19 Stovall, P. (2009). Professional virtue and professional self-awareness: A case study in engineering ethics. *Science and Engineering Ethics,* 17, 109–132. doi: 10.1007/s11948-009-9182-x; Kretser, A., Murphy, D., Bertuzzi, S., Abraham, T., Allison, D., Boor, K., Dwyer, J., Grantham, A., Harris, L., Hollander, R., Jacobs-Young, C., Rovito, S., Vafiadis, D., Woteki, C., Wyndham, J., & Yada, R. (2019). Scientific integrity principles and best practices: Recommendations from a scientific integrity consortium. *Science and Engineering Ethics*, 25. doi: 10.1007/s11948-019-00094-3; Fuller, L. L. (1981). Philosophy for the practicing lawyer. In Winston, K. I. (1981). *The Principles of Social Order: Selected Essays of Lon L. Fuller* (pp. 287–290). Durham, NC: Duke University Press

20 Ethical or moral judgment reflecting the manner by which individuals determine whether actions are morally right or wrong. Rest, J. R. (1986). The major components of morality. In W. M. Kurtines & J. L. Gerwitz (Eds.), *Morality, Moral Behavior, and Moral Development* (pp. 24–38). New York: Wiley. For considerations of cognitive moral development during the process of maturing, see Kohlberg, L. (1969). Stage and sequence: The cognitive-developmental approach to socialization. In D. A. Goslin (Ed.), Handbook of socialization theory and research (pp. 347–480). Chicago: Rand McNally. Cited by May, D. R., & Luth, M. T. (2013). The effectiveness of ethics education: A quasi-experimental field study. *Science and Engineering Ethics,* 19, 545–568, 546. doi: 10.1007/s11948-011-9349-0; Newberry, B. (2004). The dilemma of ethics in engineering education. *Science and Engineering Ethics*, 10, 343–351; Harris, C. E. Jr., Davis, M., Pritchard, M. S., & Rabins, M. J. (1996). Engineering ethics: What? Why? How? And When? *Journal of Engineering Education* (April), 93–96.

21 May, D. R., & Luth, M. T. (2013). The effectiveness of ethics education: A quasi-experimental field study. *Science and Engineering Ethics,* 19, 545–568. doi: 10.1007/s11948-011-9349-0, citing May, D. R., Luth, M., & Schwoerer, C. E. (2009). The effects of business ethics education on moral efficacy, moral meaningfulness, and moral courage: A quasi-experimental study. In *Academy of Management Best Paper Proceedings*, Chicago, IL; Maddux, J. E. (2002). Self-efficacy: The power of believing you can. In C. R. Snyder & S. J. Lopez (Eds.), *Handbook of Positive Psychology* (pp. 277–287). Oxford: Oxford Press.

22 May, D. R., Luth, M., & Schwoerer, C. E. (2010). The effects of moral efficacy, moral courage, and moral meaningfulness on moral behaviors at work. In Paper presented at the 2010 Academy of

Researchers acknowledge the benefits of ethics training. For example, 70 per cent of respondents to a survey of UK-based researchers reported that professional development and training had a positive impact on research integrity, as long as individuals were motivated towards ethical behaviour and committed to recognising scientific integrity as integral to the values of scientific research.[23] A starting point for the surveyed researchers was to ensure that training in ethics and integrity is mandatory and that the core principles are integrated into all relevant institutional policies, processes and practices.[24] In practical terms, the UK House of Commons Science and Technology Committee found the picture to be mixed – some universities have mandatory ethics education and training requirements; others don't.[25]

Appropriate ethics education sets expectations for the whole research community, encourages consistent behaviour and removes validity from the inappropriate defence of 'plausible deniability,' the claim by a researcher that they didn't realise that what they were doing was wrong.[26] Research misconduct tends to be a solo activity, with narcissistic thinking playing a role, and selfishness on the part of some researchers tempting them to feel justified in making data fit their hypotheses, perhaps seeking to become 'superstars in their fields.'[27] Education and associated mentoring roles should address with students the inevitability of failure within the scientific enterprise, seeking to temper any self-imposed assumptions about the need to consistently succeed and associated temptation to bend or breach ethical principles, by redefining as part of

---

Management meeting in Montreal, Canada, cited in May, D. R., & Luth, M. T. (2013). The effectiveness of ethics education: A quasi-experimental field study. *Science and Engineering Ethics*, 19, 545–568. doi: 10.1007/s11948-011-9349-0

23 Metcalfe, J., Wheat, K., Munafò. M., Parry, J. (2020). *Research Integrity: A Landscape Study* (p. 31). Vitae/UK Research Integrity Office/UK Reproducibility Network, www.ukri.org/files/legacy/documents/research-integrity-main-report/

24 Kretser, A., Murphy, D., Bertuzzi, S., Abraham, T., Allison, D., Boor, K., Dwyer, J., Grantham, A., Harris, L., Hollander, R., Jacobs-Young, C., Rovito, S., Vafiadis, D., Woteki, C., Wyndham, J., & Yada, R. (2019). Scientific integrity principles and best practices: Recommendations from a scientific integrity consortium. *Science and Engineering Ethics*, 25. doi: 10.1007/s11948-019-00094-3.

25 House of Commons Science and Technology Committee, Research integrity, Sixth Report of Session 2017–19, 11 July 2018 HC 350, para 59. For example, Sheffield Hallam University highlighted the mandatory ethics training for doctoral students, including creating awareness of the collective responsibility to report any apparent ethical breaches. Collusion with and/or fail to report any apparent breaches of policy and procedures therefore constitutes research misconduct in its own right.

26 Alan Finkel, Office of the Chief Scientist. 'There is a problem': Australia's top scientist Alan Finkel pushes to eradicate bad science, September 12, 2019, https://theconversation.com/there-is-a-problem-australias-top-scientist-alan-finkel-pushes-to-eradicate-bad-science-123374 (accessed 14 September 2019)

27 DuBois D.Sc. Ph.D., J. M., Anderson Ph.D. M.P.H., E. E., Chibnall Ph.D., J., Carroll J.D. M.B.E., K., Gibb J.D., T., Ogbuka M.A. M.Div., C., & Rubbelke B.S., T. (2013). Understanding research misconduct: A comparative analysis of 120 cases of professional wrongdoing. *Accountability in Research*, 20, 5–6, 320–338. doi: 10.1080/08989621.2013.822248

the educational process the concept of failure.[28] By focusing on strategies to better enable researchers to question their own motives and judgement, address bias, more fully consider others, forecast consequences and seek help, ethics education should at least help to address such risks early.[29] With this in mind, ethics education and drafting professional codes of ethics should not be the preserve only of the most senior members of the profession. Long experience is of value, but so is contemporary understanding of the front-line challenges more junior researchers experience.[30] A representative range of voices should lead to the most informed ethics syllabuses and professional codes. In terms of maximising the value of the experiences of respected scientists, who have lived experientially with the ethical and regulatory dilemmas which arise from the practice of research, if such scientists cannot regularly devote the time to in-person education, case studies drawn from their experience offer an alternative.[31] Such studies need not focus entirely on issues of misconduct, but could include examples of appropriate behaviour adopted after a period of reflection and ethical deliberation.[32]

Ethics education should be more than a rite of passage on completion of a scientific degree, but rather a career-long exercise in maintaining an effective

28 In making this point Kornfeld draws from ORI data which found that over 50 per cent of graduate students and postdoctoral fellows reported a self-imposed need to perform well and associated stress as contributing factors to their acts of research misconduct. Kornfeld, D. S. (2012). Perspective: Research misconduct: The search for a remedy. *Acad Med,* 87, 877–882, 880, citing Davis, M., Riske-Morris, M., & Diaz, S. (2007). Causal factors implicated in research misconduct: Evidence from ORI case files. *Science and Engineering Ethics,* 13, 395–414

29 DuBois D.Sc. Ph.D., J. M., Anderson Ph.D. M.P.H., E. E., Chibnall Ph.D., J., Carroll J.D. M.B.E., K., Gibb J.D., T., Ogbuka M.A. M.Div., C., & Rubbelke B.S., T. (2013). Understanding research misconduct: A comparative analysis of 120 cases of professional wrongdoing. *Accountability in Research,* 20, 5–6, 320–338. doi: 10.1080/08989621.2013.822248, citing Mumford, M. D., Connelly, S., Brown, R. P., Murphy, S. T., Hill, J. H., Antes, A. L., Waples, E. P., & Devenport, L. D. (2008). A sensemaking approach to ethics training for scientists: Preliminary evidence of training effectiveness. *Ethics Behav.,* 18, 315–339; Gibbs, J. C. (2009). *Moral Development and Reality: Beyond the Theories of Kohlberg and Hoffman.* New York: Pearson.

30 Davis, M., & Keefer, M. (2011). Getting started: Helping a new profession develop an ethics program. *Science and Engineering Ethics,* 261, 19. doi: 10.1007/s11948-011-9279-x.

31 Kretser et al note that bodies such as the U.S. Department of Health and Human Services Office of Research Integrity (HHS ORI 2017) and the Canadian Secretariat on Responsible Conduct of Research utilise "Case Studies of Misconduct" within their educational programmes. Kretser, A., Murphy, D., Bertuzzi, S., Abraham, T., Allison, D., Boor, K., Dwyer, J., Grantham, A., Harris, L., Hollander, R., Jacobs-Young, C., Rovito, S., Vafiadis, D., Woteki, C., Wyndham, J., & Yada, R. (2019). Scientific integrity principles and best practices: Recommendations from a scientific integrity consortium. *Science and Engineering Ethics,* 25. doi: 10.1007/s11948-019-00094-3.

32 Kretser, A., Murphy, D., Bertuzzi, S., Abraham, T., Allison, D., Boor, K., Dwyer, J., Grantham, A., Harris, L., Hollander, R., Jacobs-Young, C., Rovito, S., Vafiadis, D., Woteki, C., Wyndham, J., & Yada, R. (2019). Scientific integrity principles and best practices: Recommendations from a scientific integrity consortium. *Science and Engineering Ethics,* 25. doi: 10.1007/s11948-019-00094-3.

culture of scientific integrity.[33] Different stages of a scientific career will give rise to different ethical challenges, including challenges which arise with advancing seniority, supervisory and team leading roles. Also, the ethics and integrity training experienced during initial study and the early career period will need to be updated to navigate new developments in the research environment. In essence, continuing ethics development is vital to ensure that scientific integrity remains at the forefront of researchers' minds.[34] It has been questioned by commentators involved in the rehabilitation of researchers who have fallen foul of conduct provisions whether a one-size-fits-all approach to training is particularly effective – intense, individualised training may be preferable.[35] The latter is likely to be impractical in a broad-ranging, pre-emptive ethics training model.[36]

Creating an 'ethical community' in an academic institution may be one of the best mechanisms for communicating ethical rules and standards.[37] In addition to members of scientific research communities, there is scope for lawyers, philosophers and other integrity experts to contribute to ethical and regulatory education.[38]

33 Casadevall, A., Ellis, L. M., Davies, E. W., McFall-Ngai, M., & Fang, F. C. (2016). A framework for improving the quality of research in the biological sciences. *mBio,* 7(4), e0125616, cited by Kretser, A., Murphy, D., Bertuzzi, S., Abraham, T., Allison, D., Boor, K., Dwyer, J., Grantham, A., Harris, L., Hollander, R., Jacobs-Young, C., Rovito, S., Vafiadis, D., Woteki, C., Wyndham, J., & Yada, R. (2019). Scientific integrity principles and best practices: Recommendations from a scientific integrity consortium. *Science and Engineering Ethics*, 25. doi: 10.1007/s11948-019-00094-3.

34 Kretser, A., Murphy, D., Bertuzzi, S., Abraham, T., Allison, D., Boor, K., Dwyer, J., Grantham, A., Harris, L., Hollander, R., Jacobs-Young, C., Rovito, S., Vafiadis, D., Woteki, C., Wyndham, J., & Yada, R. (2019). Scientific integrity principles and best practices: Recommendations from a scientific integrity consortium. *Science and Engineering Ethics*, 25. doi: 10.1007/s11948-019-00094-3. P-hacking is given as an example of a more recent development which should form part of each scientist's ethical awareness armoury, Head, M. L., Holman, L., Lanfear, R., Kahn, A. T., & Jennions, M. D. (2015). The extent and consequences of P-hacking in science. *PLoS Biology,* 13(3), e1002106.

35 DuBois, J., Chibnall, J., Tait, R., & Vander Wal, J. (2016). Misconduct: Lessons from researcher rehab. *Nature,* 534, 173–175. doi: 10.1038/534173a. www.nature.com/news/misconduct-lessons-from-researcher-rehab-1.20029.

36 DuBois, J., Chibnall, J., Tait, R., & Vander Wal, J. (2016). Misconduct: Lessons from researcher rehab. *Nature,* 534, 173–175. doi: 10.1038/534173a. www.nature.com/news/misconduct-lessons-from-researcher-rehab-1.20029.

37 McCabe, D. L., Trevino, L. K., & Butterfield, K. D. (2001). Cheating in academic institutions: A decade of research. *Ethics & Behavior,* 11(3), 219–233, 228.

38 Zwart, H. (2017). *Tales of Research Misconduct. Library of Ethics and Applied Philosophy* (Vol 36, p. 251). Cham: Springer. Integrity experts offer the potential to add to the conceptual toolbox for addressing ethical dilemmas by combining education and the theoretical aspects of integrity challenges with detecting and forensically unpicking actual suspected fraud.

Educational models also have to contend with concerns about the risk of stifling scientific creativity. For example, Feyerabend notes that:

> The history of science, after all, does not just consist of facts and conclusions drawn from facts. It also contains ideas, interpretations of facts, problems created by conflicting interpretations, mistakes, and so on. . .. This being the case, the history of science will be as complex, chaotic, full of mistakes, and entertaining as the ideas it contains, and these ideas in turn will be as complex, chaotic, full of mistakes, and entertaining as are the minds of those who invented them. Conversely, a little brainwashing will go a long way in making the history of science duller, simpler, more uniform, more 'objective' and more easily accessible to treatment by strict and unchangeable rules. Science education as we know it today has precisely this aim.[39]

From the perspective of this line of thinking, positive ethics is preferable, concentrating upon behaviour which is ethically positive rather than focusing upon punitive measures to deal with unethical behaviour.[40] Moral efficacy, moral courage and moral meaningfulness all play an important role in underpinning a positive ethics stance.[41]

Cultural and jurisdictional differences

Standards and expectations differ between jurisdictions. Standards of ethical research conduct are not universal, with some jurisdictional and cultural differences.[42] In some jurisdictions the focus of education is primarily on

39 Paul Feyerabend, *Against Method* (Verso, New York, NY, 2010), p. 3.

40 May, D. R., Luth, M., & Schwoerer, C. E. (2009). The effects of business ethics education on moral efficacy, moral meaningfulness, and moral courage: A quasi-experimental study. In *Academy of Management Best Paper Proceedings*, Chicago, IL. Cited by May, D. R., & Luth, M. T. (2013). The effectiveness of ethics education: A quasi-experimental field study. *Science and Engineering Ethics*, 19, 545–568. doi: 10.1007/s11948-011-9349-0

41 May, D. R., Luth, M., & Schwoerer, C. E. (2010). The effects of moral efficacy, moral courage, and moral meaningfulness on moral behaviors at work. In Paper presented at the 2010 Academy of Management meeting in Montreal, Canada. Cited by May, D. R., & Luth, M. T. (2013). The effectiveness of ethics education: A quasi-experimental field study. *Science and Engineering Ethics*, 19, 545–568. doi: 10.1007/s11948-011-9349-0

42 Leonard, M., Schwieder, D. Buhler, A., Bennett, D. B., & Royster, M. (2015). Perceptions of plagiarism by STEM graduate students: A case study. *Science and Engineering Ethics*, 21(6), 1587–1608, citing, inter alia, Handa, N., & Power, C. (2005). Land and discover! A case study investigating the cultural context of plagiarism. *Journal of University Teaching and Learning Practice*, 2(3), 64–84; Ramburuth, P., & McCormick, J. (2001). Learning diversity in higher education: A comparative study of Asian international and Australian students. *Higher Education*, 42(3), 333–350; Buranen, L. (1999). But I wasn't cheating: Plagiarism and cross-cultural mythology. In L. Buranen, & A. M. Roy (Eds.), *Perspectives on Plagiarism and Intellectual Property in a Postmodern World* (p. 66). Albany, NY: State University of New York Press; Swearingen, J. C. (1999). Originality, authenticity, imitation, and

compliance, with little or no engagement with broader ethical considerations or with practical matters such as how to make decisions in problematic circumstances and appropriate ways to engage with colleagues (including senior ones) over concerns about data and other matters.[43] For example, it has been argued that in Japan respect for professors can make it difficult to doubt their integrity or competence, making the application of ethics education and willingness by researchers at all levels of seniority to question the behaviour of fellow researchers and report concerns problematic to implement.[44]

In the United States in the last few decades education in responsible conduct of research has seen significant developments, in large part due to the work of the National Institutes of Health and the National Science Foundation.[45] Cao notes some key differences between the positions in China and the United States:

> American ethical education promotes faith in freedom, democracy, and rational inquiry from various religions and Logos philosophy. Chinese moral education advocates humanism and goodness from Confucianism culture and Tao philosophy.[46]

Approaches in the United States often place greater emphasis on student self-awareness, ethical reasoning and strong decision-making abilities – the overall focus being upon specific ethics behaviours. In contrast, ethical ideology and politics are identified as playing a greater role in Chinese education – professional expertise combined with ideological loyalty to socialism and general 'moral spirit.'[47] It has also been observed that research integrity in the

plagiarism: Augustine's Chinese cousins. In L. Buranen & A. M. Roy (Eds.), *Perspectives on Plagiarism and Intellectual Property in a Postmodern World*. New York: State University of New York Press.

43 For discussion, by way of example, of the position in Australia see Alan Finkel, Office of the Chief Scientist. 'There is a problem': Australia's top scientist Alan Finkel pushes to eradicate bad science, September 12, 2019, https://theconversation.com/there-is-a-problem-australias-top-scientist-alan-finkel-pushes-to-eradicate-bad-science-123374 (accessed 14 September 2019); Gunsalus, C. K. and Robinson, Aaron D. (2018). Nine pitfalls of research misconduct. *Nature*, 557, 297–299. doi: 10.1038/d41586-018-05145-6.

44 Kupferschmidt, K. (2018). Researcher at the center of an epic fraud remains an enigma to those who exposed him. *Science*, August 17, 2018, www.sciencemag.org/news/2018/08/researcher-center-epic-fraud-remains-enigma-those-who-exposed-him

45 NIH. (1989). Requirements for programs on the responsible conduct of research in national research service award institutional training programs. Guide for Grants and Contracts, 18(45), 1; NSF. (2010). B. Responsible conduct of research in grantee standards. Cited by Kalichman, M., Sweet, M., & Plemmons, D. (2014). Standards of scientific conduct: Are there any? *Sci Eng Ethics*, 20, 885–896. doi: 10.1007/s11948-013-9500-1

46 Cao, G. H. (2015). Comparison of China-US engineering ethics educations in Sino-western philosophies of technology. *Sci Eng Ethics*, 21, 1609–1635. doi: 10.1007/s11948-014-9611-3

47 Cao, G. H. (2015). Comparison of China-US engineering ethics educations in Sino-western philosophies of technology. *Sci Eng Ethics*, 21, 1609–1635. doi: 10.1007/s11948-014-9611-3, citing Li, Z. C., & Wei, H. Y. (2008). Comparison and suggestion on engineering ethics education of

United States is taught in the context of everyday practice of science, including active learning via, for example, role-playing, moot courts and debate competitions. In contrast, the approach in China focuses more on teacher-centred, cramming models of learning, potentially at the expense of students developing ethical initiative.[48]

In the UK, the Universities UK Concordat to Support Research Integrity addresses training in general terms, requiring signatories to provide a suitable learning environment and mentoring opportunities in pursuit of the broader goal to support the cultural integrity of the research environment. Mentorship, underpinned by high-quality mentor training, is vital, given the correlation between some instances of misconduct and deficiencies in the mentoring of the individual who committed the misconduct.[49] In a 2019 update to the 2012 Concordat, it was initially suggested that it would provide for mandatory training in research ethics to 'embed a culture of research integrity,' but shortly before publication it was reported that 'mandatory' had been dropped due to fears that this approach would be unduly prescriptive and bureaucratic in terms of precise levels and frequency of ethics training.[50] As an alternative, institutions will be expected to report regarding the training they have provided as part of their annual statements.[51] Research Councils UK (RCUK) requires that postgraduate students are trained 'in the principles of good research conduct in their discipline, and understand how to comply with relevant ethical, legal and professional frameworks,' including training to address unintentional bias.

Sino-US. *Research in Higher Education of Engineering*, (1), 44–47; Zhu, Q. (2010). Engineering ethics studies in China: Dialogue between traditionalism and modernism. *Engineering Studies*, 2(2), 85–107.

48 Grinnell, F. (2009). *Everyday Practice of Science: Where Intuition and Passion Meet Objectivity and Logic*. New York: Oxford University Press; Cao, G. H. (2015). Comparison of China-US engineering ethics educations in Sino-western philosophies of technology. *Sci Eng Ethics*, 21, 1609–1635. doi: 10.1007/s11948-014-9611-3. See, also, Bain, K. (2011). *What the Best College Teachers Do*. Cambridge, MA: Harvard University Press; Herkert, J. R. (2002). Continuing and emerging issues in engineering ethics education. *Bridge*, 32(3), 8–13.

49 Wright, D. E., Titus, S. L., & Cornelison, J. B. (2008). Mentoring and research misconduct: An analysis of research mentoring in closed ORI cases. *Science and Engineering Ethics*, 14(3), 323–336; Kretser, A., Murphy, D., Bertuzzi, S., Abraham, T., Allison, D., Boor, K., Dwyer, J., Grantham, A., Harris, L., Hollander, R., Jacobs-Young, C., Rovito, S., Vafiadis, D., Woteki, C., Wyndham, J., & Yada, R. (2019). Scientific integrity principles and best practices: Recommendations from a scientific integrity consortium. *Science and Engineering Ethics*, 25. doi: 10.1007/s11948-019-00094-3. The UK House of Commons Science and Technology Committee also recommended that guidance be provided to universities on best practice in delivering training to doctoral supervisors.

50 Grove, J. (2019). UK's plan for 'mandatory' research ethics training dropped. *Times Higher Education*, September 10, 2019, www.timeshighereducation.com/news/uks-plan-mandatory-research-ethics-training-dropped

51 Grove, J. (2019). UK's plan for 'mandatory' research ethics training dropped. *Times Higher Education*, September 10, 2019, www.timeshighereducation.com/news/uks-plan-mandatory-research-ethics-training-dropped

However, monitoring of compliance is not comprehensive, primarily relying upon what is described as a 'dipstick' approach to monitoring.[52] These steps appear to fall short of the expectations of the House of Commons Science and Technology Committee.

The effectiveness of ethics education

The multi-faceted nature of scientific research, complexity within and between scientific fields and interpersonal skills necessary for the interactions involved in a complex, often 'ill structured' organisational landscape all give rise to challenges regarding the content and extent of approaches to teach prospective scientists about ethical behaviour.[53] Research findings paint a mixed picture in terms of the effectiveness of ethics education. For example, while trainee and junior scientists who had undertaken ethics training reported increased understanding, knowledge and ability to identify ethical issues, on the whole future behaviour wasn't found to have been significantly changed – someone tempted to act unethically is unlikely to change their behaviour simply because they have an increased awareness of ethics.[54] For example, ethics education has not generally been found to improve moral reasoning in terms of abstract philosophical ideas, ethical decision-making skills or ethical discussion among students outside of class.[55] Only practical knowledge of conduct practices was found to show measurable improvement.[56]

52 House of Commons Science and Technology Committee, Research integrity, Sixth Report of Session 2017–19, 11 July 2018 HC 350, para 61

53 May, D. R., & Luth, M. T. (2013). The effectiveness of ethics education: A quasi-experimental field study. *Science and Engineering Ethics*, 19, 545–568. doi: 10.1007/s11948-011-9349-0; Jonassen, D., Strobel, J., & Lee, C. B. (2006). Everyday problem solving in engineering: Lessons for engineering educators. *Journal of Engineering Education*, 95(2), 139–151.

54 Kornfeld, D. S. (2012). Perspective: Research misconduct: The search for a remedy. *Acad Med*, 87, 877–882, 877, citing Plemmons, D. K., Brody, S. A., & Kalichman, M. W. (2006). Student perceptions of the effectiveness of education in the responsible conduct of research. *Science and Engineering Ethics*, 12, 571–582; Powell, S. T., Allison, M. A., & Kalichman, M. W. (2007). Effectiveness of a responsible conduct of research course: A preliminary study. *Science and Engineering Ethics*, 13, 249–264; Antes, A. L., Wang, X., Mumford, M. D., Brown, R. P., Connelly, S., & Devenport, L. D. (2010). Evaluating the effects that existing instruction on responsible conduct of research has on ethical decision making. *Acad Med.*, 85, 519–526.

55 Thomsen, M. (2007). A course treating ethical issues in physics. *Science and Engineering Ethics*, 13(1), 117–127. doi: 10.1007/s11948-011-9349-–0, citing Antes, A. L., Murphy, S. T., Waples, E. P., Mumford, M. D., Brown, R. P., Connelly, S. et al. (2009). A meta-analysis of ethics instruction effectiveness in the sciences. *Ethics and Behavior*, 19(5), 379–402; Powell, S. T., Allison, M. A., & Kalichman, M. W. (2007). Effectiveness of a responsible conduct of research course: A preliminary study. *Science and Engineering Ethics*, 13, 249–264; Plemmons, D. K., Brody, S. A., & Kalichman, M. W. (2006). Student perceptions of the effectiveness of education in the responsible conduct of research. *Science and Engineering Ethics*, 12, 571–582.

56 Thomsen, M. (2007). A course treating ethical issues in physics. *Science and Engineering Ethics*, 13(1), 117–127. doi: 10.1007/s11948-011-9349-–0, citing Antes, A. L., Murphy, S. T., Waples, E. P.,

One meta-analysis of previous studies found that stand-alone approaches, rather than those which embedded ethics education within other subjects, had the greatest effect on moral development and ethical decision making.[57] However, other studies have found ethics education generally to be advantageous when compared with a control group absent such education, but whether the ethics course was embedded or stand-alone made no notable difference in terms of outcomes.[58] Interactive approaches involving case study examples have been found to be particularly effective in developing professional identities which had strong ethical underpinnings, as was teaching students to view ethical issues from different perspectives in terms of stakeholder experience in the interests of enhancing their 'ethical sensitivity' and 'ethical imagination.'[59] In the latter context, empathising with the perspective of others enhances the likelihood that alternative ethical solutions will be imagined.[60]

Mumford, M. D., Brown, R. P., Connelly, S. et al. (2009). A meta-analysis of ethics instruction effectiveness in the sciences. *Ethics and Behavior*, 19(5), 379–402; Powell, S. T., Allison, M. A., & Kalichman, M. W. (2007). Effectiveness of a responsible conduct of research course: A preliminary study. *Science and Engineering Ethics*, 13(2), 249–264; Plemmons, D. K., Brody, S. A., & Kalichman, M. W. (2006). Student perceptions of the effectiveness of education in the responsible conduct of research. *Science and Engineering Ethics*, 12, 571–582.

57 Antes, A. L., Murphy, S. T., Waples, E. P., Mumford, M. D., Brown, R. P., Connelly, S. et al. (2009). A meta-analysis of ethics instruction effectiveness in the sciences. *Ethics and Behavior*, 19(5), 379–402.

58 May, D. R., & Luth, M. T. (2013). The effectiveness of ethics education: A quasi-experimental field study. *Science and Engineering Ethics*, 19, 545–568. doi: 10.1007/s11948-011-9349-0. In particular, understanding of appropriate research conduct, moral judgment, moral efficacy or moral courage did not increase by a greater extent because a course was stand-alone rather than embedded within other subjects.

59 Antes, A. L., Murphy, S. T., Waples, E. P., Mumford, M. D., Brown, R. P., Connelly, S. et al. (2009). A meta-analysis of ethics instruction effectiveness in the sciences. *Ethics and Behavior*, 19(5), 379–402; Harris, C. E. Jr., Davis, M., Pritchard, M. S., & Rabins, M. J. (1996, April). Engineering ethics: What? Why? How? And When? *Journal of Engineering Education*, 93–96, discussed in May, D. R., & Luth, M. T. (2013). The effectiveness of ethics education: A quasi-experimental field study. *Science and Engineering Ethics*, 19, 545–568. doi: 10.1007/s11948-011-9349-0

60 Harris, C. E. Jr., Davis, M., Pritchard, M. S., & Rabins, M. J. (1996). Engineering ethics: What? Why? How? And When? *Journal of Engineering Education* (April), 93–96, discussed in May, D. R., & Luth, M. T. (2013). The effectiveness of ethics education: A quasi-experimental field study. *Science and Engineering Ethics*, 19, 545–568. doi: 10.1007/s11948-011-9349-0

Chapter 6

Institutional regulation

Institutional roles in research integrity and regulation

In the absence of a well-developed professional regulatory body, academic institutions play an essential part in the protection of research integrity. Universities and research institutes are indispensable to the provision of a 'supportive moral scaffold' by providing appropriately ethical research environments, demonstrating best practice and being well placed to investigate alleged research misconduct by their employees.[1] Institutional practices or guidelines influence local research culture, but personalities and management styles of research leaders have been found to be stronger drivers of research integrity, with culture and people within local research environments also being 'perceived to have strong and persistent influences.'[2]

Institutional research ethics committees play a key role in ensuring that all relevant research projects have the necessary ethical foundations.[3] To be most effective, ethics approval processes need to balance robustness with ease of use, not being unduly lengthy or complex, and to demonstrate consistency of decision making, for example, between different reviewers.[4]

1 Zwart, H. (2017). *Tales of Research Misconduct. Library of Ethics and Applied Philosophy* (Vol 36, p. 34). Cham: Springer; Universities UK (2019, October). *The Concordat to Support Research Integrity*; Grey, A., Bolland, M., Gamble, G. et al. (2019). Quality of reports of investigations of research integrity by academic institutions. *Res Integr Peer Rev*, 4, 3 https://doi.org/10.1186/s41073-019-0062-x, citing Gunsalus, C. K., Marcus, A. R., & Oransky, I. (2018). Institutional research misconduct reports need more credibility. *JAMA*, 319(13), 1315–1316. doi: 10.1001/jama.2018.0358

2 Metcalfe, J., Wheat, K., Munafò. M., Parry, J. (2020). *Research Integrity: A Landscape Study*. Vitae/UK Research Integrity Office/UK Reproducibility Network. A survey of UK researchers found that awareness of institutional ethics approval processes was very high, at 97 per cent

3 Metcalfe, J., Wheat, K., Munafò. M., Parry, J. (2020). *Research Integrity: A Landscape Study* (p. 29). Vitae/UK Research Integrity Office/UK Reproducibility Network.

4 Metcalfe, J., Wheat, K., Munafò. M., Parry, J. (2020). *Research Integrity: A Landscape Study* (p. 29). Vitae/UK Research Integrity Office/UK Reproducibility Network.

DOI: 10.4324/9780429492129-6

Institutions may employ codes of conduct as part of their research integrity processes, but it is particularly challenging to devise and implement regulatory provisions which garner widespread support among the regulated community, are effective and are readily understood. Evidence suggests that relatively small numbers of researchers may be aware of the content of their institution's code, with similarly low numbers being aware of the existence or the details of institutional processes for reporting research misconduct.[5] Some researchers express concerns that some research governance processes may negatively impact upon scientific endeavour and creativity if, for example, they are excessively bureaucratic and 'disconnected from academic realities,' such that it may be difficult or even impossible to convert policies to inform day-to-day practice, or 'reinforce broader systemic pressures,' such as emphasising productivity at speed rather than recognising and rewarding conscientiousness.[6] There are also risks that within institutions the competing pressure of enforcing research integrity with maintaining institutional reputation may result in concerns being prematurely dismissed. Examples from the United States warn against placing the power to dismiss at an early stage in the hands of too small a group and the need for transparency and appropriate record keeping in terms of the reasons for dismissal.[7] Overall, individual researchers may find themselves caught in an environment of 'conflicting imperatives and expectations.'[8]

Adding detail to codes may be tempting, although given the complexity and variety of research undertaken within a large university, this may prove challenging. Also, lessons from the regulation of other professions suggest that

5 Metcalfe, J., Wheat, K., Munafò. M., Parry, J. (2020). *Research Integrity: A Landscape Study* (p. 28). Vitae/UK Research Integrity Office/UK Reproducibility Network. www.ukri.org/files/legacy/documents/research-integrity-main-report/. Fifty per cent of respondents were aware of their institution's procedures for reporting misconduct, 43 per cent were aware that an institutional process for reporting research misconduct existed but were unfamiliar with the detail and 22 per cent claimed to be entirely unaware of the process. Researchers were also concerned about insufficient institutional protection were they to raise concerns about research integrity, with only 53 per cent stating they would be comfortable doing this without fear of reprisals. Around 50 per cent of respondents considered that institutional research strategies had either a positive impact on research integrity or combined positive and negative aspects.

6 Metcalfe, J., Wheat, K., Munafò. M., Parry, J. (2020). *Research Integrity: A Landscape Study* (pp. 21, 28, 44). Vitae/UK Research Integrity Office/UK Reproducibility Network, www.ukri.org/files/legacy/documents/research-integrity-main-report/. Elements of inconsistency may also emerge within institutions if approaches to ethics are localised and frameworks and policies are interpreted and implemented in different ways within the same institution.

7 Loikith, L., & Bauchwitz, R. (2016)., The essential need for research misconduct allegation audits. *Science and Engineering Ethics*, 22, 1027–1049. doi 10.1007/s11948-9798-6. In the UK there are historical examples from the regulation of the medical profession with problems of excessive screening out of complaints at very early stages in the regulatory process, Davies, M. (2007). *Medical Self-regulation, Crisis and Change*. London and New York: Routledge.

8 Zwart, H. (2017). *Tales of Research Misconduct. Library of Ethics and Applied Philosophy* (Vol 36, p. 35). Cham: Springer.

greater detail in ethical codes may reduce further the likelihood that the regulated community will fully read and absorb them.[9] There is also the risk that the more detailed the code, the more likely the assumptions that anything not specifically prohibited by the code is permissible. Some professions, for example, solicitors in England and Wales, have moved in the direction of shorter codes with more general statements regarding ethics and integrity, with the intention that members of the regulated community will reflect more carefully on the ethical considerations relevant to their proposed behaviour. If such approaches are successful, the regulated individual may be inclined to exercise greater caution – avoiding potentially problematic behaviours if they are in any doubt regarding their ethical appropriateness. Education to encourage ethical engagement and the deterrent effect of potential enforcement action are intended to further encourage reflection and compliance.[10]

Institutional codes and processes should complement the responsibilities of other role holders in seeking to ensure the integrity of the research process. For example, as discussed previously, if the suspicions of a journal editor or research funder are aroused regarding potential misconduct, the institution employing the researcher is often better placed than the journal editor, publisher or funder to investigate.[11] Institutions are also better placed and possess legal legitimacy to adjudicate and to ensure that those accused of research misconduct are afforded due process.[12] Institutional investigations provide the focus for considering the conduct of the researcher, while the complementary focus of the journal is to consider whether the research is trustworthy, reliable and appropriately reported. These elements give rise to challenges which need to be addressed in different ways.[13] While some leading journals, for example, *Nature* and *Science*, have been addressing issues relating to rigour and reproducibility by introducing new methods of data analysis, many universities and other employers of

9 For example, historical evidence from the medical profession in the UK suggested that knowledge of the relevant professional code was selective and limited, Davies, M. (2007). *Medical Self-regulation, Crisis and Change*. London and New York: Routledge; Case, P. (2013). Doctoring Confidence and Soliciting Trust: Models of Professional Discipline in Law and Medicine. *Journal of Professional Negligence*, 29(2), 87–107.

10 See, for example, www.sra.org.uk/sra/consultations/ofr/annexd-equality-ofr/ (accessed 12 August 2021)

11 Wager, E., Kleinert, S., Garfinkel, M., Volker Bahr, C., et al. (2017). Cooperation & Liaison between Universities & Editors (CLUE): Recommendations on best practice. *bioRxiv*. doi: https://doi.org/10.1101/139170; Grey, A., Bolland, M., Gamble, G. et al. (2019). Quality of reports of investigations of research integrity by academic institutions. *Res Integr Peer Rev*, 4, 3 https://doi.org/10.1186/s41073-019-0062-x

12 Smith, R. (2006). Research misconduct: The poisoning of the well. *Journal of the Royal Society of Medicine*, 99, 232–237, 235. doi: 10.1258/jrsm.99.5.232.

13 Wager, E., Kleinert, S., Garfinkel, M., Volker Bahr, C., et al. (2017). Cooperation & Liaison between Universities & Editors (CLUE): Recommendations on best practice. *bioRxiv*. doi: https://doi.org/10.1101/139170.

researchers may be seen to be lagging behind in terms of equivalent initiatives in their regulatory realms.[14]

While journal editors may report misconduct to institutions to facilitate further investigation, instances of institutions proactively contacting journals to suggest retraction following the outcome of an institutional misconduct investigation are rare.[15] For example, in the case of Yoshihiro Sato, it has been suggested that institutional focus on researcher misconduct, rather than balancing this with considerations of the reliability of published outputs, significantly slowed the retraction process and permitted some papers and clinical trial reports to remain unretracted and to continue to be cited by other researchers for far longer than was necessary.[16] A contrasting example is that of the Laskowski Lab at UC Davis which acknowledged the importance, in the interests of protecting the scientific record, of voluntarily retracting publications when it became clear that the data from which they were developed could no longer be trusted.[17]

Overall, universities have tended to be reluctant to investigate research misconduct.[18] Investigating misconduct and differentiating it from unintentional errors in the research process is complex and time consuming. Universities can be fearful of reputational damage and legal challenges if the accused decides to seek to protect their professional reputation in the courtroom.[19] Taking this further, universities may find themselves conflicted by contemporary research environments simultaneously tending to encourage risk taking to promote innovative research, but discouraging risk taking by requiring researchers to adhere to 'strict ethical and methodological codes and guidelines.'[20] Such conflict

14 Begley, C. G., Buchan, A. M., & Dirnagl, U. (2015). Robust research: Institutions must do their part for reproducibility. *Nature,* 525, 25–27. https://doi.org/10.1038/525025a. For example, *Science* has added statisticians to its panel of reviewing editors and checklists which require researchers to confirm whether they followed practices such as randomising, blinding and calculating appropriate sample size.

15 House of Commons Science and Technology Committee, Research integrity, Sixth Report of Session 2017–19, 11 July 2018 HC 350, para 92

16 Avenell, A., Stewart, F., Grey, A. et al. (2019). An investigation into the impact and implications of published papers from retracted research: Systematic search of affected literature. *BMJ Open*, 9, e031909. doi: 10.1136/bmjopen-2019-031909; Grey, A., Avenell, A., Klein, A. A., & Gunsalus, C.K. (2020). Check for publication integrity before misconduct. *Nature*, 577, 167–169 doi: https://doi.org/10.1038/d41586-019-03959-6

17 Laskowski Lab at UC Davis, What to do when you don't trust your data anymore, January 29, 2020, https://laskowskilab.faculty.ucdavis.edu/2020/01/29/retractions/ (accessed 30 January 2020)

18 Tourish, D. (2019). *Management Studies in Crisis: Fraud, Deception and Meaningless Research*. Cambridge: Cambridge University Press.

19 Editorial (2014). Retraction challenges *Nature*, 514, 5 (October 2). doi: 10.1038/514005a

20 Zwart, H. (2017). *Tales of Research Misconduct. Library of Ethics and Applied Philosophy* (Vol 36, p. 35). Cham: Springer.

potentially impedes institutional capacity to appropriately regulate research.[21] Moves towards a business model of science 'producing "goods" or "outputs" to be exchanged in a global market' has been enshrined in such a manner that many universities now operate in a way which negatively influences research ethics.[22] Institutions may benefit from 'perverse incentives' which allow them to enjoy 'the reflected glory of their faculty' if breakthroughs are published in prestigious journals and highlighted in the media.[23] If the desire to receive such accolades becomes too prominent, institutional messaging may tempt individual researchers to cut corners or artificially inflate their achievements. Comparisons have been drawn with the banking sector in the global financial crisis of the late 2000s. An earlier move from a salary focus to a bonus-based focus resulted in the development of inappropriate values which impeded legal and regulatory compliance.[24] While universities seek to protect brand image and prioritise external performance measures, there is a risk that ethical and regulatory control considerations will be downplayed, side-lined or, at the extreme, concerns may not even meet with an institutional response.[25] For example, in the Macchiarini case it has been suggested that Macchiarini was employed by

21 Loikith, L., & Bauchwitz, R. (2016)., The essential need for research misconduct allegation audits. *Science and Engineering Ethics*, 22, 1027–1049. doi: 10.1007/s11948-9798-6, citing Pozzi, A., & David, P. (2007). Empirical realities of scientific misconduct in publicly funded research: What can be learned from the data? In *ESF-ORI First World Conference on Scientific Integrity – Fostering Responsible Research.* http://www-siepr.stanford.edu/papers/pdf/Pozzi-David_FullText.pdf (accessed 10 December 2015); Kroll, J. (2014). *NSF OIG: Stories from the Case Files.* www.cuny.edu/research/compliance/training-education/plagiarism/Jim_Kroll_CUNY_Plagiarism_Conference_2014.ppt (accessed 10 December 2015). Some comparisons are made with the financial crisis of the late 2000s and the business model associated with accounting firms undertaking both auditing and consulting services to corporations prior to the Enron and other financial scandals which led to the enactment of the federal Sarbanes-Oxley Act of 2002. The desire to sell consulting services, it has been argued, placed accounting firms in a conflicted position with regard to robustly and critically auditing the same clients.

22 Begley, C. G., Buchan, A. M., & Dirnagl, U. (2015). Robust research: Institutions must do their part for reproducibility. *Nature,* 525, 25–27. https://doi.org/10.1038/525025a

23 Begley, C. G., Buchan, A. M., & Dirnagl, U. (2015). Robust research: Institutions must do their part for reproducibility. *Nature,* 525, 25–27. https://doi.org/10.1038/525025a

24 Finkel, A. Office of the Chief Scientist (2019). 'There is a problem': Australia's top scientist Alan Finkel pushes to eradicate bad science, September 12, 2019, https://theconversation.com/there-is-a-problem-australias-top-scientist-alan-finkel-pushes-to-eradicate-bad-science-123374 (accessed 14 September 2019).

25 Kranke, P. (2012). Putting the record straight: Granisetron's efficacy as an antiemetic 'post-Fujii'. *Anaesthesia*, 67, 1063–1067. https://doi.org/10.1111/j.1365-2044.2012.07318.x; Craig, R., Pelosi, T., & Tourish, D. (2020). Research misconduct complaints and institutional logics: The case of Hans Eysenck and the British Psychological Society. *Journal of health psychology (pre-print), citing* Huzzard, T., Benner, M., & Karreman, D. (Eds.). (2017). *The Corporatization of the Business School: Minerva Meets the Market.* London: Routledge; Grey, A., Bolland, M., Gamble, G. et al. (2019). Quality of reports of investigations of research integrity by academic institutions. *Res Integr Peer Rev*, 4, 3 https://doi.org/10.1186/s41073-019-0062-x

the prestigious Karolinska Institute in Sweden despite some negative professional references. Warning signs were side-lined at the appointment stage and when Macchiarini's employment contract was renewed in 2013 and 2015.[26] In the context of such an environment, it has been suggested that the Karolinska Institute may initially have been drawn towards attempts to manage criticism and support their 'star scientist.'[27]

Creating universally acknowledged metrics that measure scientific integrity could help to drive adherence towards ethical behaviour.[28] Mentoring, evidence of ongoing education in matters of scientific integrity, preregistering of research plans, the publication of unanticipated findings, proactively correcting the research record and other activities could be included in a lengthened list of metrics.[29] An ongoing review of the effectiveness of particular metrics in influencing behaviour in the direction of scientific integrity would aim to ensure that the list of metrics continued to be as effective as possible.[30]

When formal investigations are undertaken within institutions, appropriately independent committees, with external expert input as necessary, should be in place.[31] In practice, concerns about institutional capacity to objectively, thoroughly and transparently investigate the behaviour of employees have been

26 Editorial (2016). Macchiarini scandal is a valuable lesson for the Karolinska Institute. *Nature,* 537, 137 (September 8). doi: 10.1038/537137a

27 McKelvey, M., Saemundsson, R. J., & Zaring, O. (2018). A recent crisis in regenerative medicine: Analyzing governance in order to identify public policy issues. *Science and Public Policy*, 45(5) (October), 608–620, 617. https://doi.org/10.1093/scipol/scx085. At later stages the Karolinska Institute was able to counter some of the criticism directed at it from within and without the scientific community by adopting an approach of complete openness and transparency. Editorial (2016). Macchiarini scandal is a valuable lesson for the Karolinska Institute. *Nature,* 537, 137 (September 8). doi: 10.1038/537137a

28 Kretser, A., Murphy, D., Bertuzzi, S., Abraham, T., Allison, D., Boor, K., Dwyer, J., Grantham, A., Harris, L., Hollander, R., Jacobs-Young, C., Rovito, S., Vafiadis, D., Woteki, C., Wyndham, J., & Yada, R. (2019). Scientific integrity principles and best practices: Recommendations from a scientific integrity consortium. *Science and Engineering Ethics*, 25. doi: 10.1007/s11948-019-00094-3.

29 Kretser, A., Murphy, D., Bertuzzi, S., Abraham, T., Allison, D., Boor, K., Dwyer, J., Grantham, A., Harris, L., Hollander, R., Jacobs-Young, C., Rovito, S., Vafiadis, D., Woteki, C., Wyndham, J., & Yada, R. (2019). Scientific integrity principles and best practices: Recommendations from a scientific integrity consortium. *Science and Engineering Ethics*, 25. doi: 10.1007/s11948-019-00094-3.

30 Kretser, A., Murphy, D., Bertuzzi, S., Abraham, T., Allison, D., Boor, K., Dwyer, J., Grantham, A., Harris, L., Hollander, R., Jacobs-Young, C., Rovito, S., Vafiadis, D., Woteki, C., Wyndham, J., & Yada, R. (2019). Scientific integrity principles and best practices: Recommendations from a scientific integrity consortium. *Science and Engineering Ethics*, 25. doi: 10.1007/s11948-019-00094-3., citing National Academies of Sciences, Engineering, and Medicine. (2017). *Fostering Integrity in Research*. Washington, DC: National Academies Press, www.nap.edu/catalog/21896/fostering-integrity-in-research

31 Lerouge, I., & Hol, A. (2020). *Towards a Research Integrity Culture at Universities: From Recommendations to Implementation*. Advice Paper no. 26 – January 2020, League of European Research Universities, 17, www.leru.org/files/Towards-a-Research-Integrity-Culture-at-Universities-full-paper.pdf (accessed 11 February 2020)

raised, as has the consistency of reporting findings.[32] Sometimes those appointed to internal investigatory bodies lack the necessary expertise, relevant questions are not always asked and investigations are not expanded beyond the narrow parameters of the particular allegation.[33] Finding fault with an individual may be seen to be an end to the matter when others were involved. Psychological tendencies towards protecting group identity may also influence institutional decision making.[34] Some institutional investigations also focus upon unduly restrictive definitions of misconduct, for example, paying attention only to fabrication, falsification and plagiarism, and failing to address broader-ranging consideration such as research governance, implausible productivity and implausible data.[35] An example of some of these issues arose from findings by researchers looking at the institutional investigations into Yoshihiro Sato. Having requested reports from each of the institutions which had investigated Sato, they concluded that all of these reports were unclear about certain key issues and had neglected to address all potentially affected publications.[36] There was no evidence from the reports that any of the institutions had sought to collaborate with any of the other institutions.[37] The researchers concluded that there was growing evidence to support the proposition that investigations by

32 Grey, A., Bolland, M., Gamble, G. et al. (2019). Quality of reports of investigations of research integrity by academic institutions. *Res Integr Peer Rev*, 4, 3 https://doi.org/10.1186/s41073-019-0062-x citing, inter alia, Addressing research misconduct and detrimental research practices: Current knowledge and issues. in National Academies of Sciences, Engineering, and Medicine (2017). *Fostering Integrity in Research*. Washington, DC: The National Academies Press.

33 Gunsalus, C. K., Marcus, A. R., & Oransky, I. (2018). Institutional research misconduct reports need more credibility. *JAMA*, 319(13), 1315–1316. doi: 10.1001/jama.2018.0358

34 Gunsalus, C. K., Marcus, A. R., & Oransky, I. (2018). Institutional research misconduct reports need more credibility. *JAMA*, 319(13), 1315–1316. doi: 10.1001/jama.2018.0358, citing Valdesolo, P., & DeSteno, D. (2007). Moral hypocrisy: social groups and the flexibility of virtue. *Psychol Sci.*, 18(8), 689–690; Grey, A., Bolland, M., Gamble, G. et al. (2019). Quality of reports of investigations of research integrity by academic institutions. *Res Integr Peer Rev*, 4, 3 https://doi.org/10.1186/s41073-019-0062-x

35 Grey, A., Bolland, M., Gamble, G. et al. (2019). Quality of reports of investigations of research integrity by academic institutions. *Res Integr Peer Rev*, 4, 3 https://doi.org/10.1186/s41073-019-0062-x. It is also important that these considerations are weighed alongside the importance of maintaining the integrity of the research record. See, for example, Else, H. (2019). What universities can learn from one of science's biggest frauds. *Nature*, 570, 287–288. doi: 10.1038/d41586-019-01884-2

36 Grey, A., Bolland, M., Gamble, G. et al. (2019). Quality of reports of investigations of research integrity by academic institutions. *Res Integr Peer Rev*, 4, 3 https://doi.org/10.1186/s41073-019-0062-x

37 Else, H. (2019). What universities can learn from one of science's biggest frauds. *Nature*, 570, 287–288. doi: 10.1038/d41586-019-01884-2; Grey, A., Bolland, M., Gamble, G. et al. (2019). Quality of reports of investigations of research integrity by academic institutions. *Res Integr Peer Rev*, 4, 3 https://doi.org/10.1186/s41073-019-0062-x. Other studies of institutional research regulation have identified more positive approaches involving project participants from more than one institution, with institutional collaboration when investigating suspected misconduct. Grey, A., Bolland, M., Gamble, G. et al. (2019). Quality of reports of investigations of research integrity by academic institutions. *Res Integr Peer Rev*, 4, 3 https://doi.org/10.1186/s41073-019-0062-x

universities into research misconduct are often opaque, inaccessible, in some instances not made public at all, poorly conducted, lack adequate mechanisms to address potential conflicts of interest and are subject to inadequate oversight.[38] One way forwards, which presents a challenge to the idea of institutional self-policing, is the creation of one or more independent organisations empowered to undertake investigations and implement recommendations spanning multiple institutions and countries.[39] Such organisations, with appropriate expertise to undertake and report investigations and the authority to ensure the implementation of recommendations, could best ensure an internationally effective investigatory process.[40]

For institutional investigatory and adjudicatory processes to work effectively, policies have to be adequate and the research community have to be professionally proactive in complying with them.[41] By way of example, relating to the availability of evidence, investigations of alleged misconduct at University College London (UCL) lacked full underpinning evidence because data had not been retained. UCL policy required primary data to be kept for ten years, an insufficient period given that some of the allegations related to matters which dated back much further. Even the ten-year period had not been fully complied with, due to limited storage space and some data having become irretrievable because researchers who had left the institution had taken it with them, without copies being retained.[42]

38 Grey, A., Bolland, M., Gamble, G. et al. (2019). Quality of reports of investigations of research integrity by academic institutions. *Res Integr Peer Rev*, 4, 3 https://doi.org/10.1186/s41073-019-0062-x; Gunsalus, C. K., Marcus, A. R., & Oransky, I. (2018). Institutional research misconduct reports need more credibility. *JAMA*, 319(13), 1315–1316. doi: 10.1001/jama.2018.0358

39 Grey, A., Bolland, M., Gamble, G. et al. (2019). Quality of reports of investigations of research integrity by academic institutions. *Res Integr Peer Rev*, 4, 3 https://doi.org/10.1186/s41073-019-0062-x

40 Grey, A., Bolland, M., Gamble, G. et al. (2019). Quality of reports of investigations of research integrity by academic institutions. *Res Integr Peer Rev*, 4, 3 https://doi.org/10.1186/s41073-019-0062-x

41 The National Ethical Charter for the research professions, for example, requires that all researchers familiarise themselves with legal and regulatory provisions governing their professional activities, including detailed record keeping and preservation of data in order to guarantee experimental reproducibility, ETINED Council of Europe Platform on Ethics, Transparency and Integrity in Education Volume 1–7th Session of the Prague Forum, 2016, 149–150, https://rm.coe.int/volume-1-7th-session-of-the-prague-forum/168074427a (accessed 18 June 2019)

42 Allegation of research misconduct in respect of 32 papers published between 1990 and 2013 by researchers based at the UCL Institute of Child Health: Report of the Investigation Panel, www.documentcloud.org/documents/6178710-UCL-FOIA-Latchman-Lab-Investigations.html (accessed 6 July 2019). In the case of 22 papers, the panel were unable to conclude that research misconduct had occurred and no further investigation was to be undertaken. Some of these conclusions arose because the allegations could not be addressed without access to original data, which were no longer available. While no evidence was considered to suggest that the non-retention of original data in these cases was motivated by an intention to thwart investigations, it is of concern that in other cases this could be a motivating factor. Lessons from some aspects of the legal sphere point towards sufficiently harsh penalties for refusing to adduce evidence to discourage such behaviour.

It is also important that universities resist addressing risky ethical situations by allowing the outsourcing, sometimes referred to as 'ethics dumping,' of ethically problematic aspects of research to countries with less stringent regulatory frameworks or less developed detection infrastructures. The European Union–supported *Global Code of Conduct for Research in Resource-Poor Settings* provides the opportunity for universities and other interested parties in the research arena to adopt a common set of good practice provisions. In the words of the code:

> Those applying the Code oppose double standards in research and support long-term equitable research relationships between partners in lower-income and high-income settings based on fairness, respect, care and honesty.[43]

Researchers applying for EU funding must demonstrate that they will comply with the code.[44] At the time of writing, formal adoption of the code at individual university level remained limited.

Overall, there is limited clarity about institutional responses to potential misconduct. Information which is published in the form of misconduct reports lacks standardisation, may fail to address inherent conflicts of interest and is not quality controlled or peer reviewed, risking the creation of an environment which fails sufficiently to discourage inappropriate behaviour.[45] Responses to address this include checklists identifying that relevant data have been secured

An example from the criminal law in England and Wales would be a refusal by a driver suspected of consuming alcohol at levels above the prescribed limit to supply an evidential sample of breath. The penalty of such refusal can be harsher than that for the offence of drink driving. Examples from the civil sphere are more subtle, but can be found. For example, a court considering an allegation of negligence against a lawyer may take the view that the lawyer, rather than the client, is in the better position to produce a contemporaneous note of, say, a meeting. In the event of conflicting evidence by lawyer and client, the court's approach may be to favour the account of the client on the basis that the lawyer could have been expected to create contemporaneous supporting evidence. It can be argued that the creation and retention of scientific records fall into a similar category.

43 www.globalcodeofconduct.org/wp-content/uploads/2018/05/Global-Code-of-Conduct-Brochure.pdf (accessed 28 October 2020)

44 Nordling, L. (2018). Europe's biggest research fund cracks down on 'ethics dumping'. *Nature,* 559, 17–18. doi: 10.1038/d41586-018-05616-w

45 Gunsalus, C. K., Marcus, A. R., & Oransky, I. (2018). Institutional research misconduct reports need more credibility. *JAMA,* 319(13), 1315–1316. doi: 10.1001/jama.2018.0358; National Academies of Sciences, Engineering, and Medicine; Committee on Federal Research Regulations and Reporting Requirements: A New Framework for Research Universities in the 21st Century; Committee on Science, Technology, and Law; Board on Higher Education and Workforce; Policy and Global Affairs (2016). *Optimizing the Nation's Investment in Academic Research: A New Regulatory Framework for the 21st Century*. Washington, DC: National Academies Press, cited by Gunsalus, C. K., Marcus, A. R., & Oransky, I. (2018). Institutional research misconduct reports need more credibility. *JAMA,* 319(13), 1315–1316. doi: 10.1001/jama.2018.0358

and reviewed by appropriate experts and that such data appropriately underpin the findings of an investigatory and adjudicatory process. Such formalisation also better enables quality checking by institutional officials, university counsel and external peer reviewers.[46]

In terms of issues with transparency, institutional confidentiality protocols can undermine the effectiveness of research integrity processes if the findings of investigations are not disseminated. This weakens the value of such findings to inform and deter and may even prevent interested parties, such as editors and publishers, obtaining information which would be of value to them. If institutions are concerned that in their jurisdiction there are legal obstacles to prioritising transparency, legally permissible solutions should be sought, for example. waivers of confidentiality in contracts of employment and journal editors requiring authors to disclose any misconduct allegations or proceedings.[47] Lessons can be learned from established professional regulatory bodies. Proceedings and findings in professional conduct hearings are typically public, and members of the profession have disclosure obligations, with failure to disclose often itself constituting professional misconduct.

In the UK, the Concordat to Support Research Integrity requires employers to produce an annual statement on the number of research misconduct investigations. Around one-quarter of UK universities failed to meet this requirement, even though technically this is a prerequisite for receiving public funding. A review of the available statements has revealed that a significant number of universities undertook no investigations in certain years or in some cases at all since the Concordat came into being in 2012.[48] This gives rise to concerns that some institutions could be making insufficient efforts to detect and address misconduct, or even be sweeping misconduct under the carpet.[49] From this perspective, an increase in the number of institutional investigations could signal a healthy and proactive regulatory environment.[50]

46 Gunsalus, C. K., Marcus, A. R., & Oransky, I. (2018). Institutional research misconduct reports need more credibility. *JAMA,* 319(13), 1315–1316. doi: 10.1001/jama.2018.0358

47 Wager, E., Kleinert, S., Garfinkel, M., Volker Bahr, C., et al. (2017). Cooperation & Liaison between Universities & Editors (CLUE): Recommendations on best practice. *bioRxiv*. doi: https://doi.org/10.1101/139170.

48 House of Commons Science and Technology Committee, Research integrity, Sixth Report of Session 2017–19, 11 July 2018 HC 350 paras 25–26, citing, inter alia, James Parry, the Chief Executive of the UK Research Integrity Office and Dr Patrick Vallance, the Government's Chief Scientific Adviser

49 House of Commons Science and Technology Committee, Research integrity, Sixth Report of Session 2017–19, 11 July 2018 HC 350 paras 25–26, citing, inter alia, James Parry, the Chief Executive of the UK Research Integrity Office and Dr Patrick Vallance, the Government's Chief Scientific Adviser

50 House of Commons Science and Technology Committee, Research integrity, Sixth Report of Session 2017–19, 11 July 2018 HC 350, p. 56

Supervisory responsibility

In the regulation of traditional professions, regulatory bodies may consider the responsibility of those in senior supervisory positions in addition to or instead of direct responsibility of a more junior team member. Equivalent considerations can arise in the context of scientific research if, for example, junior staff are assigned tasks beyond their capabilities or targets are applied which are close to unachievable or if senior authority is otherwise abused. An example of the latter is the misuse of senior status by claiming credit for findings created and owned by more junior researchers.[51] If senior authority is abused, junior researchers may be tempted to act inappropriately if they feel unduly pressured. Some junior team members may also feel insufficiently confident in their knowledge of research ethics to challenge a more senior colleague and, especially if small cogs in a much larger research machine, may lack full awareness of the possible impact of their actions.[52] In one example a researcher who had fabricated data in an article stated that she had been under pressure from a superior to generate data and also expressed the view that she considered her action to be justifiable because she had observed a senior scientist in her laboratory 'clean up' data for the purposes of publication.[53] A second example involved a professor found to have encouraged a subordinate to inflate the size of an experimental sample to provide the number of tests required by the protocol.[54] A further example involved a junior researcher who had manipulated data. The researcher had previously published articles in *Cell* and *Nature* based on legitimate findings and reported 'intense self-imposed pressure' to continue performing at that level.[55]

The potential for misconduct action against senior supervisors should encourage the setting of realistic workloads and appropriate supervision. Attempts to engage with the latter have begun to emerge. For example, the Swiss Academy of Arts and Sciences *Code of Conduct for Scientific Integrity* addresses neglecting supervisory expectations and abusing a management position.[56]

51 See, for example, Matthews, D. (2015). Papers retracted after authors used unauthorised data from junior researchers. *Times Higher Education*, October 22, 2015, www.timeshighereducation.com/news/papers-retracted-after-authors-used-unauthorised-data-from-junior-researchers

52 Kornfeld, D. S. (2012). Perspective: Research misconduct: The search for a remedy. *Acad Med*, 87, 877–882, 877–79. See also, Barber, B. Trust in Science, *Minerva* (1987) 25: 123. https://doi.org/10.1007/BF01096860

53 Kornfeld, D. S. (2012). Perspective: Research misconduct: The search for a remedy. *Acad Med*, 87, 877–882, 878

54 Kornfeld, D. S. (2012). Perspective: Research misconduct: The search for a remedy. *Acad Med*, 87, 877–882, 879

55 Kornfeld, D. S. (2012). Perspective: Research misconduct: The search for a remedy. *Acad Med*, 87, 877–882, 878

56 Eornfeld, D. S. (2012). Perspective: Research misconduct: The search for a remedy. *Acad Med*, 87, 877–882, 879; Swiss Academy of Arts and Sciences (2021) *Code of Conduct for Scientific Integrity*,

Research integrity officers

The appointment by universities of integrity officers with responsibility for implementing and overseeing the institution's research integrity policy may aid effectiveness and consistency of application.[57] The importance of the work of such officers is highlighted by the costs in both monetary and reputational terms if matters are not dealt with efficiently and effectively.[58] For example, in the United States in the 1980s a number of high-profile scientific fraud cases ultimately resulted in the development of a number of regulatory safeguards, including research integrity officers (RIOs) or similar roles with different titles.[59]

RIOs should be visibly present, available to be consulted in complete confidence if concerns or suspicions are aroused and sufficiently approachable by concerned parties, however junior.[60] However, they also have to be sufficiently independent and empowered to adopt a robust stance even against powerful individuals within the organisation, with security of employment to underpin this.[61] An example of failings in these regards arose from the investigation into Dutch former professor of social psychology, Diederik Alexander Stapel. Stapel, as a dean and researcher with an international reputation, occupied a senior position and enjoyed considerable support from the university executive board, signalling a special and powerful status to more junior members of the university community.[62] Within Stapel's institution the person with

p24 https://api.swiss-academies.ch/site/assets/files/25709/kodex_layout_en_web.pdf. See also, ETINED Council of Europe Platform on Ethics, Transparency and Integrity in Education Volume 1–7th Session of the Prague Forum, 2016, 149–150, https://rm.coe.int/volume-1-7th-session-of-the-prague-forum/168074427a (accessed 18 June 2019)

57 Lerouge, I., & Hol, A. (2020). *Towards a Research Integrity Culture at Universities: From Recommendations to Implementation*. Advice Paper no. 26 – January 2020, League of European Research Universities, 17, www.leru.org/files/Towards-a-Research-Integrity-Culture-at-Universities-full-paper.pdf (accessed 11 February 2020)

58 Michalek, A., Hutson, A., Wicher, C., & Trump, D. L. (2010). The costs and underappreciated consequences of research misconduct: A case study. *PLos Medicine,* 7(8), 529–539, e100318, cited in Bonito, A. J., Titus, S. L., & Wright, D. E. (2012). Assessing the preparedness of research integrity officers (RIOs) to appropriately handle possible research misconduct cases. *Sci Eng Ethics*, 18, 605–619. doi: 10.1007/s11948-011-9274-2

59 Bonito, A. J., Titus, S. L., & Wright, D. E. (2012). Assessing the preparedness of research integrity officers (RIOs) to appropriately handle possible research misconduct cases. *Sci Eng Ethics*, 18, 605–619. doi: 10.1007/s11948-011-9274-2

60 Van Lange, P. A. M. et al. (2012). *Sharpening Scientific Policy after Stapel*. Internal Report, September 2012, 8, https://kli.sites.uu.nl/wp-content/uploads/sites/426/2019/09/Sharpening-Scientific-Policy-After-Stapel.pdf (accessed 1 May 2020)

61 A little over a third in the United States were found to have tenured positions, Bonito, A. J., Titus, S. L., & Wright, D. E. (2012). Assessing the preparedness of research integrity officers (RIOs) to appropriately handle possible research misconduct cases. *Sci Eng Ethics*, 18, 605–619. doi: 10.1007/s11948-011-9274-2

62 Levelt Committee, Noort Committee, Drenth Committee. *Flawed Science: The Fraudulent Research Practices of Social Psychologist Diederik Stapel*, November 28, 2012, 45

whom concerns were to be raised was 'the Confidential Counsellor.' Contrary to guidelines that the Confidential Counsellor should not be a member of the executive board, the office was held at the time by a board member, the Rector Magnificus. For PhD students who had concerns about Stapel, this presented them with someone in 'a very lofty and distant position' and not someone that a junior member of the academic community would feel comfortable to approach, especially without solid proof of their suspicions.[63] In the Andrew Wakefield case a PhD student in Wakefield's lab testified in the US Vaccine Court case of *Cedillo v. Secretary of HHS* that he had undertaken tests on samples which resulted in negative findings or false positives. He informed Wakefield of this and requested that his name be omitted from any publications in which any of these data were used, but appears not to have felt confident to pursue concerns more formally.[64] As illustrated in these and other cases, PhD students or other junior researchers may be in a strong position to detect potential fraud or other misconduct, but require routes by which to readily raise suspicions. Routes which an effective integrity officer system can provide.[65]

An ineffective integrity officer process may arise if there is a lack of proactivity elsewhere in the organisation, such that integrity officers receive few reports to investigate. This creates a vicious cycle – officers will gain little or no hands-on experience, and the role may be combined with other responsibilities, further reducing its visibility within the institution.[66] To consider the impact of limited experience and training, research involving testing integrity officers with hypothetical scenarios has revealed numerous weaknesses. For example, significant numbers failed to identify the need to stop destruction of data; to put safeguards in place to protect those reporting or seeking to report concerns; to appropriately investigate, secure evidence and act proactively as well as reactively in the collection of witness statements; to take steps to safeguard the wellbeing of research subjects and to halt further recruitment while investigations are underway; to institute disciplinary procedures against senior employees; and to interact with counterparts in other institutions in order to share experiences.[67]

63 Levelt Committee, Noort Committee, Drenth Committee. *Flawed Science: The Fraudulent Research Practices of Social Psychologist Diederik Stapel*, November 28, 2012, 45

64 Kirkland, A. (2012). Credibility battles in the autism litigation. *Social Studies of Science*, 42(2), 237–261, 251. https://doi.org/10.1177/0306312711435832

65 Van Lange, P. A. M. et al. (2012). *Sharpening Scientific Policy after Stapel*. Internal Report, September 2012, 8, https://kli.sites.uu.nl/wp-content/uploads/sites/426/2019/09/Sharpening-Scientific-Policy-After-Stapel.pdf (accessed 1 May 2020)

66 Bonito, A. J., Titus, S. L., & Wright, D. E. (2012). Assessing the preparedness of research integrity officers (RIOs) to appropriately handle possible research misconduct cases. *Sci Eng Ethics*, 18, 605–619. doi: 10.1007/s11948-011-9274-2

67 Bonito, A. J., Titus, S. L., & Wright, D. E. (2012). Assessing the preparedness of research integrity officers (RIOs) to appropriately handle possible research misconduct cases. *Sci Eng Ethics*, 18, 605–619. doi: 10.1007/s11948-011-9274-2

Independent research integrity advisory boards, external to institutions, offer the potential for support and expertise sharing mechanisms for RIOs.[68] By having research integrity as the sole focus and sitting outside of individual institutions, such boards can remain neutral and distinct from the conflicting and competing interests found within research organisations.[69]

The United Kingdom Concordat on Research Integrity

As introduced in Chapter 2, the Concordat on Research Integrity establishes commitments to underpin high standards of research practice, with the intention to be of both practical and symbolic value. This was developed by the UK government, Universities UK, Research Councils UK, the National Institute for Health Research, the Wellcome Trust and other stakeholders and published by Universities UK (UUK) in 2012.

The Concordat falls within the remit of institutional regulation, as both overarching compliance and individual investigation fall to individual institutional employers. However, there is an absence of coordinated leadership to drive the implementation of Concordat requirements, with Universities UK emphasising that it has a persuasive role among its members but lacks the capacity to enforce compliance.[70]

Universities UK advocated the Concordat in preference to more invasive regulation and to avoid 'presenting research integrity as an issue of compliance, rather than embedded through the lifecycle of research production and dissemination, and a cultural norm.'[71] However, more critical observations from senior researchers on the ground include observations of the following type:

> I see a lot of motherhood and apple pie. It all sounds really nice, but when I read it . . . I think, 'How would I audit compliance with this?' There are no concrete commitments in the research concordat where I could say, 'This institution has complied and that institution has not.' That is where

68 Kretser, A., Murphy, D., Bertuzzi, S., Abraham, T., Allison, D., Boor, K., Dwyer, J., Grantham, A., Harris, L., Hollander, R., Jacobs-Young, C., Rovito, S., Vafiadis, D., Woteki, C., Wyndham, J., & Yada, R. (2019). Scientific integrity principles and best practices: Recommendations from a scientific integrity consortium. *Science and Engineering Ethics*, 25. doi: 10.1007/s11948-019-00094-3.

69 Kretser, A., Murphy, D., Bertuzzi, S., Abraham, T., Allison, D., Boor, K., Dwyer, J., Grantham, A., Harris, L., Hollander, R., Jacobs-Young, C., Rovito, S., Vafiadis, D., Woteki, C., Wyndham, J., & Yada, R. (2019). Scientific integrity principles and best practices: Recommendations from a scientific integrity consortium. *Science and Engineering Ethics*, 25. doi: 10.1007/s11948-019-00094-3.

70 House of Commons Science and Technology Committee, Research integrity, Sixth Report of Session 2017–19, 11 July 2018 HC 350, paras 34–35, 37 and 57

71 House of Commons Science and Technology Committee, Research integrity, Sixth Report of Session 2017–19, 11 July 2018 HC 350, para 31

> things fall down. . . . My principal concern about all the policies and frameworks for research integrity that I ever see is that they are vague.[72]

The House of Commons Science and Technology Committee contacted the 136 Universities UK members in November 2017 and found that self-reporting of compliance with the following Concordat requirements was high: identification of 'a senior member of staff to oversee research integrity and to act as first point of contact for anyone wanting more information on matters of research integrity'; 'a named point of contact to act as confidential liaison for whistleblowers or any other person wishing to raise concerns about the integrity of research.[73] Publication of annual statements was less consistent – only 58 per cent of Universities UK members published narrative statements on research integrity between 2015 and 2017. Seventeen per cent indicated an intention to begin publishing statements, but 25 per cent expressed no such intention – in some instances because no investigations had been undertaken, although the House of Commons Committee noted that a report to this effect would provide clarity. The committee was unpersuaded by arguments that confidentiality was an obstacle to publishing an annual narrative report. Those universities treating transparency as a public image threat were missing the opportunity to project a positive image of the steps being taken to safeguard research standards and, in turn, potentially adding to the undermining of public trust.[74]

In 2013 compliance with the Concordat became a requirement before research funds can be obtained from the higher education funding councils and research councils.[75] However, the effectiveness of funding body monitoring is open to question. The House of Commons Science and Technology Committee questioned how research funders who are only supposed to distribute funds to compliant institutions found Concordat compliance to be almost 100 per cent, when other evidence clearly contradicted this.[76]

Move to the creation of UK Research and Innovation, which brought together the seven research councils with Research England and Innovate UK and offered the potential to revisit assurance processes in the future. The House

72 Dr Ben Goldacre, DataLab, Department of Primary Care, University of Oxford, giving evidence to the Science and Technology Committee, Oral evidence: Research integrity, HC 350, Monday 4 December 2017, ordered by the House of Commons to be published on 4 December 2017. Members present: Norman Lamb (Chair); Vicky Ford; Bill Grant; Clive Lewis; Stephen Metcalfe; Martin Whitfield. Questions 277–360, Q334 and Q336

73 House of Commons Science and Technology Committee, Research integrity, Sixth Report of Session 2017–19, 11 July 2018 HC 350, para 33

74 House of Commons Science and Technology Committee, Research integrity, Sixth Report of Session 2017–19, 11 July 2018 HC 350, paras 34–35 and page 57

75 House of Commons Science and Technology Committee, Research integrity, Sixth Report of Session 2017–19, 11 July 2018 HC 350, para 40

76 House of Commons Science and Technology Committee, Research integrity, Sixth Report of Session 2017–19, 11 July 2018 HC 350, para 41

of Commons Committee recommend that the Concordat be strengthened to make the expectations clearer, with explicit measurable requirements and for the signatories to produce a route map and timetable for reaching 100 per cent compliance within a year. Particular focus should be placed on strengthening training with regard to research integrity, processes for responding to allegations of misconduct, commitments to clinical trials transparency and the publication of 'negative' research results. UK Research and Innovation should publish details of universities that are not compliant.[77] To provide leadership and full consistency of research governance, government departments should also sign up to the Concordat.[78]

Compliance with the Concordat may improve as a result of institutions addressing the requirements for the Research Excellence Framework 2021 (REF). Indicators in support of statements on areas of research culture as part of the REF include research integrity benchmarks at the institutional level, as evidenced by compliance with the Concordat. Institutions are required to explain how they reach compliance.[79] Inclusion of this requirement will ideally help to emphasise the importance of research integrity to a healthy research environment and to counterbalance some of the pressures which may tempt some researchers to compromise integrity.[80] However, opinions among researchers themselves are mixed. Twenty-seven per cent of respondents to one study agreed that the REF could have a positive impact on research integrity, but 32 per cent saw the impact as negative, with others identifying both positive and negative aspects.[81] Concerns included institutional pressures to publish in a timeframe which places rigour at risk and that pressured research ecosystems may foster 'perverse' incentives, which may encourage poor research integrity.[82] In the words of one researcher:

> I think that researchers feeling forced to perform to arbitrary and often unattainable standards is probably the single biggest cause of unethical behaviour, and the REF, league tables, and metrics all contribute.[83]

77 House of Commons Science and Technology Committee, Research integrity, Sixth Report of Session 2017–19, 11 July 2018 HC 350, paras 42–46 and Conclusions and recommendations para 6.

78 House of Commons Science and Technology Committee, Research integrity, Sixth Report of Session 2017–19, 11 July 2018 HC 350, paras 42–46 and Conclusions and recommendations para 6.

79 See UK Forum for Responsible Research Metrics, *FFRRM's advice to the Research Excellence Framework (REF) 2021 panels*, 26 July 2018

80 A point discussed in the House of Commons Science and Technology Committee, Research integrity, Sixth Report of Session 2017–19, 11 July 2018 HC 350, para 57

81 Metcalfe, J., Wheat, K., Munafò. M., Parry, J. (2020). *Research Integrity: A Landscape Study* (p. 27). Vitae/UK Research Integrity Office/UK Reproducibility Network, www.ukri.org/files/legacy/documents/research-integrity-main-report/

82 Metcalfe, J., Wheat, K., Munafò. M., Parry, J. (2020). *Research Integrity: A Landscape Study*. Vitae/UK Research Integrity Office/UK Reproducibility Network, www.ukri.org/files/legacy/documents/research-integrity-main-report/

83 Metcalfe, J., Wheat, K., Munafò. M., Parry, J. (2020). *Research Integrity: A Landscape Study* (p. 27). Vitae/UK Research Integrity Office/UK Reproducibility Network, www.ukri.org/files/

Similarly, in the words of a senior research leader, the sense of personal and professional ethics on the part of researchers 'is constantly undermined by disciplinary, institutional and government drivers towards fulfilling goals and targets, even those ostensibly intended to promote ethics.'[84]

Risks that metrics may take priority over the undertaking of the highest-quality research include instilling short-term research goals; less time devoted to planning research projects; corner cutting in terms of, for example, sample sizes and the interpretation of results; and overall prioritising productivity over rigour.[85] Nobel Laureate William G. Kaelin has suggested that in some scientific fields the goals for published research have moved 'from validating specific conclusions to making the broadest possible assertions. The danger is that papers are increasingly like grand mansions of straw, rather than sturdy houses of brick.'[86] When comparing with research practises in previous decades, some ground-breaking research would be 'barely publishable today' in an environment where stakeholders, such as some funding bodies and some publishers, chase short-term impact and lack sufficient humility about the realistic possibility of predicting this.[87]

Investigation and adjudication

It is important that research institutions have a scientific integrity policy which includes an adjudicatory process for use where suspicion of detrimental research practices or research misconduct arises.[88] The UK Concordat to

legacy/documents/research-integrity-main-report/; see also, for example, Smaldino, P. E., & McElreath, R. (2016). The natural selection of bad science. *Royal Society Open Science,* 3, 160384.

84 Metcalfe, J., Wheat, K., Munafò. M., Parry, J. (2020). *Research Integrity: A Landscape Study* (p. 21). Vitae/UK Research Integrity Office/UK Reproducibility Network, www.ukri.org/files/legacy/documents/research-integrity-main-report/

85 See, for example, Nuffield Council on Bioethics, The culture of Scientific Research in the UK, December 2014, 31; Rzhetsky, A., Foster, J. G., Foster, I. T., & Evans, J. A. (2015). Choosing experiments to accelerate collective discovery. *Proc. Natl. Acad. Sci. USA,* 112, 14569–14574; Higginson, A. D., & Munafo, M. R. (2016). Current incentives for scientists lead to underpowered studies with erroneous conclusions. *PLoS Biology,* 14(11), [e2000995]. https://doi.org/10.1371/journal.pbio.2000995, Smaldino, P. E., & McElreath, R. (2016). The natural selection of bad science. *Royal Society Open Science,* 3, 160384, https://royalsocietypublishing.org/doi/full/10.1098/rsos.160384. For examples of similar challenges in other jurisdictions see Shaw, D., & Satalkar, P. (2018). Researchers' interpretations of research integrity: A qualitative study. *Accountability in Research,* 25(2), 79–93, 88. doi: 10.1080/08989621.2017.1413940

86 Kaelin Jr, W. G. (2017). Publish houses of brick, not mansions of straw. *Nature* 545, 387 (May 25). doi: 10.1038/545387a

87 Kaelin Jr, W. G. (2017). Publish houses of brick, not mansions of straw. *Nature* 545, 387 (May 25). doi: 10.1038/545387a. Noting that impact can truly be known only in retrospect and, as such, questions for reviewers of submissions should confined to whether the conclusions of the research are likely to be correct, not whether the research findings would be important if true.

88 Kretser, A., Murphy, D., Bertuzzi, S., Abraham, T., Allison, D., Boor, K., Dwyer, J., Grantham, A., Harris, L., Hollander, R., Jacobs-Young, C., Rovito, S., Vafiadis, D., Woteki, C., Wyndham, J., &

Support Research Integrity places the primary responsibility for investigating allegations of misconduct on employing organisations, requiring processes which are robust, transparent, fair and 'reflect best practice.'[89] Recommended stages include pre-screening, screening and formal investigation – with the latter being adjudicatory in nature. Ideally, each of these stages will include at least one panel member drawn from outside of the institution.[90]

In terms of approaches in practice, an example discussed in evidence to the House of Commons Science and Technology Committee is that of UCL. Described at the time of the House of Commons Committee reports as a predominantly reactive approach which involves filtering, screening and adjudication being undertaken, as appropriate, in response to complaints. A typical screening panel consists of three members drawn from within UCL, selected to ensure no conflicts of interest, but no compulsory external panel member. External input is required at the formal adjudicatory stage.[91] The screening stage at UCL addresses the question of whether there is prima facie evidence of research misconduct, an intention to deceive.[92] Lessons may be learned from historical difficulties identified with medical regulation in the UK.[93] Screening proved to be particularly problematic unless the task of identifying prima facie evidence had a sufficiently low bar – the screening process must not subvert full investigation and an adjudicatory hearing. For example, there is a risk that seeking to identify an intention to deceive is far more appropriate to a full adjudicatory hearing than at a screening stage.

Illustrative case examples

A particularly complex case example demonstrating the need for adaptability in regulatory processes relates to trachea surgeon Paolo Macchiarini, a visiting professor at UCL until 2014. Macchiarini, primarily employed by the Karolinska Institute in Sweden at the time concerns arose, was accused of misconduct involving experimental trachea transplants, with some patient deaths. Macchiarini had been lead surgeon in a series of operations in which a diseased oesophagus had been replaced with one made of a polymer material and seeded with stem cells. The results were published and follow-up reports indicated, inaccurately, that the patients were doing well.[94] Five months after the death

Yada, R. (2019). Scientific integrity principles and best practices: Recommendations from a scientific integrity consortium. *Science and Engineering Ethics*, 25. doi: 10.1007/s11948-019-00094-3.

89 Universities UK, *The Concordat to Support Research Integrity* (July 2012), pp. 18–19

90 UKRIO, Procedure for the Investigation of Research Misconduct, August 2008, https://ukrio.org/wp-content/uploads/UKRIO-Procedure-for-the-Investigation-of-Misconduct-in-Research.pdf

91 House of Commons Science and Technology Committee, Research integrity, Sixth Report of Session 2017–19, 11 July 2018 HC 350, para 86

92 House of Commons Science and Technology Committee, Research integrity, Sixth Report of Session 2017–19, 11 July 2018 HC 350, para 86

93 Davies, M. (2007). *Medical Self-regulation, Crisis and Change*. London and New York: Routledge.

94 Hawkes, N. (2018). Macchiarini case: Seven researchers are guilty of scientific misconduct, rules Karolinska's president. *BMJ*, 361, k2816 doi: 10.1136/bmj.k2816 (Published 27 June 2018)

of the first patient a formal complaint was filed by four physicians employed by the Karolinska Institute and the Karolinska University Hospital. Three of the complainants were co-authors of Macchiarini articles. They alleged that seven scientific articles contained errors relating to the condition of patients and the functioning of the implants. They also alleged failures in the obtaining of appropriate consent from patients and failure to obtain ethical permission from the Regional Ethical Board.[95] In the same month, June 2014, Professor Delaere, who had questioned in a *Lancet* article aspects of Macchiarini's work, filed a formal complaint to the Karolinska Institute.[96] The Karolinska Institute initially cleared Macchiarini of wrongdoing. A subsequent investigation found that he had committed misconduct, including failure to comply with ethics requirements, improperly dealing with the risk considerations of surgery and inaccurately recording patient outcomes. By deliberately resorting to deception to distort the findings, Macchiarini's papers presented a risk to other patients if doctors sought to rely on Macchiarini's work.[97] At UCL, even though the connection with Macchiarini was historic, it was determined that steps should be taken following receipt of a number of misconduct allegations. Given the variations in these allegations, the decision was made to adopt a more generic, rather than the usual specific, approach by means of a 'special inquiry' involving an entirely external panel and outside legal advisers.[98]

In late 2019 an experienced University of Oxford academic was found to have committed a 'serious instance of research misconduct' by failing to properly acknowledge the work of Chinese collaborators in a book she authored.[99] The book was derived in part from the time the author has spent in China living alongside people experiencing health issues linked to pollution. After publication, academic collaborators in China raised concerns that the author had failed to consult them about the use of research in which they had been involved and had insufficiently acknowledged the 'collaborative nature and co-production

95 McKelvey, M., Saemundsson, R. J., & Zaring, O. (2018). A recent crisis in regenerative medicine: Analyzing governance in order to identify public policy issues. *Science and Public Policy*, 45(5) (October), 608–620, 617. https://doi.org/10.1093/scipol/scx085

96 Delaere, P., & Hermans, R. (2009). Clinical transplantation of a tissue-engineered airway. *The Lancet*, 373, 717–718; McKelvey, M., Saemundsson, R. J., & Zaring, O. (2018). A recent crisis in regenerative medicine: Analyzing governance in order to identify public policy issues. *Science and Public Policy*, 45(5) (October), 608–620. https://doi.org/10.1093/scipol/scx085

97 *Suspected Scientific Misconduct*, Karolinska Institute Summary Report (English translation), p. 19 (accessed 20 November 2020)

98 Special_Inquiry_Final_Report_605109702_7_.pdf (ucl.ac.uk); Else, H. (2019). Scandal-weary Swedish government takes over research-fraud investigations. *Nature*, 571, 158. doi: 10.1038/d41586-018-05493-3

99 Grove, J. (2019). Oxford professor 'failed to properly acknowledge' Chinese colleagues. *Times Higher Education*, October 24, 2019, www.timeshighereducation.com/news/oxford-professor-failed-properly-acknowledge-chinese-colleagues; Bushby, E. (2019). Oxford professor failed to credit work of Chinese colleagues in award-winning book, panel rules. *The Independent*, Thursday, October 24, 2019, www.independent.co.uk/news/education/education-news/anna-lora-wainwright-book-plagiarism-oxford-university-professor-chinese-research-a9169311.html

of much of the work.'[100] The University of Oxford regulations define misconduct in research to include 'unacknowledged appropriation of the work of others' and can include acts of omission as well as acts of commission. Misconduct excludes poor-quality research, genuine errors unless due to negligence and differences in interpretation or judgement in evaluating research methods or results.[101] Responding to a *Times Higher Education* report into the Oxford investigation, the researcher is reported to have accepted that she had 'played no role in designing or conducting the research' for one chapter about which concerns had been raised and that out of 25 the pages of this chapter, 14 pages consisted of summaries of a 2013 paper by a Chinese academic collaborator and other pages were drawn from a 2016 paper co-authored by this academic and herself.[102] Acknowledgements in a methodology section at the back of the book were reported to have been considered by the Oxford disciplinary panel to be insufficient for the purposes of giving credit to research collaborators.[103] Nor did the book sufficiently acknowledge the Chinese researchers' analysis of the fieldwork done by them.[104] In the case of another Chinese academic who had interviewed local health workers and also recruited and funded students to undertake interviews, the Oxford report indicated that this academic had been

100 Grove, J. (2019). Oxford professor 'failed to properly acknowledge' Chinese colleagues. *Times Higher Education*, October 24, 2019, www.timeshighereducation.com/news/oxford-professor-failed-properly-acknowledge-chinese-colleagues; Bushby, E. (2019). Oxford professor failed to credit work of Chinese colleagues in award-winning book, panel rules. *The Independent*, Thursday, October 24, 2019, www.independent.co.uk/news/education/education-news/anna-lora-wainwright-book-plagiarism-oxford-university-professor-chinese-research-a9169311.html

101 University of Oxford, Research misconduct: Guidance on research misconduct, funder requirements and how to raise concerns, https://researchsupport.admin.ox.ac.uk/governance/integrity/misconduct#collapse390821 (accessed 30 October 2019)

102 Grove, J. (2019). Oxford professor 'failed to properly acknowledge' Chinese colleagues. *Times Higher Education*, October 24, 2019, www.timeshighereducation.com/news/oxford-professor-failed-properly-acknowledge-chinese-colleagues; Bushby, E. (2019). Oxford professor failed to credit work of Chinese colleagues in award-winning book, panel rules. *The Independent*, Thursday, October 24, 2019, www.independent.co.uk/news/education/education-news/anna-lora-wainwright-book-plagiarism-oxford-university-professor-chinese-research-a9169311.html

103 Grove, J. (2019). Oxford professor 'failed to properly acknowledge' Chinese colleagues. *Times Higher Education*, October 24, 2019, www.timeshighereducation.com/news/oxford-professor-failed-properly-acknowledge-chinese-colleagues; Bushby, E. (2019). Oxford professor failed to credit work of Chinese colleagues in award-winning book, panel rules. *The Independent*, Thursday, October 24, 2019, www.independent.co.uk/news/education/education-news/anna-lora-wainwright-book-plagiarism-oxford-university-professor-chinese-research-a9169311.html

104 Grove, J. (2019). Oxford professor 'failed to properly acknowledge' Chinese colleagues. *Times Higher Education*, October 24, 2019, www.timeshighereducation.com/news/oxford-professor-failed-properly-acknowledge-chinese-colleagues; Bushby, E. (2019). Oxford professor failed to credit work of Chinese colleagues in award-winning book, panel rules. *The Independent*, Thursday, October 24, 2019, www.independent.co.uk/news/education/education-news/anna-lora-wainwright-book-plagiarism-oxford-university-professor-chinese-research-a9169311.html

'shocked' that the book appeared to include this work without explaining that it was collaborative in nature. The researcher's response to the panel was that the use of such collaborative input was by way of a 'brief reference' with the focus being on her 'own detailed accounts of visits' to the village and personally conducted interviews. Overall, the researcher's response to a report in the *Times Higher Education* was that she 'believed at the time of publication that I had adequately consulted collaborators and acknowledged their contributions in the book. Any insufficient acknowledgement was entirely unintentional.'[105] The Oxford panel concluded that the researcher 'did not intend to deceive or mislead' but that she had been careless and failed to ensure 'due diligence with regard to the intellectual contribution of others.'[106] Research misconduct had, therefore, been established 'by the unacknowledged appropriation of the work of others and by misrepresentation of involvement in a research project.'[107] The recommendation following this finding was that the online version of the book be amended accordingly and for the researcher to be assigned an academic mentor. The complainants had called, inter alia, for the book to be recalled and were reported to have branded the sanction by the Oxford panel 'totally unacceptable.'[108] In an open letter, the objectors to the Oxford decision, members of the Forum on Health, Environment and Development,[109] expressed the

105 Grove, J. (2019). Oxford professor 'failed to properly acknowledge' Chinese colleagues. *Times Higher Education*, October 24, 2019, www.timeshighereducation.com/news/oxford-professor-failed-properly-acknowledge-chinese-colleagues

106 Grove, J. (2019). Oxford professor 'failed to properly acknowledge' Chinese colleagues. *Times Higher Education*, October 24, 2019, www.timeshighereducation.com/news/oxford-professor-failed-properly-acknowledge-chinese-colleagues; Bushby, E. (2019). Oxford professor failed to credit work of Chinese colleagues in award-winning book, panel rules. *The Independent*, Thursday, October 24, 2019, www.independent.co.uk/news/education/education-news/anna-lora-wainwright-book-plagiarism-oxford-university-professor-chinese-research-a9169311.html; Bushby, E. (2019). Oxford professor failed to credit work of Chinese colleagues in award-winning book, panel rules. *The Independent*, Thursday, October 24, 2019, www.independent.co.uk/news/education/education-news/anna-lora-wainwright-book-plagiarism-oxford-university-professor-chinese-research-a9169311.html

107 Grove, J. (2019). Oxford professor 'failed to properly acknowledge' Chinese colleagues. *Times Higher Education*, October 24, 2019, www.timeshighereducation.com/news/oxford-professor-failed-properly-acknowledge-chinese-colleagues

108 Grove, J. (2019). Oxford professor 'failed to properly acknowledge' Chinese colleagues. *Times Higher Education*, October 24, 2019, www.timeshighereducation.com/news/oxford-professor-failed-properly-acknowledge-chinese-colleagues; Bushby, E. (2019). Oxford professor failed to credit work of Chinese colleagues in award-winning book, panel rules. *The Independent*, Thursday, October 24, 2019, www.independent.co.uk/news/education/education-news/anna-lora-wainwright-book-plagiarism-oxford-university-professor-chinese-research-a9169311.html

109 An organisation which seeks to strengthen the knowledge base for responding to environment and health problems in China. www.forhead.org/

view that the decision failed to acknowledge the seriousness of the matter and the rights of the Chinese scholars in question.[110]

Final examples in this section consider questions about the boundaries between academic freedom, the need for institutional ethics approval and potential misconduct. Perhaps the best publicised example in recent times involved physicist Alan Sokal, who in 1996 published an article in *Social Text* which was an intentional hoax intended to expose alleged faulty reasoning in the postmodernist critique of science.[111] In a subsequent book, *Beyond the Hoax*, Sokal revisited this issue and the specialist and generalist media furore associated with it. More recently, a group of academics engaged in a similar exercise intended to 'understand and properly criticize' what they describe as 'an ongoing problem' within a number of research fields.[112] Twenty academic papers were submitted to a range of 'significant peer-reviewed academic journals,' papers which contained 'a variety of intentional flaws and satirical elements.' The stated aim of the research project was 'to better understand the field itself with an attempt to get absurdities and morally fashionable political ideas published as legitimate academic research' and to get 'an unvarnished look into the professional workings of the academic culture we were studying.'

No direct engagement is made here with either of these studies nor with their findings. What is of relevance to this work is the reaction to the exercises. At the time of Sokal's hoax, some opinions were expressed in support and others in opposition to his behaviour, but no formal misconduct action was taken against him. In contrast, the more recent example reportedly resulted the lead researcher facing potential disciplinary action by his employer for failing to alert his research review board and obtaining ethics approval prior to undertaking the research.[113] Arguments against such a disciplinary approach include observations that the embarrassment on the part of the editors and reviewers involved would have been better met by reflection on the implications revealed by the hoax for future rigour in those research fields.[114] An allegation of

110 www.forhead.org/, June 2, 2019, www.forhead.org/upload/201911/04/201911041334380498.pdf (accessed 3 October 2020)

111 Sokal, A. D. (1996). Transgressing the boundaries: Toward a transformative hermeneutics of quantum gravity. *Social Text*, No. 46/47, Science Wars (Spring–Summer), 217–252

112 Lindsay, J. A., Boghossian, P., & Pluckrose, H. (2018). Academic grievance studies and the corruption of scholarship. *Aero Magazine*, October 2, 2018, https://areomagazine.com/2018/10/02/academic-grievance-studies-and-the-corruption-of-scholarship/

113 Flaherty, C. (2019). Blowback against a hoax. *Inside Higher Ed*, January 8, 2019, www.insidehighered.com/news/2019/01/08/author-recent-academic-hoax-faces-disciplinary-action-portland-state; Flier, J. (2019). An exposé of lax publishing standards is not research misconduct. *Times Higher*, January 21, 2019, www.timeshighereducation.com/opinion/expose-lax-publishing-standards-not-research-misconduct

114 Flier, J. (2019). An exposé of lax publishing standards is not research misconduct. *Times Higher*, January 21, 2019, www.timeshighereducation.com/opinion/expose-lax-publishing-standards-not-research-misconduct

fabrication or falsification misses the motivational aspect of this type of study – to critique the article selection process by some journals – rather than an attempt to gain personal advantage through deception. A number of issues have been suggested as being of particular relevance; for example: was the study 'research' or more akin to journalistic investigation?; if it was research, was it human subject research, with the hoaxed editors as subjects and, if so, was appropriate approval required and informed consent obtained from the research subjects?[115]

115 Flier, J. (2019). An exposé of lax publishing standards is not research misconduct. *Times Higher*, January 21, 2019, www.timeshighereducation.com/opinion/expose-lax-publishing-standards-not-research-misconduct

Chapter 7

Regulation and the judicial process

The regulatory authority of the law stands apart from the natural and human sciences, but in practical terms science and law have features in common.[1] Both require decisions to be based on evidence. Both involve probabilistic considerations. Scientists, as with lawyers in certain jurisdictions, are expected to present their findings fully. For example, lawyers in common law jurisdictions such as England and Wales must cite all relevant legal authority of which they are aware, including that not supporting their client's position. Scientists should consider and appropriately present all of their data fully and present relevant literature even if unhelpful to their hypothesis. A key difference, however, is that lawyer obligations are underpinned by professional sanctions, hence 'must' is appropriate, whereas scientists are less clearly 'regulated,' hence 'must' becomes 'should.' In the realm of scientific misconduct legal concepts regarding burden of proof and standard of proof play a role.[2]

However, there are differences in the approaches of science and law when operating in their normal arenas. When operating together, it has been suggested that 'law–science knowledge' is a 'contingent artefact' of specific

1 Priaulx, N. M., & Weinel, M. (2014). Behavior on a beer mat: Law, interdisciplinarity & expertise. *Journal of Law, Technology & Policy,* (2), 361–391, 367. A classic account of the differences between science and law can be drawn from Kelsen. The natural sciences are concerned with cause and effect, the realm of the 'is' – A gives rise to B. In contrast, law is concerned with the realm of the 'ought'. In, for example, criminal law finding a defendant guilty of a crime may lead to punishment, but the 'crime does not cause the punishment, rather the punishment is imputed to the crime.' Paterson, J. (2003). Trans-science, trans-law and proceduralization. *Social & Legal Studies,* 12(4), 525–545, 528, discussing Kelsen, H. (1967). *The Pure Theory of Law.* Berkeley: University of California Press and Kelsen, H. (1971). *What is Justice?* Berkeley: University of California Press.

2 For example, the combined committees investigating the alleged fraud *of social psychologist Diederik Stapel* classified publications as fraudulent if in at least one of the experimental studies in a publication, fraud has been proven beyond reasonable doubt. Only those publications demonstrating the highest probability of fraud were categorised as fraudulent. Breaches of scientific rules or norms which fell below this level were categorised as 'bad science' but were not labelled 'fraudulent.' Levelt Committee, Noort Committee, Drenth Committee. *Flawed Science: The Fraudulent Research Practices of Social Psychologist Diederik Stapel,* November 28, 2012, 17–19

DOI: 10.4324/9780429492129-7

interactions of science in the legal arena, each with its own rules, procedures and traditions.[3]

Law 'provides instruments, backed by sanctions.'[4] Resort to the courts or threats to do so to seek to silence criticism, whether in the form of whistle-blowing, challenging decisions to retract papers or other eventualities, can be problematic to the smooth operation of scientific research and associated debate and disagreement.[5] For some within the scientific community, a researcher who chooses to draft lawyers into the process is encroaching upon legitimate scientific debate. For others, for example, those who face or fear misconduct allegations, it may be seen as entirely legitimate to seek to protect their careers and reputations by bringing legal expertise into a forum where they have so much at stake and may also face a significant power imbalance, notably when having to contend with institutional counsel and resources.

One potential advantage of the legal process, if matters reach the formal stage of court proceedings, is that it provides a transparent glimpse into the workings of what otherwise can be opaque processes internal to institutions.

Evidential standards in different arenas of law differ. For example, in England and Wales civil claims are based upon proof on the balance of probabilities – more likely than not. In criminal cases the standard of proof is significantly higher – beyond reasonable doubt. Some jurisdictions require clear and convincing evidence – it being substantially more likely than not to be true. The same scientist giving similar evidence as an expert witness in a civil case and a criminal case would, therefore, have that evidence tested against very different standards. For the purposes of the scientific field from which that evidence is drawn, the scientific community within that field are likely to have required even greater levels of certainty – in the guise of irrefutable evidence – than the standards of proof applied in the courtroom. A further difference between scientific proof and legal proof is that the latter, within a particular jurisdiction, will be defined consistently, whereas within scientific fields there is greater scope for definitional flexibility between specialisms. For example, a judge will precisely direct a jury about the standard of proof to be applied to the evidence they hear. The jury direction will be expected to be consistent whichever judge happens to be giving it, with an appeal process to correct errors in that regard. In contrast, in the research arena there is no equivalent process for referees determining whether the information

3 Edmond, G. (2001). The law-set: The legal-scientific production of medical propriety. *Science, Technology, & Human Values*, 26(2), 191–226, 192–193. https://doi.org/10.1177/016224390102600204

4 Paterson, J. (2003). Trans-science, trans-law and proceduralization. *Social & Legal Studies*, 12(4), 525–545, 526

5 See, for example, Johns, M., University of Pittsburgh researchers file lawsuit against journal that retracted their pulmonary disease article, *Pennsylvania Record*, September 24, 2019 (accessed 1 September 2020); Pitt researchers sue journal for defamation following retraction, *Retraction Watch*, https://retractionwatch.com/2019/12/02/pitt-researchers-sue-journal-for-defamation-following-retraction/ (accessed 1 September 2020)

presented in a manuscript is sufficiently convincing as to warrant publication. An individual journal editor may set expectations in an attempt to achieve some consistency, but this tends not to extend beyond this in wider formal or systematic terms. In some respects the courtroom environment mirrors debates within the scientific field, where scrutiny of ideas moves understanding forwards. However, evidence, including scientific evidence, in the courtroom tends to be tested over relatively brief timeframes in the cut and thrust of the legal process and a binary win-or-lose nature at the end of the process. In contrast, the search for scientific proof is a far more extended process – referees make decisions about the suitability of findings for publication, but the most meaningful scrutiny arises from prolonged consideration within the wider scientific community, including any attempts to replicate or reproduce the study being reported.

From the perspective of regulating science, a feature which some court cases can bring to this environment is the opportunity to systematically analyse the credibility of a particular research output with a speed and focus which would be difficult to replicate in other environments. For example, in claims before the US Federal Vaccine Court relating to the MMR vaccine (*Cedillo v. Secretary of HHS*; *King v. Secretary of HHS*), the permissive evidentiary rules of the vaccine court allowed research material to be adduced which had been funded by pharmaceutical companies, to enable scrutiny in the court environment for signs of poor research practice or research misconduct.[6] It has also been observed in the context of this litigation that the legal process can be used in an attempt to steer the debate. For example, expert witness evidence for the petitioners was portrayed as, inter alia, confused and drawn from a limited body of work which had not been cited by others in the field.[7] In contrast, experts on behalf of the government were categorised as having much greater experience and a significantly greater body of relevant original research publications in prestigious journals and presenting as 'paradigmatic emblems of scientific credibility.'[8]

In the United States the courts admit or exclude scientific evidence based upon the decision in *Daubert v. Dow Merrell Pharmaceuticals*, which requires federal judges to proactively screen the expert evidence to ensure its relevance and

6 Kirkland, A. (2012). Credibility battles in the autism litigation. *Social Studies of Science*, 42(2), 237–261, 249. https://doi.org/10.1177/0306312711435832. However, research and investigations undertaken as part of the litigation process may struggle to achieve the level of objectivity and disinterestedness central to ideas of scientific method.

7 Kirkland, A. (2012). Credibility battles in the autism litigation. *Social Studies of Science*, 42(2), 237–261, 249. https://doi.org/10.1177/0306312711435832; Keelan, J., & Wilson, K. (2011). Balancing vaccine science and national policy objectives: Lessons from the National Vaccine Injury Compensation Program Omnibus Autism Proceedings. *American Journal of Public Health*, 101, 11, 2016–2021. doi: 10.2105/AJPH.2011.300198

8 Kirkland, A. (2012). Credibility battles in the autism litigation. *Social Studies of Science*, 42(2), 237–261, 249. https://doi.org/10.1177/0306312711435832. See also, Keelan, J., & Wilson, K. (2011). Balancing vaccine science and national policy objectives: Lessons from the National Vaccine Injury Compensation Program Omnibus Autism Proceedings. *American Journal of Public Health*, 101, 11, 2016–2021. doi: 10.2105/AJPH.2011.300198

reliability and to ensure that it is underpinned by the methods and procedures of science.[9] Four key factors are relevant: methodology, testability, subjection to peer review and that it is accepted by the scientific community. These work within the adversarial process to provide 'vigorous cross-examination [and] presentation of contrary evidence' as the means of challenging 'shaky but admissible evidence.'[10] However, such an approach can lead to courts admitting evidence that draws an 'inference to the best explanation' drawn from a number of sources, none of which alone would be sufficient to establish causation.[11] As Huber observes: 'By requiring professional publication as a basis for expert opinion, judges will help line up the larger community of scientists to shadow the necessarily smaller community of expert witnesses.'[12] A further challenge in the courtroom is clarity of communication by scientific experts to ensure that all parties in the legal process have necessary understanding to ensure that justice is served.[13]

In England and Wales there has been no direct equivalent to *Daubert*, although there have been recommendations for moves in a similar direction with the intention to reduce the risks posed by unreliable scientific evidence, for example, recommendations by the Law Commission that in criminal cases scientific evidence should be 'sufficiently reliable to be admitted.'[14] A 2014 Practice Direction issued by the Lord Chief Justice implemented some of the Law Commission recommendations with regard to criminal law described as being similar to the *Daubert* provisions but more elaborate, for example, with regard to consideration of peer review of publications from which expert opinion is drawn and whether the opinion appropriately takes into account the margin of uncertainty as bases for the reliability of evidence.[15] However, analysis of what is 'a sufficiently reliable scientific basis' is currently limited by the absence of case law on the point.[16]

9 *Daubert v. Merrell Dow Pharmaceuticals*, 509 US 579 (1993).

10 *Daubert v. Merrell Dow Pharmaceuticals*, 509 US 579 (1993), 596.

11 Ward, T. (2015). An English Daubert? Law, forensic science and epistemic deference. *The Journal of Philosophy, Science & Law*, 15, 26–36. doi: 10.5840/jpsl20151513, 30 citing *Milward v Acuity Specialty Products*, 639 F.3d 11 (2011); Bernstein, D. E. (2013). Misbegotten judicial resistance to the Daubert revolution. *Notre Dame Law Review*, 89, 27–70; For further critical analysis see, for example, Jasanoff, S. (2005). Law's Knowledge: Science for Justice in Legal Settings. *American Journal of Public Health*, 95, S49_S58; Gatowski, S. I., Dobbin, S. A., Richardson, J. T., Ginsburg, G. P., Merlino, M. L., & Dahir, V. (2001). Asking the gatekeepers: A national survey of judges on judging expert evidence in a post-Daubert world. *Law and Human Behavior*, 25(5), 433–458.

12 Huber, P. W. (1991). *Galileo's Revenge: Junk Science in the Courtroom* (p. 202). New York: Basic Books.

13 Faigman, D. L. (1999). *Legal Alchemy: The Use and Misuse of Science in the Law* (p. 200). New York: WH Freeman and Co.

14 Law Commission of England and Wales. 2011. Expert Evidence in Criminal Proceedings in England and Wales. London

15 Ward, T. (2015). An English Daubert? Law, forensic science and epistemic deference. *The Journal of Philosophy, Science & Law*, 15, 26–36. doi: 10.5840/jpsl20151513, 30 citing Thomas of Cwmgiedd, Lord, C. J. (2014). *Practice Direction (Criminal Proceedings: Various Changes)*, www.judiciary.uk/wp-content/uploads/2014/07/Criminal-Practice-Directions-Amendment-No-2.pdf

16 Ward, T. (2020). Explaining and trusting expert evidence: What is a 'sufficiently reliable scientific basis'? *The International Journal of Evidence & Proof.*, 24(3), 233–254. doi: 10.1177/1365712720927622

The weight to be given to particular expert evidence and reaching decisions when evidence from different experts is in conflict rests with the court which, to some extent, involves determining on behalf of the wider community the degree of trust which can be placed in particular scientific ideas.[17] In English civil claims, which are usually heard by a judge alone rather than judge and jury, this determination rests with the judge. While not usually formally educated to higher levels in the scientific fields from which they hear expert evidence, judges may over time acquire some expertise in relation to scientific issues more commonly encountered.[18] However, ultimately judges are engaged in legal decision making and dispensing justice rather than doing science or engaging in scientific peer review and, as Jasanoff argues, questions can arise about the capacity of judges and lawyers to constitute 'knowledgeable' consumers of science.[19] Jasanoff also argues that the law favours a positivist view of science – the courts seeking to recover a fixed picture of scientific knowledge, side-lining or even ignoring the approach to science which sees 'claims [as] intrinsically provisional, contingent, and subject to deconstruction under critical scrutiny.'[20] The adversarial process can, therefore, encourage the creation of artificial scientific controversy, with lawyers finding causal connections which lack determined conclusions from within the scientific community.[21]

In criminal cases, weighing scientific evidence usually rests with a lay jury. This has parallels with an overarching theme of this book – how might non-experts determine which, if any, experts to trust? One line of reasoning, existing since at least the nineteenth century but advanced with approval subsequently, is that lay jurors are competent to determine whether or not:

> they have good reason to accept the expert's opinion as being one that is probably based on good reasons, even if they are not in a position to

17 Ward, T. (2020). Explaining and trusting expert evidence: What is a 'sufficiently reliable scientific basis'? *The International Journal of Evidence & Proof.*, 24(3), 233–254. doi: 10.1177/1365712720927622

18 Ward, T. (2004). Experts, juries, and witch-hunts: From Fitzjames Stephen to Angela Cannings. *Journal of Law and Society*, 31, 369–386, 385. doi: 10.1111/j.1467-6478.2004.00295.x.

19 Jasanoff, S. (1992). What judges should know about the sociology of science. *Jurimetrics J.*, 32, 345, 356; Jasanoff, S. (2008). *Science and Public Reason* (p. 192). London: Routledge. See also, Edmond, G. (2008). Judging the scientific and medical literature: Some legal implications of changes to biomedical research and publication. *Oxford Journal of Legal Studies*, 28(3), 523, at 529. doi: 10.1093/ojls/gqn021, citing Jasanoff, S. (2005). Law's knowledge: Science for justice in legal settings. *American Journal of Public Health*, 95(S1), S49–S58, The Coronado Conference: Scientific Evidence and Public Policy Paper, Available at SSRN: https://ssrn.com/abstract=849369; Edmond, G. (2004). Judging facts: Managing expert knowledges in legal decision-making. In G. Edmond (Ed.), *Expertise in Regulation and Law* (p. 136). Aldershot: Ashgate.

20 Jasanoff, S. (1992). What judges should know about the sociology of science. *Jurimetrics J.*, 32, 345, 356. See also, Jasanoff, S. (2008). *Science and Public Reason* (p. 192). London: Routledge.

21 Jasanoff, S. (1992). What judges should know about the sociology of science. *Jurimetrics J.*, 32, 345, 356. See also, Jasanoff, S. (2008). *Science and Public Reason* (p. 192). London: Routledge.

> appreciate fully what the expert's reasons are. While trust in experts is not irrational, the level of trust to be placed in a given expert is not determined by purely epistemic reasons, but depends heavily upon social judgements and attitudes.[22]

However, some jurors may place excessive trust in an expert because of their expert status and a general tendency to trust experts – to aid time-efficient decision making and to make their 'cognitive lives easier.'[23]

Given the limitations of current approaches, an alternative means for determining the validity of purported expert techniques is the use of a multidisciplinary scientific advisory panel. The panel would advise on the empirical underpinnings of aspects of forensic science methodology.[24] Experts could seek pre-approval to streamline the process and to give those seeking to instruct experts a basis on which to make a choice.[25]

Lawyers can become involved in activities which result in the alleged manipulation of scientific knowledge. For example, Huber has argued that in US torts litigation there is evidence of lawyers promoting 'bizarre and fantastic stories.'[26] Oreskes and Conway discuss what they call 'industry disinformation campaigns.'[27] Projects involving the development of scientific evidence to counter findings relating to the harm caused by second-hand smoke were operated through law firms to take advantage of attorney–client privilege, while scientists acting as expert witnesses were categorised as employees of the law firm rather than the tobacco industry.[28] In examples of this type, scientific ethics and legal ethics come into critical focus.[29] From a positivist perspective of

22 Ward, T. (2004). Experts, juries, and witch-hunts: From Fitzjames Stephen to Angela Cannings. *Journal of Law and Society*, 31, 369–386, 385. doi: 10.1111/j.1467-6478.2004.00295.x, discussing Stephen, J. F. (1860). On trial by jury, and the evidence of experts. *Papers Read before the Juridical Society*, 2, 236

23 Ward, T. (2020). Explaining and trusting expert evidence: What is a 'sufficiently reliable scientific basis'? *The International Journal of Evidence & Proof.*, 24(3), 233–254. doi: 10.1177/1365712720927622, citing Mieg, H. A. (2001). *The Social Psychology of Expertise*. New York: Psychology Press; Freckelton, I., Goodman-Delahunty, J., Horan, J. et al. (2016). *Expert Evidence and Criminal Jury Trials*. Oxford: Oxford University Press, Ch 5.

24 Edmond, G., & Roberts, A. (2011) The Law Commission's report on expert evidence in criminal proceedings. *Criminal Law Review*, 11, 844–862 846

25 Freer, E. (2020). Experts and pretenders: Examining possible responses to misconduct by experts in criminal trials in England and Wales. *The International Journal of Evidence & Proof*, 24(2), 180–207. doi: 10.1177/1365712720913336

26 Huber, P. W. (1991). *Galileo's Revenge: Junk Science in the Courtroom* (p. 202). New York: Basic Books.

27 Oreskes, N., & Conway, E. M. (2010). *Merchants of Doubt: How a Handful of Scientists Obscured the Truth on Issues from Tobacco Smoke to Global Warming*. New York: Bloomsbury, 139–140.

28 Oreskes, N., & Conway, E. M. (2010). *Merchants of Doubt: How a Handful of Scientists Obscured the Truth on Issues from Tobacco Smoke to Global Warming*. New York: Bloomsbury, 139–140.

29 See, for example, Rhode, D. (2000). Ethics in practice. In D. Rhode (Ed.), *Ethics in Practice: Lawyers' Roles, Responsibilities, and Regulation*. Oxford: Oxford University Press.

legal ethics, lawyers may find themselves adopting excessive, even immoral, approaches when acting for clients – law is prioritised over ethics, and what counts as ethics becomes defined by client interests.[30]

Overall, the key purpose of expert evidence in common law jurisdictions was neatly summed up by Mortimer J. in *Guy v Crown Melbourne Limited (No 2)*.[31] Evidence given by a senior Australian academic was characterised as being 'flawed and irresponsible' with assertions made 'without any basis in research or fact,' as well as plagiarised statements.[32] The academic's claims that he had adopted an approach less rigorous than is the norm in academic discourse because he viewed the court environment as one for education and information sharing was rejected with the following observations:

> For Professor [name] to see the provision of expert evidence to the Court as providing an 'education' in an 'information-sharing educational forum' that requires less rigour than publication in an 'academic forum' discloses at best a failure to understand and appreciate the role and responsibilities of an expert witness . . . and at worst a misplaced arrogance about the importance of discussion and debate within the academy as compared to discussion and debate between qualified experts for the purposes of assisting and informing the exercise of judicial power. The purpose of expert evidence is not to 'educate' the Court on matters, it is to provide a specialist opinion or information which is outside the experience and knowledge of a judge or jury. . . . The purpose of admitting an expert opinion on a material question of fact . . . is to assist the Court in forming its own, ultimate opinion and finding on that matter.[33]

Although a rare occurrence, at the extreme, experts giving scientific evidence could find themselves facing contempt of court proceedings and possible imprisonment if they deliberately or recklessly make false statements.[34] Experts such as registered medical practitioners may find themselves subject to investigation by their professional regulatory body, although it has been argued that

30 See for example Mescher, B. (2018). Lawyers' professional ethics: Where are the ethics? *Professional Negligence*34(1), 21–37; Dare, T. (2004). Mere-zeal, hyper-zeal and the ethical obligations of lawyers. *Legal Ethics*, 7(1), 24; Dare, T. (2000). *The Counsel of Rogues? A Defence of the Standard Conception of the Lawyers' Role*. Aldershot: Ashgate.

31 [2018] FCA 36

32 [2018] FCA 36, para 298

33 [2018] FCA 36, para 291–94, also referring to observations in *R v J-LJ* [2000] SCC 51; 2 SCR 600, Binnie J at [56]

34 *Liverpool Victoria Insurance Company Ltd v Zafar* [2019] EWCA Civ 392. In England and Wales contempt of court may be defined as behaviour taking place during, or in connection with, legal proceedings that impedes or prejudices the administration of justice or creates a real risk of that occuring. See also, Attorney General's Office (2021), The Law Officers' approach to contempt of court referrals, https://www.gov.uk/guidance/the-law-officers-approach-to-contempt-of-court-referrals

professional disciplinary proceedings may not sufficiently address expert misconduct in criminal cases.[35]

Legal considerations of plagiarism and other researcher concerns

Plagiarism within research environments risks undermining intellectual honesty and integrity, but it is generally confined to the realms of academic ethical standards, university and, where appropriate, professional regulation rather than entering the formal legal arena.[36] This is in contrast to well-established legal offences such as forgery, where the intention is to pass off one's own work as that of another, whereas plagiarism seeks to take the work of another and to pass it off as one's own.[37]

In contrast to another well-established legal wrong, copyright infringement, plagiarism rarely impacts negatively on the original author's current and future use of the work and its economic value. The nature of academic publishing is such that financial loss to the original author is not particularly quantifiable.[38] Infringement of copyright, in contrast, typically involves quantifiable losses if work is copied and sold, thereby reducing sales of the original work.[39] In legal systems based upon compensatory damages, there is usually little incentive for a plagiarised author to seek legal redress. There may also be considerable risks in pursuing a claim which, by its nature, can have little monetary value – for example, in the English legal system the losing party is usually ordered to pay the winning party's legal costs, so in cost–benefit analysis terms, the potential benefits of pursuing a claim must be sufficiently high.

35 Freer, E. (2020). Experts and pretenders: Examining possible responses to misconduct by experts in criminal trials in England and Wales. *The International Journal of Evidence & Proof*, 24(2), 180–207. doi: 10.1177/1365712720913336. See also, Davies, Mark (2014) *The law of professional immunities*. Oxford University Press, Oxford, ch.2

36 Sonfield, M. C. (2014). Academic plagiarism at the faculty level: legal versus ethical issues and a case study. *J Acad Ethics*, 12, 75–87. Doi: 10.1007/s10805-014-9205-3.

37 Sonfield, M. C. (2014). Academic plagiarism at the faculty level: legal versus ethical issues and a case study. *J Acad Ethics*, 12, 75–87. Doi: 10.1007/s10805-014-9205-3, citing Stearns, L. (1992). Copy wrong: Plagiarism, process, property, and the law. *California Law Review*, 80, 1–34, 3. It is of comparative interest that courts have been found to address as serious concerns plagiarism on the part of lawyers and judges. See, for example, the background discussion in Andrew M. Carter. (2019). The Case for Plagiarism, 9 *U.C. Irvine L. Rev.* 9, 531. In the English case of *Crinion v. I.G. Markets Ltd* [2013] EWCA Civ 587 the Court of Appeal criticised the approach of the first instance judge in taking almost all of his decision word-for-word from the written submissions of counsel.

38 Sonfield, M. C. (2014). Academic plagiarism at the faculty level: legal versus ethical issues and a case study. *J Acad Ethics*, 12, 75–87. Doi: 10.1007/s10805-014-9205-3, citing Stearns, L. (1992). Copy wrong: Plagiarism, process, property, and the law. *California Law Review*, 80, 1–34, 3

39 Sonfield, M. C. (2014). Academic plagiarism at the faculty level: legal versus ethical issues and a case study. *J Acad Ethics*, 12, 75–87. Doi: 10.1007/s10805-014-9205-3, citing Billings, R. (2004). Plagiarism in academia and beyond: what is the role of the courts? University of San Francisco Law Review, 38, 1–31.

Threats of legal action by scientists accused of plagiarism or other research misconduct can inhibit the investigation of allegations. Some editors and publishers may be reluctant to challenge suspicious behaviour, fearful of legal action, and may avoid terms such as plagiarism, however strong the evidence, adopting euphemisms such as 'textual overlap' as softer and less accusatory alternatives.[40] Editors may also prefer to use expressions of concern relating, for example, to the validity of data, methods or interpretation as a means of highlighting potential concerns without needing to take steps which may be deemed to be more risky in legal terms.[41] Such approaches may reduce the extent to which scientific communities are alerted to potentially serious problems and may leave matters relating to the scientific record unresolved.[42]

Evidence from case law also indicates that the courts in some jurisdictions will take a robust approach when litigation is deemed to challenge legitimate academic debate. For example, a senior cancer researcher, Carlo Croce, sued *The New York Times* following allegedly defamatory criticisms of some aspects of his research. The bases of the legal claims included defamation and intentional infliction of emotional distress. Dr Croce was unsuccessful at first instance and on appeal. The court concluded that a reasonable reader would have interpreted *The New York Times* article as a standard piece of investigative journalism, presenting a balanced account of each side of the issue and used appropriate language when considering whether wrongdoing may or may not have occurred.[43] In the Canadian case of *Weaver v Ball* it was observed as long recognised that:

> where someone enters the public arena, it is to be expected that his or her actions and words will be subject to robust scrutiny and criticism. . .. In such situations heated debate and even offensive comments are not in themselves markers of legal wrongs.[44]

40 Grove, J. (2019). Are legal concerns stifling scientific debate? *Times Higher Education*, November 7, 2019, www.timeshighereducation.com/features/are-legal-concerns-stifling-scientific-debate, quoting observations by David A. Sanders, a virologist and associate professor at Purdue University. The position is not entirely one-sided. Some threatened or initiated lawsuits may be legitimate attempts to protect researcher reputations in highly competitive fields, where stakes can be high in financial as well as reputational terms.

41 Vaught M, Jordan DC, Bastian H. Concern noted: a descriptive study of editorial expressions of concern in PubMed and PubMed Central. Res Integ Peer Rev. 2017;2:10. doi: 10.1186/s41073-017-0030-2.

42 Vaught M, Jordan DC, Bastian H. Concern noted: a descriptive study of editorial expressions of concern in PubMed and PubMed Central. Res Integ Peer Rev. 2017;2:10. doi: 10.1186/s41073-017-0030-2. From a sample of 5,076 records, these researchers found 230 editorial expressions of concern (EEoC) in publications indexed in PubMed. The earliest of these dated back to 1985, but the rate of use had increased more recently, with 52 per cent of the primary EEoCs being issued between 2014 and 2016.

43 *Croce v New York Times Co.*, No. 18–4158 (6th Cir. July 17, 2019) www.opn.ca6.uscourts.gov/opinions.pdf/19a0160p-06.pdf (accessed 8th November 2019)

44 2018 BCSC 205, at para [79], citing in *Lund v. Black Press Group Ltd.*, 2009 BCSC 937 at para. 123

Elements of informal self-policing within research communities have also been observed, with examples of claimants having withdrawn legal proceedings following pressure from within a scientific community against attempts to stifle rigorous debate by creating the fear of litigation.[45]

Criminal controls

With a few exceptions, research misconduct tends not give rise to criminal liability with associated penalties such as fines or imprisonment. The use of criminal law has been described as 'potentially one of the most intrusive and severe forms of regulation,' and its use in the UK in the context of research activity tends to be limited to specific areas dealing with what can involve particularly emotive issues and complex moral choices.[46] For example, research governed by the Human Fertilisation and Embryology Act 1990 (as amended) and the Human Tissue Act 2004 can be subject to criminal penalties.[47] In the United States, criminal liability can arise from the submission of false information in a US government agency grant application.[48] The misuse of public money and, associated with that, depriving a more deserving project of that money provides the rationale for an action in the criminal courts.[49]

In terms of the wider debate regarding potential advantages and disadvantages of imposing criminal liability, in general terms, the presence of criminal sanctions in the research regulation armoury, even if rarely used, may help to provide public reassurance and to counter breaches of trust by individual scientists, providing a declaration on behalf of the state about the unacceptability

45 See, for example, Alex Tsai, Stanford professor retracts $10 million libel suit against scientific critic, academic journal, *The Stamford Journal*, March 2, 2018 www.stanforddaily.com/2018/03/02/stanford-professor-retracts-10-million-libel-suit-against-scientific-critic-academic-journal/ (accessed 9 November 2019) Grove, J. (2019). Are legal concerns stifling scientific debate? *Times Higher Education*, November 7, 2019, www.timeshighereducation.com/features/are-legal-concerns-stifling-scientific-debate

46 Alghrani, A., & Chan, S. (2013). "Scientists in the dock": Regulating science. In A. Alghrani, R. Bennett, & S. Ost (Eds.), *The Criminal Law and Bioethical Conflict: Walking the Tightrope* (pp.121–139). Cambridge: Cambridge University Press at 133, 138, citing M. Brazier, 'Regulating the Reproduction Business' (1999) 7(2) Medical Law Review 166, 172

47 Human Fertilisation and Embryology Act 1990, section 41–42; Human Tissue Act 2004, sections 48–50

48 See, for example, case studies from Kornfeld, D. S. (2012). Perspective: Research misconduct: The search for a remedy. *Acad Med,* 87, 877–882, 879; Reardon, S. (2015). US vaccine researcher sentenced to prison for fraud. *Nature,* 523(July 9), 138–139. doi: 10.1038/nature.2015.17660. Although it is noted in the latter article that former biomedical scientist Dong-Pyou Han was only subject to prosecution because of the persistence of a US senator who had a history of investigating biomedical misconduct.

49 Reardon, S. (2015). US vaccine researcher sentenced to prison for fraud. *Nature,* 523(July 9), 138–139. doi: 10.1038/nature.2015.17660. Counter-arguments against the need for criminal sanctions include the observation that the future exclusion from applying for future government funding is likely to damage, possibly even destroy, the career of a researcher, so criminal prosecution offers little or no additional benefit in terms of deterrence.

of certain behaviour.[50] In terms of investigatory expertise and the funding of investigations, shifting responsibility by means of the criminal process to state-funded police and prosecution services offers some advantages, subject to police and prosecutors allocating sufficient resources to undertake the work effectively. Criminal prosecution also offers a response to research misconduct committed by those perpetrators who are unresponsive to other mechanisms for persuasion or control.[51] Such researchers may be undeterred 'unless they have every reason to fear that they are going to be caught and the consequences are going to be catastrophic,' for example, resulting in a criminal record and a financial or even a custodial penalty.[52] Criminal prosecution can, therefore, create a prophylactic effect to aid the prevention of misconduct by persuading researchers to more fully scrutinise their behaviour.[53] Conversely, there is a risk that fear of prosecution may deter openness and disclosure of error or even the seeking of advice by researchers. Criminal focus on individuals may also detract from institutional failures, but this risk can be mitigated if the possibility of institutional sanctions, such as the threat of substantial fines, encourages institutional managers to reform internal procedures to reduce misconduct risks.[54]

50 Alghrani, A., & Chan, S. (2013). "Scientists in the dock": Regulating science. In A. Alghrani, R. Bennett, & S. Ost (Eds.), *The Criminal Law and Bioethical Conflict: Walking the Tightrope* (pp.121–139). Cambridge: Cambridge University Press at 124, 139; John Elmes Should scientific misconduct be a crime?, *Times Higher Education*, June 2, 2017, quoting Ian Freckelton www.timeshighereducation.com/news/should-scientific-misconduct-be-a-crime. See also, Freckelton, Ian. (2014). Criminalising research fraud. *Journal of law and medicine*. 22. 241–54. Similar observations are made by Redman, Barbara & Caplan, Arthur. (2005). Off with their Heads: The Need to Criminalize some forms of Scientific Misconduct. *The Journal of law, medicine & ethics: a journal of the American Society of Law, Medicine & Ethics*. 33. 345–8, 346–7. 10.1111/j.1748-720X.2005.tb00498.x.

51 Freckelton, Ian. (2014). Criminalising research fraud. *Journal of law and medicine*. 22. 241–54.

52 John Elmes Should scientific misconduct be a crime?, *Times Higher Education*, June 2, 2017, quoting Ian Freckelton www.timeshighereducation.com/news/should-scientific-misconduct-be-a-crime. See also Freckelton, Ian. (2014). Criminalising research fraud. Journal of law and medicine. 22. 241–54. It is also suggested that researchers might think more carefully about being 'cavalier with the truth' and with public money if there was a realistic prospect that the police might knock on their door and criminal consequences follow.

53 Sovacool, B. (2008). Exploring scientific misconduct: Isolated individuals, impure institutions, or an inevitable idiom of modern science? *Journal of Bioethical Inquiry*, 5, 271–282, 278. doi: 10.1007/s11673-008-9113-6.. Citing Goldberg, D. (2003). Research fraud: a sui generic problem demands a sui generic solution (plus a little due process). Thomas M. Cooley Law Review, 20, 47–69; Kuzma, S.M. (1992). Criminal liability for misconduct in scientific research. University of Michigan Journal of Law Reform. University of Michigan. Law School, 25, 357–401; Redman, B., & Caplan, A. (2005). Off with their heads: the need to criminalize some forms of scientific misconduct. *The Journal of Law, Medicine & Ethics*, 33, 344–361. doi: 10.1111/j.1748-720X.2005.tb00498.x. Although as criminal prosecutions globally are very small in number, such a marginal risk may make the deterrent value negligible, Science and Technology Committee, Oral evidence: Research Integrity, HC 350, Monday 4 December 2017, Ordered by the House of Commons to be published on 4 December 2017.

54 Fenning, T.M.. (2004). Fraud offers big rewards for relatively little risk. *Nature*. 427. 393. 10.1038/427393a; Redman, Barbara & Caplan, Arthur. (2005). Off with their Heads: The Need to Criminalize some forms of Scientific Misconduct. *The Journal of law, medicine & ethics: a journal of the American Society of Law, Medicine & Ethics*. 33. 345–8, 348. 10.1111/j.1748-720X.2005.tb00498.x

In many respects, scientific research fraud is not significantly different in nature from other misbehaviour, such as financial fraud, already well established in the criminal sphere. Each typically involves the misuse of resources, and in addition scientific fraud in certain fields can directly endanger the public, for example, in the context of medical research.[55] As Smith suggests – the term research misconduct is 'the gentlemanly phrase for scientific fraud.'[56] Even if individual victims are difficult to identify with precision, the consequences of research fraud on human health can be enormous, for example, the impact of the reduced take-up globally of the MMR vaccine following the discredited research by Andrew Wakefield.[57]

Arguments against criminalising aspects of scientific misconduct include observations that outside of certain examples, such as medical research placing patients at risk, harm resulting from research misconduct is not readily measurable.[58] Criminalisation may also risk creating the impression among a regulated community that behaviour which falls outside the prescribed legal framework must be acceptable.[59] This can sit in opposition to approaches to research misconduct which seek to encourage researchers to reflect on good ethical standards, whether certain behaviours are formally proscribed or not. The criminalising of research fraud may also undermine aspects of trust which are central to research collaboration – good governance, rather than criminalisation

55 Redman, B., & Caplan, A. (2014). No One Likes a Snitch. *Science and Engineering Ethics,* 21. doi: 10.1007/s11948-014-9570-8; Freckelton, Ian. (2014). Criminalising research fraud. *Journal of law and medicine*. 22. 241–54; Redman, Barbara & Caplan, Arthur. (2005). Off with their Heads: The Need to Criminalize some forms of Scientific Misconduct. *The Journal of law, medicine & ethics: a journal of the American Society of Law, Medicine & Ethics*. 33. 345–8. 10.1111/j.1748-720X.2005.tb00498.x; Sovacool, Benjamin. (2005). Using Criminalization and Due Process to Reduce Scientific Misconduct. The *American journal of bioethics*: AJOB. 5. W1–7. 10.1080/15265160500313242.

56 Smith R. Should scientific fraud be a criminal offence? BMJ blogs, 3 December 2013. https://blogs.bmj.com/bmj/2013/12/09/richard-smith-should-scientific-fraud-be-a-criminal-offence/ (accessed 29 November 2020). See also, Editorial, Call the cops, *Nature* 504, 7 (05 December 2013) doi: 10.1038/504007a

57 Bhutta, Z.A., Crane, J. (2014) Should research fraud be a crime? *BMJ*._349_doi: https://doi.org/10.1136/bmj.g4532

58 Breen KJ (2003). Misconduct in medical research: whose responsibility? *Intern Med J*. 33: 186–91; Vogel G. (2014). Suspect drug research blamed for massive death toll. *Science*. 343:473–4; Godlee F, Smith J, Marcovitch H. (2011). Wakefield's article linking MMR vaccine and autism was fraudulent. *BMJ*. 342: c7452. See also observations by Nobel Prize winning chemist, Dan Shechtman with regard to criminalising research misconduct, David Matthews. (2019). Nobelist backs internal review for papers, 'trust' scores for scientists, *Times Higher Education*, July 29, www.timeshighereducation.com/news/nobelist-backs-internal-review-papers-trust-scores-scientists

59 Bülow, W., Helgesson, G. (2019). Criminalization of scientific misconduct. *Med Health Care and Philos* 22, 245–252. https://doi.org/10.1007/s11019-018-9865-7; Misconduct in biomedical research: final consensus statement. In: Nimmo W, ed. Joint consensus conference on misconduct in biomedical research. Proc R Coll Physicians Edinb 2000;30(suppl 7):2, cited in Bhutta, Z.A., Crane, J. (2014) Should research fraud be a crime? *BMJ*._349_doi: https://doi.org/10.1136/bmj.g4532

and punitive sanctions, may offer better solutions in this regard.[60] For example, it has been suggested that the UK Human Tissue Act 2004 could, had it existed at the time, have negatively impacted upon the research which led to the 2005 Nobel Prize in Medicine, awarded for the discovery (based on human tissue studies) of *Helicobacter pylori* as the main cause of peptic ulcers.[61] While the letter of the 2004 Act should not have prevented such research, the bureaucratic framework and fear of potential legal repercussions could have presented a deterrent effect – an 'if in doubt, don't do it' mindset among scientific researchers.[62]

The extent of current criminalisation varies between jurisdictions, and the practical reality is that the impact of potential criminal sanctions on researcher motivation and decisions about research focus remains relatively under-researched and therefore largely speculative.[63] Also, if 'scientific exceptionalism' has become so embedded that the police lack the education and expertise to address alleged scientific fraud, suspected dishonesty in science may occupy a societal vacuum, not categorised in criminal terms and so not investigated as such.[64]

Examples of criminal prosecutions

In 2009 Scott Reuben, an anaesthesiologist in the United States, was imprisoned for health care fraud, having been found to have faked data in over 20 studies. Reuben's studies impacted on the treatment of very large numbers of

60 Bhutta, Z.A., Crane, J. (2014) Should research fraud be a crime? *BMJ*._349_doi: https://doi.org/10.1136/bmj.g4532; Freckelton, Ian. (2014). Criminalising research fraud. Journal of law and medicine. 22. 241–54, quoting Research Professor Julian Crane, Director of the Wellington Asthma Research Group at the Wellington School of Medicine at the University of Otago in New Zealand and citing Branswell H, "Should Research Fraud be Treated as a Crime? Toronto Expert Says Yes", The Prince George Citizen.

61 Alghrani, A., & Chan, S. (2013). "Scientists in the dock": Regulating science. In A. Alghrani, R. Bennett, & S. Ost (Eds.), *The Criminal Law and Bioethical Conflict: Walking the Tightrope* (pp.121–139). Cambridge: Cambridge University Press at 135, citing Furness, P. (2006). 'The Human Tissue Act: Reassurance for Relatives, at a Price' *BMJ*, 333, 512.

62 Alghrani, A., & Chan, S. (2013). "Scientists in the dock": Regulating science. In A. Alghrani, R. Bennett, & S. Ost (Eds.), *The Criminal Law and Bioethical Conflict: Walking the Tightrope* (pp.121–139). Cambridge: Cambridge University Press at 135, citing Furness, P. (2006). 'The Human Tissue Act: Reassurance for Relatives, at a Price' *BMJ*, 333, 512.

63 Reardon, S. (2015). US vaccine researcher sentenced to prison for fraud. *Nature*, 523(July 9), 138–139. doi: 10.1038/nature.2015.17660.

64 Redman, Barbara & Caplan, Arthur. (2005). Off with their Heads: The Need to Criminalize some forms of Scientific Misconduct. The Journal of law, medicine & ethics: a journal of the American Society of Law, Medicine & Ethics. 33. 345–8, 347. 10.1111/j.1748–720X.2005.tb00498.x, citing Riis P. (1994). Prevention and management of fraud–in theory. J Intern Med. 235(2):107–13. doi: 10.1111/j.1365-2796.1994.tb01043.x. PMID: 8308472; Breen, K. J. (2016). Research misconduct: Time for a re-think? *Internal Medicine Journal*, 46, 728–733. doi: 10.1111/imj.13075

people for pain during and after orthopaedic surgery. In addition, medication taken by large numbers also had questionable benefits, uncertain long-term risks and may have slowed postoperative healing.[65]

Immunologist Luk Van Parijs misused funding from the US National Institutes of Health and subsequently pleaded guilty to grant fraud. The fraud related to data falsification when he was an associate professor of biology at the Massachusetts Institute of Technology (MIT), as well as concerns relating to his graduate studies at the Harvard Medical School and postdoctoral work at the California Institute of Technology.[66] Van Parijs was found to have committed over 11 incidents of data fabrication in grant applications and papers between 1997 and 2004.[67] Criminal charges were initiated, and prosecutors requested a period of imprisonment to reflect the significant value of the fraud, the criminal charges relating to a $2 million grant and to act as a deterrent to other potential research fraudsters.[68] Following his guilty plea and supporting statements from within the scientific community, Van Parijs was sentenced to home detention and community service and required to repay misused funds of $61,117 to MIT.[69] At least one supporting scientist suggested that prospective

65 White PF, Rosow CE, Shafer SL. (2011). The Scott Reuben saga: one last retraction. *Anesth Analg.* 112: 512–15; Borrell, B. A. (2009). medical Madoff: anesthesiologist faked data in 21 studies. *Sci. Am.* www.scientificamerican.com/article/a-medical-madoff-anesthestesiologist-faked-data/ (10 March); McHugh UM, Yentis SM. An analysis of retractions of papers authored by Scott Reuben, Joachim Boldt and Yoshitaka Fujii. Anaesthesia. 2019 Jan;74(1):17–21. doi: 10.1111/anae.14414. Epub 2018 Aug 24. Erratum in: Anaesthesia. 2019 Jan;74(1):113. PMID: 30144024; USDOJ: US Attorney's Office - District of Massachusetts (archive.org)

66 The United States Attorney's Office, Massachusetts, Former MIT Professor Pleads Guilty To False Statements In Federal Research Grant Application, Thursday, March 3, 2011 www.justice.gov/archive/usao/ma/news/2011/March/VanParijspleapr.html; Reich, S. E. (2011). Biologist spared jail for grant fraud. *Nature,* 474, 552. https://doi.org/10.1038/474552a; Stroebe, W., Postmes, T., & Spears, R. (2012). Scientific misconduct and the myth of self-correction in science. *Perspect Psychol Sci.*, 7(6), 670–688. doi: 10.1177/1745691612460687

67 The United States Attorney's Office, Massachusetts, Former MIT Professor Pleads Guilty To False Statements In Federal Research Grant Application, Thursday, March 3, 2011 www.justice.gov/archive/usao/ma/news/2011/March/VanParijspleapr.html; Reich, S. E. (2011). Biologist spared jail for grant fraud. *Nature,* 474, 552. https://doi.org/10.1038/474552a

68 The United States Attorney's Office, Massachusetts, Former MIT Professor Pleads Guilty To False Statements In Federal Research Grant Application, Thursday, March 3, 2011, www.justice.gov/archive/usao/ma/news/2011/March/VanParijspleapr.html; Reich, S. E. (2011). Biologist spared jail for grant fraud. *Nature,* 474, 552. https://doi.org/10.1038/474552a; Stroebe, W., Postmes, T., & Spears, R. (2012). Scientific misconduct and the myth of self-correction in science. *Perspect Psychol Sci.*, 7(6), 670–688. doi: 10.1177/1745691612460687

69 The United States Attorney's Office, Massachusetts, Former MIT Professor Pleads Guilty To False Statements In Federal Research Grant Application, Thursday, March 3, 2011, www.justice.gov/archive/usao/ma/news/2011/March/VanParijspleapr.html; Reich, S. E. (2011). Biologist spared jail for grant fraud. *Nature,* 474, 552. https://doi.org/10.1038/474552a; Stroebe, W., Postmes, T., & Spears, R. (2012). Scientific misconduct and the myth of self-correction in science. *Perspect Psychol Sci.*, 7(6), 670–688. doi: 10.1177/1745691612460687

whistle-blowers may be deterred if they thought that they may be responsible for a fellow scientist's imprisonment, but a whistle-blower against Van Parijs is reported to have signalled the opposite view and expressed concerns that the sentence was inadequate given the career damage caused to junior researchers caught up in the orbit of the scandal.[70]

Also in the United States, Eric Poehlman was sentenced to a period of imprisonment for defrauding the federal government of grant funding as a result of fabricating or falsifying data on 15 grant applications.[71] In 2015 Dong-Pyou Han, formerly a researcher at Iowa State University, was sentenced to 57 months imprisonment and fined US$7.2 million for fabricating and falsifying data in HIV vaccine trials.[72]

In the UK in 2013, Steven Eaton was imprisoned by Edinburgh Sheriff Court for three months, having been found guilty of falsifying research data for experimental anti-cancer drugs while working at the Edinburgh branch of the pharmaceutical company Aptuit.[73] Eaton had been involved in pre-clinical animal trials intended to assess the safety and side effects of new treatments. Experiments which had failed were reported as successful, which could have provided a basis from which to proceed to human trials, placing patients at risk. As part of Aptuit's quality control processes, irregularities were identified in some of Eaton's bioanalytical data. The company reported Eaton to the Medicines and Healthcare Products Regulatory Agency (MHRA). The MHRA's investigatory review extended over two years and considered hundreds of drugs tested by Aptuit. The finding was that Eaton's selective reporting of research

70 The United States Attorney's Office, Massachusetts, Former MIT Professor Pleads Guilty To False Statements In Federal Research Grant Application, Thursday, March 3, 2011, www.justice.gov/archive/usao/ma/news/2011/March/VanParijspleapr.html; Reich, S. E. (2011). Biologist spared jail for grant fraud. *Nature,* 474, 552. https://doi.org/10.1038/474552a; Stroebe, W., Postmes, T., & Spears, R. (2012). Scientific misconduct and the myth of self-correction in science. *Perspect Psychol Sci.*, 7(6), 670–688. doi: 10.1177/1745691612460687

71 The Office of Research Integrity. *Case Summary – Eric T. Poehlman*, https://ori.hhs.gov/case-summary-eric-t-poehlman (accessed 16 January 2021). See also, Dahlberg, J. E., & Mahler, C. C. (2006). The Poehlman case: Running away from the truth. *Sci Eng Ethics.*, 12(1) (January),157–173. doi: 10.1007/s11948-006-0016-9. PMID: 16501657; Tilden, S. J. (2010). Incarceration, restitution, and lifetime debarment: Legal consequences of scientific misconduct in the Eric Poehlman case: Commentary on: "Scientific forensics: How the office of research integrity can assist institutional investigations of research misconduct during oversight review". *Science and Engineering Ethics,* 16(4), 737–741.

72 Department of Justice U.S. Attorney's Office, Southern District of Iowa, Former Iowa State Researcher Sentenced for Making False Statements, Wednesday, July 1, 2015, www.justice.gov/usao-sdia/pr/former-iowa-state-researcher-sentenced-making-false-statements

73 Scientist Steven Eaton jailed for falsifying drug test results, www.bbc.co.uk/news/uk-scotland-edinburgh-east-fife-22186220; Clare Dyer, 'Bioanalyst gets jail sentence for falsifying preclinical trial data', *BMJ* 2013;346: f2514; Leung GKK. (2019). Criminalizing medical research fraud: Towards an appropriate legal framework and policy response. *Medical Law International.* 19(1):3–31. doi: 10.1177/0968533219836274

data had been ongoing for a number of years. While Eaton's actions had created potential risks for patients, the necessary investigation and suspension of certain research strands had also slowed the development of certain drugs, thus harming the public in another way. The prosecution was the first brought under the auspices of the Good Laboratory Practice Regulations 1999. The sentence was the maximum available from this legislation, and the sentencing sheriff expressed concern that his sentencing powers were inadequate given the risks Eaton's behaviour posed to patients.[74]

One of the most extreme examples in recent times of scientists being subject to criminal prosecution arose in Italy. In 2012 seven of Italy's natural disasters experts and members of an official government body, the National Commission for the Forecast and Prevention of Major Risks – six seismologists including a former president of Italy's National Institute of Geophysics and Volcanology and one government official – were sentenced to six years imprisonment for manslaughter following statements made before the L'Aquila earthquake in 2009 in which over 300 people died and over 1,000 were injured.[75] The experts had met on 31 March 2009 to assess the scientific evidence relating to imminent earthquake risk. The prosecution case was that at a subsequent press conference they communicated a reassuring message that a major earthquake was not expected.[76]

The judge explained the sentences on the basis that while the scientists were not expected to predict with certainty a forthcoming earthquake, they were expected to consider risk and to appropriately incorporate historical research literature into their advice, rather than to make reassuring statements which were superficial, vague and generic – part of a media operation to reassure the public. The judge concluded that 29 of those who died and a number of those injured would have evacuated their homes had the flawed advice not been given.[77]

From within the international scientific community the verdict and sentences were described as perverse, ludicrous and potentially placed in jeopardy the willingness of some scientists in the future to serve in public risk

74 Scientist Steven Eaton jailed for falsifying drug test results, www.bbc.co.uk/news/uk-scotland-edinburgh-east-fife-22186220; Clare Dyer, 'Bioanalyst gets jail sentence for falsifying preclinical trial data', *BMJ* 2013;346: f2514; Leung GKK. (2019). Criminalizing medical research fraud: Towards an appropriate legal framework and policy response. Medical Law International. 19(1):3–31. doi: 10.1177/0968533219836274

75 Edwin Cartlidge. (2013). Judge in L'Aquila Earthquake Trial Explains His Verdict, *Science*, January 21 www.sciencemag.org/news/2013/01/judge-laquila-earthquake-trial-explains-his-verdict. For a detailed account of the events leading up to the earthquake, see Stephen S. Hall. (2011). Scientists on trial: At fault?, *Nature* 477, 264–269 doi: 10.1038/477264a

76 Alison Abbott and Nicola Nosengo. (2014). Italian seismologists cleared of manslaughter, *Nature* 515, 171 doi: 10.1038/515171a

77 Edwin Cartlidge. (2013). Judge in L'Aquila Earthquake Trial Explains His Verdict, *Science*, January 21 www.sciencemag.org/news/2013/01/judge-laquila-earthquake-trial-explains-his-verdict

assessments.[78] The response from the convicted scientists included the observation that responsibility lay with the Italian government, which had failed to communicate nuanced scientific information to L'Aquila's citizens. They also argued that the prosecution had distorted the purpose and conclusion of the historical study and that the 'public prosecutor's superficial interpretation of scientific results to bolster his argument sets a grave precedent for not only seismology but many other disciplines as well.'[79]

In essence, the legal process, it was argued, had misrepresented the fact that individual studies are rarely the final word, but rather constitute a point for further scientific discussion and debate as knowledge advances by incremental steps.[80]

The convictions were subsequently overturned on appeal, lawyers acting for the scientists successfully arguing that no clear causal link had been established between the statements and the behaviour of the residents of L'Aquila.[81] Despite the ultimate acquittals, at least two key observations can be drawn from this case. The first is that the scientists had to fight a lengthy legal battle to clear their names, and the risk of facing a similar ordeal is likely to remain a deterrent to others when considering whether or not to engage with public service science. The second is that the anger directed at the scientists from some sections of the public remained, for example, a number of relatives of the earthquake victims were reported as remaining angry that, in their opinions, justice had not been served.[82] This may also act as a deterrent to scientists who, unlike politicians, are unlikely to have chosen their career under the assumption that they may become public figures subject in certain circumstances to public outrage.

78 Editorial, Shock and law, *Nature* 490, 446 (25 October 2012) doi: 10.1038/490446b

79 Larry Greenemeier. (2013). Faulty Justice: Italian Earthquake Scientist Speaks Out against His Conviction, *Scientific American*, September 26 www.scientificamerican.com/article/italy-abruzzo-earthquake-scientist-trial/

80 Larry Greenemeier. (2013). Faulty Justice: Italian Earthquake Scientist Speaks Out against His Conviction, *Scientific American*, September 26 www.scientificamerican.com/article/italy-abruzzo-earthquake-scientist-trial/

81 Alison Abbott and Nicola Nosengo. (2014). Italian seismologists cleared of manslaughter, *Nature* 515, 171 doi: 10.1038/515171a; Edwin Cartlidge. (2015). Italy's supreme court clears L'Aquila earthquake scientists for good, Science, Nov. 20 www.sciencemag.org/news/2015/11/italy-s-supreme-court-clears-l-aquila-earthquake-scientists-good; Edwin Cartlidge. (2016). Seven-year legal saga ends as Italian official is cleared of manslaughter in earthquake trial, *Science*, Oct. 3 www.sciencemag.org/news/2016/10/seven-year-legal-saga-ends-italian-official-cleared-manslaughter-earthquake-trial

82 Alison Abbott and Nicola Nosengo. (2014). Italian seismologists cleared of manslaughter, *Nature* 515, 171. doi: 10.1038/515171a; Edwin Cartlidge. (2015). Italy's supreme court clears L'Aquila earthquake scientists for good, Science, Nov. 20 www.sciencemag.org/news/2015/11/italy-s-supreme-court-clears-l-aquila-earthquake-scientists-good; Edwin Cartlidge. (2016). Seven-year legal saga ends as Italian official is cleared of manslaughter in earthquake trial, *Science*, Oct. 3 www.sciencemag.org/news/2016/10/seven-year-legal-saga-ends-italian-official-cleared-manslaughter-earthquake-trial

In terms of future developments, some jurisdictional moves are underway to further criminalise research misconduct. Early in 2019 Montenegro became one of the first countries to outlaw by means of legislation plagiarism, fabrication of research results and donation of authorship. Although a small jurisdiction, with a population of under 1 million and one public and two private universities, it has been suggested that other countries will watch with interest how this initiative unfolds.[83]

83 David Matthews. (2019). Balkans lead drive to criminalise academic misconduct, *Times Higher Education*, April 10 www.timeshighereducation.com/news/balkans-lead-drive-criminalise-academic-misconduct; see also The first lex specialis to tackle academic integrity in Europe will be developed in Montenegro, 10 November 2017, www.coe.int/en/web/podgorica/-/the-first-lex-specialis-to-tackle-academic-integrity-in-europe-will-be-developed-in-montenegro (accessed 18 June 2019)

Chapter 8

New approaches to matters of research integrity and regulation

This chapter cross references traditional approaches to overseeing scientific research discussed in earlier chapters with more recent developments, including in the direction of the 'democratisation' of oversight.[1]

Influences outside of science play an important role in the overall picture of scientific regulation. For example, media interest in a story can be an important influence in motivating those in the scientific field into action.[2] An example can be drawn from the case of surgeon Paolo Macchiarini at the Karolinska Institute in Sweden. The Karolinska Institute had concluded in August 2015 that Macchiarini was not guilty of scientific misconduct. Investigations were relatively quickly reopened at the Karolinska Institute following a three-part Swedish television investigation, aired in January 2016. This documentary and follow-up media comment and scrutiny appear to have revealed additional evidence not unearthed by earlier institutional investigations.[3] Macchiarini was subsequently found guilty of misconduct. As illustrated in this case, while the media can help to uncover or progress research misconduct matters, it remains problematic that a just outcome might depend upon the newsworthy nature of a particular case. Inconsistency of outcomes is a likely consequence if the thoroughness of some misconduct investigations is dependent upon media interest and investigatory resources.

The charity Sense about Science campaigns to encourage and facilitate scientific thinking among the public, politicians and others. By developing

1 H. Nowotny (1999). The place of people in our knowledge. European Review, 7(2), 247–262; H. Nowotny, P. Scott, M. Gibbons (2001). *Re-thinking science: knowledge and the public in an age of uncertainty*. Cambridge, UK: Polity; H. Nowotny. (2003). Democratising expertise and socially robust knowledge. *Sci Public Policy* 30 (3): 151–156; H. Nowotny (2005). *The public nature of science under assault politics, markets, science and the law*. New York, US: Springer

2 David A. Sanders, Each scientist must stand up, at all costs, for the truth', *Times Higher Education* 9 July 2020 www.timeshighereducation.com/features/each-scientist-must-stand-all-costs-truth

3 *Suspected Scientific Misconduct*, Karolinska Institute Summary Report (English translation), p4 (accessed 20 November 2020)

DOI: 10.4324/9780429492129-8

initiatives to facilitate honest discussions of evidence, it seeks to influence how governments, media and corporations use scientific evidence.[4] One notable example is the involvement of Sense about Science in the campaign for the reform of defamation law in England and Wales, influencing the provisions of the Defamation Act 2013, to protect open scientific discussion.

Another charitable body, the Science Media Centre, was created in 2002 following the House of Lords Science and Technology Select Committee third report on Science and Society, the aim of which was to renew public trust in science.[5] The objectives of the Science Media Centre are:

> To advance the education of the public in science and engineering and all their related branches and disciplines, particularly by the dissemination of research and information about science to the media.[6]

The Centre aims to contribute to achievement of this by promoting balanced, accurate and measured media reporting of science, health and environmental matters. Particular focus is directed to controversial news stories which pose a particular risk of disseminating misinformation and creating confusion. By working with experts from the scientific community to support their engagement with the media, and by working with journalists and press officers engaged with complex and contentious science-related stories, the Centre aims to bring all key parties together to ensure that reporting is as accurate and appropriate as possible.[7]

Identification of discrepancies in published research potentially offers an early warning of unreliability and potential misconduct. There are various examples of readers of scientific publications discovering problems overlooked in the peer reviewer and editorial processes. For example, concerns about John Sudbø, who was found to have falsified and fabricated research and 'dreamed up the lives and lifestyles of some 900 people – and used them in a study on cancer,'[8] were raised by an expert reader who noticed that the cancer patient database,

4 https://senseaboutscience.org/ (accessed 22 February 2020)
5 www.sciencemediacentre.org/about-us/ (accessed 22 February 2020)
6 www.sciencemediacentre.org/about-us/ (accessed 22 February 2020); Science Media Centre Annual Report and Financial Statements for the year ended 31 March 2019 www.sciencemediacentre.org/wp-content/uploads/2019/11/SMC-final-accounts-31-March-2019-signed.pdf (accessed 22 February 2020)
7 www.sciencemediacentre.org/about-us/ (accessed 22 February 2020); Science Media Centre Annual Report and Financial Statements for the year ended 31 March 2019 www.sciencemediacentre.org/wp-content/uploads/2019/11/SMC-final-accounts-31-March-2019-signed.pdf (accessed 22 February 2020)
8 Marris, E. (2006). Doctor admits *Lancet* study is fiction. *Nature* 439, 248–249 provides. https://doi.org/10.1038/439248b. See also, Brian Vastag. (2006). Cancer Fraud Case Stuns Research Community, Prompts Reflection on Peer Review Process, *JNCI: Journal of the National Cancer Institute*, 98(6), 374–376, https://doi.org/10.1093/jnci/djj118; Cole, Graham & Nowbar,

which Sudbø identified as being used for research published in the *Lancet*, had not been available at the time of the purported research.[9] Camilla Stoltenberg, a director of epidemiology at the Norwegian Institute of Public Health in Oslo and responsible for the Cohort of Norway, knew that, contrary to the claims made in Sudbø's paper, the cancer patient database could not have been the source of the lifestyle data.[10]

In 2016 Elisabeth Bik, when a researcher at Stanford University, led an analysis of 20,000 papers published in mBio. Four per cent contained inappropriately manipulated images. Researcher intent could not be definitively determined from the study findings. While some categories were most likely to result from honest errors, such as authors accidentally inserting the same image twice, others could have been intentional – for example, authors intentionally recycling a control panel from a different experiment because the actual control was not performed.[11] Open-access journals were not notably different from their non-open-access counterparts, although a higher proportion of problematic images were found in journals with lower impact factors. Duplications could be readily identified by simple inspection, without the need for specialist equipment, with a conclusion that greater peer reviewer and editorial scrutiny should be able to identify problematic figures prior to publication.[12]

Alexandra & Mielewczik, Michael & Shun-Shin, Matthew & Francis, Darrel. (2015). Frequency of discrepancies in retracted clinical trial reports versus unretracted reports: blinded case-control study. BMJ (Clinical research ed.). 351. h4708. 10.1136/bmj.h4708; Eaton, Lynn. (2006). Norwegian researcher admits that his data were faked. BMJ (Clinical research ed.) vol. 332,7535 193. doi: 10.1136/bmj.332.7535.193-a; ORI, Case Summary: Sudbo, Jon https://ori.hhs.gov/case-summary-sudbo-jon; Stroebe, W., Postmes, T., & Spears, R. (2012). Scientific misconduct and the myth of self-correction in science. *Perspect Psychol Sci.*, 7(6), 670–688. doi: 10.1177/1745691612460687, referring to Sudbø, J., Lee, J. J., Lippman, S. M., Mork, J., Sagen, S., Flatner, N . . .. Danneberg, A. J. (2005). Non-steroidal anti-inflammatory drugs and the risk of oral cancer: A nested case-control study. *Lancet*, 365, 1359–1366.

9 Stroebe, W., Postmes, T., & Spears, R. (2012). Scientific misconduct and the myth of self-correction in science. *Perspect Psychol Sci.*, 7(6), 670–688. doi: 10.1177/1745691612460687, referring to Sudbø, J., Lee, J. J., Lippman, S. M., Mork, J., Sagen, S., Flatner, N . . .. Danneberg, A. J. (2005). Non-steroidal anti-inflammatory drugs and the risk of oral cancer: A nested case-control study. *Lancet*, 365, 1359–1366.

10 Marris, E. (2006). Doctor admits *Lancet* study is fiction. *Nature* 439, 248–249. https://doi.org/10.1038/439248b.

11 Bik, E. M., Casadevall, A., & Fang, F. C., (2016). The prevalence of inappropriate image duplication in biomedical research publications. *mBio*, 7(3) (June), e00809–16. doi: 10.1128/mBio.00809-16

12 Evidence of this was cited in relation to the *Journal of Cell Biology*, which had instituted a policy to carefully inspect all manuscripts for image manipulation. The much lower prevalence than the average for problematic images (0.3 per cent compared with a 4 per cent average and over 12 per cent for the journal with the greatest detected proportion) indicates a positive effect from this policy. Bik, E. M., Casadevall, A., & Fang, F. C., (2016). The prevalence of inappropriate image duplication in biomedical research publications. *mBio*, 7(3) (June), e00809–16. doi: 10.1128/mBio.00809-16, citing Rossner, Mike, and Kenneth M Yamada. (2004). What's in a picture? The temptation of image manipulation. *The Journal of cell biology* vol. 166,1 11–5. doi: 10.1083/jcb.200406019

For authors intentionally seeking to commit misconduct, only a consistent approach by journals collectively will effectively address the issue. Some indication was found that an author with one detected example of duplication was more likely to have others.[13]

Journals have shown some reluctance to invest in pre-publication image checking. However, in recent years a number of science publishers have considered how automatic checking with image-checking software on a large scale might be achieved.[14] Guidance includes three categories of image manipulation. The lowest level involves the tidying up of images but not in a manner that affects the research conclusions. The highest level involves image manipulation of a level of severity where fabrication and an intent to mislead are present.[15] Publishers seeking to detect repeated images, for example, in submissions produced by 'paper mills,' are experimenting with an automated screening process, but software is not yet sufficiently developed to accurately check papers on a very large scale.[16] Such initiatives may also encounter a detection/counter-detection arms race, with increasing sophistication by organised fraudsters, for example, with artificial intelligence being used to create unique images to defeat screening software.[17] Journals may also facilitate reader reporting of discrepancies by providing forums to enable readers to share their observations.[18] This offers the potential to supplement online scientific community initiatives

13 Bik, E. M., Casadevall, A., & Fang, F. C., (2016). The prevalence of inappropriate image duplication in biomedical research publications. *mBio*, 7(3) (June), e00809–16. doi: 10.1128/mBio.00809-16

14 Richard Van Noorden, Publishers launch joint effort to tackle altered images in research papers, *Nature*, 13 May 2020 doi: 10.1038/d41586-020-01410-9; Richard Van Noorden. (2022). Journals adopt AI to spot duplicated images in manuscripts, *Nature*, **601**, 14–15 *doi:* https://doi.org/10.1038/d41586-021-03807-6

15 van Rossum, J. et al. Preprint at https://osf.io/xp58v/ (2021); Holly Else, Publishers unite to tackle doctored images in research papers, *Nature*, 28th September 2021 doi: https://doi.org/10.1038/d41586-021-02610-7

16 Else, Holly, & Van Noorden, Richard (2021). The fight against fake-paper factories that churn out sham science. *Nature,* 591, 516–519. doi: https://doi.org/10.1038/d41586-021-00733-5. See also Koppers, L., Wormer, H., & Ickstadt, K. (2016). Towards a systematic screening tool for quality assurance and semiautomatic fraud detection for images in the life sciences. *Science and Engineering Ethics*, 23(4):1113–1128. http://doi.org/10.1007/s11948-016-9841-7

17 Else, Holly, & Van Noorden, Richard (2021). The fight against fake-paper factories that churn out sham science. *Nature,* 591, 516–519. doi: https://doi.org/10.1038/d41586-021-00733-5. In terms of further discussion in this chapter, while there is no single agreed definition of artificial intelligence, more common definitions focus upon computing technologies which replicate processes associated with human intelligence. To date, applications of AI tend to be narrowly focused on specific tasks or the solution of pre-defined problems. See, for example, Nuffield Council on Bioethics Briefing Note on Artificial Intelligence AI in healthcare and research, https://www.nuffieldbioethics.org/assets/pdfs/Artificial-Intelligence-AI-in-healthcare-and-research.pdf (accessed 1 December 2021)

18 Cole, Graham & Nowbar, Alexandra & Mielewczik, Michael & Shun-Shin, Matthew & Francis, Darrel. (2015). Frequency of discrepancies in retracted clinical trial reports versus un-retracted reports: blinded case-control study. BMJ (Clinical research ed.). 351. h4708. 10.1136/bmj.h4708.

such as Retraction Watch and PeerPub, which help systematise approaches by individual readers, who by accident or design find themselves in a position to highlight concerns.[19] Social media can also play a role in this regard.[20] Academics unsure about which findings to trust from the enormous volume of research outputs arising annually may seek corroboration from colleagues they trust commenting on social media. For example, as Brigitte Nerlich, emeritus professor of science, language, and society at the University of Nottingham observes:

> Given my multidisciplinary work, I tend to only read papers that have been sort of pre-checked by others – via blogs or Twitter . . . I use experts in various fields – that I trust, and of course that's subjective – as gatekeepers. I especially trust those who speak out against hype.[21]

Commitment and funding to ensure adequate resources are likely to be key to the success of publisher-generated initiatives. For example, Smith, a former editor of the *British Medical Journal*, has noted that making it a condition of submission that editors can require sight of the raw data behind a study was of limited use in practice: 'We did so once or twice, only to discover that reviewing raw data is difficult, expensive, and time consuming.'[22] Overall, mathematical and technological approaches offer the potential to make certain aspects of image and other data checking more efficient and, if fully developed and adopted widely within the scientific community, they should offer the potential to address some of the criticisms of traditional peer review and to enable collective oversight to expand.[23]

19 PubPeer, by way of example, describes itself as an online platform for post-publication peer review. It was established in 2012 to allow registered users to comment on research misconduct. The introduction in the following year of the opportunity to comment anonymously led to what was described as 'the exposure of unexpected levels of research misconduct.' While emphasising the importance of diligence and the application of expertise of those who post, PubPeer also emphasises the importance of readers evaluating the veracity of comments on the site and considering them alongside other sources of information.

20 Matthews, D. (2019). Do researchers trust each other's work? *Times Higher Education*, August 27, 2019, www.timeshighereducation.com/news/do-researchers-trust-each-others-work

21 Matthews, D. (2019). Do researchers trust each other's work? *Times Higher Education*, August 27, 2019, www.timeshighereducation.com/news/do-researchers-trust-each-others-work

22 Smith R. (2006). Peer review: a flawed process at the heart of science and journals. *Journal of the Royal Society of Medicine*, *99*(4), 178–182. https://doi.org/10.1258/jrsm.99.4.178

23 Adam Marcus, Ivan Oransky, 'Meet the 'data thugs' out to expose shoddy and questionable research', *Science*, February 14, 2018, www.sciencemag.org/news/2018/02/meet-data-thugs-out-expose-shoddy-and-questionable-research; Biagioli, M. (2012). Recycling texts or stealing time? Plagiarism, authorship, and credit in science. *International Journal of Cultural Property*, 19, 468.

Software such as Statcheck and StatReviewer are designed to assess the consistency of authors' statistics and represent prototypes of further developments which may facilitate the verification of the internal consistency of statistical data contained in published research.[24] The team developing Statcheck found that around half of the papers tested contained one or more statistical inconsistencies, with over 10 per cent containing an error of such seriousness that the statistical significance of a published result could have changed.[25] The software was able to detect issues that a human peer reviewer had missed. The creators of StatReviewer claim that it can identify indicators of fraudulent behaviour, such as attempts to 'game some statistical rules' or the fabrication of data.[26]

Psychology theory and statistical methods may be combined to detect fabrication of quantitative data, for example, drawing on the observation that humans find it difficult to understand and estimate randomness. As a result, researchers tempted in the direction of misconduct may find it difficult to fabricate data that replicates the probabilistic nature of genuine data, a failing which may be used to aid detection.[27]

Identifying those approaches which have greatest potential to detect misconduct is important both in functional terms but also to minimise false positives, the latter placing researchers in the spotlight of potentially having violated norms of acceptable research practice when this is not the case.[28] From a lawyer's perspective the level of 'appropriate' false positives is open to debate. Legal mechanisms should be robust in avoiding unjustified findings of guilt or liability, but at the accusation stage the test aims to be robust but by its nature less

24 Adam, D. (2019). How a data detective exposed suspicious medical trials. *Nature*, 571, 462–464. doi: 10.1038/d41586-019-02241-z. As a prototype, Statcheck was limited to the strict data-presentation format used by the American Psychological Association; Monya Baker, Smart software spots statistical errors in psychology papers, *Nature*, 25 October 2015, doi: 10.1038/nature.2015.18657; Douglas Heaven. (2018). AI peer reviewers unleashed to ease publishing grind, *Nature* 563, 609–610. doi: 10.1038/d41586-018-07245-9

25 Douglas Heaven. (2018). AI peer reviewers unleashed to ease publishing grind, *Nature* 563, 609–610. doi: 10.1038/d41586-018-07245-9

26 Douglas Heaven. (2018). AI peer reviewers unleashed to ease publishing grind, *Nature* 563, 609–610. doi: 10.1038/d41586-018-07245-9

27 Chris HJ Hartgerink, Jan G Voelkel, Jelte M Wicherts, Marcel ALM van Assen, 'Detection of data fabrication using statistical tools', 19 August 2019 (pre-print), citing, inter alia, Tversky, A., & Kahneman, D. (1971). Belief in the law of small numbers. Psychological Bulletin, 76 (2), 105–110. http://doi.org/10.1037/h0031322; Wagenaar, W. A. (1972). Generation of random sequences by human subjects: A critical survey of literature. Psychological Bulletin, 77 (1), 65–72. http://doi.org/10.1037/h0032060; Tversky, A., & Kahneman, D. (1974). Judgment under uncertainty: Heuristics and biases. Science, 185 (4157), 1124–1131. http://doi.org/10.1126/science.185. 4157.1124; Nickerson, R. S. (2000). Null hypothesis significance testing: A review of an old and continuing controversy. Psychological Methods, 5 (2), 241–301. http://doi.org/10.1037/1082–989x.5.2.241

28 Chris HJ Hartgerink, Jan G Voelkel, Jelte M Wicherts, Marcel ALM van Assen, 'Detection of data fabrication using statistical tools', 19 August 2019 (pre-print)

rigorous than at an adjudication stage. For example, in criminal proceedings there should be reasonable grounds to suspect that the person has committed the offence, considering the nature and sufficiency of the evidence. However, robust testing of the evidence comes at the adjudicatory stage. A legal system in which everyone charged is convicted gives rise to suspicions that either the adjudicatory process is unfair or those making decisions to charge are unduly cautious. In the latter context, an appropriately working system will involve some 'false positives' – evidence which is deemed sufficient to charge but which on closer scrutiny at an adjudicatory stage will prove to be insufficient to establish guilt. These observations are pertinent when seeking to identify misconduct, but are more problematic when technological and statistical methods are used at the stage of accepting or rejecting submissions for publication. Approaches which are prone to false positives have the potential to prevent the publication of important research findings and to harm researcher careers in the process.[29] Overall, the risk of false positives from such methods, estimated by some sources at around one in three, leads to the conclusion that statistical methods alone should not be relied upon to detect data fabrication, but can play a valuable role as screening tools for data fabrication when accompanied by information from other evidential sources.[30] However, caution should be exercised in the latter context. For example, results from some statistical analysis may be exaggerated if the data analysed is drawn from case examples where significant evidence of misconduct has already been identified by other means, and thus the targeted data may be distorted because of this pre-selection.[31]

Initiatives are also underway to develop technological solutions to uncertainty pertaining to some aspects of reproducibility, for example, a US government–funded project to develop algorithms to generate 'confidence scores' for research reliability. The aim is to test the feasibility and utility of automated tools to make available accessible quantitative indications of the likely replicability or reproducibility of published projects. This represents the very early

29 Chris HJ Hartgerink, Jan G Voelkel, Jelte M Wicherts, Marcel ALM van Assen, 'Detection of data fabrication using statistical tools', 19 August 2019 (pre-print) citing Carlisle, J. B. (2017) Data fabrication and other reasons for non-random sampling in 5087 randomised, controlled trials in anaesthetic and general medical journals. Anaesthesia. http://doi.org/10.1111/anae.13938; Loadsman, J. A., & McCulloch, T. J. (2017). Widening the search for suspect data – is the flood of retractions about to become a tsunami? Anaesthesia, 72 (8), 931–935. http://doi.org/10.1111/anae.13962

30 Chris HJ Hartgerink, Jan G Voelkel, Jelte M Wicherts, Marcel ALM van Assen, 'Detection of data fabrication using statistical tools', 19 August 2019 (pre-print) citing, inter alia, Fanelli, D. (2009). How many scientists fabricate and falsify research? A systematic review and meta-analysis of survey data. *PLoS One,* 4(5), e5738. http://doi.org/10.1371/journal.pone.0005738

31 Chris HJ Hartgerink, Jan G Voelkel, Jelte M Wicherts, Marcel ALM van Assen, 'Detection of data fabrication using statistical tools', 19 August 2019 (pre-print). For example, as discussed in the case of Diederik Stapel, statistical evaluation was undertaken after he had confessed to fabrication. Along similar lines, the temptation should be avoided to undertake inappropriate fishing exercises in overzealous attempts to prove suspicions rather than to establish the truth.

stages of development in seeking to determine whether algorithms can provide sufficiently precise and reliable confidence scores which are equal to, or even better than, current human expert methods.[32] The Systematizing Confidence in Open Research and Evidence (SCORE) project will create a database of around 30,000 claims made in published papers. Experts will review and score a selection of these for the likelihood of their reproducibility.[33] The database will be used to create artificial intelligence tools to score the same claims as the experts and comparisons made to see how outcomes overlap.[34]

Another initiative which seeks to address the challenges of reproducibility is CASCAD, the Certification Agency for Scientific Code and Data. The co-creators of CASCAD note that many research projects involve researchers devoting weeks, months or even longer to collecting and cleaning data and refining computer code, yet these aspects of the research project are not usually subject to peer review. In recent years authors have been required by some journals to upload data to central repositories, providing the opportunity for other researchers to scrutinise the data and computations, but there is little to incentivise them to devote time to this. This approach also excludes the capacity to replicate research which relies on confidential data.[35] Faced with these challenges, CASCAD aims to present a 'trusted third party' approach. A researcher seeking evidence of reproducibility can obtain a certificate from CASCAD after a reviewer has run the code on their data to confirm that the results presented in the manuscript are sound. The certificate can be

32 DARPA Defense Sciences Office – Systematizing Confidence in Open Research and Evidence (SCORE) https://grantbulletin.research.uiowa.edu/darpa-defense-sciences-office-systematizing-confidence-open-research-and-evidence-score (accessed 9 February 2019), discussed further in Rachael Pells. (2019). Bid to use AI to predict research reproducibility launched, *Times Higher Education*, February 8, www.timeshighereducation.com/cn/news/bid-use-ai-predict-research-reproducibility-launched

33 In another study, experts were found to accurately predict the replicability of research at around the same level as actually replicability when studies were repeated. Colin F. Camerer et al, Evaluating the replicability of social science experiments in Nature and Science between 2010 and 2015, *Nature Human Behaviour*, Vol 2, September 2018, 637–644. www.nature.com/articles/s41562-018-0399-z

34 Rachael Pells. (2019). Bid to use AI to predict research reproducibility launched, *Times Higher Education*, February 8, www.timeshighereducation.com/cn/news/bid-use-ai-predict-research-reproducibility-launched

35 A small number of journals check data themselves, but this is costly in terms of time and specialised staff. Christophe Pérignon, Kamel Gadouche, Christophe Hurlin, Roxane Silberman, Eric Debonnel, Certify reproducibility with confidential data, *Science*, 12 Jul 2019: Vol. 365, Issue 6449, 127–128 doi: 10.1126/science.aaw2825; www.casd.eu/en/le-centre-dacces-securise-aux-donnees-casd/certification-de-resultats-cascad-casd/ (accessed 2 September 2019); Pérignon, C., & Hurlin, C. (2019). Data police force will help clean up research. *Times Higher Education*, August 26, 2019, www.timeshighereducation.com/science/data-police-force-will-help-clean-research; Price, S., and Flach, P. A. (2017), "Computational support for academic peer review: a perspective from artificial intelligence", Communications of the ACM, Vol. 60 No. 3, 70–79.

utilised in the reviewing and editorial recommendation and decision-making processes.[36]

Technology also presents opportunities to identify journal citation manipulation and to better ensure that new submissions do not mistakenly cite as still valid retracted papers. For over 40 years Journal Citation Reports (JCR) have provided data relating to the impact on citation metrics of self-citation and targeted interjournal citation. More recently, citation metrics have enabled the identification of journals with distorted journal impact factors due, for example, to 'excessive citation exchange between multiple donor journals.'[37] Recent developments in network science offer the prospect of indicating probabilistically the likely existence of citation cartels, in which editors collude in the mutual exchange of citations to boost journal impact factors.[38]

It is important not to rely on technology to detect what it is not good at detecting. For example, in the three decades since the early days of plagiarism detection software, the challenges have been magnified by the explosion of accessible information which can be misused.[39] Consideration of the exact replication of text has been supplemented with issues of paraphrasing without

36 Christophe Pérignon, Kamel Gadouche, Christophe Hurlin, Roxane Silberman, Eric Debonnel, Certify reproducibility with confidential data, *Science*, 12 Jul 2019: Vol. 365, Issue 6449, 127–128 doi: 10.1126/science.aaw2825; www.casd.eu/en/le-centre-dacces-securise-aux-donnees-casd/certification-de-resultats-cascad-casd/ (accessed 2 September 2019); Pérignon, C., & Hurlin, C. (2019). Data police force will help clean up research. *Times Higher Education*, August 26, 2019, www.timeshighereducation.com/science/data-police-force-will-help-clean-research

37 Szomszor, M., & Quaderi, N. (2020). *Global Research Report Research Integrity: Understanding Our Shared Responsibility for a Sustainable Scholarly Ecosystem* (p. 11). October 2020. Institute for Scientific Information, https://clarivate.com/webofsciencegroup/wp-content/uploads/sites/2/2020/10/ISI-Research-Integrity-Report.pdf (accessed 21 October 2020), citing Garfield, E. (1975). Preface and Introduction to Journal Citation Reports – Vol. 9 of the Science Citation Index, 1975; Heneberg, P. (2016). From excessive journal self-cites to citation stacking: Analysis of journal self-citation kinetics in search for journals, which boost their scientometric indicators. PLoS ONE, 11(4), https://doi.org/10.1371/journal.pone.0153730

38 Davis, P. (2012). The emergence of a citation cartel. The Scholarly Kitchen, April 10, 2012 https://scholarlykitchen.sspnet.org/2012/04/10/emergence-of-a-citation-cartel/; Fister, I., Fister, I., & Perc, M. (2016). Toward the discovery of citation cartels in citation networks. Frontiers in Physics, 4, https://doi.org/10.3389/fphy.2016.00049; Chakraborty, J., Pradhan, D. K., & Nandi, S. (2020). On the identification and analysis of citation pattern irregularities among journals. Expert Systems, article number e12561. https://doi.org/10.1111/exsy.12561, discussed by Szomszor, M., & Quaderi, N. (2020). *Global Research Report Research Integrity: Understanding Our Shared Responsibility for a Sustainable Scholarly Ecosystem* (p. 11). October 2020. Institute for Scientific Information, https://clarivate.com/webofsciencegroup/wp-content/uploads/sites/2/2020/10/ISI-Research-Integrity-Report.pdf

39 J. Hamblen and A. Parker. (1989). Computer Algorithms for Plagiarism Detection, IEEE Transactions on Education, 32(2), 94–99. doi: 10.1109/13.28038

attribution and cross language copying.[40] Bouville makes the point in terms of plagiarism detection software that the focus upon words rather than ideas can become embedded simply because that is what current technology is best at detecting, rather than alternative solutions, whether technological or otherwise, being developed.[41] One proposed approach is the identification of citation patterns – a 'semantic fingerprint' to compare textual similarities.[42] As with any other area of legal or regulatory enforcement, determined offenders will look for ways to defeat or sidestep approaches to detection, and so enforcement approaches have to be alert and adaptable. For example, plagiarisers seeking to copy ideas without attribution by changing the wording may seek to achieve this more efficiently and hide it more effectively by utilising algorithms – cheating algorithms competing against cheat-detecting algorithms.[43]

Other concerns about plagiarism software include 'black box' algorithms potentially being less effective than their producers claim, for example, with reliance on a misguided assumption that if some cases are identified, the system must have documented all cases.[44] The practical reality is that incomplete identification and false positives or false negatives are common. References and commonly cited names or phrases are obvious examples of false positives, and false negatives may arise, for example, if original sources are in other languages,

40 Szomszor, M., & Quaderi, N. (2020). *Global Research Report Research Integrity: Understanding Our Shared Responsibility for a Sustainable Scholarly Ecosystem* (p. 11). October 2020. Institute for Scientific Information, https://clarivate.com/webofsciencegroup/wp-content/uploads/sites/2/2020/10/ISI-Research-Integrity-Report.pdf (accessed 21 October 2020), citing S. M. Alzahrani, N. Salim and A. Abraham, Understanding Plagiarism Linguistic Patterns, Textual Features, and Detection Methods, in *IEEE Transactions on Systems, Man, and Cybernetics, Part C (Applications and Reviews)*, 42(2), 133–149, March 2012, doi: 10.1109/TSMCC.2011.2134847; Barrón-Cedeño, A., Vila, M., Martí, M., & Rosso, P. (2013). Plagiarism meets paraphrasing: Insights for the next generation in automatic plagiarism detection. Computational Linguistics, 39(4), 917–947. https://doi.org/10.1162/COLI_a_00153; Potthast, M., Barrón-Cedeño, A., Stein, B. *et al.* (2011). Cross-language plagiarism detection. *Lang Resources & Evaluation* 45, 45–62. https://doi.org/10.1007/s10579-009-9114-z

41 Bouville, M. (2008). Plagiarism: Words and ideas. *Science and Engineering Ethics*, 14, 311–322, 319. doi: 10.1007/s11948-008-9057-6.

42 Gipp, B., (2014). Citation-based Plagiarism Detection: Detecting Disguised and Cross-language Plagiarism using Citation Pattern Analysis. Wiesbaden: Springer. www.springer.com/gp/book/9783658063931 cited by Szomszor, M., & Quaderi, N. (2020). *Global Research Report Research Integrity: Understanding Our Shared Responsibility for a Sustainable Scholarly Ecosystem* (p. 11). October 2020. Institute for Scientific Information, https://clarivate.com/webofsciencegroup/wp-content/uploads/sites/2/2020/10/ISI-Research-Integrity-Report.pdf (accessed 21 October 2020)

43 Debora Weber-Wulff. (2019). Plagiarism detectors are a crutch, and a problem, *Nature*, 27 March doi: 10.1038/d41586-019-00893-5.

44 Debora Weber-Wulff. (2019). Plagiarism detectors are a crutch, and a problem, *Nature*, 27 March doi: 10.1038/d41586-019-00893-5.

if some sources are undigitised or sit behind inaccessible paywalls.[45] Misappropriation of work other than in published sources, for example, research proposals and unpublished manuscripts, is also likely to be hidden from search sources utilised by detection software.[46] The risks from such software weaknesses include time-pressed editors and reviewers accepting uncritically the 'score' that plagiarism software, resulting in what should be suspect papers being published, or unjustly rejecting papers if false positives have inflated the score.[47] Helgesson and Eriksson observe that low overlap percentages could disguise matters of concern – for example, a verbatim copy of one-third of a page in a four-page submission would constitute less than 10 per cent of the entire paper and could be missed if an arbitrary higher cut-off point was applied before human investigation was considered appropriate.[48] Setting the score above which investigation is undertaken at a low level would place considerable resource pressure on publishers and editors in terms of following through with human investigation.[49] The result of such technological and resource limitations may be that insufficiently developed software has the potential to do more harm than good – giving a false sense of security that published papers are free of plagiarism and falsely labelling some authors as suspected plagiarists.

Development of gaming to address the challenge of research misconduct has also been proposed, building upon ideas that educational games and simulations help to develop skills, including strategic thinking, interpretative analysis, problem solving and decision making.[50] A variety of gaming models have been utilised to aid the avoidance of research misconduct. Real-life scenarios have been used to help students gain practical experience of ethical decision making and responsibility in research – focusing on the idea that there is significant difference between ethics in theory and experiencing ethical responsibility in practice.[51] Three online mini-games developed at the University of Florida are designed

45 Debora Weber-Wulff. (2019). Plagiarism detectors are a crutch, and a problem, *Nature*, 27 March doi: 10.1038/d41586-019-00893-5.

46 Biagioli, M. (2012). Recycling texts or stealing time? Plagiarism, authorship, and credit in science. *International Journal of Cultural Property*, 19, 472.

47 Debora Weber-Wulff. (2019). Plagiarism detectors are a crutch, and a problem', *Nature*, 27 March doi: 10.1038/d41586-019-00893-5.

48 Helgesson, G., & Eriksson, S. (2014). Plagiarism in research. *Medicine, Health Care, and Philosophy*, 18, 91–101, 97. doi: 10.1007/s11019-014-9583-8.

49 Helgesson, G., & Eriksson, S. (2014). Plagiarism in research. *Medicine, Health Care, and Philosophy*, 18, 91–101, 97. doi: 10.1007/s11019-014-9583-8.

50 Gaming Against Plagiarism University of Florida, https://research.dwi.ufl.edu/page/gaming-against-plagiarism/, considering the final report from the Summit on Educational Games (Federation of American Scientists [FAS], 2006; Buhler, A.G. et al. (2011). Gaming Against Plagiarism: A Partnership Between the Library and Faculty. American Society for Engineering Education (accessed 30 December 2021)

51 Lloyd, Peter and Van De Poel, Ibo (2008). Designing Games to Teach Ethics. *Science and Engineering Ethics*, 14(3) pp. 433–447, 446.

to engage science, technology, engineering and mathematics (STEM) students with complex issues surrounding research misconduct, including data fabrication, data falsification and plagiarism.[52] In a 3D game environment, scenarios are based on real-life examples, for example, a participant placed in the role of a scientist required to draft a research proposal. As the game unfolds the player will be required to work collaboratively with other researchers, including those from other jurisdictions, consider their contributions and make decisions about what is appropriate to include. Multiple choice questions are used to test understanding.[53] Gaming Against Plagiarism (GAP) aims to influence ethical understanding and behaviour of students, peer considerations and varying cultural practices as well as highlighting the ramification of committing such misconduct. The broader goal is to ensure that participants are trained to be responsible and ethical researchers 'as members of multi-national, multi-cultural global research teams.'[54] Initiatives such as plagiarism detection competitions also offer the prospect of motivating further work to develop and refine technological detection tools.[55]

In terms of bigger-picture considerations relating to technological initiatives, it is important to maintain awareness that the commercially driven nature of much technological development may give rise to the temptation to overstate certain types of misconduct merely because they are particularly suitable for creating a larger market for software and supporting expertise, with the risk of diverting resources into areas which are not actually the most problematic or important.[56]

Artificial intelligence and peer review

A number of artificial intelligence (AI) tools are emerging which are designed to assist with the quality and time-consuming nature of peer review.[57] Such

52 Leonard, M., Schwieder, D. Buhler, A., Bennett, D. B., & Royster, M. (2015). Perceptions of plagiarism by STEM graduate students: A case study. *Science and Engineering Ethics*, 21(6), 1587–1608; Leonard, M., Buhler, A., Johnson, M., Levey, D., & Oliverio, J. (2010). Gaming Against Plagiarism (GAP) Development Proposal. National Science Foundation, Grant No. EESE IIS 1033002.

53 Gaming Against Plagiarism University of Florida, https://research.dwi.ufl.edu/page/gaming-against-plagiarism/ (accessed 1 December 2021)

54 Rami J. Haddad and Youakim Kalaani, *Gaming Against Plagiarism (GAP): A Game-Based Approach to Illustrate Research Misconduct to Undergraduate Engineering Students*, 2014 ASEE Southeast Section Conference, http://se.asee.org/proceedings/ASEE2014/Papers2014/4/45.pdf

55 Stamatatos, E., & Koppel, M. (2011). Plagiarism and authorship analysis: Introduction to the special issue. *Language Resources and Evaluation*, 45, 1–4. doi: 10.1007/s10579-011-9136-145; Biagioli, M. (2012). Recycling texts or stealing time? Plagiarism, authorship, and credit in science. *International Journal of Cultural Property*, 19, 466.

56 Stamatatos, E., & Koppel, M. (2011). Plagiarism and authorship analysis: Introduction to the special issue. *Language Resources and Evaluation*, 45, 1–4. doi: 10.1007/s10579-011-9136-145; Biagioli, M. (2012). Recycling texts or stealing time? Plagiarism, authorship, and credit in science. *International Journal of Cultural Property*, 19, 466.

57 Thelwall, M. (2019). Artificial intelligence, automation and peer review. http://repository.jisc.ac.uk/7614/1/AI_and_peer_review_briefing_paper.pdf (accessed 22 September 2020); Douglas

tools aim to undertake a range of tasks, including identifying prospective reviewers with appropriate expertise and checking the statistical content and methods within a submission.[58] Some commentators have proposed extending further the use of AI in peer review, although developments to date do not replicate or replace key aspects of human input.[59]

In 2018, open-access digital publisher, Frontiers, introduced Artificial Intelligence Review Assistance (AIRA) to evaluate multiple quality criteria on submitted manuscripts. Frontiers describe AIRA as using algorithms to recognise 'patterns in manuscripts and also check conflicts of interest, reviewer expertise and patterns of behaviour' and also checks for plagiarism and image manipulation.[60] AIRA provides a filtering tool, although editors should avoid relying uncritically on the technology to reject manuscripts in a manner which might give rise to unfairness or inequality of treatment. Full review continues to be undertaken by a human reviewer with AIRA reports providing a starting point to alert reviewers to potential issues if a manuscript reaches that stage.[61]

Software which uses natural language processing and machine learning to analyse text is being trialled with the aim of identifying whether the claims in a paper are similar to those in other publications, as well as aiming to detect more blatant plagiarism.[62] Increasing the content of databases used for cross referencing and further developing software which can extract connections between different disciplines and concepts is gradually aiming to add to the sophistication of such systems.[63]

Heaven. (2018). AI peer reviewers unleashed to ease publishing grind, *Nature* 563, 609–610 doi: 10.1038/d41586-018-07245-9

58 Thelwall, M. (2019). Artificial intelligence, automation and peer review. http://repository.jisc.ac.uk/7614/1/AI_and_peer_review_briefing_paper.pdf (accessed 22 September 2020); Douglas Heaven, AI peer reviewers unleashed to ease publishing grind, *Nature* 563, 609–610 (2018) doi: 10.1038/d41586-018-07245-9

59 Douglas Heaven. (2018). AI peer reviewers unleashed to ease publishing grind, *Nature* 563, 609–610 doi: 10.1038/d41586-018-07245-9; Thelwall, M. (2019). 'Artificial Intelligence, Automation and Peer Review.' http://repository.jisc.ac.uk/7614/1/AI_and_peer_review_briefing_paper.pdf (accessed 22 September 2020), citing Enago (2018). Can Artificial Intelligence Fix Peer Review? www.enago.com/academy/can-artificial-intelligence-fix-peer-review/; Price, S., & Flach, P. A. (2017). Computational support for academic peer review: a perspective from artificial intelligence. Communications of the ACM, 60(3), 70–79.

60 Artificial Intelligence to help meet global demand for high-quality, objective peer-review in publishing, *Frontiers Sience News*, 1 July 2020, https://blog.frontiersin.org/2020/07/01/artificial-intelligence-peer-review-assistant-aira/ (accessed 24 September 2020); Rebecca Pool, An ever-changing landscape, *Research Information*, 27 January 2020, www.researchinformation.info/feature/ever-changing-landscape (accessed 24 September 2020)

61 Rebecca Pool, An ever-changing landscape, *Research Information*, 27 January 2020 www.researchinformation.info/feature/ever-changing-landscape (accessed 24 September 2020)

62 Douglas Heaven. (2018). AI peer reviewers unleashed to ease publishing grind, *Nature* 563, 609–610 doi: 10.1038/d41586-018-07245-9

63 Douglas Heaven. (2018). AI peer reviewers unleashed to ease publishing grind, *Nature* 563, 609–610 doi: 10.1038/d41586-018-07245-9

Early-stage research has also indicated that linguistic patterns in the writing of a researcher may be of use in identifying potential fraud. For example, Markowitz and Hancock observed significant differences in several aspects of Diederik Stapel's writing that reflected changes in his writing style when reporting genuine data compared to fabricated data.[64] Such approaches are likely to have relatively limited practical utility in day-to-day detection of misconduct, but may be useful in an investigatory process as a tool to aid the determination of which outputs to focus most attention upon.

As with other areas of AI input into professional spheres, trust in the technology by all stakeholders is key. Risk factors with AI in the context of peer review include the replication of biases found within the human peer review process. If machine learning tools learn from existing papers and the human peer review input into them, idiosyncrasies and biases may find their way into the AI system.[65] For example, if an AI algorithm learns from existing texts and their human peer review scores, all or most of which are drawn from a single jurisdiction, say the UK or United States, the programme may associate markers of high-quality texts with certain linguistic attributes and perhaps other markers specific to generally well-resourced research environments.[66] AI developments have sought to engage with potential unfairness in human peer review by seeking to test whether negative review comments are made fairly and are fairly distributed or whether certain categories of researcher are unduly targeted for criticism. PeerJudge, created by researchers at the University of Wolverhampton and a private company F1000, is described by its creators as 'the first transparent AI approach to peer review sentiment detection.'[67] It seeks to identify anomalies between the text in reviews and reviewer recommendations by cross referencing reviewer comments with the recommendation to accept or reject the submission.[68]

64 Markowitz DM, Hancock JT (2014) Linguistic Traces of a Scientific Fraud: The Case of Diederik Stapel. PLoS ONE 9(8): e105937. doi: 10.1371/journal.pone. 0105937

65 Douglas Heaven. (2018). AI peer reviewers unleashed to ease publishing grind, *Nature* 563, 609–610 doi: 10.1038/d41586-018-07245-9

66 Thelwall, M. (2019). 'Artificial Intelligence, Automation and Peer Review.' http://repository.jisc.ac.uk/7614/1/AI_and_peer_review_briefing_paper.pdf (accessed 22 September 2020), citing Lepri, B., Oliver, N., Letouzé, E., Pentland, A., & Vinck, P. (2018). Fair, transparent, and accountable algorithmic decision-making processes. Philosophy & Technology, 31(4), 611–627

67 Thelwall, M., Papas, E., Nyakoojo, Z., Allen, L. and Weigert, V. (2020) Automatically detecting open academic review praise and criticism, Online Information Review 44 (5), pp. 1057–1076. doi: 10.1108/OIR-11-2019-0347

68 Thelwall, M., Papas, E., Nyakoojo, Z., Allen, L. and Weigert, V. (2020) Automatically detecting open academic review praise and criticism, Online Information Review 44 (5), pp. 1057–1076. doi: 10.1108/OIR-11-2019-0347; Jack Grove. (2020). 'TripAdvisor for peer review' targets publishing bias, *Times Higher Education*, January 2. www.timeshighereducation.com/news/tripadvisor-peer-review-targets-publishing-bias. Early findings were observations that reviewers tend to favour submissions from authors based in their own country.

Evaluation for bias and appropriate accountability on the part of AI systems is as important as it is for human decision makers.[69] Significant advances in the capability of algorithms will be needed before they may replicate more subtle aspects of human peer reviewer evaluation, and as part of this development it remains important to ensure that complexity does not result in undue opaqueness in terms of AI decision-making processes.[70]

Other developments can aid editors to identify unusual reviewer activity – for example, the setting up of fake accounts by individuals with the aim of reviewing their own submissions or submissions from collaborators.[71] Collecting and analysing data points during the peer review process may flag matters for further investigation – for example, authors and reviewers being located on the same network, being geographically proximate, using noninstitutional email addresses and turnaround times by reviewers which are unusually short.[72]

Blockchain

Traditional research and publication models are characterised by a disconnect inherent in the research workflow process. Experimental results are captured, recorded on a scientist's own systems and their implications considered. Findings are presented, usually in draft article form, and submitted to a publisher

69 Thelwall, M. (2019). 'Artificial Intelligence, Automation and Peer Review.' http://repository.jisc.ac.uk/7614/1/AI_and_peer_review_briefing_paper.pdf (accessed 22 September 2020), citing Lepri, B., Oliver, N., Letouzé, E., Pentland, A., & Vinck, P. (2018). Fair, transparent, and accountable algorithmic decision-making processes. Philosophy & Technology, 31(4), 611–627

70 Douglas Heaven. (2018). AI peer reviewers unleashed to ease publishing grind, *Nature* 563, 609–610 doi: 10.1038/d41586-018-07245-9; Thelwall, M. (2019). 'Artificial Intelligence, Automation and Peer Review.' http://repository.jisc.ac.uk/7614/1/AI_and_peer_review_briefing_paper.pdf (accessed 22 September 2020), citing Lepri, B., Oliver, N., Letouzé, E., Pentland, A., & Vinck, P. (2018). Fair, transparent, and accountable algorithmic decision-making processes. Philosophy & Technology, 31(4), 611–627

71 Szomszor, M., & Quaderi, N. (2020). *Global Research Report Research Integrity: Understanding Our Shared Responsibility for a Sustainable Scholarly Ecosystem* (p. 11). October 2020. Institute for Scientific Information, https://clarivate.com/webofsciencegroup/wp-content/uploads/sites/2/2020/10/ISI-Research-Integrity-Report.pdf (accessed 21 October 2020). Szomszor and Quaderi note that checking peer reviewer identity may be undertaken via open peer review platforms which facilitate the recording of reviewing activity. Integrating this with publication profiles further allows for the checking of reviewer legitimacy and suitability, while also allowing checking for potential conflicts of interest.

72 Szomszor, M., & Quaderi, N. (2020). *Global Research Report Research Integrity: Understanding Our Shared Responsibility for a Sustainable Scholarly Ecosystem* (p. 11). October 2020. Institute for Scientific Information, https://clarivate.com/webofsciencegroup/wp-content/uploads/sites/2/2020/10/ISI-Research-Integrity-Report.pdf (accessed 21 October 2020), citing Sikdar, S., Marsili, M., Ganguly, N., & Mukherjee, A. (2016). Anomalies in the peer-review system: A case study of the Journal of High Energy Physics. Proceedings of the 25th ACM International on Conference on Information and Knowledge Management. CIKM'16: ACM Conference on Information and Knowledge Management, 2245–2250. https://doi.org/10.1145/2983323.2983675

through its submission system. The publisher implements peer review via its own systems and, if the article is accepted, utilises these systems to effect publication and control distribution.[73] As a result, trust and control are placed in a number of different discreet elements, whereas blockchain offers the potential for a comprehensive, decentralised and transparent platform better able to facilitate greater transparency of, for example, changes to research design and an evidence trail for projects which were not pursued to publication.[74]

In essence, blockchain is a shared database which provides for secure storage of verified and encrypted digital information, with the use of cryptographic techniques to create a public ledger enabling the verification and tracing of transactions.[75] Each block of data contains links to the previous block, resulting in a digital chronology of events, with all the information in a blockchain being stored in every computer in the network, with corrupted records that differ from others in the network being removed and, overall, making it easier to track fraud.[76] An open, permissioned blockchain rather than distinct, disconnected systems would make more aspects of the research cycle open to self-correction and offer the scope to address concerns about reproducibility and scientific credibility.[77] The registration of study designs using the blockchain should prevent retrospective alternation or the suppression of findings, and 'smart contracts' offer the potential to clearly set research protocols prior to data collection, thereby preventing ex post facto hypothesising.[78]

Blockchain can also be used to underpin author identify to, for example, aid verification in the peer review process and to facilitate post-publication peer review.[79] Blockchain also offers the potential to facilitate the development of an

73 Van Rossum, J. (2017). *Blockchain for Research*. Digital Science Report, November 2017, https://figshare.com/articles/_/5607778

74 Van Rossum, J. (2017). *Blockchain for Research*. Digital Science Report, November 2017, https://figshare.com/articles/_/5607778

75 Szomszor, M., & Quaderi, N. (2020). *Global Research Report Research Integrity: Understanding Our Shared Responsibility for a Sustainable Scholarly Ecosystem* (p. 12). October 2020. Institute for Scientific Information, https://clarivate.com/webofsciencegroup/wp-content/uploads/sites/2/2020/10/ISI-Research-Integrity-Report.pdf (accessed 21 October 2020)

76 Dalmeet Singh Chawla. (2017). Technology behind bitcoin could aid science, report says *Physics Today*, 1 December. doi: 10.1063/PT.6.1.20171201a; Sherman, A. T., Javani, F., Zhang, H., & Golaszewski, E. (2019). On the origins and variations of Blockchain technologies. *IEEE Security & Privacy*, 17(1), 72–77. https://doi.org/10.1109/msec.2019.2893730

77 Joris Van Rossum, Digital Science Report Blockchain for Research Perspectives on a New Paradigm for Scholarly Communication, November 2017, Digital Science, 8 doi: https://doi.org/10.6084/m9.figshare.5607778

78 Joris Van Rossum, Digital Science Report Blockchain for Research Perspectives on a New Paradigm for Scholarly Communication, November 2017, Digital Science, 8 doi: https://doi.org/10.6084/m9.figshare.5607778

79 Along the following lines: 'Formal submission to a journal will follow a single submission protocol with select submission metadata (author name and contact information, date of submission, title, submitted journal name) written to the public blockchain that is timestamped immediately upon

'academic endorsement system (AES),' giving scientists direct access to endorsing the quality, utility, etc., of the work of others with 'academic endorsements points (AEP).'[80] AEP could then act as a metric of value, a virtual currency, with blockchains enabling an autonomous and transparent mechanism for tracking. Such a currency could be extended to valued contributions beyond traditional publication approaches by including newer means of communication, such as blogs.[81]

Potential obstacles to the adoption of blockchain revolve around the need for stakeholders in the system to buy in. This requires persuasion to move away from embedded systems which are well understood by millions of researchers worldwide. Significant adoption would necessitate fundamental transformation on the part of researchers, institutions, publishers and other stakeholders.[82] Progress in motivating a critical mass of researchers to jettison well-established systems are likely only to be successful if incremental steps are taken at a measured pace.[83]

Statements and principles relating to research integrity

A number of statements and principles have emerged in attempts to persuade the global scientific community to more fully embrace matters of research integrity and research misconduct. Such documents do not carry regulatory

verification, while other potentially confidential information will reside off-chain.' Mackey, T. K., Shah, N., Miyachi, K., Short, J., & Clauson, K. (2019). A framework proposal for Blockchain-based scientific publishing using shared governance. *Frontiers in Blockchain*. https://doi.org/10.3389/fbloc.2019.00019; Joris Van Rossum, Digital Science Report Blockchain for Research Perspectives on a New Paradigm for Scholarly Communication, November 2017, Digital Science, 8 doi: https://doi.org/10.6084/m9.figshare.5607778

80 Towards Open Science: The Case for a Decentralized Autonomous Academic Endorsement System, August 12, 2016, Zenodo. http://doi.org/10.5281/zenodo.60054

81 Van Rossum, J. (2017). *Blockchain for Research*. Digital Science Report, November 2017, https://figshare.com/articles/_/5607778. Fine-tuning to deter gaming of the system, the handling of muti-authored pieces and withdrawing endorsement in cases of fraud would need to be considered. In time, positive reviews could even form the basis for publishing decisions and/or research funding. b8d5ad9d974a44e7e2882f986467f4d3, (2016, August 12), Towards Open Science: The Case for a Decentralized Autonomous Academic Endorsement System. Zenodo. http://doi.org/10.5281/zenodo.60054. Reflecting concerns and sensitivities around challenging the status quo, the authors of this piece note: 'Our proposal aims to make parts of the scientific publishing industry obsolete, we have chosen to publish this proposal under a nom de plume in order to minimize the risk of adverse effects (e.g. unfavourable editorial decisions, or stern letters to our employers).'

82 Eefke Smit, Director, International STM Association, Standards and Technology, quoted in Joris Van Rossum, Digital Science Report Blockchain for Research Perspectives on a New Paradigm for Scholarly Communication, November 2017, Digital Science, 16 doi: https://doi.org/10.6084/m9.figshare.5607778

83 Eefke Smit, Director, International STM Association, Standards and Technology, quoted in Joris Van Rossum, Digital Science Report Blockchain for Research Perspectives on a New Paradigm for Scholarly Communication, November 2017, Digital Science, 16 doi: https://doi.org/10.6084/m9.figshare.5607778

weight nor represent official jurisdictional or organisational positions. Rather, they aim to persuade the research community to move further in the direction of self-regulation and may serve a role in focusing the attention of governments and employer organisations on the need to ensure that appropriate regulatory mechanisms are in place.

The Singapore Statement on Research Integrity

The Singapore Statement on Research Integrity was developed as part of the 2nd World Conference on Research Integrity in July 2010 and published in September 2010. Described as 'the first international effort to encourage the development of unified policies, guidelines and codes of conduct, with the long-range goal of fostering greater integrity in research worldwide,' the 340 individuals from 51 countries who participated in the conference were invited to contribute insights and observations to be considered by the drafting committee.[84] The Statement consists of Principles and Responsibilities. The Principles require:

Honesty in all aspects of research
Accountability in the conduct of research
Professional courtesy and fairness in working with others
Good stewardship of research on behalf of others

The Responsibilities are more numerous and cover:

1 *Integrity:* researchers being responsible for the trustworthiness of their research.
2 *Adherence to Regulations*
3 *Research Methods:* adoption of appropriate research methods, critical analysis of the evidence and full and objective reporting.
4 *Research Records:* maintenance of full, accurate records which facilitate replication by other researchers.
5 *Research Findings:* open and prompt sharing of data and findings.
6 *Authorship:* should only be attributed to those who satisfy relevant authorship criteria and each author should take responsibility for their contributions to all publications, funding applications and other research related outputs.
7 *Publication Acknowledgement:* of those who made significant contributions to the research but do not meet the threshold for authorship.
8 *Peer Review:* when acting as peer reviewers, researchers should provide rigorous but fair evaluations and respect confidentiality.
9 *Conflict of Interest:* disclosure of relevant information which otherwise could undermine the trustworthiness of a research proposal, output or review.

84 https://wcrif.org/guidance/singapore-statement (accessed 4 August 2020)

10 *Public Communication:* researchers should limit professional comments within the scope of expertise and clearly distinguishing these from personal opinion.
11 *Reporting Irresponsible Research Practices:* reporting to the appropriate authorities any suspected research misconduct or other irresponsible research practices that undermine the trustworthiness of research.
12 *Responding to Irresponsible Research Practices:* Research institutions, professional organizations, agencies and journals should have procedures for responding to allegations of misconduct or inappropriate research practices and protocols for protecting those who in good faith make such reports. If allegations are substantiated appropriate steps should be taken promptly, including the correction of the research record.
13 *Research Environments:* institutions should maintain environments that encourage research integrity by means of education, policies and the fostering work environments that support research integrity.
14 *Societal Considerations:* institutions and individual researchers should be mindful of their ethical obligation to weigh societal benefits against risks inherent in their work.[85]

The Hong Kong Principles

The Hong Kong Principles were developed as part of the 6th World Conference on Research Integrity with the aim of securing greater recognition for researchers who commit to robust, rigorous and transparent practices.[86] Implementation of the principles seeks to place evidence-based assessment of research rigour at the centre of researcher assessment. Behaviours which strengthen research integrity and positively contribute to the research environment are the ones to be rewarded, aiming to address research integrity rather than focusing solely on research misconduct.[87] For example, the aim is to address the issue that promotion decisions rarely give sufficient importance to activities which are integral to creating a transparent and ethical research environment.[88]

85 https://wcrif.org/guidance/singapore-statement (accessed 4 August 2020)
86 https://wcrif.org/guidance/hong-kong-principles (accessed 24 August 2020)
87 Moher, D., Bouter, L., Kleinert, S., Glasziou, P., Sham, M. H., Barbour, V., et al. (2020). The Hong Kong principles for assessing researchers: Fostering research integrity. *PLoS Biol*, 18(7), e3000737. https://doi.org/10.1371/journal.pbio.3000737
88 Moher, D., Bouter, L., Kleinert, S., Glasziou, P., Sham, M. H., Barbour, V., et al. (2020). The Hong Kong principles for assessing researchers: Fostering research integrity. *PLoS Biol*, 18(7), e3000737. https://doi.org/10.1371/journal.pbio.3000737, citing Rice, DB, Faffoul, H, Ioannidis, JPA, Moher, D. Academic criteria for promotion and tenure in faculties of biomedical sciences: a cross-sectional analysis of 146 universities [Internet]. Available from: https://doi.org/10.1101/802850.

The five Hong Kong Principles are:

1 Researchers to be assessed on responsible practices from conception of the research idea, research design, methodology, execution, and dissemination.
2 Report accurately and transparently all research, irrespective of the results.
3 Open research, including methods, materials and data should be valued.
4 A broad range of research and scholarship, including replication, translation, synthesis, and meta-research should be valued.
5 Contributions to research and scholarship, including peer review, mentoring and knowledge exchange should be valued.[89]

To gain traction and fulfil their intended role within the scientific community, such principles have to be endorsed by sufficient numbers of institutions and influential individuals. The extent of such endorsement to date has been limited.

Citizen juries

As discussed in chapter 7, the courts, including lay juries, are called upon to answer questions with a scientific element and to weigh scientific evidence to, for example, aid decision making in criminal cases. The questions faced by courts tend to be highly focused in terms of the relevance of the scientific questions being considered to the particular facts and legal issues of the case.

Drawing from the experience of juries in the courtroom, citizen panels or juries could have a much wider application to the maximising of trust in science. Non-scientists may demonstrate an interest and capacity to engage with scientific ideas when confronted with issues of direct relevance to them. Citizen panels or juries may be utilised to exploit these interests in a formalised and structured manner. To better develop such engagement, education and training in science and scientific ethics for non-scientists should help to enhance the appreciation of key scientific concepts and the ethical and regulatory issues associated with them and, overall, help to produce better-informed citizens able to appreciate and critique scientific ideas.[90]

Research integrity remains at its core a social problem within the community of scientists. In part this depends upon scientists being willing to engage in the steps necessary to maximise integrity, but the wider community can also

89 Moher D, Bouter L, Kleinert S, Glasziou P, Sham MH, Barbour V, et al. (2020) The Hong Kong Principles for assessing researchers: Fostering research integrity. PLoS Biol 18(7): e3000737. https://doi.org/10.1371/journal.pbio.3000737

90 Alan H. McGowan. (2013). Teaching Science and Ethics to Undergraduates: A Multidisciplinary Approach, *Sci Eng Ethics*. 19:535–543, doi: 10.1007/s11948-011-9338-3; Avard, M. (2006). Civic engagement in the science classroom. Journal of College Science Teaching, 15(3), 12–13.

play a part.[91] Citizen panels could be presented with details of existing scientific consensus in a particular area, including methodological considerations, the nature of evidence and other considerations which gave rise to the consensus; contrasting viewpoints from those not among the consensual majority would also be presented; the panel could then question and challenge the consensual and conflicting arguments to reach their own conclusion about the state of understanding of the particular area. In turn, such panels could help to bridge the divide between the scientific and lay communities.[92] As well as lay juries in the courtroom sometimes being called upon to consider complex scientific information, these suggestions have precedents in the form of lay participant members of professional regulatory tribunals, often called upon to consider complex matters in professional spheres such as medicine, building design and construction and law. With appropriate direction and guidance lay panels may add valuable extra voices to debates and disagreements between scientists and the public.

91 Debora Weber-Wulff. (2019). Plagiarism detectors are a crutch, and a problem, *Nature*, 27 March doi: 10.1038/d41586-019-00893-5.

92 See, for example, Kitcher, P. (2011). *Science in a Democratic Society*. New York: Prometheus.

Chapter 9

Conclusions

Those viewing issues around trust, conduct and regulation from within the scientific world may have different perspectives to those looking in from outside. Insiders bring with them a level of domain specificity associated with disciplinary knowledge and conventions, the latter often unwritten.[1] As Giddens observes, the range of options open to actors within social systems are constrained within walls created by the structural properties of the system.[2] Scientists are socialised in scientific community values which incorporate interests or biases specific to research communities. A lawyer's perspective of the regulation of scientific research offers an external view across disciplinary boundaries, allowing the sharing of interpretations and ideas between what may normally constitute alien environments. This supports calls for the further development of networking between legal and scientific fields, and in turn stimulating new ways of thinking.[3]

As with other areas of law and regulation, determining what to regulate can be as important as how to implement regulation. An opening challenge is that definitions of research misconduct lack consensus, codification or even clear understanding within and between research communities.[4] Plagiarism provides an example of this. Whether plagiarism is harmful to the scientific record is

1 Priaulx, N. M., & Weinel, M. (2014). Behavior on a beer mat: Law, interdisciplinarity & expertise. *Journal of Law, Technology & Policy*, (2), 361–391.

2 Giddens, Anthony. (1984). *The Constitution of Society: Outline of the Theory of Structuration*, Polity Press. *ProQuest Ebook Central*, 176–77; Sovacool, B. (2008). Exploring scientific misconduct: Isolated individuals, impure institutions, or an inevitable idiom of modern science? *Journal of Bioethical Inquiry*, 5, 271–282, 275. doi: 10.1007/s11673-008-9113-6.

3 See, for example, Cloatre, E. and Pickersgill, M.(eds) (2014) *Knowledge, Technology and Law: At the Intersection of Socio-Legal and Science & Technology Studies*. Routledge; Cloatre, E. and Pickersgill, M. (2013) The material life of science and law. Blog post: www.sciculture.ac.uk/2013/12/09/1085/.

4 Redman, Barbara & Caplan, Arthur. (2005). Off with their Heads: The Need to Criminalize some forms of Scientific Misconduct. *The Journal of law, medicine & ethics: a journal of the American Society of Law, Medicine & Ethics*. 33. 345–8. 10.1111/j.1748–720X.2005.tb00498.x.

DOI: 10.4324/9780429492129-9

subject to disagreement.[5] Towards one end of the viewpoint spectrum, plagiarism is seen as a category of dishonesty which undermines the integrity of science and the scientific community. The standards to which scientific researchers are subject and judged against should be no different from the standards applied to others who are entrusted to be honest.[6] In contrast, towards the other end of the spectrum, observations include '"Plagiarism" is the name of the collective neurosis of academic life'[7] and 'there is no reason to consider "tedium and redundancy" to be "academic crimes."'[8] Faced with multiple works presenting similar ideas, readers are free to decide for themselves who expressed the idea first, with any inappropriate claim to novelty being refuted by the existence of earlier work.[9]

With regard to self-plagiarism, it has been argued that 'in a saner world [it] would be regarded as an ordinary exercise of the author's copyright.'[10] Developing further the intellectual property analogy, it has been said that the norms of plagiarism are an 'extra-legal' and 'illegitimate' way for academics to assert property rights in ideas in a legal arena where no such obligation exists: 'Copyright cannot and should not protect ideas, and plagiarism norms are simply copyright by other means . . . a kind of quasi-property right in attribution.'[11] Debates of this type neatly illustrate the challenges created by seeking to import legal ideas and ideas about regulatory certainty into non-legal arenas and the associated risks of distorting those alternative arenas.

The manner in which misconduct is defined also creates the field on which conflicting visions between society and the scientific community are fought out.[12] Those seeking to minimize the regulation and oversight of research may focus on describing scientific misconduct in terms of a narrative of 'individual impurity,' something 'intentionally carried out by deranged individuals' and

5 See, for example, discussion in Bouville, M. (2008). Plagiarism: Words and ideas. *Science and Engineering Ethics*, 14, 311–322. doi: 10.1007/s11948-008-9057-6.

6 Redman, Barbara & Caplan, Arthur. (2005). Off with their Heads: The Need to Criminalize some forms of Scientific Misconduct. *The Journal of law, medicine & ethics: a journal of the American Society of Law, Medicine & Ethics*. 33. 345–8. 10.1111/j.1748–720X.2005.tb00498.x

7 Steve Fuller. (2020). Plagiarism hunters, please lay down your weapons, *Times Higher Education*, February 5. www.timeshighereducation.com/opinion/plagiarism-hunters-please-lay-down-your-weapons

8 Frye, B. L. (2020). Plagiarize this paper (October 1, 2019). *IDEA: The IP Law Review*, 60(294), 311. Available at SSRN: https://ssrn.com/abstract=3462144

9 Frye, B. L. (2020). Plagiarize this paper (October 1, 2019). *IDEA: The IP Law Review*, 60(294), 311. Available at SSRN: https://ssrn.com/abstract=3462144

10 Steve Fuller. (2020). Plagiarism hunters, please lay down your weapons, *Times Higher Education*, February 5. www.timeshighereducation.com/opinion/plagiarism-hunters-please-lay-down-your-weapons

11 Frye, B. L. (2020). Plagiarize this paper (October 1, 2019). *IDEA: The IP Law Review*, 60(294). Available at SSRN: https://ssrn.com/abstract=3462144

12 Sovacool, B. (2008). Exploring scientific misconduct: Isolated individuals, impure institutions, or an inevitable idiom of modern science? *Journal of Bioethical Inquiry*, 5, 271–282, 275. doi: 10.1007/s11673-008-9113-6.

therefore very rare, of limited consequence and best addressed by identifying and removing those individuals.[13] At the heart of many scientists' conception of the scientific world is the conviction that there must be freedom to think, experiment and base relationships on trust. Such trust can make scientists easier to deceive if they have a fraudster in their midst, but this can be counterbalanced with arguments that it is such trust which aids efficiency and the speed at which science can advance.[14] A suspicious and untrusting attitude may impede advances in scientific knowledge without necessarily reducing the risk of problematic testimony.[15] Given the importance of epistemic cooperation, there is a delicate balance to be drawn between the place of trust and the need for appropriate safeguards against untrustworthy members of the research community.[16] Some concerns from within the scientific community can find support in the jurisprudential critique relating to juridification – the tendency towards increasing formal law and regulation in modern society.[17] 'Regulatory reach' has already extended into areas previously considered to be beyond the appropriate reach of law.[18] There is a risk that legal input goes beyond supplementing socially integrated constructs, and instead the field being regulated loses distinctiveness and is converted by the medium of law, the superimposition of legal norms being accompanied by associated functional disturbances.[19] As a result, controls, whether formal or informal, may be disliked within the scientific community and have even be described as 'abhorred . . . as affronts to

13 Redman, Barbara & Caplan, Arthur. (2005). Off with their Heads: The Need to Criminalize some forms of Scientific Misconduct. *The Journal of law, medicine & ethics: a journal of the American Society of Law, Medicine & Ethics*. 33. 345–8. 10.1111/j.1748-720X.2005.tb00498.x; Sovacool, B. (2008). Exploring scientific misconduct: Isolated individuals, impure institutions, or an inevitable idiom of modern science? *Journal of Bioethical Inquiry*, 5, 271–282, 272. doi: 10.1007/s11673-008-9113-6.

14 See, for example, observations by Barber, B. (1987). Trust in Science, *Minerva* 25: 123. https://doi.org/10.1007/BF01096860

15 See, for example, Hardwig, J. (1991). The role of trust in knowledge. *Journal of Philosophy*, 88(12), 693–708, 707.

16 Hardwig, J. (1991). The role of trust in knowledge. *Journal of Philosophy*, 88(12), 693–708, 707.

17 Habermas, Jurgen (1987) [1981]. *Theory of Communicative Action, Volume Two: Lifeworld and System: A Critique of Functionalist Reason* Translated by Thomas A. McCarthy. Boston, Mass.: Beacon Press.

18 Veitch, S., Christodoulidis, E., Goldoni, M. (2018). *Jurisprudence*. London: Routledge, ch 9

19 Habermas, Jurgen (1987) [1981]. *Theory of Communicative Action, Volume Two: Lifeworld and System: A Critique of Functionalist Reason* Translated by Thomas A. McCarthy. Boston, Mass.: Beacon Press. Beacon Press; Gunther Teubner, 'Juridification: Concepts, Aspects, Limits, Solutions', in Gunther Teubner (ed), *Juridification of Social Spheres* (de Gruyter 1987); Veitch, S., Christodoulidis, E., Goldoni, M. (2018). *Jurisprudence*. London: Routledge, ch 9. Citing Gunther Teubner, 'Juridification: Concepts, Aspects, Limits, Solutions', in Gunther Teubner (ed), *Juridification of Social Spheres* (de Gruyter 1987); Teubner, G. (1992). Regulatory Law: Chronicle of a Death Foretold, 1 *Social & Legal Studies* 451–475

the valued solidarity and co-operation of scientists with each other,' which in turn may precipitate poor morale and mutual suspicion.[20]

Influential stakeholders such as the UK Russell Group of research-intensive universities, have responded to calls for the external imposition of rules by arguing that an emphasis on rule compliance can be counterproductive by encouraging minimum compliance, rather than incentivising striving for the highest level of behaviour.[21] From these perspectives, the prospect of systematic checking for misconduct will sit uncomfortably as demonstrating an inherent lack of trust, a presumption of guilt even, from what is a predominantly honest community of researchers.[22] Those researchers who consider themselves to be at the cutting edge of their discipline may add to such perceptions by challenging approaches to misconduct or error, perpetuating a mythology of the 'maverick genius' within science.[23] For example, Hans Eysenck responded to a critic as follows:

> Pedantic to the last degree, any error, however slight, random, and unimportant from the point of view of the grand design, is a sin against the Holy Ghost, to be hunted down, exposed and eradicated. This battle is age-old, and few creative scientists escape it.[24]

The Macchiarini case further illustrates the dangers of the continuation of the maverick genius approach in modern research environments. Macchiarini's misconduct had effects beyond his immediate circle and the integrity of the research record. Even though Macchiarini was the focus of culpability, a number of role holders took steps that they thought were appropriate to protect the integrity of the Karolinska Institute and the wider research environment. Notably, the stepping down of a vice-chancellor and chair of the university board of governors. Four professors from the Nobel Assembly at Karolinska Institute withdrew from participating in the work of the assembly while the Macchiarini case was being investigated, in case they found themselves drawn into the investigation. The Nobel Foundation, although independent of the

20 Barber, B. (1987). Trust in Science, *Minerva* 25: 123. https://doi.org/10.1007/BF01096860.

21 Chris Havergal. (2019). UKRI agrees to create research integrity watchdog, *Times Higher Education*, June 10, www.timeshighereducation.com/news/ukri-agrees-create-research-integrity-watchdog

22 Bouville, M. (2008). Plagiarism: Words and ideas. *Science and Engineering Ethics*, 14, 311–322, 319. doi: 10.1007/s11948-008-9057-6.

23 The idea of the 'genius scientist' is often pictured as a rule-breaking risk taker in the pursuit of breakthrough discoveries, with progress being driven by 'the genius of a few,' John Rasko and Carl Power, Dr Con Man: the rise and fall of a celebrity scientist who fooled almost everyone, The Guardian, Friday 1 September 2017 www.theguardian.com/science/2017/sep/01/paolo-macchiarini-scientist-surgeon-rise-and-fall

24 Eysenck, HJ (1993b) Reply to Van Der Ploeg, Vetter, and Kleijn. *Psychological Inquiry* 4: 70–73.

institute, is quoted as observing that mistakes in the handling of the Macchiarini case could affect the way the Nobel Prize is perceived.[25]

If calls from within the research community to resist greater external imposition of regulation are to be effective, prompt and committed changes arising from within that community may be one way to achieve this. A specific scientific 'profession' with a regulatory infrastructure, compulsory ethics and regulatory education, a regulatory code, an ombudsperson and even a professional 'oath' offer possible ways forward. Such a self-regulatory model would allow the research community to utilise its expertise, expertise which external regulators would find challenging to match, to police the community. A more structured and trustworthy research ecosystem would focus less on individual researchers expected to voluntarily underpin research integrity and more on creating and nurturing an environment which aims at continuous improvement and values and rewards research integrity.[26] Research ethics and research integrity within such an environment are virtues which can be enhanced with ongoing education and training and by creating a climate which incorporates awareness and openness.[27] Ethics education and professional ethical codes of conduct can be used to cement such an environment in a manner which enhances the best interests of society, rather than unduly focusing on the narrower self-interest of the scientific community.[28]

Excessive focus on compliance monitoring and seeking to attribute blame can be counterproductive, but appropriate and effective monitoring may avoid what has been described in the context of some existing regulatory models as 'fractured, inefficient, inconsistent' systems.[29] Monitoring which offers a high

25 Henry Fountain, Official Quits Nobel Panel Over Inquiry Into Surgeon, *New York Times*, Feb. 7, 2016, www.nytimes.com/2016/02/08/world/europe/official-quits-nobel-panel-over-inquiry-into-surgeon.html (accessed 26 November 2020); Karolinska Institute, The Macchiarini case: Timeline https://news.ki.se/the-macchiarini-case-timeline (accessed 26 November 2020)

26 Metcalfe, J., Wheat, K., Munafò. M., Parry, J. (2020). *Research Integrity: A Landscape Study* (p. 44). Vitae/UK Research Integrity Office/UK Reproducibility Network, www.ukri.org/files/legacy/documents/research-integrity-main-report/. See also, for example, Kretser, A., Murphy, D., Bertuzzi, S., Abraham, T., Allison, D., Boor, K., Dwyer, J., Grantham, A., Harris, L., Hollander, R., Jacobs-Young, C., Rovito, S., Vafiadis, D., Woteki, C., Wyndham, J., & Yada, R. (2019). Scientific integrity principles and best practices: Recommendations from a scientific integrity consortium. *Science and Engineering Ethics*, 25. doi: 10.1007/s11948-019-00094-3.

27 Editorial, 'Research integrity is much more than misconduct', *Nature* 570, 5 (2019) doi: 10.1038/d41586-019-01727-0; Bird, Stephanie. (2006). Research ethics, research integrity and the responsible conduct of research. *Science and Engineering Ethics*. 12. 411–412, 412 10.1007/s11948–006–0040–9.

28 Sovacool, B. (2008). Exploring scientific misconduct: Isolated individuals, impure institutions, or an inevitable idiom of modern science? *Journal of Bioethical Inquiry*, 5, 271–282, 276. doi: 10.1007/s11673-008-9113-6.

29 Gunsalus, C. K., McNutt, M. K. et al. (2019). Overdue: A US advisory board for research integrity. *Nature*, 566, 173–175 doi: https://doi.org/10.1038/d41586-019-00519-w

probability of detection utilised alongside the invocation of high ethical standards in combination are likely to be most effective.[30]

If regulatory targets are adopted, caution must be exercised to avoid measuring what is easy to measure, rather than what is most important to measure, and to avoid encouraging behaviour calculated to meet targets rather than to achieve the most important ethical and regulatory outcomes.[31] Consideration should also be given to perverse institutional incentives and other characteristics of modern scientific practice which may make ethically questionable behaviour more likely.[32] From this perspective the focus of research misconduct should be less on 'rotten apples' and more on 'rotten barrels' arising from inappropriate organisational culture, where appropriate a narrative of 'institutional failure' or a narrative of 'structural crisis.'[33] A focus entirely on individual self-regulation will be insufficient to meaningfully address such organisational challenges.[34]

Also associated with these bigger-picture changes are considerations of science itself, scientific method and achieving appropriate consistency in that regard. Arguments that science lacks a sufficiently common and coherent value system, with different sections of the research community developing their own cultural and social positions and even contradictions in their scientific practise may inhibit developments of the type discussed in this work.[35]

Producing significant change within a well-established group culture is challenging, but possible if determined efforts are made. For example, within the medical field, over the period of a few decades, clinical research has moved from being subject to limited oversight to a much more rigorous oversight

30 Metcalfe, J., Wheat, K., Munafò. M., Parry, J. (2020). *Research Integrity: A Landscape Study* (p. 44). Vitae/UK Research Integrity Office/UK Reproducibility Network, www.ukri.org/files/legacy/documents/research-integrity-main-report/; Quandt, R. (2012). Some models of academic corruption. *European Journal of Law and Economics*, 72, 29. doi: 10.1007/s10657-010-9162-2 at 72. For counter arguments relating to the costs of control see Falk, A., & Kosfeld, M. (2006). The hidden costs of control. American Economic Review, 96, 1611–1630.

31 See, for example, Geoffrey Hosking (2010), Trust: Money, Markets and Society, (Calcutta: Seagull Books), 7–9

32 Sovacool, B. (2008). Exploring scientific misconduct: Isolated individuals, impure institutions, or an inevitable idiom of modern science? *Journal of Bioethical Inquiry*, 5, 271–282, 272. doi: 10.1007/s11673-008-9113-6.

33 Faria, R. (2015). Scientific misconduct: how organizational culture plays its part. Tijdschrift over Cultuur& Criminaliteit, 5(1), 38–54, 51; Sovacool, B. (2008). Exploring scientific misconduct: Isolated individuals, impure institutions, or an inevitable idiom of modern science? *Journal of Bioethical Inquiry*, 5, 271–282, 272. doi: 10.1007/s11673-008-9113-6.

34 Sovacool, B. (2008). Exploring scientific misconduct: Isolated individuals, impure institutions, or an inevitable idiom of modern science? *Journal of Bioethical Inquiry*, 5, 271–282, 276–277. doi: 10.1007/s11673-008-9113-6.

35 Cetina, Karin Knorr. (1999). *Epistemic Cultures: How the Sciences Make Knowledge*. Harvard University Press; Sovacool, B. (2008). Exploring scientific misconduct: Isolated individuals, impure institutions, or an inevitable idiom of modern science? *Journal of Bioethical Inquiry*, 5, 271–282, 276–277. doi: 10.1007/s11673-008-9113-6.

regime. Changes deemed at the time they were proposed to be highly controversial and seen by some, for example, those with vested interests to maintain the status quo or more generally averse to change, have become well established.[36] The suggestion that junior researchers may be more idealistic than their more senior colleagues presents the prospect that newer generations may be open to more radical change.[37]

All stakeholders, notably universities and other research institutions, research integrity professionals, research funders, publishers, learned societies and policy makers, have a role to play.[38] For example, universities could decouple job security and job enhancement from productivity and reward ethically focused activity.[39] Funders could motivate institutions, research supervisors and individual researchers to act ethically and to take appropriate care by including a refund clause, triggered by certain eventualities or behaviours, in all grant award terms and conditions. To encourage ethically appropriate institutional investigation where a problem with research is suspected, such provisions could provide for less than full clawback of funding or even no clawback at all if the institutional investigation was demonstrably timely, comprehensive and transparent.[40]

In terms of modern research practice, the reality is that research is often carried out by teams of scientists, in many instances international and interdisciplinary.[41] Alongside modern technologies enhancing global communication and facilitating global team building, new ethics and regulatory challenges may also arise as new developments emerge in other areas of technology, for example, in

36 Begley, C. G., Buchan, A. M., & Dirnagl, U. (2015). Robust research: Institutions must do their part for reproducibility. *Nature,* 525, 25–27. https://doi.org/10.1038/525025a

37 Shaw, D., & Satalkar, P. (2018). Researchers' interpretations of research integrity: A qualitative study. *Accountability in Research,* 25(2), 79–93, 90. doi: 10.1080/08989621.2017.1413940

38 Metcalfe, J., Wheat, K., Munafò. M., Parry, J. (2020). *Research Integrity: A Landscape Study* (p. 51). Vitae/UK Research Integrity Office/UK Reproducibility Network, www.ukri.org/files/legacy/documents/research-integrity-main-report/

39 Inge Lerouge and Antoine Hol, *Towards a Research Integrity Culture at Universities: From Recommendations to Implementation.* Advice Paper no. 26 – January 2020, League of European Research Universities, 8; Foster, J. G., Rzhetsky, A., & Evans, J. A. (2013). Tradition and innovation in scientists' research strategies. *American Sociological Review,* 80(5) (February). doi: 10.1177/0003122415601618, citing Gertner, Jon. 2012. *The Idea Factory: Bell Labs and the Great Age of American Innovation.* New York: Penguin.

40 Leonid Schneider, What if universities had to agree to refund grants whenever there was a retraction? *Retraction Watch.* http://retractionwatch.com/2015/01/19/universities-agree-refund-grants-whenever-retraction/ (accessed 4 February 2021). As noted in the comments to this piece, there are risks that the approach would be cumbersome and bureaucratic. Institutions and authors may be tempted to refuse to cooperate with journal investigations, and institutions may use power and influence over academic editors to minimise the use of retractions seeking, for example, corrections instead.

41 Zwart, H. Challenges of Macro-ethics: Bioethics and the Transformation of Knowledge Production. *Bioethical Inquiry* 5, 283–293 (2008). https://doi.org/10.1007/s11673-008-9110-9

relation to big data or artificial intelligence.[42] The enormity of the worldwide research enterprise makes the task of regulation particularly challenging. Institutional and professional self-regulatory models can break this down into more manageable chunks. However, large-scale cases requiring significant investigatory and adjudicatory resources can overwhelm such bodies, as can variations in jurisdictional approaches to research ethics and enforcement. As international research teams collaborate and compete globally, transnational organisations, 'moral "players" in the global field of science ethics' with development of globally agreed principles of research ethics become increasingly important.[43] An ultimate goal is the embedding of an overarching culture of integrity at the international level and ranging across all scientific disciplines.[44]

Whichever approach is adopted, transparency is key. In the words of one editor: 'Throw open the windows, let everyone see everything. I do have a belief in the fundamentality of science to correct itself. We can't do that under the blanket of secrecy.'[45] Only with the collective attention of the scientific community upon a fully transparent field and a willingness to fully police that field can maximum confidence be had in the integrity and trustworthiness of science.[46]

Evidence of progress with regard to the scientific community more fully committing to addressing issues of ethics and misconduct includes early stage development of a specialist area of research – misconduct studies. This can facilitate the sharing of expertise and the critical analysis of all aspects of research misconduct and potential solutions.[47] Similarly, publishing outlets which welcome negative findings can help to balance against publishing trends towards 'interesting' results at the cost of a relative absence of less novel, negative or null findings, thereby depriving the research community of important knowledge which can avoid wasting the time of other researchers in pursuing futile

42 Metcalfe, J., Wheat, K., Munafò. M., Parry, J. (2020). *Research Integrity: A Landscape Study* (p. 46). Vitae/UK Research Integrity Office/UK Reproducibility Network, www.ukri.org/files/legacy/documents/research-integrity-main-report/

43 Zwart, H. (2008). Challenges of Macro-ethics: Bioethics and the Transformation of Knowledge Production. *Bioethical Inquiry* 5, 283–293. https://doi.org/10.1007/s11673-008-9110-9.

44 For exploration of such ideas at a national level see Gunsalus, C. K., McNutt, M. K. et al. (2019). Overdue: A US advisory board for research integrity. *Nature*, 566, 173–175 doi: https://doi.org/10.1038/d41586-019-00519-w

45 Kelly Crowe, BMJ editor Fiona Godlee takes on corruption in science, CBC News · Posted: Apr 19, 2016, www.cbc.ca/news/health/bmj-fiona-godlee-science-1.3541769 (accessed 28 November 2020)

46 O'Neill O. A question of trust (BBC Reith Lectures). 2002. www.bbc.co.uk/radio4/reith2002/ (accessed 29 November 2020)

47 In a more focused discussion, 'plagiarism studies' was suggested, Biagioli, M. (2012). Recycling texts or stealing time? Plagiarism, authorship, and credit in science. *International Journal of Cultural Property*, 19, 468. It should be feasible to have sub-specialisms resting under a broader umbrella title, although it will be important that appropriate lines of communication are maintained to maximise sharing of expertise across such sub-specialisms.

projects.[48] An example of a specialist publication was the *Journal of Negative Results in Biomedicine*, an open-access, peer-reviewed journal published between 2002 and 2017. The journal offered a specialist outlet for negative data and unexpected or controversial findings which may have otherwise not found space for publication. The closure of this journal may be viewed in positive terms, as its demise is attributed to an increasing number of mainstream journals which have increased their willingness to publish articles reporting negative or null results.[49]

Ultimately, the extent to which greater regulation enhances or impairs trust is open to debate. Some voices from within the scientific community see regulation as fostering negative aspects of managerialism, stifling creativity and increasing the focus on narrow targets.[50] Accountability to regulators and, sometimes, government could lead to a decline rather than an increase in public trust.[51] In contrast, voices from within other professions can be heard calling for greater regulation or decrying the loss of hard-won regulatory coverage, fearful that with a weakening of regulatory status will come a reduced level of trust and respect, accompanied with a reduced capacity to undertake the professional role.[52] The scientific research community may also risk harm to its status without full commitment to an appropriate ethics and regulatory model.

48 Kretser, A., Murphy, D., Bertuzzi, S., Abraham, T., Allison, D., Boor, K., Dwyer, J., Grantham, A., Harris, L., Hollander, R., Jacobs-Young, C., Rovito, S., Vafiadis, D., Woteki, C., Wyndham, J., & Yada, R. (2019). Scientific integrity principles and best practices: Recommendations from a scientific integrity consortium. *Science and Engineering Ethics*, 25. doi: 10.1007/s11948-019-00094-3.

49 Kretser, A., Murphy, D., Bertuzzi, S., Abraham, T., Allison, D., Boor, K., Dwyer, J., Grantham, A., Harris, L., Hollander, R., Jacobs-Young, C., Rovito, S., Vafiadis, D., Woteki, C., Wyndham, J., & Yada, R. (2019). Scientific integrity principles and best practices: Recommendations from a scientific integrity consortium. *Science and Engineering Ethics*, 25. doi: 10.1007/s11948-019-00094-3.

50 See, for example, observations in ALLEA, Loss of Trust? Loss of Trustworthiness? Truth and Expertise, ALLEA discussion paper #1, May 2018 https://allea.org/wp-content/uploads/2018/05/ALLEA_Discussion_Paper_1_Truth_and_Expertise_Today-digital.pdf

51 ALLEA, Loss of Trust? Loss of Trustworthiness? Truth and Expertise, ALLEA discussion paper #1, May 2018 https://allea.org/wp-content/uploads/2018/05/ALLEA_Discussion_Paper_1_Truth_and_Expertise_Today-digital.pdf

52 For a brief discussion in the context of the regulation of solicitors in England and Wales, see Jonathan Goldsmith, How deregulation harms our trade in legal services, *Law Society Gazette*, 11 June 2018; In the context of financial regulation, see Charles Randell, *Rolling the rock: The cycle of deregulation, crisis and regulation*. Speech by Charles Randell, Chair, Financial Conduct Authority, delivered at the Association for Financial Markets in Europe (AFME) Annual Conference on 2 October 2018. https://www.fca.org.uk/news/speeches/rolling-rock-cycle-deregulation-crisis-and-regulation (accessed 1 December 2021)

Appendix

Case studies

Introduction

Throughout this work a number of case examples have been integrated into the discussion. In this appendix, for reference purposes, the background detail of some of these examples is built upon. The cases are presented alphabetically.

Niels Birbaumer

Niels Birbaumer, a German neuroscientist holding positions at the University of Tübingen in Germany and the Wyss Center for Bio and Neuroengineering in Switzerland, was found in 2019 by Germany's primary research agency to have committed scientific misconduct in research relating to a purported brain-monitoring technique able to read certain thoughts of paralysed people.[1] The agency had been alerted to concerns by a postdoctoral whistle blower at Tübingen who was unable to reproduce the research findings from the published data. An independent expert commissioned by the Deutsche Forschungsgemeinschaft (DFG), the central self-governing organization of the German research community, and two additional whistle-blowers fed into the investigatory process.[2] Two papers arising from the research were found to be incomplete and the analysis within flawed. There was also a lack of transparency in the research methodology, which involved vulnerable research subjects, and questions regarding whether all relevant findings had been included.[3]

1 Abbott, A. (2019). Prominent German neuroscientist committed misconduct in 'brain-reading' research. *Nature*, September 21, 2019. doi: 10.1038/d41586-019-02862-4

2 Abbott, A. (2019). Prominent German neuroscientist committed misconduct in 'brain-reading' research. *Nature*, September 21, 2019. doi: 10.1038/d41586-019-02862-4

3 University of Tübingen, accusing the renowned brain researcher misconduct, *HealthMedicinentral,* http://healthmedicinentral.com/personal-health/university-of-tubingen-accusing-the-renowned-brain-researcher-misconduct/ (accessed 26 September 2019). See also blog discussion Neuroskeptic, The Fall of Niels Birbaumer, July 2, 2019, http://blogs.discovermagazine.com/neuroskeptic/2019/07/02/the-fall-of-niels-birbaumer/#.XYk1OHdFw2w (accessed 26 September 2019)

Birbaumer was forbidden from applying for DFG grants and from serving as a DFG evaluator for five years and retraction of the two papers recommended.[4] A member of Birbaumer's team and first author of the two papers, Ujwal Chaudhary, was also found to have committed scientific misconduct and prohibited from applying for DFG grants and from serving as a DFG evaluator for three years.[5] The University of Tübingen also investigated Birbaumer and Chaudhary's work and found that they had committed scientific misconduct.[6] Birbaumer and co-authors are reported to have declined to agree to the retractions, stand by their data and analyses and were challenging legally the misconduct findings.[7]

Ranjit Kumar Chandra

Ranjit Kumar Chandra was a nutrition researcher who claimed to have made ground-breaking findings in relation to both children's health and the health of the elderly. He fell from the position of highly regarded researcher at Memorial University of Newfoundland (MUN), author of over 200 papers, member of the Order of Canada, to having a number of retractions and facing significant costs at the end of an unsuccessful defamation lawsuit.[8] The latter in particular makes this an instructive case study, as it was Chandra's decision to pursue defamation proceedings which brought additional evidence into public view and revealed failures in scientific governance.

4 Abbott, A. (2019). Prominent German neuroscientist committed misconduct in 'brain-reading' research. *Nature*, September 21, 2019. doi: 10.1038/d41586-019-02862-4; The PLOS Biology Editors (2019) Retraction: Brain – Computer Interface – Based Communication in the Completely Locked-In State. PLOS Biology 17(12): e3000607. https://doi.org/10.1371/journal.pbio.3000607; The PLOS Biology Editors (2019) Retraction: Response to: "Questioning the evidence for BCI-based communication in the complete locked-in state". PLOS Biology 17(12): e3000608. https://doi.org/10.1371/journal.pbio.3000608

5 Abbott, A. (2019). Prominent German neuroscientist committed misconduct in 'brain-reading' research. *Nature*, September 21, 2019. doi: 10.1038/d41586-019-02862-4

6 Abbott, A. (2019). Prominent German neuroscientist committed misconduct in 'brain-reading' research. *Nature*, September 21, 2019. doi: 10.1038/d41586-019-02862-4

7 The PLOS Biology Editors (2019) Retraction: Brain – Computer Interface – Based Communication in the Completely Locked-In State. PLOS Biology 17(12): e3000607. https://doi.org/10.1371/journal.pbio.3000607; The PLOS Biology Editors (2019) Retraction: Response to: "Questioning the evidence for BCI-based communication in the complete locked-in state". *PLOS Biology*, 17(12), e3000608. https://doi.org/10.1371/journal.pbio.3000608. Shortly before publication of this work news was emerging of a settlement of the legal dispute between Birbaumer and DFG. As a result of the settlement, no judicial determination had been made regarding the facts. The DFG had agreed to the early lifting of the sanctions imposed on Birbaumer but in other respects the DFG press release reported that the parties maintained their respective opinions with regard to the core tenets of the disputed matters. www.dfg.de

8 See Who is Ranjit Kumar Chandra? A timeline of notoriety https://retractionwatch.com/2016/07/26/who-is-ranjit-kumar-chandra-a-timeline-of-notoriety/ (accessed 2 January 2020); for link to full text of the law suit decision see www.cbc.ca/news/canada/newfoundland-labrador/chandra-paying-legal-fees-1.3322284 (accessed 2 January 2020)

Chandra's research began to be drawn into question in the 1990s. In 1995 allegations were raised by the chief of the Department of Pediatrics at MUN regarding a study in the *Annals of Allergy* and whether it and unpublished follow-up studies had been undertaken in the manner specified by Chandra.[9] A nurse recruited to identify research subjects among recent mothers was described as being amazed at seeing the published results, knowing that the recruitment had not taken place, but was deterred from attempting to blow the whistle by concerns about potential legal action.[10] This, it has been argued, was a common factor – those in a position to raise informed concerns about Chandra's work were reluctant to risk their own reputations, careers and financial wellbeing.[11] An inquiry by MUN into the *Annals of Allergy* and other studies was undertaken, but Chandra is reported to have threatened to sue. The results were deemed by MUN to be a product of a flawed investigation and so not published at the time. It subsequently became public as a result of Chandra's libel lawsuit.[12]

In 2000 Chandra submitted to the *British Medical Journal* a paper which purported to demonstrate that a vitamin supplement patented by Chandra could improve cognition in elderly patients. Editorial doubts resulted in the paper being submitted for review to a reviewer with particularly relevant statistical expertise and expertise in research misconduct, as well as a reviewer with expertise in the specialist field of the paper. The paper was rejected because of concerns that the research and its timeframe exceeded the capabilities of a single author and that the amount of psychometric testing involved in the study was beyond the author's expertise. One reviewer is reported to have suggested that the paper 'had all the hallmarks of being entirely invented.'[13] The paper was subsequently published in *Nutrition* in 2001. A 2002 article supporting Chandra's research was published in a journal, *Nutrition Research*, founded and edited by Chandra. The named author, Amrit Jain, could not be traced by interested parties beyond a paid-for mailbox in Canada, and it was later suggested that it

9 See Who is Ranjit Kumar Chandra? A timeline of notoriety, https://retractionwatch.com/2016/07/26/who-is-ranjit-kumar-chandra-a-timeline-of-notoriety/ (accessed 2 January 2020)

10 O'Neill-Yates C. The secret life of Dr. Chandra. NCB, 31 January – 2 February 2006. Available from You Tube at the time of writing (6 January 2020). See also BMJ review by Terry Hamblin, 2006 Feb 11; 332(7537): 369.

11 Sterken, E. (2006). The impact of scientific misconduct on child health. *Public Health Nutrition*, 9(2), 273–274. doi: 10.1079/PHN2006951. Sterken, Director INFACT Canada, acknowledges that her own organisation was not in a position to place its own financial status in jeopardy without clear evidence.

12 See Who is Ranjit Kumar Chandra? A timeline of notoriety, https://retractionwatch.com/2016/07/26/who-is-ranjit-kumar-chandra-a-timeline-of-notoriety/ (accessed 2 January 2020)

13 Smith, R. (2005). Investigating the previous studies of a fraudulent author, *BMJ*. 331: 288 doi: https://doi.org/10.1136/bmj.331.7511.288; Roberts, S. (2006). Dealing with scientific fraud: A proposal. Public Health Nutrition, 9(5), 664–665. doi: 10.1079/PHN2006963, citing White C. (2004). Three journals raise doubts on validity of Canadian studies. *BMJ*. 328: 67 and also Chandra's reply Chandra R. (2004). Validity of Canadian studies: author's response. *BMJ*. 328: 465

could be a pseudonym for Chandra.[14] A letter to *The Lancet* in 2003 raised a number of statistical concerns relating to the 2001 *Nutrition* paper. The letter was accompanied by a refutation from Chandra.[15] In 2005 *Nutrition* retracted the 2001 article on the basis that:

> The numerous serious questions raised about the methodology call into question the study's veracity. Professor Chandra's reply to repeated correspondence concerning these problems did not in our view satisfactorily provide supporting information nor explain discrepancies in his data.[16]

In the early to mid-2000s the concerns surrounding Chandra also came to the attention of various journalistic sources,[17] culminating in a 2006 Canadian Broadcasting Corporation documentary.[18]

Following this publicity MUN began an investigation into the 2001 *Nutrition* paper to determine whether it complied with the scientific, ethical and/or integrity standards of MUN.[19] The report, by Dr William Pryse-Phillips, retired professor of medicine, dated October 2009 but published ten years after the *Nutrition* retraction once litigation was at an end, identified over 40 problems with the article and concluded that it was not in compliance with MUN standards.[20]

14 Owen Dyer. (2015). Prominent Canadian researcher loses libel case against documentary makers. *BMJ*. 351 doi: https://doi.org/10.1136/bmj.h4129 (Published 30 July 2015); Who is Ranjit Kumar Chandra? A timeline of notoriety https://retractionwatch.com/2016/07/26/who-is-ranjit-kumar-chandra-a-timeline-of-notoriety/ (accessed 2 January 2020)

15 Carpenter, K, Roberts, S, Sternberg, S. Nutrition and immune function: a 1992 report. *Lancet* 2003; 361: 2247 www.thelancet.com/journals/lancet/article/PIIS0140-6736(03)13755-5/fulltext. See also Roberts, S. (2006). Dealing with scientific fraud: A proposal. Public Health Nutrition, 9(5), 664–665. doi: 10.1079/PHN2006963

16 RETRACTED: Effect of vitamin and trace-element supplementation on cognitive function in elderly subjects. *Nutrition*. 17(9) September 2001, 709–712 www.sciencedirect.com/science/article/pii/S0899900701006104; *Nutrition*. 2005 Feb;21(2):286. doi: 10.1016/j.nut.2004.12.002 (accessed 6 January 2020), discussed in Who is Ranjit Kumar Chandra? A timeline of notoriety, https://retractionwatch.com/2016/07/26/who-is-ranjit-kumar-chandra-a-timeline-of-notoriety/ (accessed 2 January 2020) and See also Roberts, S. (2006). Dealing with scientific fraud: A proposal. Public Health Nutrition, 9(5), 664–665. doi: 10.1079/PHN2006963

17 See, for example, Mahoney J. Leading vitamin scientist faces fire over data. Globe and Mail, 11 December 2003; Brody J. A top scientist's research is under attack. New York Times, 6 May 2004; Walsh N. Questions continue over research claims. CBC News, 10 June 2004, cited by Roberts, S. (2006). Dealing with scientific fraud: A proposal. Public Health Nutrition, 9(5), 664–665. doi: 10.1079/PHN2006963

18 O'Neill-Yates C. The secret life of Dr. Chandra. NCB, 31 January – 2 February 2006. Available from You Tube at the time of writing (6 January 2020). See also BMJ review by Terry Hamblin, 2006 Feb 11; 332(7537): 369.

19 www.mun.ca/research/PRYSE-PHILLIPS_REPORT1126.pdf, see also discussion in Who is Ranjit Kumar Chandra? A timeline of notoriety, https://retractionwatch.com/2016/07/26/who-is-ranjit-kumar-chandra-a-timeline-of-notoriety/ (accessed 2 January 2020)

20 http://today.mun.ca/news.php?id=9846 (accessed 6 January 2020); full report at www.mun.ca/research/PRYSE-PHILLIPS_REPORT1126.pdf (accessed 6 January 2020)

Following this report and MUN's concerns about Chandra's 1992 *Lancet* article, *The Lancet*, which had previously identified no evidence to justify retracting the piece, undertook further investigation and subsequently retracted the paper.[21] The 1995 MUN inquiry, which became public as part of Chandra's defamation litigation, also revealed information which led to the retraction of Chandra's 1989 article in the *British Medical Journal*.[22] The investigation leading to the 1995 report found a total absence of raw data, could not identify anyone involved in recruiting research subjects, the co-authors had little or nothing to do with the work and there were no hospital records to support the study.[23]

Peter Eklöv and Oona Lönnstedt

Peter Eklöv and Oona Lönnstedt were found guilty of research misconduct by the Swedish Central Ethical Review Board.[24] This accompanied the retraction of a paper published in *Science*.[25] The board concluded that Lönnstedt had intentionally fabricated data and had not conducted the experiments to the extent presented in the *Science* paper. Eklöv was Lönnstedt's supervisor, as well as co-author, and had allegedly failed to check that the research had been undertaken as described and so bore part of the responsibility but was not guilty of fabrication. According to Uppsala University, the employing institution, internal misconduct processes at the time did not incorporate unintentional behaviour of this type.[26] However, a follow-up investigation after the Central Ethical Review Board decision, at which point a fuller evidential picture was available, led Uppsala to revisit the matter and to conclude that Lönnstedt and Eklöv were guilty of research misconduct.[27] Lönnstedt and Eklöv requested

21 Chandra RK, Effect of vitamin and trace-element supplementation on immune responses and infection in elderly subjects. *Lancet*. 1992; 340: 1124–1127; Retraction – Effect of vitamin and trace-element supplementation on immune responses and infection in elderly subjects, The Lancet, Volume 387, Issue 10017, 30 January – 5 February 2016, Page 417 www.thelancet.com/pdfs/journals/lancet/PII0140-6736(92)93151-C.pdf

22 Chandra RK, Puri S, Hamed A. (1989). Influence of maternal diet during lactation and use of formula feeds on development of atopic eczema in high risk infants. *BMJ*. 299:228–30; www.bmj.com/content/299/6693/228; Retraction: Influence of maternal diet during lactation and use of formula feeds on development of atopic eczema in high risk infants. *BMJ* 2015; 351 doi: https://doi.org/10.1136/bmj.h5682 (Published 28 October 2015)

23 See retraction note at: Chandra RK, Puri S, Hamed A. (1989). Influence of maternal diet during lactation and use of formula feeds on development of atopic eczema in high risk infants. *BMJ*. 299:228–30; www.bmj.com/content/299/6693/228; Retraction: Influence of maternal diet during lactation and use of formula feeds on development of atopic eczema in high risk infants. *BMJ* 2015; 351 doi: https://doi.org/10.1136/bmj.h5682 (Published 28 October 2015)

24 Quirin Schiermeier. (2017). Investigation finds Swedish scientists committed scientific misconduct, *Nature*, 07 December 2017 www.nature.com/articles/d41586-017-08321-2

25 Lönnstedt, O. and Eklöv, P. *Science* 352, 1213–1216 (2016); retraction 356, 812 (2017).

26 Quirin Schiermeier. (2017). Investigation finds Swedish scientists committed scientific misconduct', *Nature*, 07 December 2017 www.nature.com/articles/d41586-017-08321-2

27 www.uu.se/digitalAssets/640/c_640434-l_1-k_ufv-2016-1074-decision.pdf (accessed 25 October 2020). For a discussion regarding apportionment of blame between the two researchers see

that the *Science* paper be retracted, stating that while they continue to strongly defend themselves against allegations made about their work, their findings will not be trusted as long as a suspicion of misconduct remains.[28]

The subject matter of the paper was a purported finding which suggested that microplastic particles in the ocean were harmful to certain fish larvae. Members of the wider research community had expressed concerns about missing research data and had questioned whether the experiments reported were feasible and could actually have been undertaken and whether the time-scale was accurate.[29] From this perspective, even in the absence of deceit, the nature of the purported research would have had questionable scientific value in the eyes of some within the wider research community.[30] It has also been suggested that indications from the research paper – that the research was not sufficiently aligned with the real-world environment being considered – could have alerted reviewers of the draft article.[31]

The Lönnstedt and Eklöv case is particularly instructive in terms of whistle-blowing within the scientific community. Scientists from various countries raised concerns. While it has been argued that the paper itself contained errors, eyewitnesses in the research environment played a key role, as they were able to identify significant disparities in the way the experimental work was reported by the authors compared with the actual observed research activity. The commitment needed by the whistle-blowers was significant. They had used their own records, text messages, social media posts and suchlike to piece together Lönnstedt's whereabouts on particular dates. These investigations indicated that she had been on Gotland to undertake her study for less than two weeks, rather than the three weeks described in the study. The formal misconduct investigations followed this lead by using receipts, travel records and email correspondence.[32]

Enserink, M. (2017). Researcher in Swedish fraud case speaks out: 'I'm very disappointed by my colleague'. *Science*, December 8, 2017, www.sciencemag.org/news/2017/12/researcher-swedish fraud-case-speaks-out-i-m-very-disappointed-my-colleague.

28 Cressey, D. (2017). Controversial microplastics study to be retracted. *Nature*, 02 May 2017. https://doi.org/10.1038/nature.2017.21929

29 Nancy Bazilchuk, 'Swedish research article retracted by prestigious international journal', *ScienceNordic*, May 11, 2017, http://sciencenordic.com/swedish-research-article-retracted-prestigious-international-journal

30 See discussion by Leonid Schneider https://forbetterscience.com/2017/07/09/fishy-peer-review-at-science-by-citizen-scientist-ted-held/ (accessed 20 April 2019)

31 See e-letters from Alastair Grant, professor of ecology at University of East Anglia, UK, and James Armitage, research associate at University of Toronto Scarborough, Canada https://science.sciencemag.org/content/352/6290/1213/tab-e-letters. Discussed by Leonid Schneider https://forbetterscience.com/2017/07/09/fishy-peer-review-at-science-by-citizen-scientist-ted-held/ (accessed 20 April 2019)

32 Enserink, M. (2017). Researcher in Swedish fraud case speaks out: 'I'm very disappointed by my colleague'. *Science*, December 8, 2017, www.sciencemag.org/news/2017/12/researcher-swedish-fraud-case-speaks-out-i-m-very-disappointed-my-colleague.

The follow-on ramifications of this case are also noteworthy. James Cook University (JCU) in Australia, at which Lönnstedt undertook her PhD between 2010 and 2014, launched an investigation into her research record with a panel consisting of scientific experts and a former federal court judge.[33] Lönnstedt had co-authored 15 papers during her time at JCU, and concerns had been raised about possible missing data from three of these. After reviewing the evidence, the panel concluded that Dr Lönnstedt had not committed research misconduct in prohibition of the JCU Research Code during her time at JCU, there being no evidence of 'intent and deliberation, recklessness or gross and persistent negligence.'[34] There were a number of breaches of the Research Code arising from failure to observe full requirements of animal ethics approvals, but in themselves these did not constitute misconduct. Some inadequate reporting of data was identified, but the panel concluded that this was an issue of professional standards rather than misconduct. Similarly, failure to ensure that data were appropriately lodged on completion of the PhD was deemed to be poor practice rather than misconduct.[35] It is a positive sign that once a researcher has been found to have committed misconduct, a wider-scale investigation followed to determine the integrity of other aspects of their research record.

Hans Eysenck

The late Professor Hans J. Eysenck has been described as 'Britain's most productive, but sometimes controversial, psychologist' and among the most commonly cited psychologists in the world.[36] The Eysenck case has been described as 'a stain on the record of psychology,' not least because certain results remained in peer-reviewed literature for decades, with failure to follow up allegations.[37] The studies in question influenced behaviour in terms of smoking and lifestyle

33 Emeritus Professor Alan Rix, Chair; Professor Bronwyn Gillanders; The Hon. Geoff Giudice AO; Emeritus Professor Tony Underwood. *Report of the Independent External Research Misconduct Inquiry: Oona Lönnstedt*, June 2020 www.jcu.edu.au/news/releases/2020/august/report-of-the-independent-external-research-misconduct-inquiry-oona-lonnstedt (accessed 1 March 2021)

34 *Report of the Independent External Research Misconduct Inquiry: Oona Lönnstedt*, June 2020, 4 www.jcu.edu.au/news/releases/2020/august/report-of-the-independent-external-research-misconduct-inquiry-oona-lonnstedt (accessed 1 March 2021)

35 *Report of the Independent External Research Misconduct Inquiry: Oona Lönnstedt*, June 2020, 4 www.jcu.edu.au/news/releases/2020/august/report-of-the-independent-external-research-misconduct-inquiry-oona-lonnstedt (accessed 1 March 2021)

36 Andersen, N., Corr, P. J. and Furnham, A. (2020). A Bibliometric Analysis of H. J. Eysenck's Research Output: Clarifying Controversy. *Personality and Individual Differences*, doi: 10.1016/j.paid.2020.109935; Smith Richard. (2019). Hans Eysenck: controversialist or worse? *BMJ*. 365: l1897; Rushton, J. P. (2001). 'A scientometric appreciation of H. J. Eysenck's contributions to psychology'. *Personality and Individual Differences*. 31: 17–39, p. 20. https://doi.org/10.1016/S0191-8869(00)00235-X.

37 Craig, R., Pelosi, T., & Tourish, D. (2020). Research misconduct complaints and institutional logics: The case of Hans Eysenck and the British Psychological Society. *Journal of Health Psychology*.

choices, which in turn led some commentators to argue that the research was 'a contributory factor in premature illness and death' of an unknown and unknowable number of individuals.[38]

Concerns about Eysenck were ongoing for a significant period of time. In the early 1990s psychologists and other experts focusing on research into fatal illnesses and personality questioned whether data had been altered or produced artificially.[39] For example, there were numerous instances of identical questionnaire responses unlikely to be explained by chance, leading to the conclusion that interviews were re-used either intentionally or by systematic accident.[40] In 1995 Anthony Pelosi, a medical practitioner, wrote to the British Psychological Society (BPS) expressing concerns about Eysenck.[41] The complaint expressed concerns about certain publications by Eysenck, the feasibility of some of the claims made and the timeframe needed to undertake the randomised trials involving very large numbers of participants.[42] The complaint was dismissed by the BPS Investigatory Committee and so did not progress to the stage of a full hearing.[43] In the letter from the BPS to Dr Pelosi, it was noted that the decision

(pre-print); Pelosi, A. J. (2019). Personality and fatal diseases: Revisiting a scientific scandal. *Journal of Health Psychology,* 24(4), 421–439; Pelosi, AJ (1998) The responsibility of academic institutions and professional organisations after accusations of scientific misconduct. The COPE Report, BMJ Publishing, London.

38 Pelosi, A. J. (2019). Personality and fatal diseases: Revisiting a scientific scandal. *Journal of Health Psychology,* 24(4), 421–439; Pelosi, AJ (1998) The responsibility of academic institutions and professional organisations after accusations of scientific misconduct. The COPE Report, BMJ Publishing, London.

39 Craig, R., Pelosi, T., & Tourish, D. (2020). Research misconduct complaints and institutional logics: The case of Hans Eysenck and the British Psychological Society. *Journal of Health Psychology*. (pre-print), citing Fox, B. H. (1991). Quandaries created by unlikely numbers in some of Grossarth-Maticek's studies. *Psychological Inquiry*, 2, 242–247; Pelosi AJ and Appleby L (1992) Psychological influences on cancer and ischaemic heart disease. *British Medical Journal* 304: 1295–1298; Van Der Ploeg HM (1991) What a wonderful world it would be: A re-analysis of some of the work of Grossarth-Maticek. *Psychological Inquiry* 2: 280–285; Van Der Ploeg, HM (1992) Psychological influences on cancer and ischaemic heart disease *British Medical Journal* 304(6842): 1632–1633. doi: 10.1136/bmj.304.6842.1632-b

40 Van Der Ploeg, HM, Vetter, H (1993) Two for the price of one: The empirical basis of the Grossarth-Maticek interviews. Psychological Inquiry 4: 65–69, 66, cited by Pelosi, A. J. (2019). Personality and fatal diseases: Revisiting a scientific scandal. *Journal of Health Psychology,* 24(4), 421–439. Eysenck replied, denying any systematic errors and arguing that some errors were likely in any large epidemiological study. Eysenck, HJ (1993b) Reply to Van Der Ploeg, Vetter, and Kleijn. Psychological Inquiry 4: 70–73.

41 Pelosi, A. J. (2019). Personality and fatal diseases: Revisiting a scientific scandal. *Journal of Health Psychology,* 24(4), 421–439.

42 Referring to commentary in the *British Medical Journal*: Pelosi AJ and Appleby L (1992) Psychological influences on cancer and ischaemic heart disease. *British Medical Journal* 304: 1295–1298; Eysenck H (1992) Psychosocial factors, cancer and ischaemic heart disease. *British Medical Journal* 305: 457–459; Pelosi AJ and Appleby L (1993) Personality and fatal diseases. *British Medical Journal* 306: 1666–1667.

43 Craig, R., Pelosi, T., & Tourish, D. (2020). Research misconduct complaints and institutional logics: The case of Hans Eysenck and the British Psychological Society. *Journal of Health Psychology*. (pre-print)

had been confirmed by the independent non-psychologist representative of the disciplinary board.[44] Whilst effective lay membership of professional regulatory bodies has often been identified as an important balancing feature against, for example, overprotectiveness of professional members towards those accused, in the case of the subtleties involved in identifying erroneous research or research misconduct, placing the final decision in the hands of non-experts may prove to be particularly problematic if they lack expertise to fully assess the nature and detail of allegations.[45]

Hans Eysenck died in 1997. This explains in part why the intensity of pressure for further investigation diminished to some extent. Pelosi also explained that, having received notice from the BPS that they had ended their considerations of the allegations against Eysenck, he was unsure about what, if any, further routes of action were available.[46] Eysenck continued to be celebrated, and his work continued to be influential.[47] However, a notable resurgence in the raising of concerns arose from around 2016 onwards when celebrations to commemorate the centenary of Eysenck's birth were being planned. Pelosi's interest was rekindled when he was invited to contribute to a special issue of *Personality and Individual Differences*, a journal founded by Eysenck. Pelosi's article was not published in the special issue, but in 2019 it was accepted for publication in the *Journal of Health Psychology*.[48] An accompanying editorial in the *Journal of Health Psychology* discussed the 'questionable science' facilitated by Eysenck and a 'programme of flawed research' which remains highly cited and continues to have a misleading impact upon the scientific record.[49] For example, large and important epidemiological studies have incorporated hypotheses drawn from Eysenck's work, and personality assessments have been featured in clinical research on cancer patients.[50]

44 Pelosi, A. J. (2019). Personality and fatal diseases: Revisiting a scientific scandal. *Journal of Health Psychology,* 24(4), 421–439.

45 Craig, R., Pelosi, T., & Tourish, D. (2020). Research misconduct complaints and institutional logics: The case of Hans Eysenck and the British Psychological Society. *Journal of Health Psychology*. (pre-print)

46 Pelosi, A. J. (2019). Personality and fatal diseases: Revisiting a scientific scandal. *Journal of Health Psychology,* 24(4), 421–439; Pelosi, AJ (1998) The responsibility of academic institutions and professional organisations after accusations of scientific misconduct. The COPE Report, BMJ Publishing, London.

47 For example, Eysenck featured prominently in commemorations of 100 years of British psychology by the Science Museum in London in 2001. Bunn, G.C., Lovie, A.D., and Richards, G.D. Eds. (2001) *Psychology in Britain: Historical Essays and Personal Reflections*. Leicester: BPS Books in association with the Science Museum.

48 Cathleen O'Grady, Misconduct allegations push psychology hero off his pedestal, *Science*, July 15, 2020, www.sciencemag.org/news/2020/07/misconduct-allegations-push-psychology-hero-his-pedestal

49 Marks, D. F. (2019). The Hans Eysenck affair: Time to correct the scientific record, Editorial. *Journal of Health Psychology*, 24(4), 409–420. https://doi.org/10.1177/1359105318820931

50 Pelosi, A. J. (2019). Personality and fatal diseases: Revisiting a scientific scandal. *Journal of Health Psychology,* 24(4), 421–439, citing Nabi, H, Kivimaki, M, Zins, M, et al. (2008) Does personality

Debate and disagreement within the relevant research community continues. On the one hand, long-standing concern and critique, on the other hand, commemorative academic centenary celebrations praising Eysenck's work. Critics of Eysenck claim that the praise his work continues to receive is 'damaging to Psychology, science and medicine, and can be harmful to patients and the general public who may be offered false hope and ineffective therapies as a consequence.'[51] The 'Eysenck affair' has also been identified as highlighting wider difficulties around the integrity of science and its governance.[52] In an open letter to the president and principal of King's College London, Eysenck's employer between the 1950s and the 1980s, Marks noted that even though Professor Eysenck died in 1997, 'the issue of alleged falsified science remains current to the present day.' The letter included the following:

> It is recorded on the King's College London website that 'King's has adopted the UKRIO Code of Practice for Research'. In line with the COPE guidelines I am referring this matter to you as the President of the relevant academic institution. I bring to your attention the research programme led by the late Professor Hans J Eysenck at the Institute of Psychiatry over a 40-year period. The evidence reviewed in the attached documentation suggests the late Professor's research involved systematic breaches of conduct
>
> . . .
>
> The case to be answered is fully documented in Dr. Anthony Pelosi's peer-reviewed article: 'Personality and fatal diseases: revisiting a scientific scandal'. As the Editor responsible for the peer review and publication of Dr. Pelosi's article, I have every confidence that Dr. Pelosi's evidence and conclusions are reliable and true. In light of the policies and statutes of King's College London concerning research integrity I bring this case to your attention for investigation. A full and thorough investigation would be good for science, for the research integrity of your esteemed institution and for the welfare of patients and the general public.[53]

---

predict mortality? Results from the GAZEL French prospective cohort study. *International Journal of Epidemiology* 37: 386–396; Nagano, J, Ichinose, Y, Asoh, H, et al. (2006) A prospective Japanese study of the association between personality and the progression of lung cancer. *Internal Medicine* 45: 1453.

51 Marks, D. F. (2019). The Hans Eysenck affair: Time to correct the scientific record, Editorial. *Journal of Health Psychology*, 24(4), 409–420. https://doi.org/10.1177/1359105318820931

52 Marks, D. F. (2019). The Hans Eysenck affair: Time to correct the scientific record, Editorial. *Journal of Health Psychology*, 24(4), 409–420. https://doi.org/10.1177/1359105318820931

53 Marks, D. F. (2019). The Hans Eysenck affair: Time to correct the scientific record, Editorial. *Journal of Health Psychology*, 24(4), 409–420. https://doi.org/10.1177/1359105318820931

An open letter along very similar lines was sent to the chief executive of the British Psychological Society and included:

> I hope that the Society will add its voice to those who are requesting that the relevant publishers and journals should correct or retract Eysenck's publications wherever they can be shown to contain questionable data-sets or claims that are known to be false.[54]

An appendix listing 61 allegedly suspect publications was included with each letter.

In May 2019 an inquiry by a committee set up by the Institute of Psychiatry, Psychology & Neuroscience at King's College London concluded that 26 of Eysenck's co-authored papers, published between 1988 and 2000, were 'unsafe.'[55] The committee expressed concerns around two issues:

> First, the validity of the datasets, in terms of recruitment of participants, administration of measures, reliability of outcome ascertainment, biases in data collection, absence of relevant covariates, and selection of cases analysed in each article. Second, the implausibility of the results presented, many of which show effect sizes virtually unknown in medical science. For example, the relative risk of dying of cancer for individuals with 'cancer-prone' personality compared with healthy personality was over 100, while the risk of cancer mortality was reduced 80% by bibliotherapy. These findings are incompatible with modern clinical science and the understanding of disease processes.[56]

Following the King's College findings other retractions and expressions of concern were made relating to publications not listed by King's College. However, other papers which raised questions remain un-retracted, and it has been noted that expressions of concern can send an ambiguous message if they are used in lieu of retraction.[57]

54 Marks, D. F. (2019). The Hans Eysenck affair: Time to correct the scientific record, Editorial. *Journal of Health Psychology*, 24(4), 409–420. https://doi.org/10.1177/1359105318820931

55 King's College London (2019) King's College London enquiry into publications authored by Professor Hans Eysenck with Professor Ronald Grossarth-Maticek, www.kcl.ac.uk/news/statements/docs/hans-eysenck-enquiry-final-may-2019.pdf (accessed 6 October 2020). A pre-publication copy of Pelosi's review in *Journal of Health Psychology* and the accompanying editorial had been sent to the Principal of KCL in late 2018. Marks, D. F., & Buchanan, R. (2020). King's College London's enquiry into Hans J Eysenck's "unsafe" publications must be properly completed. *Journal of Health Psychology,* 25(1), 3–6. doi: 10.1177/1359105319887791. Some surprise has been expressed that KCL chose not to investigate Eysenck's sole authored papers.

56 Marks, D. F., & Buchanan, R. (2020). King's College London's enquiry into Hans J Eysenck's "unsafe" publications must be properly completed. *Journal of Health Psychology,* 25(1), 3–6. doi: 10.1177/1359105319887791

57 Cathleen O'Grady, Misconduct allegations push psychology hero off his pedestal, *Science,* July 15, 2020 www.sciencemag.org/news/2020/07/misconduct-allegations-push-psychology-hero-his-pedestal

It has been suggested that the King's College inquiry was insufficient in that it ignored many publications that emerged from the same disputed research programme.[58] Calls continue for further investigation into Eysenck's publications, potentially erroneous associations with prestigious organisations and for the BSP to reconsider the complaint made by Pelosi.[59]

Eysenck's work remains influential within student texts and has continued to be cited widely and uncritically, in the words of one commentator: 'poison[ing] the well' of science.[60]

The Eysenck case provides an example of a researcher who may have become 'too famous' to be seriously challenged, with high status and a prominent reputation within a field potentially providing an insulating effect. In the case of Eysenck, a delay exceeding two decades, during which time the scientific record remained uncorrected and new research may be built upon unstable foundations.

Marc Hauser

Marc Hauser was a psychologist at Harvard University undertaking research into the evolution of language and cognition. Hauser was found to have made false statements about experimental methods and fabricated and falsified data in six federally funded studies.[61] Hauser resigned his position at Harvard University in 2011 and acknowledged that he had made mistakes but denied deliberate misconduct, explaining that he had allowed himself to succumb to an excessive

58 Marks, D. F., & Buchanan, R. (2020). King's College London's enquiry into Hans J Eysenck's "unsafe" publications must be properly completed. *Journal of Health Psychology,* 25(1), 3–6. doi: 10.1177/1359105319887791; Hawkes, N. (2019). Inquiry into eminent psychologist failed to list many unsafe papers, biographer claims. *British Medical Journal,* l6329. doi: 10.1136/bmj.l6329.

59 For example, Pelosi notes that Eysenck and Grossarth-Maticek were not justified in referring to their psychotherapy trials as the 'Maudsley Intervention Project,' as the trials were not considered by the Maudsley Hospital and Institute of Psychiatry ethics committee, nor formed part of that organisation's research strategy. Pelosi, A. J. (2019). Personality and fatal diseases: Revisiting a scientific scandal. *Journal of Health Psychology,* 24(4), 421–439, citing Checkley, S (1993) Personality and fatal diseases. *British Medical Journal* 307: 329; Marks, D. F., & Buchanan, R. (2020). King's College London's enquiry into Hans J Eysenck's "unsafe" publications must be properly completed. *Journal of Health Psychology,* 25, 3–6; Colman A, Marks D, McVittie C and Smith R (2019) A role in auditing Hans Eysenck? *The Psychologist,* September, p. 2; Smith R (2019) Hans Eysenck: Controversialist or worse? *British Medical Journal.* 365. doi: https://doi.org/10.1136/bmj.l1897.

60 Smith, R. (2006). Research misconduct: The poisoning of the well. *Journal of the Royal Society of Medicine,* 99, 232–237, cited by Pelosi, A. J. (2019). Personality and fatal diseases: Revisiting a scientific scandal. *Journal of Health Psychology,* 24(4), 421–439, citing Kissane, DW, Al-Asady, Y (2015) Cancer, the mind and the person: What we know about the causes of cancer. BJPsych Advances 21: 281–288.

61 U.S. Department of Health and Human Services Office of Research Integrity, New Research Misconduct Finding: Marc Hauser, https://ori.hhs.gov/new-research-misconduct-finding-marc-hauser (accessed 7 May 2019); Siri Carpenter. (2012). Harvard Psychology Researcher Committed Fraud, U.S. Investigation Concludes, *Science,* September 6 2012. www.sciencemag.org/news/2012/09/harvard-psychology-researcher-committed-fraud-us-investigation-concludes

workload with the result that he lost sight of important details.[62] As head of the laboratory, he accepted responsibility for errors which arose within the lab, whether or not he was directly involved.[63]

At its height Hauser's work in the field of the biological roots of cognition and morality resulted in an output which averaged one peer-reviewed article per month. In 2007 he was subject to an internal investigation at Harvard when concerns were raised by members of his laboratory.[64] This investigation, which considered work dating back to 2002, concluded that Hauser was solely responsible for eight instances of scientific misconduct.[65] These included the false description of experimental methodology, miscoding of some data and the failure of the experiment to support the initial hypothesis.[66] Hauser was also subject to investigation by the Office of Research Integrity (ORI).[67]

Woo Suk Hwang

A significant case of data fabrication arose from the publication in 2004 by Seoul National University scientist Woo Suk Hwang and his research team of two papers in *Science* which claimed to have succeeded in cloning human stem cells.[68] The particular breakthrough significance of this in medical terms

62 Siri Carpenter. (2012). Harvard Psychology Researcher Committed Fraud, U.S. Investigation Concludes, *Science*, September 6, 2012. www.sciencemag.org/news/2012/09/harvard-psychology-researcher-committed-fraud-us-investigation-concludes

63 Marc Hauser "Engaged in Research Misconduct". *Harvard Magazine*. https://harvardmagazine.com/2012/09/hauser-research-misconduct-reported (accessed 7 May 2019)

64 Siri Carpenter. (2012). Harvard Psychology Researcher Committed Fraud, U.S. Investigation Concludes, *Science*, September 6, 2012. www.sciencemag.org/news/2012/09/harvard-psychology-researcher-committed-fraud-us-investigation-concludes

65 FAS Dean Smith Confirms Scientific Misconduct by Marc Hauser. *Harvard Magazine*. https://harvardmagazine.com/2010/08/harvard-dean-details-hauser-scientific-misconduct (accessed 8 May 2019)

66 Marc Hauser "Engaged in Research Misconduct". *Harvard Magazine*. https://harvardmagazine.com/2012/09/hauser-research-misconduct-reported (accessed 7 May 2019)

67 Couzin-Frankel, J. (2014), Harvard misconduct allegation of psychologist released. *Science*, 30 May 2014, https://www.science.org/content/article/harvard-misconduct-investigation-psychologist-released

68 Hwang WS, Ryu YJ, Park JH, Park ES, Lee EG, Koo JM, Jeon HY, Lee BC, Kang SK, Kim SJ, Ahn C, Hwang JH, Park KY, Cibelli JB, Moon SY. Evidence of a pluripotent human embryonic stem cell line derived from a cloned blastocyst. Science. 2004 Mar 12;303(5664):1669–74. doi: 10.1126/science.1094515. Epub 2004 Feb 12. Retraction in: Kennedy D. Science. 2006 Jan 20;311(5759):335. Erratum in: Science. 2005 Dec 16;310(5755):1769. PMID: 14963337; Hwang WS, Roh SI, Lee BC, Kang SK, Kwon DK, Kim S, Kim SJ, Park SW, Kwon HS, Lee CK, Lee JB, Kim JM, Ahn C, Paek SH, Chang SS, Koo JJ, Yoon HS, Hwang JH, Hwang YY, Park YS, Oh SK, Kim HS, Park JH, Moon SY, Schatten G. Patient-specific embryonic stem cells derived from human SCNT blastocysts. Science. 2005 Jun 17;308(5729):1777–83. doi: 10.1126/science.1112286. Epub 2005 May 19. Retraction in: Kennedy D. Science. 2006 Jan 20;311(5759):335. Erratum in: Science. 2005 Dec 16;310(5755):1769. PMID: 15905366.

was that cell lines produced in this manner would be compatible immunologically, reducing the risk of tissue rejection and could offer a major impact in terms of the fight against degenerative disorders such as diabetes and Parkinson's disease.[69]

Concerns about these papers emerged in late 2005. These concerns included the manner in which the egg donors had been recruited and other transparency issues.[70] Seoul National University began to investigate, and in December 2005 the university announced that Hwang's data were fabricated. The university's investigatory committee had asked three laboratories to test whether the cells reported in Hwang's paper matched the cells from the donors. The laboratories could not find a match. Hwang admitted to falsifying data, was dismissed from Seoul University and was subject to other action, including being banned from securing research funding in South Korea.[71] Both papers were retracted by *Science*, but prior to this, other researchers had devoted time and grant money attempting to reproduce Hwang's research.[72]

69 Cyranoski, D. (2009). Woo Suk Hwang convicted, but not of fraud. *Nature* 461, 1181. https://doi.org/10.1038/4611181a; Shamoo, A.S., & Resnik, D.B. (2009). Responsible conduct of research (2nd ed.). New York: Oxford University Press; Zwart, H. (2008). Challenges of Macro-ethics: Bioethics and the Transformation of Knowledge Production. Bioethical Inquiry 5, 283–293. https://doi.org/10.1007/s11673-008-9110-9; Saunders, R., and J. Savulescu. (2008). Research Ethics and Lessons from Hwanggate: What Can We Learn from the Korean Cloning Fraud? *Journal of Medical Ethics*, 34(3). 214–221. *JSTOR*, www.jstor.org/stable/27720044.

70 Zwart, H. (2008). Challenges of Macro-ethics: Bioethics and the Transformation of Knowledge Production. Bioethical Inquiry 5, 283–293. https://doi.org/10.1007/s11673-008-9110-9; Cyranoski, D. (2004). Korea's stem-cell stars dogged by suspicion of ethical breach. *Nature* 429, 3. https://doi.org/10.1038/429003a; van der Heyden, M A G et al. (2009). Fraud and misconduct in science: the stem cell seduction: Implications for the peer-review process. *Netherlands heart journal: monthly journal of the Netherlands Society of Cardiology and the Netherlands Heart Foundation* vol. 17,1: 25–9. doi: 10.1007/BF03086211

71 Resnik, D. B. (2014). Data fabrication and falsification and empiricist philosophy of science. *Sci Eng Ethics*, 20, 423–431. doi: 10.1007/s11948-013-9466-z; Resnik, David B et al. (2006). Fraudulent human embryonic stem cell research in South Korea: lessons learned. *Accountability in research*. 13(1): 101–9. doi: 10.1080/08989620600634193; van der Heyden, M A G et al. (2009). Fraud and misconduct in science: the stem cell seduction: Implications for the peer-review process. *Netherlands heart journal: monthly journal of the Netherlands Society of Cardiology and the Netherlands Heart Foundation* 17(1): 25–9. doi: 10.1007/BF03086211; Saunders, R., and J. Savulescu. (2008). Research Ethics and Lessons from Hwanggate: What Can We Learn from the Korean Cloning Fraud? *Journal of Medical Ethics*, 34(3). 214–221. *JSTOR*, www.jstor.org/stable/27720044; Cyranoski, D. (2009). Woo Suk Hwang convicted, but not of fraud. *Nature* 461, 1181. https://doi.org/10.1038/4611181a.

72 Kennedy D. Editorial retraction. Science. 2006 Jan 20;311(5759):335. doi: 10.1126/science.1124926. Epub 2006 Jan 12. PMID: 16410485; Cyranoski, D. (2009). Woo Suk Hwang convicted, but not of fraud. *Nature* 461, 1181. https://doi.org/10.1038/4611181a; van der Heyden, M A G et al. (2009). Fraud and misconduct in science: the stem cell seduction: Implications for the peer-review process. *Netherlands heart journal: monthly journal of the Netherlands Society of Cardiology Society of Cardiology and the Netherlands Heart Foundation*. 17(1). 25–9. doi: 10.1007/BF03086211; Resnik, David B et al. (2006). Fraudulent human embryonic stem cell research in South Korea: lessons learned. *Accountability in research*. 13(1). 101–9. doi: 10.1080/08989620600634193

The Hwang case offers some insight into research and ethics cultures within different jurisdictions, including if, and if so how, scientists found to have committed research misconduct should be accepted back within the research community. Hwang has been reported to have been rebuilding his research career.[73]

Dr Abderrahmane Kaidi

Dr Abderrahmane Kaidi, a specialist in cancer biology and DNA damage working in the School of Cellular and Molecular Medicine, resigned from the University of Bristol in 2018 during an investigation into allegations that he had fabricated results, misled his laboratory head and misled his co-author at the University of Cambridge in terms of experiments purported to have been undertaken.[74] Dr Kaidi had previously been a postdoctoral fellow at the University of Cambridge. Both the University of Bristol and the University of Cambridge found malfeasance. Dr Kaidi is reported to have accepted sole responsibility for misrepresentation and fabrication of data in two published papers which were subsequently retracted, one from *Nature*, published in 2013, and the other from *Science*, published in 2010.[75] The *Science* retraction notice stated that 'the University of Cambridge has concluded that there was falsification of research data used in the Report,' while the *Nature* retraction notice stated that the authors were retracting the paper due to 'issues with figure presentation and underlying data.'[76] Concerns were expressed from within the scientific community that both papers had been widely cited and as such had distorted the research record in an important area of cancer research.[77]

The Kaidi case reinforces concerns that pressure to attract research funding may encourage some researchers in the direction of misconduct.

73 Leo Kim (2008) Explaining the Hwang Scandal: National Scientific Culture and its Global Relevance, Science as Culture, 17:4, 397–415, doi: 10.1080/09505430802515023; Cyranoski, D. (2009). Woo Suk Hwang convicted, but not of fraud. *Nature* 461, 1181. https://doi.org/10.1038/4611181a; Tong-hyung, K. (2009) Hwang Claims to Have Cloned Pig Stem Cells, *The Korean Times*, 15 May 2009, http://www.koreatimes.co.kr/www/news/tech/2009/05/129_44979.html

74 Authors have papers in Nature and Science retracted on the same day https://retractionwatch.com/2019/04/11/authors-have-papers-in-nature-and-science-retracted-on-the-same-day/ (accessed 10 August 2018); Nick Mayo. (2019). Articles pulled after data fabrication in Cambridge DNA lab, *Times Higher Education*, April 12. www.timeshighereducation.com/news/articles-pulled-after-data-fabrication-cambridge-dna-lab

75 Holly Else. (2019). Top journals retract DNA-repair studies after misconduct probe, *Nature*, 15 April, www.nature.com/articles/d41586-019-00406-4

76 Abderrahmane Kaidi & Stephen P. Jackson, Retraction Note: KAT5 tyrosine phosphorylation couples chromatin sensing to ATM signalling, *Nature*, volume 568, 11 April 2019, 576, www.nature.com/articles/s41586-019-1142-2; Holly Else. (2019). Top journals retract DNA-repair studies after misconduct probe, *Nature*, 15 April. www.nature.com/articles/d41586-019-00406-4

77 Holly Else. (2019). Top journals retract DNA-repair studies after misconduct probe, *Nature*, 15 April. www.nature.com/articles/d41586-019-00406-4

In terms of investigatory transparency, it was noted in a *Nature* report following the retraction that 'the University of Cambridge declined to comment on how many of Kaidi's papers it had examined as part of its probe.' It therefore remained unclear whether concerns might extend beyond the two retracted papers.[78]

Professor David Latchman

This case study provides an example of issues which can arise if a senior scientist in a supervisory role has insufficient time or engagement with the projects being supervised to enable them to detect misconduct. If successful members of a scientific community over-extend themselves in terms of their ability to juggle numerous commitments, then the consequences, both to the scientific record and researcher reputation, can be significant.

Allegations were made by an anonymous whistle-blower and referred to postings on PubPeer – a website which provides a space for scientists to anonymously question research studies.[79] For over a decade Professor David Latchman ran a laboratory at University College London (UCL), supervising around 20 scientists. He continued this role on a fractional basis, 0.1 FTE appointment, after becoming Master of Birkbeck, University of London. During his time overseeing the laboratory, a number of problematic papers were published. The issues included cloning of images, presenting an old image as drawing from new data and flipping or copying images to make them look new. Professor Latchman was not responsible for fabricating data, nor did he have knowledge of the behaviour, but he was accused of being insufficiently attentive to the management of the laboratory and in respect of the group's publications and thus permitting the emergence and continuation over an extended time period of a lab culture which fell outside accepted standards of research integrity. His involvement as senior author or co-author of publications where misconduct was identified was also found to constitute recklessness.[80] This included being named as last author and therefore deemed to have

78 Holly Else. (2019). Top journals retract DNA-repair studies after misconduct probe, *Nature*, 15 April. www.nature.com/articles/d41586-019-00406-4

79 https://pubpeer.com/

80 The term 'reckless' was not used by the panel in the specific manner adopted by the English courts when discussing, for example, recklessness in criminal law, but the panel drew from the Oxford English Dictionary definition – inter alia, as 'Heedless of or indifferent to the consequences of one's actions'; 'Careless in executing a task, duty, etc.; inattentive, lacking in diligence.' UCL Institute of Child Health: Report of the Investigation Panel www.documentcloud.org/documents/6178710-UCL-FOIA-Latchman-Lab-Investigations.html (accessed 6 July 2019). For further discussion see, for example, Sample, I. (2019). Research misconduct claim upheld against former head of UCL lab. *The Guardian*, July 1, 2019, www.theguardian.com/science/2019/jul/01/research-misconduct-claim-upheld-against-former-head-of-ucl-lab; Peter Aldhous, Documents Reveal Widespread Data

ultimate responsibility for the data arising therefrom.[81] The screening panel noted that they could not rule out that the extent of misconduct might be greater than those cases identified, given that much of the data in other papers was not presented in primary form and, therefore, its validity could not be assessed. The work in many of those papers was considered to be 'very sloppy,' and the conclusions reached in the papers were not always persuasively supported by the data presented.[82]

The findings of a disciplinary hearing included the observations that fraud could be difficult to detect by supervising scientists and had been missed by journal referees. However, UCL had permitted a very senior staff member to run a very large research group on a small fractional contract while having the burden of considerable responsibilities at another institution. Latchman also served on the National DNA Database Ethics Group and a number of other boards and committees, further dividing his time.[83] Institutional consideration needed to be given to the time commitment required from laboratory leaders and to the potential compromise to leadership autonomy if laboratory leaders expect to be named as authors or accept offers of authorship on papers.[84] Professor Latchman, along with other authors and editors, was directed to correct the research record by means of retractions or clarifications. No further penalty was imposed upon Professor Latchman.[85]

In response to these findings, a spokesperson for Professor Latchman argued that to detect fraud of the nature alleged would require an unreasonable and disproportionate degree of scrutiny to be applied to all research.[86] Professor

Fraud In A Leading UK Scientist's Lab www.buzzfeednews.com/article/peteraldhous/david-latchman-scientific-misconduct (accessed 10 July 2019).

81 UCL Institute of Child Health: Report of the Investigation Panel, www.documentcloud.org/documents/6178710-UCL-FOIA-Latchman-Lab-Investigations.html (accessed 6 July 2019).

82 UCL Institute of Child Health: Report of the Investigation Panel, www.documentcloud.org/documents/6178710-UCL-FOIA-Latchman-Lab-Investigations.html (accessed 6 July 2019).

83 Owens B. (2015). UCL geneticist faces questions over image duplication. *Lancet*. Feb 14; 385(9968):593. doi: 10.1016/s0140-6736(15)60219-7. PMID: 25713854.

84 UCL Institute of Child Health: Report of the Investigation Panel, www.documentcloud.org/documents/6178710-UCL-FOIA-Latchman-Lab-Investigations.html (accessed 6 July 2019).

85 UCL Institute of Child Health: Report of the Investigation Panel, www.documentcloud.org/documents/6178710-UCL-FOIA-Latchman-Lab-Investigations.html (accessed 6 July 2019). Some secondary commentary was critical of the speed at which this was occurring. See, for example, Peter Aldhous, Documents Reveal Widespread Data Fraud In A Leading UK Scientist's Lab www.buzzfeednews.com/article/peteraldhous/david-latchman-scientific-misconduct (accessed 10 July 2019)

86 Sample, I. (2019). Research misconduct claim upheld against former head of UCL lab. *The Guardian*, July 1, 2019, www.theguardian.com/science/2019/jul/01/research-misconduct-claim-upheld-against-former-head-of-ucl-lab; Peter Aldhous, Documents Reveal Widespread Data Fraud In A Leading UK Scientist's Lab www.buzzfeednews.com/article/peteraldhous/david-latchman-scientific-misconduct (accessed 10 July 2019)

Latchman's focus was, instead, upon the ethical education of researchers early in their careers and appropriate penalties to deter misconduct.[87]

An additional feature of the Latchman case is the reflection it casts on institutional transparency. The *Guardian* newspaper reported that UCL initially refused to release the reports from the two misconduct investigations, one in 2014 and the other in 2015.[88] The *Guardian* had requested the documents under the Freedom of Information Act 2000 and subsequently escalated the matter to the United Kingdom Information Commissioner's Office.[89] UCL has given assurances that in future it will promote greater transparency and publish 'more detailed appropriate summaries of research misconduct investigations,' stating:[90]

> We are aware of calls from the research community for total transparency and for the publication of research misconduct reports in full. UCL is supportive of this approach and will be working closely with Government, regulators and key bodies such as UK Research and Innovation, UK Research Integrity Office and the League of European Research Universities to ensure that it is doing all that it can to meet the demands of transparency in this area of significant public interest.[91]

Viktor Ninov

Viktor Ninov had been described as the 'rising star of heavy element research' and 'the most successful element makers of all time' at the University of California, Berkeley, where he worked. When Ninov was recruited by Berkeley he brought with him a computer program, Goosy, that promised to provide an edge with data analysis.[92] Ninov produced data showing that krypton and lead

87 UCL Institute of Child Health: Report of the Investigation Panel, www.documentcloud.org/documents/6178710-UCL-FOIA-Latchman-Lab-Investigations.html (accessed 6 July 2019); Sample, I. (2019). Research misconduct claim upheld against former head of UCL lab. *The Guardian*, July 1, 2019, www.theguardian.com/science/2019/jul/01/research-misconduct-claim-upheld-against-former-head-of-ucl-lab; Peter Aldhous, Documents Reveal Widespread Data Fraud In A Leading UK Scientist's Lab www.buzzfeednews.com/article/peteraldhous/david-latchman-scientific-misconduct (accessed 10 July 2019)

88 Sample, I. (2019). Research misconduct claim upheld against former head of UCL lab. *The Guardian*, Monday, July 1, 2019, www.theguardian.com/science/2019/jul/01/research-misconduct-claim-upheld-against-former-head-of-ucl-lab

89 https://ico.org.uk/

90 UCL Institute of Child Health: Report of the Investigation Panel, www.documentcloud.org/documents/6178710-UCL-FOIA-Latchman-Lab-Investigations.html (accessed 6 July 2019).

91 UCL Institute of Child Health: Report of the Investigation Panel, www.documentcloud.org/documents/6178710-UCL-FOIA-Latchman-Lab-Investigations.html (accessed 6 July 2019).

92 Kit Chapman, 'The element that never was', *Chemistry World*, 10 June 2019 www.chemistryworld.com/features/victor-ninov-and-the-element-that-never-was/3010596.article; Park, Robert. (2008). Fraud in Science. *Social Research: An International Quarterly*. 75. 1135–1150; Schwarzschild,

nuclei had fused together to form a new element, element 118, before radioactively decaying into elements 116 and 114 in sequence. On 27 May 1999 the Berkeley team announced the discovery in *Physical Review Letters*. All research team participants were included as co-authors.[93]

However, attempts to replicate the experiment both at Berkley and elsewhere in the world were unsuccessful. Fellow scientists also described becoming confused by Ninov's behaviour, for example, at conferences, some found him unusually evasive when he was asked about his new elements.[94]

Concerns resulted in an internal investigation chaired by another nuclear physicist at Berkley, I-Yang Lee. The conclusion reached was that 'so far, the most likely reason for the difference between the two experiments is the magnet settings.'[95]

Investigation of the Goosy software gave rise to suggestions that, depending on who used it, different answers emerged. Close analysis of the different pieces of information associated with the Goosy files revealed data and temporal anomalies. Investigations revealed that log data produced by Goosy typically had between 63 and 68 lines per page, whereas the page purporting to record

---

Bertram. (2002). Lawrence Berkeley Lab Concludes that Evidence of Element 118 Was a Fabrication, *Physics Today*. 55, 9, 15. https://doi.org/10.1063/1.1522199; Dalton, R. (2002). California lab fires physicist over retracted finding. *Nature* 418, 261. https://doi.org/10.1038/418261b; Charles Seife. (2002). Heavy-Element Fizzle Laid to Falsified Data. *Science*. 19 July. 297(5580). 313–315 doi: 10.1126/science.297.5580.313

93 Kit Chapman, 'The element that never was', *Chemistry World*, 10 June 2019 www.chemistryworld.com/features/victor-ninov-and-the-element-that-never-was/3010596.article; Park, Robert. (2008). Fraud in Science. *Social Research: An International Quarterly*. 75. 1135–1150; Schwarzschild, Bertram. (2002). Lawrence Berkeley Lab Concludes that Evidence of Element 118 Was a Fabrication, *Physics Today*. 55, 9, 15. https://doi.org/10.1063/1.1522199; Dalton, R. (2002). California lab fires physicist over retracted finding. *Nature* 418, 261. https://doi.org/10.1038/418261b; Charles Seife. (2002). Heavy-Element Fizzle Laid to Falsified Data. *Science*. 19 July. 297(5580). 313–315 doi: 10.1126/science.297.5580.313

94 Kit Chapman, 'The element that never was', *Chemistry World*, 10 June 2019 www.chemistryworld.com/features/victor-ninov-and-the-element-that-never-was/3010596.article; Park, Robert. (2008). Fraud in Science. *Social Research: An International Quarterly*. 75. 1135–1150; Schwarzschild, Bertram, Lawrence Berkeley Lab Concludes that Evidence of Element 118 Was a Fabrication, Physics Today 55, 9, 15 (2002); https://doi.org/10.1063/1.1522199; Dalton, R. California lab fires physicist over retracted finding. *Nature* 418, 261 (2002). https://doi.org/10.1038/418261b; Charles Seife. (2002). Heavy-Element Fizzle Laid to Falsified Data Science 19 Jul 2002: Vol. 297, Issue 5580, pp. 313–315 doi: 10.1126/science.297.5580.313

95 Kit Chapman, 'The element that never was', *Chemistry World*, 10 June 2019 www.chemistryworld.com/features/victor-ninov-and-the-element-that-never-was/3010596.article; Park, Robert. (2008). Fraud in Science. *Social Research: An International Quarterly*. 75. 1135–1150; Schwarzschild, Bertram. (2002). Lawrence Berkeley Lab Concludes that Evidence of Element 118 Was a Fabrication, *Physics Today*. 55, 9, 15. https://doi.org/10.1063/1.1522199; Dalton, R. (2002). California lab fires physicist over retracted finding. *Nature* 418, 261 (2002). https://doi.org/10.1038/418261b; Charles Seife. (2002). Heavy-Element Fizzle Laid to Falsified Data. *Science*. 19 July. 297(5580). 313–315 doi: 10.1126/science.297.5580.313

the discovery had 76 lines, leading to suspicions that new readings been pasted in with a text editor. Further scrutiny indicated that a 200-MB file had been processed in five seconds – notably quicker than the computer's capability – suggesting that the program was not actually analysing data during this run. Analysis of the older experimental data was more problematic, as Ninov had worked alone and recorded his results by hand. These records were described as 'so meagre that they fall outside the normally accepted standards for scientific research.'[96] Checking of the original tapes from 1999 failed to reveal the chains Ninov had reported.[97]

In October 2001 independent investigators reported that original 1999 Goosy files, available due to automatic backing up, showed modifications and additions. The conclusion was that 'at least one of the 118 element decay chains published in 1999 and the single 2001 candidate decay chain were fabricated.'[98] Ninov denied any misbehaviour, but a misconduct hearing concluded that he was the only research participant with sufficient involvement in all matters under investigation to be responsible. If, as he claimed, someone else could have accessed his systems and been responsible for the fabrication, the investigation concluded that 'Ninov would almost surely have detected it.'[99] In

96 Kit Chapman, 'The element that never was', *Chemistry World*, 10 June 2019 www.chemistryworld.com/features/victor-ninov-and-the-element-that-never-was/3010596.article; Park, Robert. (2008). Fraud in Science. *Social Research: An International Quarterly*. 75. 1135–1150; Schwarzschild, Bertram. (2002). Lawrence Berkeley Lab Concludes that Evidence of Element 118 Was a Fabrication, *Physics Today*. 55, 9, 15. https://doi.org/10.1063/1.1522199; Dalton, R. (2002). California lab fires physicist over retracted finding. *Nature* 418, 261. https://doi.org/10.1038/418261b; Charles Seife. (2002). Heavy-Element Fizzle Laid to Falsified Data. *Science*. 19 July. 297(5580). 313–315 doi: 10.1126/science.297.5580.313

97 Kit Chapman, 'The element that never was', *Chemistry World*, 10 June 2019 www.chemistryworld.com/features/victor-ninov-and-the-element-that-never-was/3010596.article; Park, Robert. (2008). Fraud in Science. *Social Research: An International Quarterly*. 75. 1135–1150; Schwarzschild, Bertram. (2002). Lawrence Berkeley Lab Concludes that Evidence of Element 118 Was a Fabrication, *Physics Today*. 55, 9, 15. https://doi.org/10.1063/1.1522199; Dalton, R. (2002). California lab fires physicist over retracted finding. *Nature* 418, 261. https://doi.org/10.1038/418261b; Charles Seife. (2002). Heavy-Element Fizzle Laid to Falsified Data. *Science*. 19 July. 297(5580). 313–315 doi: 10.1126/science.297.5580.313

98 Kit Chapman, 'The element that never was', *Chemistry World*, 10 June 2019 www.chemistryworld.com/features/victor-ninov-and-the-element-that-never-was/3010596.article; Park, Robert. (2008). Fraud in Science. *Social Research: An International Quarterly*. 75. 1135–1150; Schwarzschild, Bertram. (2002). Lawrence Berkeley Lab Concludes that Evidence of Element 118 Was a Fabrication, *Physics Today*. 55, 9, 15. https://doi.org/10.1063/1.1522199; Dalton, R. (2002). California lab fires physicist over retracted finding. *Nature* 418, 261. https://doi.org/10.1038/418261b; Charles Seife. (2002). Heavy-Element Fizzle Laid to Falsified Data. *Science*. 19 July. 297(5580). 313–315 doi: 10.1126/science.297.5580.313

99 Kit Chapman, 'The element that never was', *Chemistry World*, 10 June 2019 www.chemistry world.com/features/victor-ninov-and-the-element-that-never-was/3010596.article; Park, Robert. (2008). Fraud in Science. *Social Research: An International Quarterly*. 75. 1135–1150; Schwarzschild, Bertram. (2002). Lawrence Berkeley Lab Concludes that Evidence of Element 118 Was a Fabrication,

2002 Ninov was dismissed from the Lawrence Berkeley National Laboratory, having been found guilty of misconduct.[100]

While Ninov alone was found to have committed misconduct, other team members at Berkeley were criticised for weaknesses in their oversight and checking processes and over-reliance on the integrity of a leading scientist.[101]

The Ninov case and Schön case (discussed later in this appendix) emerged in quick succession and were reported to have caused a sufficient stir within the physics community that ethics and professional conduct guidelines for physicists were expanded.[102]

Eric T. Poehlman

University of Vermont researcher Eric Poehlman was sentenced to a period of imprisonment for defrauding the United States federal government of grant funding as a result of committing scientific misconduct by 'engaging in the misleading and deceptive practices,' notably fabricating or falsifying data on grant applications as well as in publications. The work ranged across areas of scientific research, including metabolism and aging, energy expenditures during the menopausal transition, energy balance and body fat distribution. Poehlman eventually settled a comprehensive range of criminal, civil and administrative allegations relating to his scientific misconduct over a period spanning a decade

Physics Today. 55, 9, 15. https://doi.org/10.1063/1.1522199; Dalton, R. (2002). California lab fires physicist over retracted finding. *Nature* 418, 261. https://doi.org/10.1038/418261b; Charles Seife. (2002). Heavy-Element Fizzle Laid to Falsified Data. *Science*. 19 July. 297(5580). 313–315 doi: 10.1126/science.297.5580.313

100 Kit Chapman, 'The element that never was', *Chemistry World*, 10 June 2019 www.chemistryworld.com/features/victor-ninov-and-the-element-that-never-was/3010596.article; Park, Robert. (2008). Fraud in Science. *Social Research: An International Quarterly*. 75. 1135–1150; Schwarzschild, Bertram. (2002). Lawrence Berkeley Lab Concludes that Evidence of Element 118 Was a Fabrication, *Physics Today*. 55, 9, 15. https://doi.org/10.1063/1.1522199; Dalton, R. (2002). California lab fires physicist over retracted finding. *Nature* 418, 261. https://doi.org/10.1038/418261b; Charles Seife. (2002). Heavy-Element Fizzle Laid to Falsified Data. *Science*. 19 July. 297(5580). 313–315 doi: 10.1126/science.297.5580.313

101 Kit Chapman, 'The element that never was', *Chemistry World*, 10 June 2019 www.chemistryworld.com/features/victor-ninov-and-the-element-that-never-was/3010596.article; Park, Robert. (2008). Fraud in Science. *Social Research: An International Quarterly*. 75. 1135–1150; Schwarzschild, Bertram. (2002). Lawrence Berkeley Lab Concludes that Evidence of Element 118 Was a Fabrication, *Physics Today*. 55, 9, 15. https://doi.org/10.1063/1.1522199; Dalton, R. (2002). California lab fires physicist over retracted finding. *Nature* 418, 261 (2002). https://doi.org/10.1038/418261b; Charles Seife. (2002). Heavy-Element Fizzle Laid to Falsified Data. *Science*. 19 July. 297(5580). 313–315 doi: 10.1126/science.297.5580.313

102 APS News, January 2003, Volume 12, No.1, www.aps.org/publications/apsnews/200301/guidelines.cfm; APS News, May 2003, Volume 12, No. 5, https://aps.org/publications/apsnews/200305/upload/may03.pdf (accessed 1 December 2020)

from the early 1990s to the early 2000s and agreed to a number of retractions or corrections.[103]

In terms of the coming to light of concerns, a junior member of Poehlman's laboratory became concerned that Poehlman had altered data relating to a study on aging. A US Office of Research Integrity investigation found that Poehlman had published articles from the 1990s, the findings of which were based upon fabricated or falsified data and had used falsified data in the making of grant applications. As well as personally disseminating fraudulent findings and giving misleading evidence to a University of Vermont Investigation Committee, Poehlman reportedly drew other researchers into the orbit of his misconduct by providing them with falsified data in the knowledge that this would be used to prepare presentations and articles.[104] Poehlman is reported to have explained in a letter to the judge that his motivation was a desire to advance his career and to increase the chances of grant capture by misrepresenting what he described as 'minor' pieces of data.[105]

Yoshihiro Sato

The research fraud committed by Yoshihiro Sato, a bone-health researcher in Japan, was substantial in its scope, and the influence of Sato's publications on medical treatment guidelines were significant. Sato's work was widely cited, featuring meta-analyses, and time and money were wasted by other researchers undertaking follow-up studies.[106]

Sato undertook clinical trials of drugs and supplements to consider whether they might help to prevent bone fractures. Other researchers began to raise concerns from the mid-2000s, when it became increasingly clear that the speed

103 National Institutes of Health, Grantee Misconduct: Dr. Eric T. Poehlman www.nih.gov/news-events/grantee-misconduct-dr-eric-t-poehlman. In some instances the retractions were slow to materialise, Retraction Watch, *12 years after researcher found guilty of misconduct, journal retracts paper,* https://retractionwatch.com/2017/06/21/12-years-researcher-found-guilty-misconduct-journal-retracts-paper/ (accessed 16 January 2022)

104 The Office of Research Integrity. *Case Summary – Eric T. Poehlman*, https://ori.hhs.gov/case-summary-eric-t-poehlman (accessed 16 January 2021). See also, Dahlberg, J. E., & Mahler, C. C. (2006). The Poehlman case: Running away from the truth. *Sci Eng Ethics.*, 12(1) (January),157–173. doi: 10.1007/s11948-006-0016-9. PMID: 16501657; Tilden, S. J. (2010). Incarceration, restitution, and lifetime debarment: Legal consequences of scientific misconduct in the Eric Poehlman case: Commentary on: "Scientific forensics: How the office of research integrity can assist institutional investigations of research misconduct during oversight review". *Science and Engineering Ethics,* 16(4), 737–741.

105 Kintisch E. (2006). Poehlman sentenced to 1year of prison. *Science.* 28 June. www.science.org/content/article/poehlman-sentenced-1-year-prison

106 Kupferschmidt, K. (2018). Researcher at the center of an epic fraud remains an enigma to those who exposed him. *Science*, August 17, 2018, www.sciencemag.org/news/2018/08/researcher-center-epic-fraud-remains-enigma-those-who-exposed-him

with which Sato recruited and assessed participants for his trials gave rise to suspicions.[107] It subsequently became clear that between 1996 and 2013 Sato had plagiarised, fabricated data and manipulated co-authorships in numerous studies. Retractions of more than 60 publications followed.[108]

In a 2005 paper published in *Neurology*, Sato made remarkable claims that a drug, risedronate, reduced the risk of hip fractures in women following a stroke by 86 per cent. In a letter to the journal three researchers from the University of Cambridge expressed surprise that the authors had managed to recruit 374 patients suitable to be research subjects in only four months.[109]

In 2007, a letter in the *Archives of Internal Medicine* raised concerns about the validity of Sato's research.[110] In one highlighted study Sato had enrolled 280 male stroke patients in only two months; in another study, 500 women with Alzheimer's disease were purportedly recruited in a similarly short timeframe, with suspicions being compounded because Sato stated that he had diagnosed all of the Alzheimer's patients himself.[111] Concerns were raised about a further 11 studies in other journals.[112]

Professor Alison Avenell, a clinical nutritionist at the University of Aberdeen, together with three colleagues in New Zealand, Mark Bolland, Andrew Grey and Greg Gamble, discovered that Sato had fabricated data for dozens of clinical trials published in international journals.[113] Avenell's suspicions were aroused in 2006 when she was reviewing papers for an analysis of whether vitamin D reduces the risk of bone fractures. Two papers by Sato gave rise

107 Else, H. (2019). What universities can learn from one of science's biggest frauds. *Nature,* 570, 287–288. doi: 10.1038/d41586-019-01884-2

108 Else, H. (2019). What universities can learn from one of science's biggest frauds. *Nature,* 570, 287–288. doi: 10.1038/d41586-019-01884-2

109 Poole KE, Warburton EA, Reeve J (2005), Risedronate therapy for prevention of hip fracture after stroke in elderly women. *Neurology* 65(9):1513–4; author reply 1513–4 https://n.neurology.org/content/risedronate-therapy-prevention-hip-fracture-after-stroke-elderly-women; Kupferschmidt, K. (2018). Researcher at the center of an epic fraud remains an enigma to those who exposed him. *Science*, August 17, 2018, www.sciencemag.org/news/2018/08/researcher-center-epic-fraud-remains-enigma-those-who-exposed-him

110 Halbekath, Jutta & Schenk, Stefanie & Maxen, Andreas & Meyer, Gabriele & Mühlhauser, Ingrid. (2007). Risedronate for the Prevention of Hip Fractures: Concern About Validity of Trials. *Archives of Internal Medicine*. 167. 513–4; author reply 514. 10.1001/archinte.167.5.513-b.

111 Kupferschmidt, K. (2018). Researcher at the center of an epic fraud remains an enigma to those who exposed him. *Science*, August 17, 2018, www.sciencemag.org/news/2018/08/researcher-center-epic-fraud-remains-enigma-those-who-exposed-him

112 Kupferschmidt, K. (2018). Researcher at the center of an epic fraud remains an enigma to those who exposed him. *Science*, August 17, 2018, www.sciencemag.org/news/2018/08/researcher-center-epic-fraud-remains-enigma-those-who-exposed-him

113 Grey, A., Bolland, M., Gamble, G. et al. (2019). Quality of reports of investigations of research integrity by academic institutions. *Res Integr Peer Rev*, 4, 3 https://doi.org/10.1186/s41073-019-0062-x

to concerns. The papers described different trials – one in stroke victims, the other in Parkinson's disease patients – but the study and control groups in each paper had identical mean body mass indexes. Further scrutiny then revealed other anomalies.[114]

Avenell, Bolland, Grey and Gamble formed a research team in 2008 to undertake a meta-analysis on calcium supplements. They were surprised by the impact Sato's work could have on the outcome. Bolland was described as being 'stunned' by the low dropout rate in Sato's large cohort studies and the large effects of almost any treatment Sato investigated. Bolland is quoted as saying: 'There is nothing that I can think of that produces a 70% to 80% reduction in hip fractures, yet Sato was able to do it consistently in all his trials.'[115]

The researchers chose to write up their findings for submission to the *Journal of the American Medical Association* (JAMA), which they identified as the highest-profile journal Sato had published in and one they considered might be well placed in resource terms to undertake a detailed investigation. The researchers reported that after a two-year wait in which the editor-in-chief had attempted unsuccessfully to contact Sato and his employer, the journal was willing to publish an 'expression of concern' only – a note which would flag Sato's article as suspicious – rather than publishing the full paper from Bolland et al.[116]

In June 2015 *The Journal of Bone and Mineral Research* retracted one of Sato's papers, after which some other journals followed suit. This coincided with Avenell, Bolland, Grey and Gamble making what they anticipated to be one last effort to have their paper published by submitting it to *Neurology*, where Sato had published three papers.[117] The paper was accepted.[118] By this time 10

114 Kupferschmidt, K. (2018). Researcher at the center of an epic fraud remains an enigma to those who exposed him. *Science*, August 17, 2018, www.sciencemag.org/news/2018/08/researcher-center-epic-fraud-remains-enigma-those-who-exposed-him

115 Kupferschmidt, K. (2018). Researcher at the center of an epic fraud remains an enigma to those who exposed him. *Science*, August 17, 2018, www.sciencemag.org/news/2018/08/researcher-center-epic-fraud-remains-enigma-those-who-exposed-him. Statistical analysis of Sato's purported treatment and control groups also failed to reveal the distribution of p-values expected from randomly selected groups, but rather very significant levels of similarity when key variables were considered.

116 Kupferschmidt, K. (2018). Researcher at the center of an epic fraud remains an enigma to those who exposed him. *Science*, August 17, 2018, www.sciencemag.org/news/2018/08/researcher-center-epic-fraud-remains-enigma-those-who-exposed-him. Rejection of the manuscript by two further journals in which Sato had published followed. A further journal, not one in which Sato had published, also rejected the manuscript, indicating that it would be inappropriate to become involved.

117 Kupferschmidt, K. (2018). Researcher at the center of an epic fraud remains an enigma to those who exposed him. *Science*, August 17, 2018, www.sciencemag.org/news/2018/08/researcher-center-epic-fraud-remains-enigma-those-who-exposed-him

118 Bolland, M. J., Avenell, A., Gamble, G. D., & Grey, A. (2016). Systematic review and statistical analysis of the integrity of 33 randomized controlled trials. *Neurology*, 87(23) (December), 2391–2402. doi: 10.1212/WNL.0000000000003387

of the 33 trials the researchers had investigated had been retracted, and further retractions have occurred since. The *Neurology* paper prompted investigations by institutions which had employed Sato. In light of the publication Sato admitted that three of his studies were fraudulent, requested that they be retracted and absolved his co-authors from any involvement, although the delays prior to retraction had left Sato's papers available to be referenced hundreds of times and included in 20 systematic reviews or meta-analyses, providing his purported findings with continued, potentially harmful, influence.[119]

After their challenging journey attempting to blow the whistle, Avenell, Bolland, Grey and Gamble concluded that investigations of this scale should be undertaken by institutions, journals or an independent body, perhaps being funded by a levy on journals, rather than be left to the perseverance of individuals.[120]

Jan Hendrik Schön

Jan Hendrik Schön, a physicist employed by Bell Labs, Lucent Technologies as a nanotechnologist, was dismissed for falsifying, duplicating and destroying data – being found guilty of 16 out of 24 counts of scientific misconduct by a review committee (the remaining eight cases were described as 'troubling' but did not provide sufficient evidence of misconduct).[121] Schön was found to have duplicated figures and deleted data points that disagreed with his

119 Else, H. (2019). What universities can learn from one of science's biggest frauds. *Nature*, 570, 287–288. doi: 10.1038/d41586-019-01884-2; Kupferschmidt, K. (2018). Researcher at the center of an epic fraud remains an enigma to those who exposed him. *Science*, August 17, 2018, www.sciencemag.org/news/2018/08/researcher-center-epic-fraud-remains-enigma-those-who-exposed-him

120 Kupferschmidt, K. (2018). Researcher at the center of an epic fraud remains an enigma to those who exposed him. *Science*, August 17, 2018, www.sciencemag.org/news/2018/08/researcher-center-epic-fraud-remains-enigma-those-who-exposed-him

121 The committee was established in late May 2002 to investigate 'the possibility of scientific misconduct, the validity of the data and whether or not proper scientific methodology was used in papers by Hendrik Schön, et al., that are being challenged in the scientific community.' Report of The Investigation Committee on the Possibility of Scientific Misconduct in the Work of Hendrik Schön and Coauthors, September 2002 http://w.astro.berkeley.edu/~kalas/ethics/documents/schoen.pdf (accessed 11 November 2020). The committee was chaired by leading academic physicist Malcolm Beasley of Stanford University; other members of the committee were Supriyo Datta of Purdue University, Herwig Kogelnik of Bell Labs, Herbert Kroemer of the University of California, Santa Barbara, and Donald Monroe of Agere Systems. The committee adopted the US Federal Policy on Research Misconduct as its guiding set of principles, definitions and recommended practices. Management at Bell Labs had been made aware of some problems with Schön's work in the autumn of 2001, but at that point sloppiness and poor record keeping, rather than fraud, were considered to be the likely explanation. Levi, B. G. (2002). Investigation finds that one lucent physicist engaged in scientific misconduct. *Physics Today*, 55(11) (November 1). https://doi.org/10.1063/1.1534995

predictions. Graphs in three unrelated papers appeared to be identical, including what should have been random noise.[122]

Retractions of articles followed. Prior to this, Schön, who at the time of the investigations was approximately four years postdoctoral, had been identified as a rising-star researcher with a significant volume of outputs published in leading journals. For over two years, the world of condensed matter physics was described as being 'enthralled' by findings emerging from Bell Labs, reporting a technique to 'make organic materials behave in amazing new ways: as superconductors, as lasers, as Josephson junctions, and as single-molecule transistors.'[123] Schön wrote at a prolific rate, averaging a paper every eight days during 2001.[124] If authentic, Schön's work would have represented 'a remarkable number of major breakthroughs in condensed-matter physics and solid-state devices.'[125] In the words of one commentator:

> He created high-performance transistors from plastic and other organic (carbon-based) materials, a radical break from the standard silicon-based technology that underlies modern computers. He created light-emitting transistors and an organic electrical laser. Finally, he forged (in both senses) boldly into the realm of nanotechnology, the brave new world of tiny molecule-sized machines by claiming to have built a transistor from a single molecule. Any one of these inventions would have been a brilliant accomplishment – and a valuable asset for Bell Labs and its erstwhile owner, Lucent Technologies. But not a single result was real.[126]

122 Physicist found guilty of misconduct, *Nature*, 26 September 2002; Report of The Investigation Committee on the Possibility of Scientific Misconduct in the Work of Hendrik Schön and Coauthors, September 2002, 3 http://w.astro.berkeley.edu/~kalas/ethics/documents/schoen.pdf (accessed 11 November 2020). The most significant problematic results were achieved when neither co-authors nor other colleagues were present to witness the research activity, Report of The Investigation Committee on the Possibility of Scientific Misconduct in the Work of Hendrik Schön and Coauthors, September 2002, 3 http://w.astro.berkeley.edu/~kalas/ethics/documents/schoen.pdf (accessed 11 November 2020)

123 Levi, B. G. (2002). Investigation finds that one lucent physicist engaged in scientific misconduct. *Physics Today*, 55(11) (November 1). https://doi.org/10.1063/1.1534995

124 Report of The Investigation Committee on the Possibility of Scientific Misconduct in the Work of Hendrik Schön and Coauthors, September 2002, 8 http://w.astro.berkeley.edu/~kalas/ethics/documents/schoen.pdf (accessed 11 November 2020).

125 Report of The Investigation Committee on the Possibility of Scientific Misconduct in the Work of Hendrik Schön and Coauthors, September 2002, 9 http://w.astro.berkeley.edu/~kalas/ethics/documents/schoen.pdf (accessed 11 November 2020)

126 Plastic Fantastic: How the Biggest Fraud in Physics Shook the Scientific World, by Eugenie Samuel Reich. New York: Palgrave Macmillan, 2009, Roberta Garner, 'Book Reviews', 2012, *Science & Society*, 76(1). 115–135.

The breakthrough nature of Schön's findings meant that numerous physicists were investing considerable time in their efforts to reproduce them. Graduate students were reported to have based their doctoral research on Schön's experiments, subsequently placing their education and career development at risk.[127]

Schön disputed the allegations made against him, but he had failed to systematically maintain records and was unable to provide primary data – claiming that he had deleted files to free up computer memory. Devices which could have been used to confirm his results were unavailable, Schön claiming that they had been damaged in measurement, damaged in transit or discarded.[128] His explanations failed to persuade the review committee. His suggestion that data substitution resulted from honest mistake was also unpersuasive. The committee concluded that, at a minimum, Schön demonstrated a 'reckless disregard for the sanctity of data in the value system of science.' Schön admitted that some substitutions of single curves or even parts of single curves were done to 'achieve a more convincing representation of behavior that was nonetheless observed.' The committee concluded that such practices were unacceptable and constituted scientific misconduct.[129]

The panel also observed that even if some of the claims made by Schön ultimately turned out to be accurate and his falsifying and fabricating activities had been fuelled by impatience, this would not invalidate the conclusion that scientific misconduct occurred. The intentional data manipulation and misrepresentation themselves were the basis for the findings, not the ultimate validity of the claims made – the reporting of scientific results must be honest.[130]

Fallout from within the scientific community included concerns that the peer review process failed to detect concerns about Schön's papers. Discussion also focused upon competition among some journals to publish the most cutting-edge research and the tensions between ensuring rigorous pre-publication review and the desire to see the latest findings published without delay.[131]

127 Cassuto, L. (2002). Big trouble in the world of 'Big Physics'. *The Guardian*, Wednesday, September 18, 2002, www.theguardian.com/education/2002/sep/18/science.highereducation

128 Report of The Investigation Committee on the Possibility of Scientific Misconduct in the Work of Hendrik Schön and Coauthors, September 2002, 3 http://w.astro.berkeley.edu/~kalas/ethics/documents/schoen.pdf (accessed 11 November 2020)

129 Report of The Investigation Committee on the Possibility of Scientific Misconduct in the Work of Hendrik Schön and Coauthors, September 2002, 3 http://w.astro.berkeley.edu/~kalas/ethics/documents/schoen.pdf (accessed 11 November 2020)

130 Report of The Investigation Committee on the Possibility of Scientific Misconduct in the Work of Hendrik Schön and Coauthors, September 2002, 17 http://w.astro.berkeley.edu/~kalas/ethics/documents/schoen.pdf (accessed 11 November 2020)

131 David Kaiser, Physics and Pixie Dust, *American Scientist*, November-December 2009, 97(6), 496, Review of Eugenie Samuel Reich, Plastic Fantastic, 2009, Palgrave Macmillan; Blume, M. Keeping up scientific standards. *Nature* 459, 645–646 (2009). https://doi.org/10.1038/459645a; Eugenie Samuel Reich, *Plastic Fantastic: How the Biggest Fraud in Physics Shook the Scientific World*,

Schön used his knowledge of the research and publication processes in attempts to better conceal his fabrications. He would begin with existing findings and fabricate data which expanded upon these to support the results he sought to justify. When peer reviewers raised points, he generally sought to keep these reviewers on side, fabricating further data or modifying existing data to address their concerns.[132]

The personal aftermath for Schön included the revocation of his PhD by the University of Konstanz, a decision subsequently upheld by a German appellate court. No evidence of misconduct was found relating to the PhD research, but the university was able to rely upon a state law allowing degrees to be revoked when the recipient proves 'unworthy.' In Schön's case, he had seriously undermined the principles of acceptable scientific practice and in so doing brought into disrepute the principle that a PhD carries with it the public perception of high levels of trustworthiness as a member of the scientific community.[133]

In summary, the Schön case provides insight into pressures in the commercial world of scientific research. While Schön may have felt under pressure to produce results to further his own career, numerous other parties had incentives to resist 'questioning results that were too good to be true' – including managers under pressure to demonstrate results and so drawn towards 'innocent complicity.'[134]

Diederik Alexander Stapel

Diederik Alexander Stapel was a professor of social psychology. A joint university committee investigation into his work found evidence of fraud in over 30 articles and other work.[135] Stapel's data and findings were described as being often 'too good to be true,' and his research hypotheses were almost always

Palgrave Macmillan: 2009; Cassuto, L. (2002). Big trouble in the world of 'Big Physics'. *The Guardian*, Wednesday, September 18, 2002, www.theguardian.com/education/2002/sep/18/science.highereducation

132 Plastic Fantastic: How the Biggest Fraud in Physics Shook the Scientific World, by Eugenie Samuel Reich. New York: Palgrave Macmillan, 2009, Roberta Garner, 'Book Reviews', 2012, *Science & Society*, vol. 76, no. 1, pp. 115–135; Blume, M. Keeping up scientific standards. *Nature* 459, 645–646 (2009). https://doi.org/10.1038/459645a; Eugenie Samuel Reich, *Plastic Fantastic: How the Biggest Fraud in Physics Shook the Scientific World*, Palgrave Macmillan: 2009.

133 Press release, 31 July 2013 www.bverwg.de/pm/2013/56 (accessed 12 November 2020); See also report by Gretchen Vogel, Jan Hendrik Schön Loses His Ph.D., *Science*, Sep. 19, 2011 www.sciencemag.org/news/2011/09/jan-hendrik-sch-n-loses-his-phd

134 Plastic Fantastic: How the Biggest Fraud in Physics Shook the Scientific World, by Eugenie Samuel Reich. New York: Palgrave Macmillan, 2009, Roberta Garner, 'Book Reviews', 2012, *Science & Society*, vol. 76, no. 1, pp. 115–135.

135 Levelt Committee, Noort Committee, Drenth Committee. *Flawed Science: The Fraudulent Research Practices of Social Psychologist Diederik Stapel*, November 28, 2012

confirmed.[136] The fraud involved the manipulation of existing datasets and fabrication of new ones. The committee concluded that fraud had occurred while Stapel worked as a professor in Tilburg (2006–2011), but also during his earlier work in Groningen (2000–2006) and dated at least from 2004.

Stapel had used his prestigious reputation and powerful institutional position to facilitate his fraudulent activity.[137] Initial stealth was gradually replaced by what appeared to be greater confidence by Stapel that the risk of him being challenged was low.[138] In one variant of the fraud the research preparation would appear to be normal, with questionnaires developed and the number of subjects determined.[139] Stapel then utilised student assistants to collect the data. Stapel then amended these data or fabricated his own dataset before passing it on to a PhD student for analysis.[140] In another variant, Stapel sent datasets to fellow researchers which he claimed had been in existence for a considerable time, but which in reality he had fabricated. These researchers were asked to analyse the data and to write up the study.[141] Many of Stapel's co-researchers were based in different universities and different countries and were not aware of the misconduct or were not in a good position to monitor Stapel's handling of data. Such collaborations may have helped to boost Stapel's reputation, thus creating an upward spiral of unsuspecting researchers willing to work with him. One case was identified where, in response to comments from a journal, the original dataset was withdrawn by Stapel and then appeared to have been augmented with additional observations, the result of which was that the 'hypotheses were neatly confirmed.'[142] Had Stapel limited his behaviour to utilising this final misconduct variant, his fraud would have been difficult to prove or even to detect.[143]

It was of particular concern that Stapel had implicated doctoral researchers in his fraudulent activity by supplying them with fictitious data to feed into their

136 Levelt Committee, Noort Committee, Drenth Committee. *Flawed Science: The Fraudulent Research Practices of Social Psychologist Diederik Stapel*, November 28, 2012

137 Levelt Committee, Noort Committee, Drenth Committee. *Flawed Science: The Fraudulent Research Practices of Social Psychologist Diederik Stapel*, November 28, 2012, 37

138 Stapel's roles had included scientific director and dean of the faculty, as well as external editing roles.

139 Levelt Committee, Noort Committee, Drenth Committee. *Flawed Science: The Fraudulent Research Practices of Social Psychologist Diederik Stapel*, November 28, 2012, 31–32

140 Levelt Committee, Noort Committee, Drenth Committee. *Flawed Science: The Fraudulent Research Practices of Social Psychologist Diederik Stapel*, November 28, 2012, 31–32

141 Levelt Committee, Noort Committee, Drenth Committee. *Flawed Science: The Fraudulent Research Practices of Social Psychologist Diederik Stapel*, November 28, 2012, 32

142 Levelt Committee, Noort Committee, Drenth Committee. *Flawed Science: The Fraudulent Research Practices of Social Psychologist Diederik Stapel*, November 28, 2012, 40

143 Stroebe, W., Postmes, T., & Spears, R. (2012). Scientific misconduct and the myth of self-correction in science. *Perspect Psychol Sci.*, 7(6), 670–688. doi: 10.1177/1745691612460687

doctoral research.[144] As the investigatory committee noted, Stapel may have been particularly impressive to doctoral researchers by combining charisma with the impression he gave of being a renowned academic in his field, yet he remained willing to devote time to helping his doctoral students with the basics of data collection. In turn, the status and trust he enjoyed may have alleviated concerns on the part of some students that the data Stapel provided was 'too good to be true.'[145] Conversely, a few students who did attempt to voice concerns stated to the investigating committee that Stapel used his power and influence to deflect awkward questions.[146] Stapel fostered a close and intensive working relationship with junior researchers, with many PhD students viewing him as a personal friend. They had meals together, visited the cinema and suchlike. However, there were also reports of a more threatening manner when critical questions were asked, the PhD student being made to feel that such questions constituted a lack of trust, challenging the authority and superior knowledge of the senior partner in their relationship.[147]

Stapel's provision of fraudulent data impacted upon completed doctoral theses, and at least one thesis was withdrawn shortly before it was due to be defended because the student learned of the data fraud. The committee concluded that none of these cases involved culpability or complicity, the PhD students having been 'misled with great subtlety,' such that there should be no repercussions on the awarded doctoral degrees, but the fraudulent nature of the data used should be made known.[148] Such an approach, whilst demonstrating balance and fairness in terms of assigning culpability, could not alleviate the likelihood that the future careers of these doctoral students seems likely to be hampered by their association with Stapel and the fact that their doctorates will have reduced value within the scholarly community.[149]

144 The questionable use of research students also appears in other case studies. For example, one of the observations arising from the case of Hans Eysenck and Grossarth-Maticek was the claim that over 100 research students had undertaken large numbers of interviews to measure personality traits without any measurement error, Pelosi, A. J. (2019). Personality and fatal diseases: Revisiting a scientific scandal. *Journal of Health Psychology,* 24(4), 421–439, citing, inter alia, Fox, B. H. (1991). Quandaries created by unlikely numbers in some of Grossarth-Maticek's studies. *Psychological Inquiry*, 2, 242–247; Lee, PN (1991) Personality and disease: A call for replication. *Psychological Inquiry* 2: 251–253.

145 Levelt Committee, Noort Committee, Drenth Committee. *Flawed Science: The Fraudulent Research Practices of Social Psychologist Diederik Stapel*, November 28, 2012, 40–42

146 Levelt Committee, Noort Committee, Drenth Committee. *Flawed Science: The Fraudulent Research Practices of Social Psychologist Diederik Stapel*, November 28, 2012, 44

147 Levelt Committee, Noort Committee, Drenth Committee. *Flawed Science: The Fraudulent Research Practices of Social Psychologist Diederik Stapel*, November 28, 2012, 44

148 Levelt Committee, Noort Committee, Drenth Committee. *Flawed Science: The Fraudulent Research Practices of Social Psychologist Diederik Stapel*, November 28, 2012, 33

149 Stroebe, W., Postmes, T., & Spears, R. (2012). Scientific misconduct and the myth of self-correction in science. *Perspect Psychol Sci.*, 7(6), 670–688. doi: 10.1177/1745691612460687

Stapel had abused not only the trust relationship which is key to established scientists working together but also the even greater trust relationship that has to exist between research student and supervisor.[150] In the case of Stapel the markers of apparent trustworthiness went even deeper:

> The last thing that colleagues, staff, and students would suspect is that, of all people, the department's scientific star, and faculty dean, and the man who personally taught his department's scientific ethics course, would systematically betray that trust.[151]

As well as being a valuable case study illustrating manipulative behaviour by a very senior academic, the Stapel case provides further evidence of failures in wider-ranging mechanisms to detect misconduct. For example, in 1999 a formal international visitation committee had given this same research environment about which the Stapel inquiry had been highly critical an exceptionally high score, suggesting outstanding international excellence.[152]

Andrew Wakefield

Dr Andrew Wakefield was a lead author of a paper published in *The Lancet* in 1998 which explored a link between the MMR (measles, mumps, and rubella) vaccine in children, bowel disorder and the onset of autism.[153] In a small study of 12 children with autism or related conditions colonoscopy studies were examined, resulting in the suggestion that the study revealed evidence of a new form of inflammatory bowel disease. In eight of the cases parents were reported to have associated behavioural symptoms of autism with their child receiving

150 Levelt Committee, Noort Committee, Drenth Committee. *Flawed Science: The Fraudulent Research Practices of Social Psychologist Diederik Stapel*, November 28, 2012, 37–38

151 Levelt Committee, Noort Committee, Drenth Committee. *Flawed Science: The Fraudulent Research Practices of Social Psychologist Diederik Stapel*, November 28, 2012, 43

152 Zwart H. (2017) The Catwalk and the Mousetrap: Reading Diederik Stapel's *Derailment* as a Misconduct Novel. In *Tales of Research Misconduct. Library of Ethics and Applied Philosophy* (Vol. 36). Cham: Springer.

153 Wakefield AJ, Murch SH, Anthony A, Linnell J, Casson DM, Malik M, Berelowitz M, Dhillon AP, Thomson MA, Harvey P, Valentine A, Davies SE, Walker-Smith JA. Ileal-lymphoid-nodular hyperplasia, non-specific colitis, and pervasive developmental disorder in children. Lancet. 1998 Feb 28;351(9103):637–41. doi: 10.1016/s0140-6736(97)11096-0. Retraction in: Lancet. 2010 Feb 6;375(9713):445. Erratum in: Lancet. 2004 Mar 6;363(9411):750. PMID: 9500320. Wakefield had co-authored previous papers exploring similar themes and which had also been criticised on the basis of certain alleged methodological weaknesses, Thompson NP, Montgomery SM, Pounder RE, Wakefield AJ. (1995). Is measles vaccination a risk factor for inflammatory bowel disease? Lancet. Apr 29;345(8957):1071–4. doi: 10.1016/s0140-6736(95)90816-1. PMID: 7715338. For critique of the latter, see for example Farrington P, Miller E. (1995). Measles vaccination as a risk factor for inflammatory bowel disease. Lancet. May 27;345(8961):1362. PMID: 7752764.

the MMR vaccine a few days before.[154] The paper did not identify a causal link between the MMR vaccine and autism and/or bowel disorders, beyond speculation suggesting the need for further studies, but Wakefield made the assertion of a link in a news conference.[155] The press reported the research as suggesting a link between the MMR vaccine and autism. This was seen as a catalyst for a rise in the numbers of parents choosing to reject the MMR vaccine for their children, leading to a fall in vaccine coverage below that needed for herd immunity. Wakefield's expert testimony gained prominence, even though other experts in the field did not agree with his opinions.[156]

Serious concerns regarding the original research grew, including suggestions of selection bias in terms of an overrepresentation of research subjects whose parents were already of the opinion that the MMR vaccine was responsible for their children's autism.[157] Wakefield was also found to have financial conflicts of interest, having patented a single measles vaccine which would likely have gained in popularity in the absence of the combined MMR vaccine.[158] In 2004 the *Lancet* paper analysis was retracted by most of Wakefield's co-authors as being unduly suggestive of a link between the MMR vaccine and autism.[159] In 2010 Wakefield's name was erased from the medical register in the UK as a result of professional regulatory proceedings by the General Medical Council. The basis of this decision included unethical behaviour in dealing with the children who were research subjects for what became the *Lancet* study, fraudulent reporting of results and acting in conflict of interest. Following this decision of the General Medical Council the *Lancet* fully retracted the original study.[160] Further details emerged of alleged behaviour on the part of Wakefield

154 Goldenberg, Maya J. (2016). Public misunderstanding of science? Reframing the problem of vaccine hesitancy. *Perspectives on Science*, 24(5), 552–581. https://doi.org/10.1162/POSC_a_00223.

155 As Stephen John points out in his discussion of the case, Wakefield claimed that the triple MMR vaccine might cause autism in a small number of cases, John, S. (2011). Expert testimony and epistemological free-riding: The MMR controversy. *The Philosophical Quarterly*, 61, 496–517. doi: 10.1111/j.1467-9213.2010.687.x

156 Hobson-West, P. (2003) Understanding vaccination resistance: moving beyond risk. *Health, Risk & Society*, 5(3), 273–283. doi: 10.1080/1369857031000160697 8; John, S. (2011). Expert testimony and epistemological free-riding: The MMR controversy. *The Philosophical Quarterly*, 61, 496–517. doi: 10.1111/j.1467-9213.2010.687.x

157 Goldenberg, Maya J. (2016). Public misunderstanding of science? Reframing the problem of vaccine hesitancy. *Perspectives on Science*, 24(5), 552–581. https://doi.org/10.1162/POSC_a_00223.

158 Deer, B. (2004). Revealed: MMR research scandal. *The Sunday Times*, February 22. www.thetimes.co.uk/tto/health/article1879347.ece

159 Murch, S. H., Anthony, A., Casson, D. H., Malik, M., Berelowitz, M., Dhillon, A. P., Thomson, M. A., Valentine, A., Davies, S. E., & Walker-Smith, J. A. (2004). Retraction of an interpretation. *Lancet*, 363(9411) (March 6), 750. doi: 10.1016/S0140-6736(04)15715-2. Erratum for: *Lancet*, 1998 Feb 28;351(9103),637–641. PMID: 15016483.

160 Retraction–Ileal-lymphoid-nodular hyperplasia, non-specific colitis, and pervasive developmental disorder in children. *Lancet*, 375(9713) (February 6, 2010), 445. doi: 10.1016/S0140-6736(10)60175-4. PMID: 20137807.

when investigative reporter Brian Deer produced a report for the *British Medical Journal* and more recently an unauthorised biography.[161]

The Wakefield case is among the most controversial case studies discussed in this work because of the ongoing heated debate between sections of the public who support Wakefield's ideas and members of the scientific community who continue to adduce evidence in support of counter-arguments to the ideas propagated by Wakefield. Furthermore, 12 years elapsed between publication and full retraction of the problematic *Lancet* paper, during which time it remained citable and retained the potential to influence further research and the approach taken by medical practitioners towards patients.

161 Deer, B. (2020) *The Doctor Who Fooled the World: Andrew Wakefield's War on Vaccines*. Scribe, Melbourne, London; Deer, B. (2011). How the case against the MMR vaccine was fixed. *British Medical Journal*, 342, c5347. doi: 10.1136/bmj.c5347; Deer, B. (2011) How the vaccine crisis was meant to make money. *British Medical Journal*, 342, c5258 doi: 10.1136/bmj.c5258; Deer, B. (2011). The Lancet's two days to bury bad news. *British Medical Journal*, 342, c7001 doi: 10.1136/bmj.c7001

Index